LEEWARD

GEOFFREY LEHMANN was born in Sydney in 1940. Aged sixteen, he began an Arts/Law course at the University of Sydney, where he performed indifferently, but co-edited literary magazines with poet Les Murray, with whom he co-published his first book of poetry, *The Ilex Tree*. He was the first Australian poet to be published by the leading English poetry publisher Faber & Faber, and his *Spring Forest* was shortlisted for the TS Eliot Prize. His *Poems 1957–2013* (UWAP 2014) won the Prime Minister's prize for poetry. He has edited five poetry anthologies, including *Australian Poetry Since 1788*, co-edited with Robert Gray (UNSW Press 2011). He is co-author of a leading taxation textbook, was a partner at PriceWaterhouseCoopers, has been involved in the design of Australian tax legislation, and was Chairman of the Australian Tax Research Foundation.

LEEWARD

GEOFFREY LEHMANN
LEEWARD
a memoir

NEWSOUTH

A NewSouth book

Published by
NewSouth Publishing
University of New South Wales Press Ltd
University of New South Wales
Sydney NSW 2052
AUSTRALIA
newsouthpublishing.com

© Geoffrey Lehmann 2018
First published 2018

10 9 8 7 6 5 4 3 2 1

This book is copyright. Apart from any fair dealing for the purpose of private study, research, criticism or review, as permitted under the *Copyright Act*, no part of this book may be reproduced by any process without written permission. Inquiries should be addressed to the publisher.

ISBN: 9781742236131 (paperback)
          9781742244426 (ebook)
          9781742248875 (ePDF)

 A catalogue record for this book is available from the National Library of Australia

Design Josephine Pajor-Markus
Cover design Lisa White
Cover image High tide – full moon Peter Kingston
Cover image photograph and author photograph Piers Laverty
Printer Griffin Press

All reasonable efforts were taken to obtain permission to use copyright material reproduced in this book, but in some cases copyright could not be traced. The author welcomes information in this regard.

This book is printed on paper using fibre supplied from plantation or sustainably managed forests.

For Gail

ACKNOWLEDGMENTS

I wish to acknowledge the encouragement and great support given by my publisher, Phillipa McGuinness of NewSouth, and by Kathy Bail, CEO of NewSouth.

I was very lucky to have as my text editor Fiona Sim, who has been exceptional in her many suggestions, and had an uncanny ability to sense exactly where changes were needed.

My wife Gail Pearson suggested more than five years ago that I write this book. Since then she has provided emotional support and constructive criticism during many drafts and revisions.

I also thank the following individuals for reading and critiquing earlier drafts: my children Harry, Lucy and Julia; Gail's sisters Cecily and Deborah; my friends Robert Gray (in particular with the structure of the book), Donald Kirby, Ruth Burgess, Rex Burgess and Nick Hordern; and my agent Fiona Inglis of Curtis Brown.

Auguste and Andrea Blackman asked me to contribute to a family memoir about Charles and Barbara Blackman. This book includes an edited extract from that contribution.

I thank Peter Kingston for allowing the use of his wonderful linocut on the cover and Piers Laverty for photographing it.

For permission to use copyright material I gratefully acknowledge the following people: John Eldershaw for permission to

Acknowledgments

use extracts from his father's memoirs; Sally McInerney for the quotation from her poem 'Cattle Incident'; Professor Margaret Harris for permission to quote from Christina Stead's *Seven Poor Men of Sydney*.

CONTENTS

Acknowlegments *vi*
The red-roofed cottage *1*
The skinny house *9*
The *Liberty* *25*
The holiday in Queensland *34*
Mosman Prep *43*
'Fifty-three' *58*
Diana *68*
The house at Gordon *82*
Bella *91*
Shore School *118*

Iris *135*
Sydney University *147*
Johann *170*
The Sydney Push *187*
Studebaker years *203*
Leo *228*
Concrete nymphs *245*
Ten years *298*
Gail *351*
Brother and sister *399*
Currarong *411*

THE RED-ROOFED COTTAGE

In May 1942 three Japanese midget submarines sneaked into Sydney Harbour; one sank a ferry and the others were depth-charged. There were distant explosions echoing across the water in the night. My sister was summoned from her attic bedroom. I was woken and led from my cot in my parents' bedroom on the ground floor. The four of us assembled in the downstairs hallway in the dark. Some time after the detonations stopped we went back to bed. I was not quite two. It is my first memory.

During the war the windows of our house were masked by brown paper, so light could not escape. I watched searchlights sweep across the night sky. My father had a gas mask and sometimes wore a khaki warden's uniform; he was too old to be a soldier, I was told.

Many years before I was born, peering down into the viewfinder of a large, cumbersome Zeiss camera, which hung suspended from his neck on a leather strap, my father recorded what he saw in black and white on large glass negatives. In my early childhood, he was still using this camera to photograph the groups of picnickers he took in his boat the *Liberty* on weekend daytrips up the Lane Cove River, an estuary of Sydney Harbour. He developed the negatives and prints in his darkroom, lit by a dim red electric globe which fascinated me as a child. Then he sold the photographs to the picnickers, or gave them away. He did not talk about the financial details.

The glass negatives he favoured were already antiquated technology by the 1940s. As a child I sensed there was something beautiful and strange about these obsolete glass objects. None survive, but I have a couple of his group portraits: thirty or more picnickers, adults and children, none of whom I can recognise, sitting and standing in dappled shadow under trees.

Born in June 1940, not long after the start of World War II, I was a statistical outlier. My mother was two weeks short of her forty-fourth birthday. A year or so before, she had miscarried, and my parents believed, perhaps regretfully, that my elder sister Diana would be their only child.

For my first ten years I grew up in Lavender Bay, with the smell of salt water, in houses facing the grey curved eye of the Sydney Harbour Bridge. There was a distant rumble, like thunder, when trains went across. At the end of the day a southerly buster often blew up, and the twenty or so moored yachts and motor launches pointed, like compass needles, down the bay into the wind. On rare occasions our bay was visited by a Chinese junk – with varnished planks and red sails like something out of a child's picture book; it came and was gone.

I have no memory of living in my first childhood house, 'Leeward', a two-storey grey weatherboard building at the head of the bay and backed by a wild escarpment of weeds and lantana. The ground shook when trains empty of passengers emerged from a tunnel set into a hill, then went across a viaduct to railway yards at the water's edge.

'Leeward' was the rented house my parents – Leo and Iris – moved into when they married in 1935. My father had been courting Iris for about two years and waiting until 'she'd got some sense'. One day he asked how old she was. Her answer shocked

The red-roofed cottage

him – she was almost too old to have children. They married 'hastily' – as my father saw it – six months later. She was a thirty-nine-year-old spinster and he was a bachelor aged forty-four. When I was in my twenties my father would say: 'Son, I got married too young – the older you are when you get married, the shorter the time you have to put up with it.'

Using his large, cumbersome Zeiss camera he photographed the Orphan Rock, then famous as a scenic wonder, on their short honeymoon visiting the Blue Mountains and Jenolan Caves. He developed his glass negative and enhanced a large sepia print with natural tints. My mother gave up her job and joined a lending library, confident that keeping house for my father would allow a lifetime of reading books.

'Leo, there's always a bed for you in Walker Street, if you want to move back', Leo's sister Agnes told the newly married couple in her stentorian squawk. Until his marriage, my father had lived with Agnes and his brother Carl in the house in Walker Street, North Sydney where he was born. Agnes worked in a steam laundry most of her life. She wore the plainest of clothes and her metallic grey hair was tied back in a bun. A favourite word was 'obstropolous'. She pronounced 'going' as *goin'* and 'opposite' as *oppo-sight*. With her rounded shoulders, long trunk, short legs and loud voice, she was sceptical of my mother's educated accent and delicate looks. Iris, she decided, had a bad case of 'imaginitis'.

'Leeward' was less than a mile from the Walker Street house and was next to the Lavender Bay wharf. Each morning, from Monday to Friday, just after seven, my father's launch, the *Liberty*, set out from there with twenty or so workmen on board. If the sky was unclouded, the boat and water were festive with early morning sunlight. Their destination was the engineering works of the Adelaide Steamship Company at Balmain, a dilapidated harbourside suburb, which was yet to become fashionable.

At about 4.30 in the afternoon, the launch returned with the workmen to the wharf. Shadows would be forming. The sun would be disappearing over the hill. Between those two boat trips, which started and finished his day, my father's launch took men and supplies to and from ships anchored in the harbour for the steamship company.

Working-class Lavender Bay was a foreign planet for my mother. To get to the shops in Blues Point Road, she walked, clutching a string shopping bag, up a set of steep steps from 'Leeward' to King Georges Road. On her right was the tunnel from which empty trains sometimes thundered out. As she climbed higher, she could look across a wasteland of dense lantana. Local boys played among the dry, acrid foliage, in a warren of secret tracks through prickly branches that tore at skin and clothes if they were clumsy. One day Iris was walking up these steps – perhaps before Diana was born. A boy and girl were among the bushes, the girl's 'scanties' around her feet. My mother called out to them to stop. The boy stood up and waved his penis at my mother: 'D'yer want some too?'

Only a couple of months into married life, my mother made a disconcerting discovery. She was pregnant. But even after my sister was born, she held onto her fantasy of the book-reading housewife. One morning my father had gone off to work and Diana, two months old, was asleep in her cot. Locking the front door of 'Leeward', my mother hurried up to North Sydney station and boarded a train. Her plan was to steal a couple of hours in the city – to borrow more books from her lending library, or sit down in an arcade and have tea and a cake. Chatting to a woman sitting beside her in the train – a stranger – she confided she had left her baby asleep. The woman looked at her: 'You can't do that!' My mother got off at the very next station, Milsons Point, and ran down the hill. She unlocked

The red-roofed cottage

the front door. The house was silent and my sister still asleep.

When I was born, the nurses nicknamed me 'Buddha', because of my large, melon-shaped head. Its size was later emphasised by my father's cutting my hair very short, and at primary school I collected nicknames such as 'Baldy', 'Bighead' and 'Boofhead'. 'Boofhead' was an Australian comic-strip character, with short black hair, clipped in the style preferred by my father, and was the nickname that I carried with me into high school, often shortened to 'Boof'. (By a strange coincidence the Australian cricketer Darren Lehmann also has the nickname 'Boofhead'.)

One morning, not long after the start of World War II, my parents were heading down Lavender Bay on the *Liberty*. My father pointed to three houses halfway along the bay on a steep site planted with large Moreton Bay fig trees. He indicated a white and beige wooden cottage with a red galvanised iron roof; higher up still, a decayed double-storey mansion, and next to it a strange edifice, one room wide and four stories high. Catching the ferry into the city, my mother had already given this singular building a name: 'the skinny house'.

'Iris, I'm buying those houses', my father told her. She was astonished. In the six years since their marriage, nothing had changed her first impression that she had married a working class man of modest means.

For two decades my father had been depositing his earnings from the *Liberty* at the Erskine Street branch of the Bank of New South Wales – an elaborate sandstone building from the Victorian era, where I spent hours of my childhood, waiting on leather-bottomed wooden chairs. The houses had been part of a deceased estate since the nineteenth century and were selling cheaply, my father said. The Japanese army had already reached New Guinea. Waterfront properties were being sold at knock-down prices.

My father paid cash. The amount – several thousand pounds – was a lot more than the accumulated sum of the annual earnings he recorded for income tax purposes in a small black cash book – which I still have – noting his receipts and expenses week by week in longhand in blue-black ink.

We moved from 'Leeward' into the white and beige cottage with its red iron roof. Its postal address was 1 Lower Bayview Street, McMahons Point. My father made a wooden placard with silvery metal letters spelling 'IVANHOE' for the front gate. Iris loved the novels of Walter Scott and had chosen this name.

A sloping path, bordered by blue plumbago, led downhill from the gate and stopped at some steps built into the rock-face. At the bottom of this small cliff, there was a small paved area and the red-roofed cottage.

When I was a few years older, I wheeled a tricycle up and down the path. I remember my father rebuilding it in concrete with a couple of workmen: the wooden formwork, the cement mixer turning, the sieves and drying concrete. I also remember watching him tip kerosene into the preheating tray of a blowtorch, then light it. For a minute or so a yellow, smoky flame billowed around the flame tube. As this flickered out, he moved the pumping rod quickly up and down. There was a roaring sound and a concentrated blue flame I could barely see in full sunlight.

Before her marriage Iris had lived with her mother Bella in a flat at Rose Bay. After my parents married, Bella moved to a flat at 'Burundah Hall' in East Crescent Street, a building of liver-coloured bricks and cream stucco decorations several doors up from the skinny house. I have a memory of cool halls with terrazzo floors. One afternoon as Bella opened her door I may have handed her a tribute of blue plumbago flowers. My grandmother wore old-ladies'-style long black dresses and had a black piano. She played it as we sat there in the afternoon sunlight, which I remember as yellow-tinted.

I have a scatter of memories of my early childhood in 'Ivanhoe'. In one, I'm about three years old and running around aimlessly one morning on the front lawn facing the harbour. There is a small orange tree. A disused brick outhouse with a primitive water closet at the bottom of some steps is a haven for mosquitoes. One weekend morning my father is pursuing my sister with a leather strap – this is unusual, he is rarely provoked and I'm scared he'll get angry with me. In another memory, on a weekend afternoon, my sister and I are a year or so older. Diana is sitting on a chair at the back of the house under the shadow of the cliff. There is the snip snip of scissors and her hair falling on the concrete as my father gives her a basin cut, then panic and blood as his scissors gash her ear.

Mrs Holmes owned the block of flats next to the red-roofed cottage and lived in the ground floor flat. She was the widow of Reginald Holmes, a boat builder who was shot three times, and killed, before he could give evidence in the 'shark arm murder case'. (In April 1935 the tattooed arm of a petty criminal, Jim Smith – Holmes's acquaintance – was vomited up by a tiger shark in the Coogee Aquarium Baths.) I was invited once or twice to play with her granddaughter Georgina, and was envious of Georgina's large painted rocking horse. Mrs Holmes had a heavy smoker's sallow face and years later burned to death in bed, having fallen asleep with a lighted cigarette.

A large neutered tomcat, a tabby with a white bib, used to walk inquiringly around our garden. He was Mrs Holmes's cat. My father called him Skipper and we called him Puss. I used to play with him and he eventually moved in with us, disappointing

Mrs Holmes. My courting of this cat amused and mildly embarrassed my father (on account of Mrs Holmes) and he held me responsible for alienating Puss from his owner.

The war ended. The brown paper was torn off the windows, neon shop signs were lit again and my mother took Diana and me into the city, to see the shops and lights, and join in the bustle and excitement. Long past our bedtime, on VJ night (Victory over Japan), my father took us in the *Liberty* out under the Harbour Bridge, cutting the engine when we reached the main body of Port Jackson, near Pinchgut Island. Other boats and ships surrounded us, bobbing in the liquorice water. Everyone was tooting. Nearby toots were answered by toots far away. Coloured lights played on great arcs of spray shooting up from fireboats. Fireworks were exploding and rockets painting the night sky, as acrid smoke drifted across the harbour.

After the war, we moved from red-roofed 'Ivanhoe', further up the hill to the skinny house. Puss moved up the hill with us.

THE SKINNY HOUSE

I was five years old. Late in the afternoon I walked up the hill and watched furniture being carried into empty rooms, and my father checking the stove. There was a pop as he applied a match to gas escaping from each burner, and blue rings of flame lit up in the darkened kitchen. I was surprised to discover he owned this house, and the decayed mansion next door which we called by its street number, 'Fifty-three'. Until then, the cottage lower down the hill and its patch of lawn, with a low wire fence separating it from the other two houses, had been the limit of my world. I sensed a new freedom. I could roam over a hillside. Property ownership was a novel concept.

We stayed in the skinny house for the next five years. Those years, according to Freud, were my 'latency phase', an interlude where nothing much happens, after my more exciting 'oral', 'anal' and 'phallic' phases, and before my perturbed 'genital phase'.

Those five years, a mere Freudian interlude, were when I first fell in love with women; I discovered music, plants and books; I had my first ideas about politics and the universe. The places I knew then are where I return to at night in my sleep. They have a singularity and strangeness; they are where I first became fully aware.

I was too young to understand we had moved from 'Ivanhoe', which had three bedrooms, to a house that had only two (my mother may have welcomed the fact that I would continue sleeping in the marital bedroom). The skinny house was large and imposing. This thrilled me. Viewed from the water, the skinny house was an oddity – just one room wide and four stories high. The side-on view was less odd – it was three rooms deep. On the title deed it was named 'The Shingles', but my father had replaced the old shingle roof with glazed red terracotta tiles. Our new address was 51 East Crescent Street, McMahons Point.

My first walk up the hill to the skinny house may have been blissful, but I was filled with despair by a small wasteland between the windowless southern wall of 'Fifty-three' and the skinny house. A dank gutter, about 60 centimetres deep, ran along the base of the blank wall, a haven for mosquitoes. Their larvae could be seen wriggling in the water. A derelict outdoor brick toilet and a fibro laundry of indeterminate age inhabited this wasteland between the houses.

This run-down laundry was where my mother now did the washing. My sister was a girl, four and a half years older than me, and was expected to help. I was a spectator: my mother shaking flakes of soap from a packet into a copper lit by a circle of little blue flames; wisps of steam as she stirred the clothes and bed sheets with a short wooden pole; soapy water spilling on the concrete floor as she hoisted the washing with the pole into a polished cement basin for rinsing; finally a mangle, turned by my mother, cranking each garment and sheet into a second basin.

The damp clothes were stowed in a pale wicker basket, marked with large faded red initials. Woollen jumpers were spread out on clipped privet bushes. Other items were hung out on a

The skinny house

wire clothesline strung between two wooden posts. Props (long branches, forked at the top) supported the line where it might sag under the weight of wet clothes.

Nothing was expected of me, except to dry dishes, dress myself for school and do my homework – my school days began soon after we moved into the skinny house.

I had self-imposed tasks. My mother's thin lips could not hide a smile when I announced I wanted a bucket of hot water to wash the rocks. I carried this, slopping and spilling, down the hill, a cake of soap and piece of old cloth in my other hand. At a certain point the steps were flanked by rocks which had weathered to a dull grey. I had seen the colour of newly cut stone, when my father built a rockery. After washing the rocks, I sat there and imagined pink and gold tints just beneath the surface. Then they dried and were grey as before.

Another self-imposed task was making wine from my aunt's grapes. My father's sister Agnes still lived about a mile away in Walker Street, in a dilapidated timber cottage on poles, built by her father. A large open workshop under the house – a dim cavern of old tools and building materials with an earth floor – was separated from the garden by latticework between the poles. The house was set back behind trees, bamboo and shrubs, and to reach it we crossed a wooden bridge across a creek. It was a place of enchantment. Before he died, in 1891, my grandfather planted vines that fruited heavily with inedible red wine grapes. I persuaded my father we should make them into wine. A row of tall Vacola jars stood for months on the ledge of our laundry window, filled with dark fermenting juice, clouds of white scum forming on the red surface. The smell must have got to my mother. They were emptied out.

I also tried making olive oil from the hard green olive-like seeds of the Lord Howe Island palms at 'Fifty-three'. A slurry was all I got after persuading my mother to let me boil them in a pot for an hour. Olive oil was not used for culinary purposes at the time and came in a pharmaceutical manufacturer's bottle with brown-green print on a cream label. We were given a tablespoon of olive oil to swallow if we were sick. Very sick children were made to gag on castor oil (which was ghastly and is now used only for industrial purposes, such as brake fluid).

When we sounded croupy, eucalyptus oil was mixed with boiling water in a basin, and we breathed in hot eucalyptus steam, nostrils stinging, a tea-towel draped over our head like a tent, inside a white world where nothing else existed.

My knees collected scabs from falls caused by the steep slope of the land. A favourite spot for falling down was where an asphalt path was crumbling into a ditch beside the cellars. If I hit my forehead, my father would say, 'Iris, he's got another egg', and I would be rushed inside, where butter was applied to the swelling.

The skinny house, where my 'eggs' were ministered to, was demolished fifty years ago.

Freud's account of the unconscious has lasted better than his phases. The cellars of the skinny house were like Freud's unconscious: vast, dark and exciting. The door to this subterranean realm was of heavy wood panelling, painted a faded pastel green, and bolted and padlocked. It opened onto a series of cellars. As my father pulled a cord to light up the cobwebbed corridor, brown moths, startled, flapped past, as big as small birds, and brushed us with their wings. He filled these dim rooms with used timber and iron pipes, stacked on wooden frames raised on bricks, to stay clear of the earth. There were a few remnant boards where there had been a wooden floor. Walls of crumbling sandstone rubbed

The skinny house

away at a touch. A small rivulet, red with iron oxide, had carved a narrow channel in the soft earth. A disused stairway, leading up into the main part of the house, had been blocked off. The cellars, formerly servants' quarters, had been condemned for human habitation. Digging for buried treasure there, we found shattered pieces from a nineteenth century dinner set.

The main cellar, at the end of the corridor, had a cement floor and was my father's workshop. On the wall above a mantelpiece, painted outlines of plates and jugs indicated where valuable items were to be put back by the servants after use. He had a power saw with a steel bench and a lathe. Benches along the walls had drawers full of wrenches, hammers, chisels, planes and screwdrivers. He also had a small kiln. A trombone and a frame for restringing tennis racquets were hanging on the wall, but he did not play tennis or the trombone. In my early twenties, having been chased by a Labrador dog when picking up a girlfriend, I called on my father in his cellars to get a water pistol. He pulled open his drawer of water pistols: 'What do you want it for, son? A dog?'

He felt it was his duty to educate me in the use of tools. I went with him by train (we had no car) across Sydney to buy his saw-bench. We were led up a grassy suburban backyard into a shed, a home handyman's Aladdin's cave, glinting with tools neatly arranged on shelves, where we were shown the bench that was for sale – with its machined, polished steel and green paint. The owner no longer needed it, he explained, and indicated his new and more elaborate saw-bench, which my father inspected respectfully and perhaps with envy. I was glad not to be the man's son. I preferred my father's eccentric clutter.

One of the repetitive sounds of my childhood was the whining roar of a circular saw, rising to a crescendo as it ripped through timber – deafening, despite fingers blocking my ears – and the relief when the blade had cut through, singing as it revolved freely in the air. My father spent weeks in his underground workshop, machine-sawing rosewood planks into long slender slats. I was disappointed when he coated the red, finely grained wood with gloss cream paint, a tint named 'new ivory', and the slats became venetian blinds for his flatettes in the decayed mansion next door.

I accompanied him to auctions where he bought large, framed engravings of grazing cows, lions, and desert scenes. This was a way of getting cheap window glass when he enclosed the verandas of his flatettes. He indicated I should touch the point of a glass cutter — an industrial diamond, he explained. Then he ran the glass cutter along the length of a sheet of glass, guided by a rule, and pulled the glass apart bare-handed. He spent hours machine-buffing the white painted letters 'ULVA' (United Licensed Victuallers Association) from hotel glasses.

His tenants all had ice chests (supplied by my father). I would watch the iceman park his van and hurry in with blocks of ice suspended on steel tongs. We, however, had no ice chest or refrigerator. My father insisted on cheaper alternatives for us. Every day, except Sunday when the shops were closed, my mother walked up the hill to Blues Point Road and bought fresh meat. For a year or so after the war, she handed over small cream-coloured coupons from a ration book. The butcher's shop smelt of dried blood and sawed bones. Diana and I stood beside her in the sawdust on the red-painted concrete floor. The price was rung up on a mechanical till with a keyboard, and when we got home, we stored the meat in a ventilated metal meat safe. We ate cheaper cuts: chuck steak for stews, lamb chops, offal, and perhaps rump steak once a week, as a treat. We had roast legs of lamb and mint sauce made with brown vinegar, sugar and mint from our garden.

Our mother also handed over a coupon at the grocery shop for butter. We stored butter and milk in an evaporative butter cooler. A muslin cloth, weighted with glass beads, was draped over a perforated metal cylinder resting in a rim of water.

Sometimes I'd see the long brown neck of a draft horse, leather blinkers over its eyes, swallowing from a water trough on the corner of Blues Point Road and East Crescent Street. Milk was delivered by horse and cart, the large hooves of the draft horse, surmounted by white fetlocks like woolly socks, clip-clopping on the road outside our house in the early morning.

My father suspected the milkman of watering the milk; bottled milk, which could not be adulterated, was more expensive, so my father persisted in leaving out a large grey-blue enamel billy up at street level, to be filled. Rushing out when he heard the milkman, and taking the lid off the billy, he would inspect the surface of the milk for traces of cloudiness, where added water may not have mixed in. We drank this milk early in the day, while it was still cool and before it was insipid and warm. The milkman's horse deposited manure in the street, like clumped grassy kidneys. My father, a keen vegetable grower, promptly fetched his shovel.

In later years, he sold the ice chests from his flatettes as scrap metal and installed refrigerators. Armed with a pressure gauge and steel canisters of refrigerator gas, he became an expert refrigerator mechanic. Then to his disgust, manufacturers stopped making open-unit refrigerators. The sealed units, which replaced them, enclosed the motor and compressor in a welded steel casing, and had to be sent back to the factory for maintenance.

My father kept repairing his fleet of older-style refrigerators, with their rust spots and perishing rubber seals, until the last years of his life. He had an old self-latching refrigerator, which sat at a slight angle on a brick path outside his laundry, open to the sun and rain, a death-trap for any child who might crawl inside and have the door slammed on them.

LEEWARD

Like all McMahons Point houses, the skinny house faced the water. A set of stone steps led up to the level above the cellars and a stone-paved front veranda looking out across Lavender Bay. On each side of the landing there was a balustrade with a heavy wooden handrail supported by two intertwining iron dolphins. The dolphins, my father said, had been the table legs in the dining saloon of Ben Boyd's yacht, the *Wanderer*, wrecked off Port Macquarie in the 1850s.

This level had a dining room and kitchen, and a large drawing room. After our evening meal in the kitchen my father, wearing second-hand spectacles, did paperwork sitting in the dining room at an oak dining table. There were matching oak chairs upholstered with artificial leather. My sister and I sat there too, doing homework, and would be joined by my mother after she had cleaned up in the kitchen. Puss (Mrs Holmes's former cat) perched on the windowsill gazing in, beside an aspidistra growing in a brass pot. If he was sick, the pink tip of his tongue protruded, endearingly I thought. We could see from across the bay the blazing lights of Luna Park, with its carousels reflected in the water.

My father had an ability to spend much of his life asleep, and his midday nap was on a settee under the window. My mother's niece Evelyn Boardman used this settee as her bed, when she stayed with us for a few weeks, as a young trainee teacher. Evelyn smoked cigarettes, had a firm, decisive voice and full lips and cheeks. She was already more sophisticated than my non-smoking, delicate mother. At seven years of age, I was intrigued.

Our winter heating cost us nothing thanks to the North Shore Gas Company. We collected coke from our beach, floating in on the tide from Balls Head Bay, where it was dumped into Sydney Harbour by the gasworks, as waste (my father explained).

The skinny house

On winter nights we had a coke fire in a small iron fireplace in our dining room. I crouched on a mat, gazing into blue and red flames and flickers of yellow. The fireplace was set under a mantelpiece of greenish-black marble, streaked with white. A black marble French clock, with a round white enamel face, and another much smaller clock balanced on the tip of a metal elephant's trunk, rested on the shelf.

We listened to the evening news – always from the government broadcaster, the ABC – from a freestanding radio in a timber veneer console next to the fireplace. At night (if I peered in at the back of the console), the valves were like tiny lit up towers in a futuristic city, signalling to each other.

I was a priggish eight-year-old, my mother's loyal disciple, and uninterested in the vulgar entertainment across the bay at Luna Park. One afternoon I was listening to a broadcast of a Wagner opera, intrigued by the music and the pedantic, high-pitched voice of the German-accented announcer from Bayreuth. I was listening avidly, but with little comprehension. My mother kept reminding me I was supposed to be at a boy's birthday party down the road. I knew she despised the people in our working-class neighbourhood. There was a knock on the door, and a child asking my mother where I was. She called out to me several times. No, I told her. I wanted to go on listening to the opera. She made some excuses and sent the boy away.

An operatic company visited Sydney after World War II. On the morning when tickets came on sale, my mother trekked with my sister and me into the city. We lined up in a queue of hundreds, stretching around a city block. She bought tickets for a matinée performance of Gounod's *Faust*. As Mephistopheles descended into Hell, he was surrounded by an instantaneous circle of orange neon light. Even a five-year-old realised someone had flicked a switch.

Our kitchen walls were a cream colour. There was an emu on the white oven door of a gas stove in an old chimney-place. All family meals were eaten around a dark wooden kitchen table with a cream glass top, except Christmas dinner and the rare occasions when we entertained relatives in the dining room. My parents never asked friends to dinner.

'Eat up', was a refrain of my childhood. Until the age of seven or eight, I was often spoon-fed, almost force-fed. I detested my mother's corned beef. It was streaked with yellowish-white fat, had a rancid smell and contained fragments of boiled string and bitter-sweet cloves. My father grew many of the vegetables we ate: he allowed his round beans to ripen until they were stringy and bitter. The fatty, leathery taint of his broad beans made me feel ill. His chokoes, a favourite food of his – prolific and easy to grow – had the flavour of transparent flesh mixed with wood fragments (the seeds).

The most nauseating meal of all (I thought) was the midday salad on weekends: iceberg lettuce cut into thin ribbons, tomatoes chopped in small bits, gratings of raw carrot and aged cheddar, beetroot and fragments of hard-boiled eggs. Tossed with sugar, salt and brown vinegar, this concoction had a wet, gritty texture. Even food I liked, my mother made uninteresting. She boiled potatoes and pumpkin until they became bland three-dimensional replicas of themselves.

Not every meal was a battleground. My mother cooked a wonderful steak and kidney pie with a lining and lid of suet pastry made from beef dripping. We ate a great variety of meats: lamb, rabbit, tripe, crumbed brains and liver – all of which I enjoyed, apart from corned beef. The strong ammoniated flavour of liver was a challenge, but I ate it – co-operatively, I thought. Favourite dishes of my father's were pickled ox tongue, served hot; and oxtail soup, which he spent days cooking up, its rich, fatty smell pervading the house. My mother was silently critical of this dish as some kind of working-class aberration.

'The cat knows it's Tuesday', my mother announced on Tuesday mornings. This was the day when the rabbit-oh called by in his small panel van and we ate rabbit in a white sauce with parsley. Rabbit scrags were given to Puss. Puss was fed in the kitchen with chopped-up meat or fish then milk in a china saucer, licking his whiskers when he finished. Unaware cats can't taste sweetness, I occasionally flavoured his milk with a sweet 'lime' cordial dyed chemical green, that I loved, called 'Green Ice'.

My mother drank frequent cups of milky tea with sugar, always with a bad conscience. Tea gave her freckles, she said. Proud of her 'fair English complexion' and ten years old when she came to Australia, she thought people who grew up here looked coarse. I was a smiling, freckle-faced urchin sitting at the foot of the La Perouse monument in a photograph my father took. My mother hated freckles and tore it up.

Every December Diana and I went with our father to the Andronicus shop near Circular Quay to order two boxes of chocolates for Christmas – long cardboard boxes, the colour of milk coffee, decorated with brown and white lettering and heraldic insignia. On Christmas Day, when we were allowed to open one of them, Diana and I would read the printed description of the fillings many times, before choosing.

We once went to the very top of the large Farmer & Co department store on the corner of George and Market Streets – to the smallgoods department. It was an unexpected outpost in a shop that mostly sold clothes. There was a hushed atmosphere, the smell of bacon and large blocks of cheese. Speaking across a long curved glass-fronted refrigerator to a man in a white chef's outfit, my father solemnly ordered a chicken for Christmas – a luxury item, something my sister and I had never eaten before.

The downstairs hall of the skinny house ended in our largest room. Our drawing room had two French doors opening onto a wooden veranda. Very occasionally we sat in a lounge suite with elaborately carved black wooden arms and crests, upholstered with a grey-blue, heavy-duty tapestry, or I might sit on the floor with a train set or playing snakes and ladders. There was a small black piano inherited from my mother's mother, and later a yellowish walnut veneer upright Lipp, with brass candle holders, and two coats of arms on the gold painted soundboard.

The piano was bought ceremoniously in 1949 with money bequeathed to my mother by her uncle John Cragin Rainer, a childless itinerant agricultural worker who had the same name as his operatic father. The Lipp was owned by a genteel old lady. Dressed in our best clothes, our family came to her Neutral Bay apartment, my father advising my mother, who was nervous about such an extravagant purchase, and the old lady expressing regret at giving it up. There was an undisclosed logic to my mother's extravagance. Diana was recently out of hospital, where she had been treated for a congenital condition. She would be learning the piano. This was her reward – a reward that became a chore.

My father was convinced a second-hand violin he bought at auction was a valuable instrument. He peered inside it with his eyeglass, looking for signs left by some famous maker. I was allowed to produce screeching sounds on it. My parents were not interested in paying for me to have lessons. I was a boy.

On Sunday afternoons we listened to 78s on my father's small HMV portable record player: the voice of the Australian tenor Peter Dawson or Christian Sinding's piano piece, 'Rustle of Spring'. My mother was embarrassed by my father's favourite 78, which he played (I suspect) to provoke her:

The skinny house

Hallelujah, I'm a bum,
Hallelujah, bum again,
Hallelujah, give us a handout
To revive us again…

We played hit songs from the 1920s such as 'How about a little kiss Cecilia/ Just a kiss you'll never miss Cecilia…' I thought this song was idiotic but songs such as this reminded my mother of glamorous days before she met my father.

The drawing room had a tall upright mirror with a gilt base that stood in the corner on a low L-shaped book case. My mother chose the books: Dickens, Baroness Orczy's *The Scarlet Pimpernel*, one volume of HG Wells's two-volume *A Short History of the World*, two bulky dark green volumes of *The Poetical Works of Robert Browning* and a slimmer grass-green volume, *Mrs Browning's Poems*. Rather than their poems, my mother was more interested in the Brownings' courtship – she used to talk about the 1934 film *The Barretts of Wimpole Street*.

I was intrigued by a small nineteenth century volume with black and white illustrations and viridian green cloth binding. I insisted my mother read me stories from this jewel-like book. She had to make these up, as there was nothing in this book for a child, but I have no memory of any of these invented tales.

A narrow stair led from the downstairs hall up to a small landing on which stood a rickety black lacquer side table, decorated with rural Chinese scenes. The landing was lit feebly at night by an electric globe hanging in a reddish-orange silk lampshade with tassels. Three rooms led off the landing. My sister had a large sunny bedroom at the back of the house facing the street. Next to it there was a bathroom with a hot water geyser – we had no running hot water. At the front of the house my parents slept in a bedroom where I also slept until the age of ten.

My bed was stationed next to one of two glass French doors, opening onto a wooden veranda with a cast iron railing, looking out over Lavender Bay. The veranda shook when we stepped out onto it. My parents had an elaborate walnut veneer bedroom suite, purchased when they married and my father was flush with earnings from the *Liberty*. Their double bed stood in the centre of the room. I saw shapes like blurred human-sized mummies in the doors of my mother's large wardrobe and Arthur Rackham grotesqueries in all the walnut veneer surfaces.

My mother sometimes wore a Chinese blue and orange silk dressing gown. She also had an elaborate green silk gown embroidered with large roses, which I never saw her wear, though once I secretly slipped it on myself.

The fourth storey of the skinny house was a desiccated room up a final narrow and dusty set of stairs – my father's attic, where he repaired watches. I sometimes went there with him in the early evening, breathing in its hot acrid air, which had heated up during the day. I sat in a bay window on a wooden bench, looking east, across the water. Two other tiny, dusty windows with gothic arches looked north and south. The woodwork was sun-bleached, painted a pale chalky green, and the wooden walls were papered with a nineteenth century wallpaper with a pattern of small flowers. A black eyeglass popped into his right eye socket and held there as if by magnetism, my father explained the workings of mainsprings and balance wheels, pointing out the jewels on which the small mechanisms pivoted.

I had no interest in his explanations. But I was fascinated by the low bright light suspended over his work bench, illuminating the soft white cloth spread over it, with the watches and precision tools scattered across it, including a large gold fob watch and a cuttlefish shell used for soldering. There were old clocks, an amethyst necklace in a jewel case, and a broken ivory chess set with heraldic figures in white and red. A plywood box was filled with old postcards. I used to rummage through these, admiring postage stamps of the Australian states, dating back before federation, and glancing at handwritten messages from unknown people to unknown people.

Early one morning I guiltily sneaked up into my father's attic. He may have heard me fossicking about upstairs. I heard his feet shuffling up the creaking wooden stairs. He opened the attic door and gave me a look of quiet disapproval.

He loved owning things. I have a list he wrote in blue-black ink on a small sheet of lined paper, from about 1960. The purpose is obscure:

8 day
(4) wall clocks (1) seth Thomas weight power
English [illegible] (2) Mainspring Powered
8 day mantel striking clock, WestMinster chime,
Alarm clocks, small watchmakers bench,
lathe, & Tools, foot power buff & emery wheel,
(2) Portable Wireless, Violin, silver plated trombone,
cameras, 1/4 Plate Reflex Zeiss 4.5 lens (2) Rolleiflex 2.8
   & 3.8
Telescopic Tripods, 6' condenser, automatic focusing
enlarger, paper hangers straight edge & brushes,
Pocket Watch R. G. silver & nickel open face & hunters
Ladies & Gents wrist watches movements
'Omega' english [illegible] & swiss fractional H.P. Elec
   Motors
Tecnico lawn mower, Vacuum cleaners, Typist

> desk (Teak) & spring back chair, Tape recorder
> Elec radiators pressure cookers,
> aluminium Pots, pans, pictures, blankets
> sheets, lounge covers, curtains, bedspreads,
> carpet runners,
> 12 flatette's furniture?

I have no idea where most of these objects went, but I still have the silver and nickel fob watch with a hunting scene.

I slept on a horsehair mattress in a silky oak bed my father made. Although he extolled horsehair mattresses as firm and good for the posture of growing males, I grew up with rounded shoulders, not unlike his.

Falling asleep at night, I heard the muted and distant screams from the Big Dipper across the bay as the roller-coaster clattered up the first steep climb and rocketed down, then around, and up and down diminishing crests. Most local children had been there but it was a forbidden place for my sister and me. My mother's disapproval was cultural. A waste of money, said my father.

The lights of Luna Park flickered on the water. As I shut my eyes I seemed to be in a large auditorium, with dim orange, green and reddish shapes revolving slowly as I subsided pleasantly into sleep. I was unaware of the sex, if any, my parents may or may not have had on the bed in the centre of the room. I did not know there was such a thing.

THE *LIBERTY*

As a child, I watched my father collecting pennies from the workmen he took on the *Liberty* from Lavender Bay to Balmain. One of the refrains of my childhood was his 'Look after the pennies and the pounds look after themselves'. My mother had an antiphonal response (perhaps not said when he was around), her sarcastic 'Penny-wise, pound-foolish'. Her family, the Rainers, had been penny-foolish and pound-foolish.

As well as learning about thrift and hard work from my father's motor launch, I had my first exposure to bohemian life among his weekend picnickers, the family of Kleber Claux, anarchist and nudist.

♔

'Iris', my father announced as we were breakfasting one morning years after he had sold his boat and we had moved from the McMahons Point houses, 'I dreamt last night it was raining and I had to go down to the boat and empty all the rafts'.

I have what may be the first certificate for the *Liberty* issued to my father, dated 1921, on a large cardboard sheet. It was to be 'exhibited in a conspicuous part of the Motor Boat' and lists the required number of life jackets, rafts and life buoys (stowed on the roof) and the 'local limits within which this motor boat is certified to ply for hire'.

The *Liberty* had a white hull and brown superstructure. My father sat in a driver's cabin at the front, almost on top of an eight-cylinder engine painted dark green, warm and throbbing and smelling of engine oil. There was an open-air back deck with a curved, ribbed wooden seat (licensed to seat eight). The main cabin had banks of seats (licensed to seat fifty-eight) and an out-of-tune honky-tonk piano with many dead notes. At the end of the day my father, who was the sole crewmember, tied his launch up at a stout timber mooring pile not far from his beach, and rowed ashore.

The name *Liberty* symbolised freedom and proprietorship. My father had printed invoice forms headed 'L. Lehman' – the double N was reduced to a single N, as this made his name look less German – and endorsed with his phone number B2560. (This became XB2560 when Sydney phone numbers were about to exceed one hundred thousand.) He kept a record of his takings from year to year in blue-black copperplate in a small notebook. But he did not record his earnings from repairing watches (a trade he taught himself).

Eventually my father received a large 'assets betterment' assessment from the Tax Office for undisclosed income. As a child aged about nine, I accompanied him to the office of a Mr Bickford, a hail-fellow-well-met sort of man, and heard my father explain his undisclosed earnings. Mr Bickford was a bit rough, I thought.

My father allowed me to witness all of this, perhaps so I did not repeat his mistake when I grew up. Filling in his tax return, he once pointed out it was prepared in accordance with the *Income Tax and Social Services Contribution Act*. 'You see son, I pay tax now and I'm entitled later on to the old age pension.' The promise of a universal old age pension made payment of income tax more attractive. The words 'Social Services Contribution' were later dropped from the title of the legislation, along with automatic entitlement to the pension. He never did receive it.

Almost thirty years after our visits to Mr Bickford, I prepared the will of the company secretary of one of my largest clients. I had known him for some years, and we had become friends. He was a bachelor, on the board of a chamber music society and a trustee of an Anglican city church. While chatting – after he had signed his will – he mentioned he had known a Lehmann, who drove a launch around the harbour. He had helped with his tax affairs. I had a moment of sudden recognition.

'Fred, that was my father! I used to come in with him to see you, when he had to pay that big fine to the Tax Office.' Fred Jackson had tactfully not mentioned this. I suddenly realised he was the person I believed as a child was Mr Bickford (Fred's employer at the time). My impression of Fred's 'roughness' may have been play-acting to relax my working-class father.

I have a memory of half a dozen or so boats at sunset careened in a placid reach of the inner harbour when for a few days each year the *Liberty* had its bottom scraped. At other times my father brought the boat ashore to his beach and worked on the hull himself. One afternoon when it was careened on his beach, he staged for family and friends a demonstration of the shockproof nature of watches that had Incabloc mechanisms, throwing and bouncing them off the hull.

He built a long wooden photographic enlarger (mentioned in his itemised list) and developed and printed his own photographs in the dim red light of his darkroom. Long exposure times were needed for night photography. For a year or so he tried to photograph the Harbour Bridge at night, with its lights reflected in completely still water. One night the harbour was like a sheet of glass for some minutes and the photograph was perfect. He sold the prints to a local shop. On nights like those, when there was no wind and the harbour was still, lying in my small bed at 'Ivanhoe' I could hear the lions at Taronga Zoo, several miles and bays away, their roars carrying across the water.

My father's photography may have been an adjunct to his boat business — to sell photographs to his weekend picnickers. This would explain his professional-sized Zeiss camera with its glass negatives and black silk shutter — a horizontal slit as the aperture.

Our family went on many of these weekend group picnics in the *Liberty*. The usual destination was 'Fairyland', a picnic ground owned by the Swan family in what is now Lane Cove National Park. The picnickers unwrapped cut lunches from dishcloths in baskets, and held egg-and-spoon and obstacle races in a large grassy area. My father used to call on the Swans, an elderly couple in their timber house set back from the picnic ground. They had a complicated gold-plated clock on a table — to my childish eyes a toy golden city, which emerged as its protective cloth was removed.

Because the river was tidal, the *Liberty* often got stuck on the way back, late in the afternoon. Wearing a pair of old shorts, my father would jump into the river, wading up to his chest, investigating and pushing, watched by the boatload of picnickers. One of the men would be deputised to sit at the controls while my father called out instructions from the water.

As the boat headed home at the end of the day, the mangroves of the Lane Cove River were left behind, and we were in the open waters of the harbour under a sky flecked with small orange clouds. I liked being in the front cabin with my father, beside the large, quietly vibrating green-painted engine. I pronounced engine as 'injun' and for years believed this was the correct pronunciation. 'I can hear singing in the injun, Daddy.' And I started singing to myself.

'He's singing. He's tired,' my father announced to my mother. I hated being told I was tired, and stopped.

A group of artists and bohemians periodically hired the boat for weekend picnics. This group included a family who were nudists and artists' models, the Claux family – my parents pronouncing their name as 'Clocks'. My childhood memory of the Claux children is of beautiful dark-haired adolescents with striking eyes. The son exhibited in the Wynn Prize landscape competition when he was a teenager, and died in 1950 at the age of twenty-one. Deborah Beck's book *Hope in Hell* has a 1948 photograph of the daughter, Moira. Naked to the waist, she is sitting surrounded by velvet drapery and holding a sword. The Claux family was my first exposure to the bohemian way of life.

Christina Stead's novel *Seven Poor Men of Sydney* describes a bohemian group going on a picnic in the late 1920s. I believe she is describing the same group my father began to take on picnics up the Lane Cove River in the 1920s, and which continued into the 1940s (but in the 1920s this group did not include the bearded nudist-anarchist Kleber Claux, who was yet to arrive in Australia). My father may be Stead's 'owner of the boat'. She wrote:

> They disembarked in some pleasure-grounds up the Lane Cove River … The sun set later on in a pomegranate sky; the smooth narrow river was like cloth of gold … When dark came rapidly … the owner of the boat lighted lanterns along the roof and they sat in the dark, feeling the breezes, listening to the creaking of wood and the lapping of the shore-water.

The harbour was the great spectacle of my childhood. Its surface brightened and darkened with winds and clouds, and the sun moving across the sky. Boats went to and fro, their wakes washing noisily against the barnacled piles of wharves. From my father's boat I used to watch water rats poking about under inner-harbour wharves – large whiskered animals in motley, some grey, some with dark pelts and light-coloured golden bellies, accosting each other and running about. I loved the shifting patterns of petrol spills on the water, like the rainbow hues of carnival glass.

Mornings of thick fog were a muffled rhapsody, with fog horns blaring, some close by and others far away, a symphony of too much information jamming the ears, boats suddenly looming up out of the mist, and dampness settling on everything as droplets of moisture. My father meanwhile had to stay levelheaded and steer through great billows and apparitions of fog in the direction of Balmain. The harbour was his workplace, his face furrowed from peering ahead at the water, watching for what might be approaching or crossing his path. A one-man boat crew required agility: as a wharf approached, leaving the controls and throwing a rope to curl around a bollard.

My father shouted a greeting to his friend Archie Bryant whenever their boats passed, Archie's boat with its varnished forecastle smarter looking than my father's with its dull brown paint. 'Archie doesn't own his boat', was my father's invariable comment.

He used to point out the Adelaide Steamship Company's *Manunda*, a large passenger ship with a single cream funnel – a hospital ship in the war. He explained the plimsoll marks on the sides of ships and encouraged me to follow him up rusty ladders onto their decks. As I stood on the edge of his boat which was moving and pitching, reaching across a treacherous strip of water in which I could not swim, I hated trying to get a grip on these ladders.

The *Liberty*

My father talked to managers in offices on the wharves, such as short plump Mr Bagley, standing with thumbs in the pockets of his navy blue waistcoat, in his glass-partitioned office on a wharf that had a ginger Manx cat, a rodent hunter *par excellence*, that held its face up waiting to be patted.

Late one afternoon my father took me into the front bar of the Blues Point Hotel. I was about six years old. Some mates of his were drinking there. He sat me on a tall stool and placed a glass of beer in front of me: 'Here, drink this son. It's good for you.' I took one small sip and recoiled – it was like salt water on fire. The men along the bar laughed.

For a few Christmases after the war my father took us to Manly in the *Liberty*. We tied up to a wharf, slept on-board and went swimming in a nearby public baths. Although he owned some black woollen swimming trunks, with the Jantzen bathing girl discreetly sewn into the corner – the standard men's swimwear for that era – my father usually wore a pair of oversize khaki work shorts that ballooned in the water.

He had no personal vanity. He looked in a mirror only to shave, and had no interest in trimming the small tufts of dark hair sprouting from his ears and nostrils. In the last twenty years of his life he wore second-hand clothes, picked up in auction rooms.

I was painfully slow learning to swim. My father encouraged me to float on my back, holding his hand under my shoulders, the water popping and tingling in my ears. At other times, when I was hesitating, he emerged from the water spluttering and roaring and waving his arms, and I backed away up the beach. Then one day, dog-paddling by myself in the Manly Baths during one of our Christmases, I found I was swimming in deep water. At last I could swim! Although not well.

During our Manly Christmases we slept on canvas stretchers. The *Liberty* rocked gently, tugging at the ropes securing it to the wharf, night-lights visible through the sheets my mother hung up against the windows for privacy. One Christmas morning, I found pieces of a Meccano set, sharp angles distorting the shape of the white pillowcase that hung by my stretcher. My father and I spent hours scrutinising printed diagrams and screwing pieces together.

The cabin was pungent with the fumes of fat and kerosene when he pan-fried fish on the blue flame of a Primus stove. Early one morning I hauled up his wire fish trap, set the previous night. There were dozens of small tailor, yellowtail and a silver fish with black stripes. I tipped them, panting, on the deck and started throwing them back in the water, as my father appeared in the hatchway, too surprised to protest as I threw the last of his catch into the harbour.

My father once took a party of my sister's school friends around Sydney Harbour on the *Liberty* – girls aged about ten from Ravenswood Methodist Ladies' College in Gordon. My sister's closest friend at school recalled this party when we met fifty years later. She and her school friends, who still regularly met, wanted to see Diana again, she said. But Diana showed no interest when I mentioned this invitation. My sister never talked about her school days and never went to old girls' reunions. After her death I met her school friend again. She told me her classmates, who still met regularly, had admired Diana's fortitude – she was one of their best runners.

A few years after the end of World War II, 'Leeward' (the grey weatherboard house rented by my father when he married my mother) caught fire and was burned to the ground. My sister and father talked about it with shocked disbelief as we ate dinner that night. I had no memory of living there and the fire meant nothing to me.

Since the early 1920s my father's profits from the *Liberty* and watch-repairs had been several times the average weekly earnings.

The *Liberty*

His frugally accumulated savings had allowed him to lash out and buy a couple of good-quality suits when he was single. He may have been wearing one of these at the party where my mother and he first met.

In 1948 my father sold his launch and stopped working for the Adelaide Steamship Company. He was fifty-six. The *Liberty* was converted to a houseboat by its new owner, a retired man, and a year or so later was burned to the waterline, when a Primus stove accidentally tipped over.

My father's occupation noted on documents had been 'launch proprietor'. It was now 'property owner'.

THE HOLIDAY IN QUEENSLAND

We were walking through the crowds at the first post-war Royal Easter Show in 1946. I had a blue balloon bobbing at the end of a string – the only balloon my parents ever bought me. A monkey in a cage reached out and scratched it. There was a bang and it burst, and I cried bitterly. I had enjoyed it for just two or three minutes.

We filed past displays in the Agricultural Hall – jars of preserved fruit, wool, sheaves of wheat, green and red apples, and massive pumpkins in many shades and fantastic shapes. The art deco exhibition halls set in manicured lawns and beds of orange marigolds and pink petunias symbolised our post-war revival, a self-conscious blend of the bush and the city, the wholesome Australia of Chesty Bond singlets and the two reigning radio quiz shows: the American Bob Dyer with his call of 'Happy motoring, customers' at the end of his Atlantic show – Atlantic was an American-owned petroleum company – and Jack Davey with his 'Hi ho everybody' and mellifluous voice – Davey began his radio career as a crooner and was often the voice-over in Australian newsreels.

The Royal Easter Show had a seedy side, a long alley of itinerant sideshows, spruikers in top hats, fat ladies and freaks

The holiday in Queensland

in tents, ghost trains and dodgem cars, which my sister and I glimpsed as our parents hurried us on elsewhere. Even as a five-year-old, I despised the confected wholesomeness of Jack Davey and the Royal Easter Show. As soon as I was a teenager I refused to go. I may have been more interested if I had been allowed to visit Sideshow Alley.

In 1948 my father was flush with funds from selling the *Liberty*. That year, when we went to the Show, he made inquiries at a Queensland Government stand about sugarcane farming and took home some literature. It is hard to imagine my mother with her Englishified ways as a sugarcane farmer's wife, but she had entrusted herself and her children's lives to this man who was like an alien to her, and I heard no arguments. My father was keen to go on a quick reconnoitre in Queensland.

There may have been another undiscussed reason for this expedition – my sister's congenital condition, which was 'fixed' by a series of surgical operations. Her months away from home in the children's hospital were over. She was well again, and it was time for a family celebration.

Plans for our family holiday in Queensland began months in advance. We visited the Queensland Tourist Bureau. All four of us sat down at a desk, for discussions with a bureau official, and collected colour brochures for the Barrier Reef islands. Two weeks in September were chosen.

We took our cheap, carefully labelled brown fibre suitcases to the Trans Australia Airlines depot in Phillip Street and waited for the airport bus. Once we were past the shops and office blocks and inner-city slums, the bus took us through a bleak industrial landscape of factories and large grey hangars, devoid of human beings, with just the occasional boarded-up house. There was an overpowering symphony of smells: rotten egg gas, rancid fat smells from boiling-down works, ammonia and tannery smells. I was secretly thrilled and dubbed this devastated stage set 'the street of a thousand smells'.

Kingsford Smith Airport was a flat windswept place. To board the plane, we climbed up a metal stairway on wheels. How my mother managed this, with her fear of heights, I'm not sure. With urgings from Leo and clutching the handrail tightly I suspect. The air hostesses, in navy blue uniforms and caps, and blonde hair tied back in buns, helped strap us in and solicitously pointed out the paper bags we were to vomit in, if we were airsick. They handed out barley sugar lollies as an extra insurance. We touched down at Brisbane and took off again for Townsville.

Waiting on the Townsville railway platform that night, I read a comic-book version of Wilkie Collins's *The Moonstone*. The train pulled slowly in to the platform, its engine hissing like a sea-monster, the warning bell slowly clanging and the carriages lit up like strips of honeycomb, jolting and groaning, as they eased to a halt.

We struggled down a corridor with our luggage and found our compartment, easing back the sliding glass door, and stowed our bags in steel-mesh luggage racks suspended above leather bank-seats facing each other. Our compartment had varnished timber walls with sepia photographs of tourist sites set in panels above the seats, and glass water beakers suspended on metal brackets.

The smell of the tropical night air and the sounds of the steam train, like the heavy panting of a horse, as it careered across the landscape, were intoxicating for an eight-year-old. We travelled past burning sugar cane, a rim of fire moving up the sides of hills in the dark. Pineapple fields were briefly lit up by the windows of our train and quickly engulfed in darkness.

The holiday in Queensland

Next day, with suitcases parked beside us, waiting on the pier at Bowen, there was a further surprise. The pier stood on pilings well above the water. It was built for 12 foot tides, dwarfing our Sydney Harbour tides of no more than 6 feet.

As we set out for Hayman Island late in the morning, I mentally compared my father's old workboat the *Liberty* with the palatial motor launch, its chrome fittings and varnished timber cabin. My father was chatting to the skipper and crew. He liked talking to strangers – a knack honed by dealing with passengers on the *Liberty* – but it embarrassed my mother. I looked over the side as an occasional large purple-brown jellyfish with stinging skirts went past and the turbulent wake spread out behind us. The water was an electric turquoise blue – much of the tropical Pacific lacks algae and is a marine desert. After some hours we were abreast of the Whitsunday Passage. My father pointed to the distant spouting of a whale. In the late afternoon we dropped anchor a couple of hundred metres out from the island, a heavily wooded volcanic outcrop in the ocean.

I was wearing sandshoes as we waded ashore through warm tropical water only a foot deep across a long stretch of sand. On our right there was a bleached coral reef. I referred to this moment in a poem which I wrote when I was fifteen:

> I remember
> The warm sleepy waters of the lagoon
> The ripples and spray splashing from my legs
> Breaking the calm.
>
> I remember
> The blue nightfall, the golden horizon,
> The sand crunching beneath my feet

As I waded ashore
Slowly approaching the dark looming island ahead.

I remember
The pride at being the first
To reach the ghostly shore, the night darkened palm,
And my fears when I thought I was lost
When those who came,
Came long behind me.

We were shown to a basic family hut among pandanus palms, one of a row along the beachfront. Our evening meal was with other guests in an airy dining hall full of cane furniture and tropical-coloured cotton cushions. For dessert we had pawpaw, grown on the island. I had my first cautious taste of its wet, aromatic flesh, and liked it. My father boasted about my soprano voice, and one night I sang 'Silent Night, Holy Night' for the manager.

The island's motor launch took us on day excursions. We viewed coral and fish through a glass-bottomed tender, moored beside cliffs crowned by hoop pines. There was a stampede of adults to commandeer the best positions around the glass viewing panel, their large bodies crouched together, peering down and jolted by the rocking of the waves. When I was able to get a glimpse, I saw large fans of red-brown coral with white tips in the blue-green depths of a remote world – something I could never be part of.

One afternoon we were taken to an uninhabited island. I was bathing by myself in a sandy bay away from the main group of people. In the water floated a glittering blue glass-like bubble, with long tendrils. As it drifted closer, I screamed out, my thigh burning. My father hurried across and carried me out of the water – my first encounter with a bluebottle.

Insects thrived in the tropical warmth. I watched large brown butterflies with cream markings fluttering around a bush in lazy circles, and a cat leaping, trying to catch them. My bare legs collected scabs from sand-fly bites. There was a family panic when our hut was invaded by a large hornet, my father chasing it away and announcing when it was safe to come back.

Despite the island management's advance publicity – 'It's close to the outer reef' – our first encounter with a living coral reef was a disappointment. After travelling for an hour by motor launch we disembarked and scattered across an exposed khaki-yellowish mass of coral, much of it dead, stretching for acres. It felt like a gigantic graveyard.

The only exciting thing for a child was the occasional giant clam, its richly coloured mantle exposed between open jaws. With the tropical sun beating down on my small canvas hat and water squelching in my sandshoes, I plodded aimlessly across a wilderness of barely surviving coral, through the shimmer and glare reflected off pools and wet surfaces. It seemed we would never reach the far-off line of white waves breaking on the ocean edge of the reef. Some of our group did. We didn't.

I have two hand-tinted photographs, taken by my father, of this place. In one I am wearing a blue-tinted canvas hat (it was white) and standing in a flat expanse of stag-horn coral tinted a dirty yellow. In the other I am hatless. In both photos I am in profile, a small boy in a large landscape looking despondent. John Blight's sonnet 'The Coral Reef' encapsulates this type of reef at low tide: 'this mass of death' and 'its vast progression'. I was relieved when we were told to return to the motor launch.

Near our hut, hidden among the stilt-roots of a pandanus, my father found some trochus shells with reddish banding and spiral pearl interiors, a melon-coloured bailer, some bleached clams, and a large glazed orange-pink spider shell. Despite a whiff of decay, he bundled them into one of our suitcases. He disapproved of collecting live shells, and (I suspect) enjoyed frustrating some unknown despoiler of the reef who was planning to come back for them after they dried out.

The island management warned against going on foot around the eastern shoreline. There was a risk of being trapped between 12 foot (3.6 metre) tides and the cliffs. One afternoon we put on stout sandshoes and slipped away. We walked along the main beach past a mass of bleached coral at the southern end, where a channel separated Hayman from Hook Island. We rounded the corner and were now out of sight.

My mother was unafraid at first. Glancing down, she saw rubbery black strips about 9 inches (20 cm) long, resting in the sand, just below water level. She thought they were tree roots. Then she noticed them swaying slightly in the wash of a wavelet. One of these torpid creatures had extruded a white, cotton-like, sticky mess. She let out a gasp of horror. 'Iris, they're bêche-de-mer. Sea slugs,' my father laughed. 'The Chinese eat them.'

My mother's feet had bunions and corns, from fashionable tight-fitting shoes, worn in her youth. She insisted on stopping halfway, sitting on a boulder. She may have been attended by my sister, then twelve years old. More probably Diana continued with my father and me.

Our father had chosen for our walk an afternoon when there was one of those tides referred to by W Saville-Kent in his 1893 book *The Great Barrier Reef of Australia* as 'extremely low spring-tides'. Our visit to the large, half-dead outer reef had in no way prepared us for what we now saw. We had stumbled upon a living coral garden, a long strip on the sloping leeside of the island, away from the wind, and sheltered by the nearby bulk of Hook Island.

The garden was vast, some of it exposed to the air or pricking the surface of the water: tan-coloured boulders of brain coral;

large fans of pink-brown table-top corals with pale yellow or pink growing tips, like the tiers of a wedding cake; pillar corals; cabbages; stags' horns of blue, green and violet, with splashes of rose pink and lilac; ledges that dropped into pools of blue water with sandy bottoms where iridescent fish streaked, some spotted, some with black or orange bands.

I was enchanted by the striped lionfish with its poisonous reddish-brown and white spines, patrolling like a sedate little zebra. A huge blue brute of a fish, as big as my eight-year-old self, glided past just a few feet away, making its way through the maze of connected pools. A groper, my father explained. He took several photographs with his cumbersome Zeiss reflex.

We walked carefully past the open jaws of clams, some a brilliant turquoise, others a rich browny-crimson, and may have given one a prod with a stick, to watch it clamp shut, with a small jet of water. We also stayed clear of the black spines of the sea urchins. I felt they were watching us, strangely alert and intelligent.

As we made our way along the steep shoreline, we came across what looked like small plastic columbines, draped across the rocks, and other much larger creatures like a giant rubbery leaf, pale green and buff yellow, exposed to the air, almost a metre across. These large, languid creatures were mysterious and alien. In adulthood I began to wonder whether I had imagined them. Then I found them in Saville-Kent's book: the Great Barrier Reef Giant Anemone or Haddon's Carpet Anemone.

The Great Barrier Reef is an oasis in a marine desert. Like a great city, its species have multiplied and specialised. Judith Wright's *The Coral Battleground* (1977) notes that Fred Grassie found more than 100 species of polychaete worms in a single 5.8 kg lump of Barrier Reef coral, which was more than the total number of species he had found elsewhere in the world. The reef is in constant motion, bleaching and renewing itself. At the start of an interglacial period, sea levels rise more than 100 metres – and the 1600 kilometre length of the Great Barrier Reef moves in a procession over miles of coastal land. When an ice age returns and sea levels drop, the reef retreats again.

When we ate in the dining hall that evening, we told no-one where we had been. After our week on the island we briefly stayed in Bowen and had a night at the open-air cinema. Bowen is in a rain shadow and we watched the screen sitting back in canvas deck chairs with no roof, apart from the stars. A night in 1948 at the cinema involved two feature films and newsreels. For the newsreels Jack Davey would have been the mellifluous voice-over.

When we got back to Sydney there was no further discussion about cane farming, and my mother did not become a cane farmer's wife.

I woke up one morning months later. I was still sleeping in my parents' bedroom. The sun was streaming in through the French doors from across Lavender Bay. I was quietly crying – crying for the memory of Queensland nights, the coral garden and the tropical blue water that was a marine desert.

MOSMAN PREP

My parents went to state schools, my father leaving school aged twelve and my mother aged thirteen. What happened I do not know, but my sister had a difficult time at her state primary school in North Sydney. My mother persuaded my father that Diana should go to Ravenswood Methodist Ladies' College at Gordon. She then persuaded him to send me to Church of England Preparatory School, Mosman. I went to Anglican schools for my entire school life.

Before I could be enrolled, we were interviewed by the headmaster AH (Tibby) Yarnold, then approaching eighty, who founded Mosman Prep in 1904. My mother, Diana and I went to his house in Mosman, where he lived with his pale-haired daughter and her husband, his deputy headmaster EC MacDougall, a plump man with bright red cheeks, who was marvellously good natured and adept at managing boys. While I was at primary school I did not realise how small Mr MacDougall was. We were all young and small. But even for primary school boys it was obvious Tibby was tiny and spider-like, with round spectacles that were large for his face. An outstanding scholar, he would have been headmaster of a top secondary school, except for his size. At our interview I announced: 'I've seen the Devil'. My mother had to explain this was Mephistopheles in Gounod's *Faust*.

The Mosman Prep coat and navy blue cap carried an embroidered white and blue crest and the motto *Non Nobis Solum* – 'not for ourselves alone'. In order to buy my uniform, we went to David Jones department store in the city. A uniformed attendant, twisting a brass handle back and forth, took us up in the lift, stopping and reciting the goods on each floor. I stood with my feet under an X-ray machine, to check the fit of my school shoes. I wriggled my toes and watched the bones move, lit up in a dim green light. On one of these David Jones visits, my sister and I discovered our mother's fear of heights, as we egged her on to leave the shop by the escalator. She stood paralysed, watching the cascading steps, and called out to her mother. We retreated to the lift.

I started school in 1946. The asphalt playground and red-brick and cream stucco castellations of the main building seemed gigantic. For a year my mother came with me on the tram to Mosman, a distance of 4 kilometres. She must also have accompanied me on the tram trip back home. From the start of my second year of primary school – I was then six and a half – I travelled by myself. Each day my mother gave me twopence for fares and a packed lunch in my small leather satchel and I set off, like a little adult, for the long walk up the hill to the tram stop outside North Sydney railway station.

Many old toast-rack trams were still in service. The conductor swung along the outside running board, with the leisurely lope of a foxtrot dancer, peering into each compartment and announcing 'Fez pleaz' and thumbing tickets from a clipboard. He stowed the money in a leather pouch hanging from his shoulder. Penny tickets, which the children bought, had a pale yellow band. Home from school one afternoon, I proudly handed my mother back a penny. When the conductor swung past, opened the glass door and peered in, I had sat there, staring ahead. Never do that again, my mother told me.

After school, walking home down Blues Point Road, I was aware of the stale reek of wine from a wine saloon. Glancing through the swing doors, I glimpsed women sitting at tables, each with a glass, often alone. Wine was a ladies' drink and I assumed they were alcoholics. Occasionally I passed a drunk slumped in a backstreet gutter. I was ready to run for my life at any hint of trouble.

McMahons Point had become working class. A few genteel people stayed on in fine old houses and gardens with harbour views. Old Mr and Mrs Bushell (from the Bushell's Tea family) lived across the road from us and walked their two Scottie dogs, who wore tartan dog-coats in winter. Dark-skinned, pretty girls lived in a house at the top of the steps leading down to the Bushells. They walked around in shabby dresses with no shoes. A grey cat – a Russian blue – used to greet me on their brick front fence. I spent minutes stroking it, before walking down the last part of the hill.

There was a shortage of teachers after the war and our first teacher was Miss Janet Cooper, about eighteen years old. Sixty years later at an old boys' reunion there were excited murmurs when her name was mentioned – I was not the only boy who had a childish crush on her. My one unhappy memory from her class is the little bully who sat next to me and stabbed my hand with a pencil. A tiny piece of graphite he left in the palm of my right hand is still there. As a left-hander who switched, I often did not know which hand was which. I used to consult the piece of graphite.

Boys addressed each other by their surname and Miss Cooper was 'Sir'. Our lady teacher in our next grade, an older woman who lacked the brunette glamour of Janet Cooper, was also 'Sir'.

In my third year there was an unpleasant surprise. We had no physical discipline from our lady teachers. Returned soldiers were still finding their way through teachers' college and in 1948 we had a relic of the profession, a tyrannical old teacher in his seventies, with a high yellow skull and wisps of white hair stuck like raw wool to his head. He had a tobacco-stained moustache and hawked from the back of his throat. Mr Hall's favourite expression was: 'Stop that humbuggin' about'. Boys who misbehaved were sent to the back of the class; they lowered their short pants a few inches, bent over and Mr Hall's long cane swept and whistled through the air, delivering two or three 'cuts'. I was caned a couple of times in this manner.

The ultimate disciplinarian was the tiny and ancient headmaster. If an infringement was serious, the boy was told to go to Mr Yarnold's office. This was a small book-lined room, where he sat reading, with a view through an open door to a small garden with a Rose of Sharon hibiscus covered with white flowers turning pink, like vanilla and strawberry ice creams. The boy presented himself and announced the prescribed punishment. Mr Yarnold stood up, and with no expression on his face took out his cane and delivered some short cuts to the outstretched hand.

The toilet block was a windowless, roofed building. It had an entrance with no door, and stank of ammonia. During the mid-morning play lunch and lunch hour, we stood before a perpendicular sheet of black rusting iron, higher than our heads and long enough to accommodate eight boys peeing side by side. We competed to see whose urine went highest. Sitting on a toilet was something done behind a closed door in a cubicle, and the unsavoury product was quickly flushed away.

Bottoms were our rudest body part, because what we did with them was hidden. Mention of 'bottoms' was greeted with a childish guffaw. A group of us was lingering after school in a large exercise shed where we used to swing back and forth across a set of monkey bars. A game of 'Show us your bottom' began. We took it in turns, briefly exposing ourselves. The plumpest boy tried to excuse himself. We had all humiliated ourselves and we cajoled and wheedled relentlessly until he gave in.

'Shagging' was something the six- and seven-year-olds did on the front playground. We did not know this word's vernacular meaning. They enjoyed tickling; their most vulnerable spot was the genitals and they faced each other, feinting and parrying like fencers. Older boys enjoyed more grown-up forms of assault. 'Itchy powder' – hundreds of small seeds from the seed balls of plane trees – was stuffed down a boy's collar from behind. The sadists delivered 'rabbit killers' with the edge of the hand to the back of an unsuspecting boy's neck.

Party invitations in envelopes would sometimes be handed around the classroom. The Mosman cinema was a popular venue. One boy's father owned Mynor, the manufacturer of 'Green Ice' cordial (that I fed to Puss). During one party, we inspected the bottling factory. Another father owned Classic Comics – my copy of *The Moonstone* was part of this series. He hired a double-decker bus to take all the children to a picnic ground. As the little boys scrambled up the back stairs to get the best seats on the top deck at the front, I decided their rushing was pointless and was the last to board. I was relieved my parents did not hold a class party for me.

I used to travel on the tram with the only Mosman Prep boy living in the North Sydney region. Living in a 'slum' area was something we shared. Before going to his mother's house, he was minded after school by his grandmother in one of a row of decayed workmen's cottages, in a lane behind a large furniture shop. As she began washing him, standing in a basin on a table, I quickly said good-bye.

The 'lads' of McMahons Point had competitions roaring down the steep hill of King George Street in home-made timber billy carts. A boy I'll call 'Lars' lived with his parents in 'Roma', a large old white-painted residential from the Victorian era. Lars wanted my help with a money-making scheme that would let him buy the expensive ball-bearing wheels for one of these billy carts.

He was a pupil at the school attached to St Francis Xavier's church, next to the railway station. He took me inside the dimly lit church one afternoon, dipped his fingers in holy water, crossed himself and genuflected. I realise now this was a small pantomime to impress me with his rectitude. Lars did not understand Protestants regarded Catholics as inherently dishonest, and this demonstration made me suspicious.

He took me to meet friends of his, tough local boys, billy cart owners, crouched among lantana bushes on overgrown wasteland, and handing around a roll-your-own cigarette made with tobacco salvaged from cigarette butts. They insisted I take a puff and laughed when I coughed on the smoke. Lars suggested I have the name 'Bashful'. I sensed this word was an insult, and was glad they did not bash me up.

One winter morning Lars arrived at our house with a hand trolley. He was about to execute his plan, which I had not understood until then. We toured the neighbourhood and collected lengths of timber from old wood piles. He was a bossy boy and kept demanding 'Bashful' drag the trolley around while he knocked on doors and sold firewood to housewives. Even when an angrily shouting man chased us off his property, it did not occur to me we were selling stolen wood. I had no interest in the rewards Lars insisted he would give me. Dragging the trolley around was a chore and I disliked Lars's bossiness.

A few days later he invited me back to 'Roma'. I waited in the grand, dilapidated central hall outside the door of his flat, and thought it was odd he did not ask me in to meet his parents. Lars may have worried I might blurt something out. Eventually he came out and handed me some purple Indian postage stamps and 'cigarette cards' – he knew I was interested in these. This was the final settling up he had planned. Lars was a boy with principles.

I woke up in bed one morning a few weeks later and almost cried. Lars and I were thieves! Lars probably chose me as his accomplice because I was a naive private school boy, and he was tempted by my father's piles of wood, the largest in Lavender Bay. But I must have made it clear they were not to be touched.

'Cigarette cards' were carefully folded cigarette packets, made to look like a card. Before World War II, actual cigarette cards depicting sportsmen, actresses, animals and birds were inserted into cigarette packets and keenly collected. With the World War II paper shortage this was discontinued and never resumed. So schoolboys began collecting empty cigarette packets and fashioning them into substitute cigarette cards – like other wartime substitutes.

Among the cigarette packets Lars gave me was a double Three Threes State Express. Unlike the cheaper packs of ten, popular with working men, a double pack held twenty cigarettes. Lars's double Three Threes was a nondescript dark crimson-red. But it was an absolute rarity – I had never seen one before. I knew I could sell this at school for sixpence – not something I told Lars.

Until then boys at Mosman Prep had traded 'cigarette cards' in small isolated transactions. One morning I brought my entire collection to school. Boys swarmed around me as I sold them during the morning break and lunch hour. I typically sold for four or five pence a double packet of Clifton (moderately rare and glamorously blue), single packets of red or blue Capstan for a penny (these had a small ship's capstan pictured in the right bottom corner and were a working man's cigarette), a brown single Capstan for threepence (these were rare), and so on.

Boys were attracted by the variety of packages. Kensitas showed a bow-tied waiter in a red circle holding out a pack on a plate. Craven 'A' was a red packet with a black cat's head in a white ellipse. The most romantic pack was a double Player's Navy Cut. A bearded sailor's head was framed by a white lifebelt on a seascape at sunset – the only pack I ever coveted. I did not have one.

Not long after the school lunch hour began, I had sold my entire collection. My takings were four shillings and eight pence halfpenny. As we went back into our classes, a ban on the sale of 'cigarette cards' was announced. This ban left me with an uneasy feeling. That was the end of my interest in 'cigarette cards' – once they had no monetary value.

A few weeks later, a red and white object washed up on my father's beach. It was a waterlogged cardboard replica of a Craven 'A' packet, about 2 feet (60 cm) high, a model from a tobacconist's window display. A couple of months earlier, it would have astonished my schoolboy customers: worth two shillings at least. I picked it up reverently, examined its condition – it had the salt and oil slick smell of the harbour – then dropped it back on the beach, with the other flotsam and jetsam.

We also collected cicadas. They were deafening in summer, 'Greengrocers' in every tree and on every bush, so we had to block our ears. 'Yellow Mondays' were less prolific, and 'Floury Bakers' and 'Cherry Noses' were moderately rare. 'Black Princes', small and noisy, were a great prize. In wild bushland we occasionally heard a black 'Double Drummer', the bass baritone of cicadas, high up in a group of trees. Most of us thought it was cruel to keep cicadas in bottles. We loved to hold them, and feel their prickly feet crawl up our arms; then we threw them in the air and they took off like little rockets, croaking and peeing as they flew away.

Primrose Park was a favourite place for cicadas and where we also played cricket in summer. I was an outer fieldsman, and for much of the time just stood there in a pleasant green haze. I was rarely asked to bowl and did not survive for long at the crease to bat. What was far more interesting was a disused sewer works at the end of the park, a vast concrete Babylonian ruin. Late in the afternoon some of us lingered after the stumps were pulled up. When the teachers were all gone, we headed for the sewer works, jumping down into old settling vats for human sewage, now harmless grass. We ran around, our voices echoing among the concrete walls and tunnels until it was time to go home, trudging up the hill as the sun declined in a dusty, peach-coloured sky.

In winter we played rugby union. I became inner centre in the backs. This was where I could do least harm. My role was simply to receive the ball, run with it a short distance and pass it to the outer centre, who passed it to the wing. Wings were speedy. For a few weeks I became mildly notorious as a tackler, running and throwing myself in a crouching position at the thighs of a boy from the opposing team who was running with the ball. I later lost my nerve. I chipped a tooth, tackling too high. 'It serves you right', the referee told me.

Mr O'Brien, a cheerful, no-nonsense thirty-year-old, taught us in my fourth year of primary school. We started Latin and French, pronounced in a healthy, Australian way. 'Dans', for example, was pronounced 'danz'. I shared a desk with Alan Bishop, a gentle, thoughtful boy with a round face and red hair (the future husband of a well-known Australian politician, Bronwyn). After school we sometimes went back to his house in Mosman. He had a bike – a novelty for me.

On the last day of the year we went on a class expedition to Taronga Zoo. We had our report books to take home, little books with bright blue covers and a dozen pages showing our progress from month to month, signed by teachers and the headmaster. Alan and I were leaning over a metal fence to look down at a rocky pit inhabited by a tribe of spider monkeys. Alan's report book was sitting in his shirt pocket and fell into the monkey pit. A spider monkey sidled up stealthily, attracted by the bright blue cover. Little hands picked it up and tore it in shreds. Alan burst into tears. I wondered what he would tell his parents. Alan had no memory of this event when he had become a judge and I reminded him forty years later.

I was walking up to Spit Junction with a new friend after school. He began talking about how rich his family was. He asked for a loan, explaining how he would soon be able to pay me back. I had been taught to expect strict honesty – he need not have given me this long-winded explanation. I had a two shilling coin in my pocket – a significant sum for me – and handed this to him. In the following weeks I asked several times for my money back. He ignored me. I learned a lesson from Lars and this boy. I was careless about money only once later in my life.

Another friend was Christopher Tadgell. Waiting in a queue for a school bus, we were discussing Strauss waltzes. As a nine-year-old Wagnerian, I argued Strauss waltzes were not serious enough to be good music. Christopher disagreed. He enjoyed waltzes. In 1982 we caught up again at an Australian High Commission dinner in New Delhi. He was preparing *The History of Architecture in India*. Christopher has published over twenty books on the history of architecture. One Amazon reviewer writes: 'Tadgell gives equal weight to all cultures…'

Mosman Prep appreciated music. We learned the Jacobite song 'Charlie is my darling, my darling, my darling./ Charlie is my darling, the young Chevalier.' It did not occur to anyone this song was seditious. One afternoon the whole school gathered in the large assembly hall and we heard the *1812 Overture* from a small portable gramophone. It was very rousing. We went to concerts for schools in the Sydney Town Hall. When the orchestra began Tchaikovsky's *Waltz of the Flowers* there was a ripple of soprano excitement, girls and unbroken boys' voices whispering: it was the theme of a radio serial, *The Search for the Golden Boomerang*.

․․․

The year 1950 was our second last year of the primary school syllabus. Our new teacher was a nervous young man. We were the first class he had ever had – perhaps his last. He became 'Beaky' because of his nose. His classes were a rabble; he had difficulty speaking above the uproar. We began talking insurrection: our parents pay school fees; we'll get them to get rid of this hopeless person, and so on. I was complicit in this hypocritical talk. He was replaced by a young teacher who stared us down. French classes with our new teacher, Mr Walters, were a surprise. He spoke French with strange nasalised vowels and a uvular 'r'. It sounded very affected. Did French people really speak like this? Mr Walters was my first encounter with an intellectual – not a word I knew then. Despite this, he had a good control of our class.

(In the 1980s I got to know Ray Walters again at the University of New South Wales, where he was a lecturer. I was teaching law in the commerce faculty. I had no sense of any age difference between us. It seemed bizarre that he was my teacher in primary school. Ray convened a book group and invited me to a discussion of Proust's *À la recherche du temps perdu*. I had the pale blue and red volumes of the Scott Moncrieff translation – considered superior to Proust's original by Joseph Conrad. I sat in my office between classes, reading Proust – my third attempt. In about six weeks I read the 1500-odd magical pages from start to finish.)

We were given weekly elocution lessons by Mrs Sheila Hancox – I think that was her name. Taking off her hat, which had a net veil, she made an entrance like a *grande dame* in long floral dresses. She had us deliver little speeches, while she sat on a chair on the dais, appraising and correcting. I decided to 'improve' my accent. By the end of the year, a boy I got on well with, who had a broad Scots accent, ribbed me for talking like a stuck-up English boy. For years afterwards I was asked 'When did you come out from England?'

My mother used to read to me from Alexandre Dumas' *The Count of Monte Cristo*. She liked to quote the mysterious count's remark that 'punctuality is the politeness of kings'. I started reading Dumas myself. On my tenth birthday my mother left on my bed twenty-four volumes of Dumas in a cardboard box. I could not believe it as I unfolded sheets of brown packing paper and extracted book after book with crimson cloth binding and gold lettering on the spine. She had only a small allowance from my father and must have bought these books out of the modest bequest from her farm labourer uncle John (as well as the Lipp piano for Diana's piano lessons). That was the high point of my love affair with my mother.

I became a fanatical reader – Dickens, Conan Doyle, Jeffery Farnol and Defoe (authors recommended by my mother) – as well as Dumas. One morning I was reading a book in the tram. As I got out and headed down the hill to Mosman Prep, still reading my book, I walked into a telegraph pole.

In mid-1950, it was decided our class of forty was too big. (That may have contributed to the Beaky catastrophe.) Classes of about thirty-two were the norm. I was one of six boys chosen to move up to a class of older boys who were taught the 6th class primary school curriculum. We were to be given special tuition until we caught up. I had been six months younger than the average age of the other boys. I was now eighteen months younger, the baby of the class. One of the boys who moved up with me was David Raphael, who later became a tax lawyer, like me, and the only primary school friend who is still alive and with whom I have stayed in touch.

A few boys in that class had some understanding of sex. Once our class went for a couple of days to the Blue Mountains. One evening we went on a bush walk beside some cascades, and were singing 'Ten green bottles hanging on a wall…' I overheard stifled guffaws as one boy recited to another: 'Tom and Mary went to the dairy/ Tom pulled out his long and hairy…' I did not hear the rest of the rhyme. It was disgusting and incomprehensible. Despite my sexual naivety, when I was playing the part of a girl in a school play, as we were about to go on stage I popped a couple of socks into my dress to simulate breasts. The boy who had the male role opposite me thought this was a great lark.

At the end of 1950, most of our 6th class went off to secondary high schools – many to Shore School. About twelve of us stayed on and did our first year of high school at Mosman Prep. Our teacher was the deputy headmaster, Mr MacDougall, the plump, red-faced, easygoing son-in-law of Mr Yarnold. Thus 1951 was one of the pleasantest years in my school life.

When I was much younger I had lost a penny, when I agreed to play 'Heads I win, tails you lose'. I had now taught myself a few tricks. During the lunch hour, we played a geographical game. If one of us said 'Assam' the next person had to find a place beginning with M. If the reply was 'Madras', the reply to the reply might be 'Sussex'. A place name ending with X was always a problem for the next boy whose turn it was, although we all knew some obscure place names beginning with X, such as Xaquixaguana. I had a place name which I saved up. When asked to respond to 'Middlesex' by a smiling boy who was confident all the X's were exhausted, I replied 'Xcalax'. I spelled the name. There was an incredulous silence. I opened the lid of my desk and produced a battered red nineteenth century atlas my father had picked up at auction. It was starting to fall apart. I pointed to 'Xcalax' in the index – a place in South America.

Another boy and I were given special coaching by 'Tibby' Yarnold, as we were sitting for a scholarship to Shore later in the year. Tibby loved the classics. He concentrated on polishing up our Latin. He could see I was fascinated by ancient history and gave me Sayce's 1889 book *The Hittites*. One of the prizes he chose for me at the end of the year was Guerber's *Myths of Greece and Rome*. I fell in love with the ancient gods and heroes and treasured this in my high school years.

Mr Yarnold and I shared a connection, which I discovered years later. I do not know if he was aware of it. His father was the Anglican rector at Christ Church Lavender Bay. In 1891 his father recruited my grandfather to go on a mission to New Guinea as the carpenter, and was a witness on the death certificate when my grandfather came back later in the year, extremely ill with malaria, and died just after his return.

I was an unbaptised war baby. Mosman Prep was Anglican and we went to chapel once a week at St Clement's, a large redbrick church next to the school. I enjoyed a few of the more rousing hymns and was vaguely intrigued by the change in colour of the church's cloth vestments with each liturgical season: white and gold, and at other times red or green. But I had the feeling this was all meaningless pomp, and I hated going down on my knees.

Mosman Prep

As a boy soprano, it was suggested I join the regular choir at St Clement's for the Sunday service. Perhaps because we lived a long way away, at McMahons Point, nothing came of this. I was secretly relieved. Churches were gloomy places.

Parents (which meant mothers) were invited to come to our weekly chapel service. My mother was starved for female friends. She began appearing at the back of the church with a few other mothers. These mid-week services were one of her few social outlets. She could mix with other ladies of her own class (as she saw it). But these women had refrigerators and middle-class husbands, and lived in respectable neighbourhoods. She could not invite them back to her house.

At the end of each term, there was a Sunday service which we had to attend with our families. My parents and Diana came. The church would be packed with the boys' families and the usual members of the congregation. In my last year at Mosman Prep, 1951, I read the lesson from the Bible at these crowded services in my boy soprano voice and faux English accent. No one had explained to me that italicised words in the King James Bible were words added to the divine text by the translators. I puzzled over their significance and whether I should give them extra emphasis. I read the lessons, I hoped, with a graceful expression and an uneasy emphasis when I came to italicised words.

My pride in being chosen as the lesson reader for these large end-of-term congregations was not spoiled by having become an atheist. One afternoon I was in my father's fibro laundry, the ramshackle two-room outhouse in the wasteland between the skinny house and 'Fifty-three'. I was in the junk room that was not used as a laundry, and looking up at the sky through a dusty window. I was ten years old. I idly reasoned that if a passing cloud crossed the sun, this would tell me whether there was a God. I did not wait to see what happened to the cloud. I decided God did not exist.

'FIFTY-THREE'

Perhaps like many childhoods, some images from my McMahons Point 'latency phase' seem to come from a time when I was just barely awake. One night we shone a powerful torch across the bay at the railway yards next to Luna Park, and saw a dim gleam answer back from the blank windows of a darkened train.

On another very still night we rowed across to a submarine moored beside the railway yards. We were scrambling up and boarding when naval officers appeared and warned us to leave. Puffing up my seven-year-old lungs, I uttered boastful threats.

The harbour was a great conveyer of floating rubbish. Coke and timber turned up on our beach; also dead cats, rotting fruit, the odd coconut, and unidentifiable flotsam oily with grime. Towards the end of the war, a rusted-out naval mine, about 4 feet (1.2 m) in diameter, appeared on rocks at the far end of the beach and sat there for years, then was gone as mysteriously as it arrived. At low tide I used to scramble far out among seaweed-green rocks to visit the home of a green eel. It poked its head out, and quickly retracted.

One night during World War II, a sandstone cliff-face collapsed. The rumble woke my parents and Diana. Next morning they stood at the top of this small cliff and looked down. Dislodged by the roots of a Port Jackson fig, large blocks of sandstone had fallen onto the bottom level beside the beach, dragging down sixty-year-old iron railings. The new yellow cliff face was soon smothered with Crofton weed – rank-smelling, with chocolate-red stems, dark triangular leaves and small, furry white flowers.

I have no memory of the collapse. In my early childhood Diana and I picked bunches of nasturtiums at the cliff bottom – orange, yellow and crimson, with blotches and stripes. Along with white arum lilies, they grew in the damp soil among the fallen sandstone blocks. The pale green tangle of their stems brushed against my legs as I waded among them. I liked the way a silver dewdrop sat in the middle of each leaf.

When we moved up the hill to the skinny house, I became obsessed with 'Fifty-three', our mansion next door. We did not ever live there. It became the life we never had.

My father's three-quarters of an acre (0.3 ha) was a botanical lost property office. Fruit trees were scattered across the various levels: a peach, a nectarine and a guava with small, acrid red fruit. A loquat with dark metallic leaves and barely edible yellow fruit grew beside the rocks I used to wash. The beautiful plants were mixed in with weeds – fleabane had prolific seeds and asthma weed had grey hairy leaves and thin brittle stems growing from cracks.

This profusion of beautiful and less beautiful plants was the start of a life-long fascination. Each afternoon after catching the tram home from Mosman Prep, I began haunting a flower shop beside North Sydney railway station. I stared at the plants in the window. I wandered in and gazed at the colourful pictures on seed packets. The shop owner had a standard greeting for me: 'How are you today, boss?'

The grounds of 'Fifty-three' were the epicentre of this botanical eclecticism. We did not speculate about who had planted all these trees and flowers. The original owners of the skinny house seem to have had a maritime connection – with their souvenir from Ben Boyd's yacht. We assumed their descendants owned the three houses until my father bought them.

Recently I searched up 'Leddicott'. This was the name 'Fifty-three' had on the title deeds. It became the property of John Davies, a George Street draper, in the late 1870s. He named it after his father's property in Shobdon, Herefordshire. His wife, Jane, was a colonial soprano and poet, whose *nom-de-plume* was 'Desda'. She wrote a children's book and the words for 'Cooey! An Australian Song'.

It seems Davies bought the skinny house and built 'Leddicott' on the vacant land next door. The cottage lower down the hill may already have been there, or was built as an afterthought. I suspect Desda may have been responsible for the great variety of plants which entranced me as a child.

There was yet another name, 'Bellevue', on an embossed metal plate fitted to 'Leddicott's' front gate. Had Desda argued for this more glamorous name? The iron gate was painted a fading green and stood between stone pillars with rounded tops. An asphalt path led past a stand of banana palms, masses of yellow chrysanthemums that flowered in autumn, and ended at a Norfolk Island pine. There, a flight of stone steps led up to the front door of 'Fifty-three', painted a faded green like the gate. The door had a yellow cut-glass handle and two long glass panes.

I used to watch the striped yellow-green abdomens of hoverflies circling above a bed of shasta daisies and dwarf papyrus. Every year the banana palms produced only black, stunted fingers of fruit, and an apricot tree no fruit at all. Desda's biggest mistake, if it was hers, was to plant a jacaranda which never flowered. Jacarandas are picky about salt air.

Margaret Cohen – the poet Douglas Stewart's wife – did a pen-and-ink drawing of the front door of 'Fifty-three' just before the house was demolished (the Stewarts's wedding gift when I married in 1969). It shows a cast-iron railing panel with a distinctive 'flower' – perhaps a stylised waratah – as its centre-piece. A cast-iron balcony railing with these panels surrounded three sides of the upper storey and much of the ground floor.

My father used to bowl a tennis ball to me – tennis balls were less likely to break a window – when we played cricket on the ground floor veranda. This was paved with black and salmon-coloured tessellated tiles. I patted the ball back with my 'Bert Oldfield' cricket bat – a birthday gift.

My father kept a close watch for encroachments on our southern boundary with a slipway. When Diana and I picked nasturtiums by the beach, we were aware of men moving about in the cavernous works, the sound of hammering, the piercing light from a welding torch, a motor starting up and throbbing as a boat was slowly hauled up. On special occasions an ungainly man in a full rubber diving suit, swaying from side to side, descended into the water to carry out repairs, breathing from a compressed-air hose.

Each year my father pruned a pussy willow hedge that stood between the garden of the skinny house and 'Fifty-three'. Along from this hedge, three hollyhocks – yellow, white and a deep double pink – were fed by the stream that leaked through his cellars and emerged as seepage over a rounded rock shelf. They crawled with bees in summer.

Birds loved my father's vegetable beds. He cut large cat faces out of tin and painted them black, with white whiskers, staring eyes and laughing mouths, then dangled them from poles in the beds. The birds took no notice. He next suspended a large trawl net above his beds. In the morning he walked out on our front bedroom balcony (that trembled when you stepped on it) and pulled on a hundred feet (30 m) of rope. The beds were down a steep hill from the skinny house. Birds flew up as the net rose and fell.

I was never punished. I was four or five. My father was away somewhere on his boat. A patch of cannas, with bright yellow flowers, grew near the beach. The sappy plants towered over my head and I ran through a jungle of intersecting paths, trampling them, obsessed – I couldn't stop – until I had flattened them all. I was astonished and scared. Later in the day my father's boat came back. I stood shamefaced among the slaughtered stems. He laughed: I'd done some good work, he said.

I was now a couple of years older. A friend and I daubed ourselves with tar from a pot of warm tar left by the slipway workers. I was panicking when I traipsed up the hill for the evening meal. I got a mild reprimand from my mother, who lit the hot water geyser in the bathroom and had to scrub it all off. There were tar marks on the side of the bath for weeks.

For thirty years my father's eldest brother Carl, a small inoffensive man with white hair, had been courting Lily, who had fine white facial hairs. When this odd couple visited, Lily gave us tea cups and saucers from her workplace, a wholesaler – seconds of expensive brands, slightly chipped or cracked. Afterwards my mother was scornful about these gifts and pointed out that Carl was a former admirer of Hitler.

My father used to invite Carl for inspection tours of his vegetable beds. One day he suggested Carl should help himself to some parsnips. I hated their strong flavour. My father was pottering elsewhere, and I kept egging Carl on to take more. Carl looked at me doubtfully, but did not stop. In the end he had a big armful of long creamy-white roots and green leaves and not one plant was left in the bed. When my father caught up with us, Carl nodded at me: 'The boy told me to take them.'

The respectability of roses was reassuring for my mother. She planted three tea-roses in the front garden of the skinny house. I hated one of these. 'President Hoover' had creamy, spiral flowers like old women with heavy make-up. I did not associate my mother with older women, and thought she was beautiful, despite her thin lips.

I never saw her unclothed but I could not avoid seeing her ageing body imprisoned in bulky undergarments: flesh-coloured brassieres and corsets, and big ugly bloomers. Every morning, as I shared their bedroom, I heard my father snoring – a stentorian snore, that rose to a strangling crescendo, stopped, then started again. When I asked him how old he was, his reply, year after year, was a joke: 'Son, I'm twenty-five'. I worried about my parents' mortality.

I was about eight years old and playing with neighbouring children near the vegetable beds. A sudden sun-shower started and they chanted 'It's raining, it's pouring, the old man is snoring'. The phrase the children were singing – 'the old man' – seemed cruel and mocking. Their parents were younger than mine. The sun-shower and children chanting reminded my of a recurring dream I used to have. In my dream, my parents had died and I would wake up with tears on my face.

My father planned to support the family with rents from his houses when he sold the *Liberty* in 1948. He may have expected wartime rent control would disappear. But legislation entrenching rent control was passed in the same year. He was fifty-six, had a wife who did not work, and now two children at private schools. He may have worked his boat for a few years longer if he had realised two decades of near-penury lay ahead.

The first tenants in the red-roofed cottage were an English family. They were replaced by the Leitners. 'Old Man Leitner' as my father called him was a Jew, bald with a hearing aid, who survived the Nazis because he had an Aryan wife. She had a goitre (an iodine deficiency caused this, my parents explained, which could happen to people living far away from the sea).

The Leitners lived with a fair-haired daughter, Lotte, who had a ginger-haired toddler. They also lived with a son, Freddy, a handsome man with a broken, flattened nose and a beautiful Italian wife, Juliana. Freddy had fought for the Germans in Italy, my parents said. They suspected his broken nose was not an accident. Old Leitner had an aquiline nose.

There was no shortage of would-be tenants. My father chose the Leitners because he warmed to 'Old Man Leitner'. They conversed in loud voices – old Leitner holding a hand up near his ear that had no hearing aid, and my father partly deafened by thirty years of engine noise as he criss-crossed the harbour in the *Liberty*. The Leitners installed large knitting machines in the front veranda of the cottage and pulled the handles backwards and forwards hour after hour. Knitted woollen stuff piled up in baskets beside the machines. Freddy worked for a debt collection firm and at night came up to our house to make business phone calls.

We were invited down the hill to inspect Juliana's newly-born son. We tiptoed into their front bedroom where he was asleep. (This had been my parents' bedroom, where I slept until I was five.) Pointing to her stomach, Juliana asked *sotto voce*: 'Am I still as fat?' I did not understand the mechanics of pregnancy. I was abashed. For me, she was the most beautiful woman I knew – more beautiful than my eighteen-year-old cousin and even Miss Cooper. I stammered: 'Yes'. She laughed. I realised I had made a mistake.

The Leitners were good tenants, but my father had to work hard to get a living from his main source of income, 'Fifty-three'. He glassed in the front veranda of the downstairs flatette on the southern side. My sister and I helped him hang new wallpaper. At one stage the tenants in this flat – according to my father – hid some old boots under the house, to become mildewed and claim to the Fair Rents Court that their flat was damp. Their claim may have been true. The wall of their kitchen was built into the side of the hill and was permanently dank.

A middle-aged couple, the Scanlans, sometimes invited my father in for a cup of tea in their northern downstairs flat. This had been one long room – the former ballroom, my father said – now divided by a folding screen, varnished cedar on the living-room side, and pale green on the side facing their kitchen. They explained to me scenes from the Knights of the Round Table depicted on the tile surround of their marble fireplace.

Mrs Humphries, well into her seventies, with prominent false teeth and purple-tinted, permed white hair had the upstairs northeast flat. Her balcony had not been glassed in and the original railing was still in place. She had just a room.

Old Mr Matthews occupied a room at the back of Mrs Humphries's flat. He smelt of sweet, stale tea and stood at the door of his room in a dressing gown – a bookish, smiling sort of man. He became increasingly frail and moved out. My father glassed in his part of the veranda, creating a narrow L-shaped kitchen on the corner of the building. It was the last bit of veranda my father glassed in. I was with him while he was cutting up rosewood slats for the venetian blinds, and sawing the fibro panels – carcinogenic asbestos dust floating in the air – on which the windows were to stand.

'Fifty-three' had just two bathrooms, including toilets, shared by all the tenants: one upstairs and one downstairs. All the flatettes and both bathrooms had bulky grey-painted metal gas meters that had to be fed with pennies. The door to each flatette had a yellow cut-glass handle. The tiled downstairs hallway had white arches held up by plaster female heads with flowing hair, and a wide cedar staircase leading to the upstairs hallway. Windows in common areas had red and blue panes, or clear glass with stencilled frosting.

My father was often on the slate roof of 'Fifty-three', replacing broken slates and patching sheets of lead in the valleys. In later years, when his houses were almost deserted, he complained about thieves stealing the lead off his roof.

I never penetrated far into the low, dark cellars of 'Fifty-three' where my father stored the large framed engravings he bought for their glass, and old brass beds he bought for resale as scrap metal (while salvaging the small hand-painted ceramic decorations). But friends and I fossicked in the former stables of 'Fifty-three', inspecting the hundreds of empty liquor bottles stacked there by the tenants. We ignored spiders and the smell of alcohol dregs, fascinated by colourful labels and different bottle shapes. When the bottle-oh came, we heard the clashing noise of glass tipped into hemp bags.

My father kept inventories for each flatette's contents, down to the knives, forks and spoons. Each item added up and brought in extra pennies every week. He bought everything at auction, and had me shake hands with Mr Ellis the auctioneer at his favourite Bridge Street auction rooms. I slept in second-hand pyjamas, and my childhood bed-sheets were stamped 'US Army'.

'Fifty-three'

I sometimes accompanied him to the tenancy courts, where he was fighting battles about rents. When he advertised a vacant flatette, he was deluged with begging letters. Our family sat around the dining room table of the skinny house, reading and discussing each letter. My father held up one: 'Listen to this: "Please let me have a go at your flat".' He laughed: 'Have a go at your flat! We don't want him!' This shortage of accommodation and my father's stupid battles in tenancy courts, I was beginning to realise, were the result of government rent controls. By the age of ten I was a believer in free markets as well as an atheist.

I was about to go to a high school where my classmates would be much older and my friendships weaker. Much of my childhood was solitary. There was a 20 foot (6 m) high stone embankment between the two levels of East Crescent Street. I used to stand at the bottom with a tennis racquet, hitting a ball against the rock face, and imagine I was adopted.

DIANA

'I like being a woman', my sister Diana once said.

A few years after Diana's death I was with my Japanese daughter-in-law Manami and grandson Rui, inspecting apartments. They were spacious and newly built, in landscaped gardens with a sprinkling of older brick buildings, tastefully restored. It was sunny. Everything was calm, architect designed, with a lot of greenery.

I began to have an odd sense of *déjà vu*. Some of the older buildings looked familiar. Then I found a plaque. This had been the site of the Children's Hospital in Camperdown, where I spent hours sitting on lawns at age seven, waiting with one parent to visit my sister in her hospital bed, while the other was visiting her or talking to doctors. My sister did not have a fatal disease; she had something wrong that was not explained to me, and over some months had a series of operations.

Other parents of fatally ill children may have been even more anxious than my worried parents, and also waited on these lawns or stood by the beds of their children in these older buildings that were once hospital wards.

I do not know when my parents found out my sister was born with a congenital defect. When it was discovered, they concealed it from relatives and friends, and there was a long history of silence and secret shame that my sister maintained after our parents died, and until her own death. One of her repeated directions was: there was to be no autopsy and her body was not to be used for medical research.

⚊

Diana was born in December 1935, eleven months after my parents' marriage. She was baptised 'Diana Isabel Lehmann' five months later. I was born during the war and my parents never got around to having me baptised. At the Anglican schools where I was a pupil, when the issue of my being confirmed in the Church of England was raised, I would point out there was an impediment: I'd never been baptised – I was quietly proud of this fact.

As a child, I teased my parents about the set of initials they'd burdened my sister with: DIL. My father photographed Diana many times during her first four years, and wrote her age in ink on the photographs. In one she is in a swimming costume on the beach next to 'Leeward' – a normal little girl, hair still wet and salt water droplets clinging to her skin. In another she is sitting by herself in a white organdie dress at a child's tea party, fair haired and with a cheeky smile. My father made her small cream table and chairs and painted Minnie Mouse designs on them.

I have copies of two letters sent by my mother to her cousin in Melbourne. The first is dated August 1938 and is from 'Leeward':

My Dear Molly,

How are you all? Well, I hope. It has been a cold winter has it not.

Leo took this snap of Diana one Sunday morning – she is

2yrs 7 mths – or at least she was then – she is into the 8th month now. Her father made the furniture, which is a deep cream. There is nothing Diana likes so much as to have a 'tea par' she calls it – with nothing to eat mind you. She abbreviates all big words. She always calls Grandma 'Ma'. I say to her 'Where shall we go today?' and she says 'Ma's'.

Hoping you are all well

Love from Iris.

There is no anxiety in these letters. My sister looks like any other little girl. My impression is she had an idyllic childhood in the first four-and-a-half years of her life and my parents were unaware of any problem.

Then I was born.

Because my father worked his boat on weekdays, there was no-one to look after Diana while my mother was in hospital giving birth. Bella, the 'Ma' of Iris's letter, lived a few streets away, was in her mid-seventies and not too elderly to play the piano. Most grandparents would have been delighted to look after a granddaughter aged four-and-a-half. But not Bella, it would appear.

Whatever the reason, Diana was sent off for a short stay at a children's home. A few days became prolonged when my mother's milk failed and my anxious mother along with the baby (me) was sent to a Tresillian Centre to revive her milk. For a woman who was afraid of anything to do with the human body, getting her milk back was traumatic – sleepless nights, hot and cold compresses several times a day, and nurses inspecting and pummelling her dry breasts until at last milk came. (When I was twelve years old, I was the involuntary audience for my mother's repeated stories about this ordeal.)

Meanwhile my sister was still at the children's home, feeling abandoned, as the days became weeks. Weekend visits from her father did not alter the feeling of abandonment – something that lingered with her for the rest of her life. My sister rarely talked about her emotions, but this was a time she sometimes mentioned.

My mother and I came home, and my sister came home. But life at 'Leeward' was not the same. My mother was now forty-four and absorbed in caring for this unexpected baby – this pre-menopausal statistical outlier. I don't know what the sleeping arrangements were at 'Leeward'. But when we moved along the bay to 'Ivanhoe' in about 1941, I slept downstairs in my parents' bedroom in a cot, and Diana slept upstairs in her own bedroom. This baby – me – lived in the most privileged room in the house, the parents' bedroom. Diana was exiled upstairs.

My mother used to call me 'my pet lamb'. My father may have worried she was turning me into a sissy. He used to call me 'Tiger' and recite:

What are little girls made of?
Sugar and spice and all things nice.
What are little boys made of?
Slugs and snails and puppy-dog tails.

I hated being made of slugs and snails and puppy-dog tails. I would have much preferred sugar and spice. The 'sugar and spice' may have been a doting father's overture for Diana. She was still the apple of his eye (and remained so until his death). He called her 'Princess' and continued to take many photographs of her.

In about 1945 we moved up the hill to the 'skinny house'. My parents' bedroom was upstairs at the front of the house, facing the harbour, and my sister's bedroom was at the back, facing the street. She was now on the same floor as the rest of us and her bedroom was large and sunny. I was envious. Although this time I was in a proper bed, once again I was sleeping in the same room as our parents. I suspect Diana resented this – I was still the favoured child and she was the exile.

Diana was hostile and bossy and I got back at her by nicknaming her 'Stinker' – but not to her face. She was bigger and stronger. I recruited younger friends, Jimmy and Ivan. I'd call out to them, 'Look! Stinker's coming. Let's hide.' We started collecting Lord Howe Island palm seeds, which were like large green bullets, and storing them in the decaying stumps of Moreton Bay figs my father had cut down. Our plan was to bombard my sister. We enjoyed climbing up on the stumps, which were taller than we were, and preparing for an aerial Armageddon.

That day never came. But my enmity still festered. Diana and I were down on our beach sitting on the sand, and our father was fixing things on the *Liberty*. It was a peaceful morning. I noticed a piece of wood with a nail in it, part of a fruit box that had washed up. My sister's back was turned and I weakly thwacked her with it, drawing blood. My father saw something was wrong and rowed ashore. I cried so loudly and piteously that he must have thought, 'Here's Diana picking on her younger brother again', and he began to berate her.

My sister's heartbeat developed an unpredictable arrhythmia. When her heart began beating quickly, our entire family hurried up Blues Point Road and took a tram to Dr Dey's surgery opposite St Leonards Park. The arrhythmia always stopped by the time we reached Dr Dey. My sister began to grow rapidly and became tall for a girl of her age, with heavy acne and perhaps facial hair. I took no notice of the details but it seemed to me she was growing suddenly like the giant Alice of the illustrations in *Alice in Wonderland*.

Her odd appearance drew unwelcome attention. She may

have been threatened in the train on the way to school. She was certainly attacked by some of the Lavender Bay children. My father brought her home in tears. A small cut to her face was bleeding. What happened was not explained and I did not ask.

When she was about eleven, she was hospitalised for some weeks at Camperdown Children's Hospital and her adrenal glands were cut out, the only treatment at that time. (There may have been some surgical reconstruction as well. I became aware of this possibility after my sister's death.) Her doctor was Lorimer Dods, Australia's first Professor of Child Health. For the rest of her life Diana had to take cortisone.

My sister was deeply ashamed of her disorder. It affects about one in 10 000. In the nineteenth and early twentieth century, before surgeons began removing adrenal glands, women who grew beards masqueraded as men. In Joseph Furphy's *Such Is Life*, a boundary rider, Nosey Alf, with a disfigured face, sings and plays the violin in the moonlight in his lonely hut, and the narrator Tom Collins fails to recognise 'he' is Molly Cooper. Nosey Alf had a light down above his lip and was not one of those bearded women. But he was one of that group of women whose bodies forced them to live as men.

As a child I had only a vague idea of what Diana had gone through. I was under the impression she had been operated upon more than once. She sometimes described to me what it was like – one child confiding to another in thrilling and ghastly language – the sickly-sweet smell of the gas (she referred to it as chloroform) and the sinking feeling as she lost consciousness, like a lift rapidly descending, and the nausea when she woke up. These experiences in the operating theatre made her want to be dead. I do not know how much she understood as a child. But enough was explained so that she submitted to the treatment, which was radical at the time.

Our bodies have two adrenal glands, duplicates of each other, one above each kidney. I imagine she had surgery twice: first, one gland was cut out, her condition was observed, and then the other was cut out. The protracted treatment, the anxious waiting between operations and the ordeal of the eleven-year-old girl were all experienced by me at second-hand.

Dr Dods was a careful diagnostician. He used to examine the elastic of my sister's school hatband for traces of fungus that might be aggravating her teenage acne. (In my twenties I suffered from recurrent conjunctivitis in my right eye. Diana, applying what she had learned from Dr Dods, suggested my eye trouble was caused by my hair, parted on the left and flopping across into my right eye.)

Our mother trained my sister to be intensely private, but she liked prying into other people's lives and looked up Dr Dods's address in the telephone directory. On a weekday during school holidays when it was unlikely anyone would see us, my mother, Diana and I travelled by public transport to the eastern suburbs and stood outside his house. We looked across a brick fence down into his garden. He lived in a cream brick cottage with a second story. I can still see his house, as though I am still standing there. I was ashamed of my mother's indecent curiosity and wanted to run away and hide.

Diana was at Ravenswood school when she was absent from class for weeks and inexplicable things were done to her in a hospital. She may have wondered what was in the minds of her classmates – if they noticed when her body began developing strangely – and what they thought about her absences, if they thought about them at all. My sister rarely mentioned Ravenswood later in her life, although I think she enjoyed her last few years there and had school friends who would have liked to stay in touch.

Academically, she was about the middle of her class. Our family attended school sports days and the end-of-year prize giving. Her growth spurt stopped. By her final school year, she was normal height, with a trunk slightly longer than usual and legs slightly shorter. The heavy acne eventually faded.

The sister–brother hostility also faded. My sister appreciated she had been given piano lessons by Miss Bosworth, an advantage I was denied as a boy. She set about teaching me to read music, and showed me how to practise scales. I became moderately proficient in some easy scales, but without formal lessons I did not progress. The only piece I remember her playing (expressionlessly, as an exercise in finger gymnastics) was Beethoven's 'Für Elise'. I began to hate the opening notes of this piece. I suspect she was simply indifferent to it. When the piano lessons stopped later in high school, she never opened the piano again. After our father died in 1968, we divided the furniture up, and my mother and Diana were happy to leave the yellow walnut veneer Lipp piano with me – someone who couldn't play it.

With the onset of puberty I also had pimples – not as extreme as Diana's – and she shared with me her tube of Teenaid, a pink ointment, a proprietary medicine manufactured by the communist father of the artist Keith Looby, who later became a friend of mine.

Diana's favourite subject in her last years at school was ancient history. I read her text book avidly. After we moved to the Sydney suburb of Gordon, she arranged for us both to join Gordon public library. I started reading *Science Digest* and popular psychology and acquired a smattering of Freud, Jung and Adler.

On Saturday mornings, under Diana's leadership, she and I began borrowing books from a bigger library in the city ('in town' as we called it). The Sydney Municipal Library was in the Queen Victoria Building and permeated by the sickly scent of wine from the Penfold cellars in the basement. This, however, neutralised the dusty smell of thousands of old books. I was excited by the pseudoscience of Velikovsky's *Worlds in Collision* and a book about Colonel Fawcett's fatal search for a lost city of gold in the Amazonian jungle.

When Diana was awarded a Commonwealth Scholarship there was family talk of her studying physiotherapy at university. It would have taken longer than a secretarial course. My mother was a trained stenographer and may have wanted a daughter who followed uncritically in her footsteps. My mother's ambitions were focused on me. It was an era of low expectations for women and Diana was encouraged to go to a secretarial school, which she did.

Diana never expressed regret at her lost career as a physiotherapist. My regret at the time may simply have been egotistical. After a year at Miss Hale's Secretarial College, she was happy to become a legal secretary.

There may also have been an unacknowledged family dynamic at work. My mother's own mother, Bella, had groomed her to become the spinster child who would support and care for her until she died. Then the docile Iris at the age of thirty-eight broke free and unexpectedly married. Iris may have had an inkling Diana could be a companion into her old age. Unlike Bella's failed attempt, my mother's probably unconscious entrapment of her daughter succeeded.

There was a paradox in this. My mother was a timid person and Diana was strong-willed and determined. But Diana had a body which betrayed her as she matured. She wanted to hold onto her early years of innocence. Her mother was a link with that time. I, too, became a willing conspirator. I didn't have to worry about my mother – she was cared for by Diana. They found love and comfort together.

The late 1950s were some of Diana's happiest years. During the week there was the novelty of being a secretary at an old established law firm. She would come home with stories about the senior partner old Mr Crowther, her boss Mr Edwards, and the employed solicitors and articled clerks. Sunday was a washing day and almost every Saturday the four of us went by train and bus – our father couldn't afford a car – to a beach or place of interest. Later in life Diana longed to re-create this period and did not seem to understand why I did not.

She later became a voluntary aid or VA at Lady Gowrie Hospital for veterans. On her scheduled weekends she dressed in a pale blue uniform with a red cross stitched onto a white patch and walked out of the house in her tightly-laced black nurse's shoes.

When I was about nineteen I had a dream. Diana and I were flying past a coastline of sandstone cliffs, side by side with our arms stretched out. We were suspended high in the air above a calm grey-blue sea.

Diana formed three good friendships at Miss Hale's: Shirley Lee, a forthright ethnically Chinese girl who lived in Dixon Street in Chinatown; Gerda Pick, who was the daughter of Jewish refugees from Europe; and Roseanne Fuller, a beautiful girl with brown eyes and hair who inherited her looks from her mother, but not her mother's wildness. I often saw Mrs Fuller about the city, small and dressed in a Gypsy fashion: multiple black pleated skirts, bangles and long earrings. She was a legal registration clerk – an occupation that attracted free spirits, as they did the rounds of court offices and registries with bundles of documents in fair and foul weather.

Roseanne had a remarkable calm and equanimity. Diana's friendship with her lasted throughout Diana's life. My sister drifted apart from Shirley Lee – they may have had differences. She remained friendly with Gerda Pick but the link became tenuous after Gerda moved to Melbourne. Both Gerda and Roseanne married and had children.

I was about thirteen when my sister took me to lunch with Gerda and her parents at their northern beaches house. We ate outside on a raised patio and Gerda's mother served cold meat with a salad – a few slices of tomato, half a boiled egg and two or three iceberg lettuce leaves, neatly set out on each plate. I tested the bits of salad warily. It wasn't like my parents' mashed salads sluiced with brown vinegar, sugar and salt. I remarked afterwards to Diana that the Picks' salad was one I could eat. I was relieved – I was no longer weird.

Diana began taking me to Keatings Dance Studio above Newtown railway station when I was about fifteen. We learned the jazz waltz, the quick step and foxtrot. I was one of the youngest there, a slow and clumsy learner, an adolescent version of the child who fell over on the steep paths of the skinny house. The bored female dancing instructors, with permed blond or brown hair, led me around, in their lightly perfumed cloud. Though half in love with them, I regarded these eighteen- and nineteen-year-old women as intellectual inferiors.

My sister started going to dances by herself. She had admirers – one of them a young solicitor. I sensed there were men she fell in love with, but she held back. She could not tell them about the events of her childhood. One night she came home from a dance, upset. She had allowed herself to be monopolised by two Italian men. They told her 'how kind' she was to dance with them, and 'you should have a boyfriend'. Then they quarrelled over who should have the next dance. They told her 'come out with me on the weekend … become my friend … you're the only girl who likes me…' Eventually one asked her to marry him, and she left hastily.

There had been no family holiday since the 1948 Hayman Island trip. As soon as she had saved money from her first job,

Diana paid for a family holiday in Melbourne, taking my mother and me – our father did not come. We stayed in a temperance hotel and music from *My Fair Lady* – just out – was playing in a foyer decorated with enormous blue-dyed feathers in a brass bowl. Iris was able to see her sister Eva and brother Tommy, and revisit the site of the old St Kilda Palais de Danse which had burned down. We stayed at a guesthouse in Sorrento, a beach resort outside Melbourne, where Iris had holidayed in her twenties with her mother Bella – in the era of silent movies, glamorous nights and eligible young men who had courted our inhibited mother.

More family holidays (minus our father) at Nambucca Heads and Forster were to follow. For the Nambucca Heads holiday, we caught a train to Macksville, then a bus through timber-getting country, picking up and dropping off children after school. I saw a beautiful Aboriginal girl with a green shawl, sitting at the back of the bus. I wrote a poem about her in which I saw: 'in a jungle of vivid green/ The strange unfolding of a dark brown iris.'

The single-storey guest house at Forster looked across the water. A couple on their honeymoon sat across the room by themselves for the evening meal. The bride's face was lightly flushed, and when they left after a couple of nights I was downcast. We hired a small open boat. I had to pull-start the inboard motor with a leather belt, and we chugged across great shallow lakes under glaring January skies, avoiding sand shoals. When I started my second year of university, I stopped coming on these holidays.

Diana obtained her first and last passport. Labelled 'British Passport Australia', this described her as 5 feet 4 inches (1.6 m) tall with blue eyes and brown hair. In August 1961 she and her friend Roseanne passed through the Suez Canal. Diana visited the house in Wales where our grandmother Annie Jones grew up. They travelled in Europe and their ship arrived back in Australia before Christmas. In Switzerland one night, in a restaurant with a tour group, Diana jumped up from her table afraid, when a man crawled up on all fours, pretending to be a cow and grunting around her legs. The other diners tittered. Diana was reliving her panic as a child, when our father used to crawl up on all fours to the kitchen table and pretend to snip the hem of her frock with phantom scissors, reciting:

And cut her petticoats all about
And made the old woman to shiver and sneeze.

My sister never travelled overseas again. She began to suffer unpredictable nausea attacks and illnesses, even on short car trips. She never drove a car. She was convinced losing her adrenal glands and the cortisone she took had unbalanced her bodily chemistry.

Diana began taking colour slides of the family, 'warts and all' photographs, in our old clothes: my father sitting in a dilapidated cane chair in the sun wearing a pair of old shorts and a singlet; me in pyjamas, unshaven and lying idly in bed, a model of adolescent ennui and affectation.

There was a lunar eclipse of Venus in 1962. It was a clear and brilliant night and my sister decided to photograph the moon as it inched across the planet. Hurrying down the old wooden steps of our Gordon house she unfolded her tripod on the lawn and set her camera for a time exposure. About a quarter of an hour later she reappeared in the house, with camera and tripod, disappointed. Her attempt had failed. It was a technical impossibility.

Diana's social life was narrowing. I bought a length of tangerine Thai silk for our mother to make into clothes for her. 'Where can I wear it?' Diana insisted. 'I'm too ill to go out.' The silk was folded up and put back in its brown wrapping paper for storage in a cupboard.

Diana

When I married at age twenty-nine, my mother and sister began hinting I should have no children. Dr Himmelhoch, our family doctor, told me the gene for my sister's condition was rare, both parents had to have it, and the child had to get two copies. I might not even have the gene. He told me the name of my sister's condition: congenital adrenal hyperplasia.

I imagined it might be worse for girls. When my first child, a girl, was born, I had a pang of dismay. It being the early 1970s, a time when husbands did not usually attend births, I arrived in the delivery room shortly after Julia was born. With a proud smile and holding my naked daughter by the feet, Dr Himmelhoch displayed her to me upside down. I did not realise at the time what he was showing me: this is a normal little girl.

THE HOUSE AT GORDON

All the houses of my childhood have vanished, except one – the cottage at Gordon, my last childhood house, where I fell out of love with my mother.

In the late 1940s my sister and I were at private schools. Our mother was concerned we should live in a suburb suitable for private school children. She may also have been hoping to form friendships with other mothers. It was awkward telling them she lived in McMahons Point. My father was North Sydney born and bred, but happy to move. His habits of speech were changing. He still made mistakes – pronouncing 'monk' to rhyme with 'honk' – but he was no longer dropping his 'g's' at the end of words like running; and there were fewer 'bonzers' and 'buggers' (though he had never used words like 'bugger' in my mother's presence).

Our family went to look at possible houses along the North Shore line. Our northbound train had to go through two tunnels. The windows chattered in their frames, and the sound of steel wheels on steel rails ricocheted off the tunnel walls. I imagined thousands of pieces of broken glass were being shaken around until we emerged into daylight and an abrupt silence.

As we emerged from the second, shorter, tunnel, the North Shore Gas Company's khaki-grey gasometer, as high as a six-storey building, loomed up from a valley of untidy bushland, and beyond it the gasworks that dumped coke in the harbour that we gleaned for our winter fires.

I brought *Middy Malone* comic books on these train trips. I could not read, but revelled in their full-colour illustrations on large pages of thick, good quality paper, and learned about pirates and sailing ships and the Sargasso Sea. (Their author and illustrator was an Australian socialist cartoonist, Syd Nicholls, who started his own publishing company when no-one would publish his *Middy Malone* stories. Nicholls may well have been one of the bohemian picnickers my father took up the Lane Cove River.) I knew parts of *Middy Malone* off by heart. Once, as my father was reading it to me in the train, I anticipated the next panel and announced 'and the sails began to creak'. My father laughed.

We found a house in Gordon. There were still price controls just after World War II and the owner wanted more than the regulated price. When contracts were exchanged, my father gave Mrs Freeman a diamond ring (bought at auction for about a third of the retail price) to clinch the sale.

The Gordon house had 'protected' tenants and we had to wait for them to move out, which they did two or three years afterwards. Their only child carved his initials 'VB' into the cream painted stucco of the Gordon house. Not long after they left, Victor was killed when his motorbike collided at an intersection with a car driven by an old man.

The house next door to our Gordon house was also owned by Mrs Freeman. She had sold it and moved out by the time we moved to Gordon. The new owners were a former naval man, who was Irish, and his Russian wife. They had a daughter, Helen.

My father set about clearing the long backyard – chopping down hundreds of tall privet bushes and dozens of wild tobacco or bug trees, with their unpleasant smell and large furry leaves. The Russian lady was upset when my father began hacking down this mini-forest. Her words, leaning over the fence, to admonish him – 'Chop! Chop! And down they come!' – became a family joke.

The house once belonged to Launcelot Harrison and his wife Amy Mack. He was a professor of zoology and published light verse under the pseudonym 'Alter Ego'. She wrote children's books. An old lady, Miss Austin, was often out weeding in the front garden of her large house on the corner of our street. She told me the poet Louise Mack lived in our house. Louise was Amy's sister and wrote 'To Sydney': 'O little City, let me tell – / A secret woven of your wiles…'

After my father had chopped down the mini-forest, thousands of bulbs sprang up in the grass and flowered in the following spring – yellow ixias and white sparaxis with a russet reverse – the ghosts of the Harrisons. This bookish couple also bequeathed us a small arbour in the back garden: a tall red-flowered *Chaenomeles* (flowering quince) and plum trees with small white flowers, followed by small, bitter, red fruit. When the plums and quince were flowering – white-flowered branches arching over red-flowered prongs – Puss lounged among the falling petals, his tabby coat sticky and honey-scented.

The move to Gordon had a downside for Puss. When the weather warmed and he looked out of sorts – an unambiguous symptom was his back legs faltering – we searched him for ticks. If we located a paralysis tick, bloated like a small, blue-grey bag, my sister or I held him down, and our father poured turps on the tick before removing it with tweezers. The powerful smell of turps hung around Puss like a cloud he could not escape. As soon as he was released he ran off into the garden and stayed away for hours. One day we could not find the tick. My mother was the only person with him as he died. She was distraught when we got back late in the afternoon.

The house at Gordon

The house had a rusty galvanised iron roof that had once been red and the front section of the house was stuccoed brick painted cream. One of the two front bedrooms became my sister's, and the other my parents'. We had a dining room 30 feet (9 m) long and a 1919-style bathroom, primitive even by the standards of 1951, with no hot water apart from a gas-heated geyser. In a wooden box fixed to the wall, next to the toilet seat, were neatly cut-up squares of newspaper – substitute toilet paper, then still a luxury.

The rear section was weatherboard and had weatherboard ceilings varnished a handsome red colour and weatherboard internal walls painted a dull ochreous yellow, like solidified fat. There were three rooms at the back: a small sewing room, a large kitchen and, next to it, my own bedroom – at last!

I became a prolific reader. I sat up in bed reading the red and gold Dumas volumes my mother gave me. I had no understanding of the 'mistresses' Dumas wrote about and my mother studiously ignored this aspect of his books. I once read all night – Dumas's *The Black Tulip*. As the sun came up, I switched off the light, relieved my all-night reading was undetected.

A long path led to the back door and kitchen. It was bordered by a tangled wave of wisteria, grey and ugly in winter, and with heavily scented pale purple flowers in spring. I began to take an interest in the garden – not the sort of interest parents would normally welcome. Weeding had no appeal. I just wanted to plant things.

Where the bulbs died down, the grass was long and rank. We attacked it with a scythe. Scything requires a precise motion, like a ballet dancer's movements. My sister and I learned from our father how to swing the handle, balanced between two hands, the grass toppling neatly at the light touch of the long, curving blade.

Our mother took Diana and me on a picnic in the Botanic Gardens. We were walking along a curved path under tall trees when I saw Kurume azaleas for the first time. I was excited. They were like stamps in a child's stamp album: masses of small neat brilliant flowers. Some were bi-colour, white with pink or mauve edges. Later in the week I went back and took as many cuttings as I dared. I treated them with cutting powder but only one thrived – 'Hinode-giri' which had become a large shrub with cerise flowers when my sister and I sold the Gordon house twenty years later.

When we moved to the Gordon house, our weekend expeditions to places of interest began in earnest. My sister later looked back on this time as the halcyon days of her youth. My father had an unstated plan to swim at every beach in the Sydney region. We would take a picnic lunch packed in a wicker basket, and might buy an ice cream, if we were lucky, before coming home late in the afternoon.

My father mentally ticked off the beaches one by one. South of the Harbour Bridge we went swimming at Watsons Bay, Bondi (where excrement from the sewer outlet sometimes floated past), Tamarama, Bronte and Maroubra. The narrow surfing beach of Tamarama, surrounded on three sides by cliffs, was treacherous and we sometimes had to struggle through a deep gutter of water to reach a sandbank where surf was breaking normally. We travelled once or twice all the way south to Cronulla by train for a swim.

We went on bush walks at Kurnell along sandy paths. 'Here, suck this' my father used to say, picking the leaf of a sarsaparilla vine, refreshing with a dark, bitter-sweet taste. A leaf from a similar looking vine had no flavour at all. Walking along the cliff-face he pointed at dolphins or 'porpoises' as he called them – diving and swimming in the brightly lit waves, not far from the shadow of the cliffs.

We also went on train journeys further south to Thirroul and Austinmer, but never got as far as Wollongong. These southern train journeys, setting out from Central Station, began with a descent into 'the bottleneck', where dozens of rail tracks crossed and trains travelling in the opposite direction thundered overhead on tall brick viaducts. Once we were out of this maze of brick arches, as we rushed along, our heads turned at every mile to read the dark blue enamel plate advertising the distance from Sydney and Griffiths Teas in white letters.

The train took us on through forests of eucalypts with naked cream trunks and angophoras with orange-pink trunks. Tree ferns and cabbage palms, and the red floral head-dresses of Gymea lilies on 3-metre-high green maypoles were scattered like jewels in this primeval landscape. This was the train journey DH Lawrence describes in *Kangaroo*.

We also caught trains heading north to Mt Kuring-gai and Mt Colah, for bushwalks. These 'mounts', insignificant hills even by Australian standards, only 30 kilometres from Sydney, are now suburbs. We were bought frothy milkshakes at the Mt Kuring-gai general store. Placing the metal containers on the linoleum-covered counter, the fleshy armed proprietress turned to my sister and me: 'How do you kids like being in the country, eh?'

On our walks we encountered the tiny white star-like flowers of heaths, held on stiff stems with metallic green leaves. If we were lucky, we saw the small cupped pink flowers of a stand of *Boronia serrulata* on a sandstone ledge. Or 'native rose', as my father called them – 'common when I was a child', he explained, and since then pillaged for the cut-flower trade.

Sometimes our bush walks were close to home. We once saw an echidna burying itself in bush sand at our feet on the walk down to Rocky Creek. The creek became a waterfall with a large green swimming hole at its foot. If we did not swim, we left Iris behind, reading a book. As we continued downstream, the valley widened and became a natural amphitheatre. An old white-bearded dosser camped there under a long shelf of rock. In December thousands of yellow and red Christmas bells flowered on the valley floor. They have vanished along with the dosser.

The end of our walk was the upper reaches of Middle Harbour, a string of tidal pools that were a refuge for injured, gashed fish. High above us a white sea eagle hovered on thermals.

Coming from the bright colours and fragrances of the untidy Garden of Eden at McMahons Point, the Australian bush felt alien and drab. But I slowly realised the flowers were not all scentless. Some had an overpowering honey fragrance. I became fascinated by the great mosaic of plants, their subtle variations and ancientness, a Joseph's coat of species living happily together. They were perfect gardens that cared for themselves.

I shall not list the dozen or so northern beaches we visited, except to say that Harbord (or Freshwater, its other name) could be as treacherous as Tamarama. We came by public transport and had to change in 'bathing pavilions' if we wanted to swim. These 'pavilions' were brick buildings with showers and benches. Many had large courtyards open to the sun, where men stretched out on a towel and sunbaked with or without swimming trunks. I was yet to reach puberty and knew nothing about sex, but I thought it odd when a youth of about sixteen walked across the courtyard with an erection. I was glad to be with my father and not by myself in these places.

Our mother sat on the sand in her straw bonnet and cotton dress, minding the towels and clothes, with a small umbrella open at her back to provide shade, as Diana and I waded into the water

The house at Gordon

with our father. Once a month Iris was joined by my sister, and only my father and I went swimming.

My father installed a thirty-year-old Maytag washing machine in the cavernous laundry under the Gordon house. The Maytag was a square metal tub on thin metal legs and did little, except rock the clothes back and forth in the suds. We then spun the clothes in a small aluminium spin dryer rotated by water pressure from a laundry hose. Not unlike a steel beer barrel, open at one end, and spinning rapidly above a tub, this was another of my father's bargains from the Bridge Street auction rooms.

My mother was afraid of these machines. My father became the impresario of our Sunday washdays, with my mother standing by anxiously. One of my sister's colour slides is of Leo, like a man in a Diego Rivera painting, with a broad back and an arm reaching across to hang out a sheet.

When we moved into the Gordon house I made friends with Helen, the ten-year-old girl next door. I was an ignorant, innocent child, and I believe she was too. She would come in from her parents' house and we would sit on the ground and invent games to play. I was at an all-boys school and she was the first girl of my own age I had as a friend. One evening my mother said: 'You're not to play with that girl next door. And I've told her mother that too.'

I was stunned. I could not believe my mother, who was my confidant and supporter, was telling me this. I felt she was being unjust – to me and to my new friend. I never spoke to Helen again – I was an obedient child. At night I used to lean on the railing of our side veranda that overlooked Helen's house, and whistle improvised tunes, imagining she might hear. My feelings towards my mother began to change.

About three years later I was lying in bed one night. My mother came into my bedroom and observed my hand move under the bedclothes as I quickly placed it by my side. She regarded me with a look of dismay. She said as she left the room: 'You're not the boy I thought you were.'

BELLA

In late 1905, a group of relatives gathered on a wharf in Melbourne. They were there to welcome Dr and Mrs Rainer back to Australia. Twelve years earlier, the newly-married couple had set out for England – William to complete his medical studies and Bella, a bride known for her 'mahogany red hair', to entertain and keep house for him. Now he was a doctor and they had five children. Looking up from the wharf at the ship's deck, the relatives were shocked. The pale faces of the five children gazing down over the railing – one of them was my mother – were frightened and bewildered.

The following year my mother, ten years old, found her father dead on a couch in the Queensland mining town of Eidsvold. She (and her mother and siblings) had only just been reunited with her father, who had gone north ten months earlier. Later that day she went in to look at his body for a last time. She thought his teeth were beautiful and opened his mouth for a last look. There was a smell of onions.

'Smile and when you smile another smiles and soon there's miles and miles of smiles and life's worthwhile because you smile.'

Going through my sister's documents I found she had written this out on a piece of paper, possibly after our mother died in 1983. It was a favourite saying of my mother's. Diana seems to have treasured these words as a fond memento. I felt a flash of anger – with our mother, not my sister. I hated that saying – its banality, its falsity. I was ashamed I could still feel such anger. I stopped loving my mother when I was ten.

Also in among my sister's documents were Bella's – my mother's mother's – three scrapbooks. One was filled with newspaper photographs and cuttings about kings and queens and the British nobility. She prided herself as an expert on the lives of the aristocracy, checking their genealogy in her blue covered Whitaker's *Peerage*. She spent thirty years cutting out newspaper stories about the rich and famous, and pasting them into this scrapbook. Keeping track of the goings-on of these strangers was her full-time profession. Apart from briefly working as a governess before her marriage, Bella never worked again. After her husband's early death, she expected her children to support her for the rest of her life – children she sent out to work after the minimum years of schooling. I threw this scrapbook away.

The other two scrapbooks had material that was more personal and I kept them. I was hoping to glean confirmation of family stories. Both were tall books covered in ultramarine blue cloth. The less interesting scrapbook had been volume II of *Geography and Atlas of Protestant Missions*. A bookshop stamp indicates Bella bought it cheaply at a sale, after she moved to Sydney. She then filled it with the overflow of newspaper cuttings, collected over decades.

Pasted on the *Atlas*'s inside cover is a newspaper account of the wedding of my mother's younger sister Eva just after World War I:

> An interesting wedding took place at Holy Trinity Church, Balaclava ... The bride wore white crepe de chene [sic] and georgette with a satin train lined with shell-pink ... Miss

> Iris Rainer, sister of the bride, was bridesmaid, wearing pale pink crepe de chene and georgette draperies, with a white georgette hat... After the ceremony the bride's mother held a reception at 'Wickliffe House,' St. Kilda ... Both bridegroom and best man were in uniform.

I was amused by the euphemistic 'the bride's mother held a reception...' Her children, not Bella, would have paid for this. She sent Iris out to work as a seamstress in a factory at the age of thirteen.

There was an unspoken rivalry between Iris and Eva. Bella had accepted the offer of distant female relatives to take Eva as a 'free' boarder at their young ladies' college in Sydney. Bella was keen on how things 'looked'. Eva would get a private school education. Eva saw it quite differently. She was being expelled from her family. Only once a year at Christmas was she allowed back to Melbourne to be with them. Her 'private school education' was demeaning; she was treated as a domestic drudge, waiting at meals on the other young ladies seated around a long table.

When Eva's school years were over, she came back to Melbourne from her exile in Sydney. Slightly shorter than my mother, she was now a buxom, fair-headed young woman, a fresh-faced practical girl. During her courting days she was 'too keen' on her future husband, my mother used to say. It is not clear what this excessive keenness was. But it made my mother uncomfortable.

Eva and Jack soon had four children. My mother was envious. It was almost another twenty years before the bridesmaid escaped from Bella and became a bride.

In her Melbourne years after World War I, Bella was active in charities. A cutting records her attendance at a 'linen tea', where guests donated sheets, pillow slips and towels for a hospital. Another cutting, headed 'Mrs. Moss Entertained', lists Bella as a member of an 'entertainment committee' of the National Council of Women of Victoria. They held a farewell lunch after raising money for Mrs Moss to attend a women's conference in Geneva.

Several pages later, Bella pasted a newspaper photograph of a handsome woman, with pearl drop earrings and necklace: 'Mrs I. H. Moss, who has been appointed Australia's substitute delegate to the Assembly of the League of Nations'.

Bella left no explanation as to why she kept these two mementoes of Mrs Moss, whose life was such a brilliant success, compared with her own. When my mother inherited the scrapbooks she wrote 'Father could have married she was in love with him' beside the article headed 'Mrs. Moss Entertained', and underneath the newspaper photograph she wrote: 'Father could have married but she was Jewish. She loved our father. I. I. L.' My mother's surmise that Mrs Moss was Jewish is wrong. She married a Jewish man, but she was 'cremated with Presbyterian forms'.

A favourite story of my mother's was about my grandfather's romantic assignation with Alice Wilson shortly before she married. My mother was vague about the details. My grandfather would then have been a twenty-two-year-old medical student. He was yet to inherit a fortune from his uncle, and was too young to marry the seventeen-year-old Alice Wilson, who was about to become Mrs Moss. Alice may have made something of my grandfather if they had married. It is more likely she had a lucky escape.

Bella's earlier scrapbook is labelled 'Album' in large gold lettering and decorated with gold-leaf flowers, a butterfly and birds. It was a genuine scrapbook and not a Protestant Atlas converted to this purpose. There is an inscription in a large flowing hand on the inside cover:

Bella. Dora. Mooney.
Park Street
South Melbourne
May 25th 1888

Most of the pages are a hodgepodge of newspaper cuttings. One page is carefully arranged like a small garden of remembrance. In its centre Bella pasted a checkerboard cross of cut-up black and grey squares, placed above a small mound of similar squares. Beside it is a newspaper death notice which she dated 'July 11th 1887'. The man who died was William Norman Matheson 'in his twenty-eighth year'.

Centred directly under the black and grey cross, is a small neatly handwritten card on which is written:

Je vous aime
&
you know
it – (I love you)
Blow you
W. N. M.
1885

My grandmother tried, not very effectively, to scratch out the 'Blow you'.

On the opposite page is an account of the death of William Matheson's mother, two months after her son. The son 'died very suddenly after a short illness'. A notice of letters of administration pasted onto this page states William Matheson died intestate leaving an estate of £47 122 – an amount that could have purchased seventy average-priced houses in that era.

If William Rainer had married Alice Wilson, and Bella had married William Matheson (and he had not died young), my grandparents may have been saved from a love match which was a disaster for both of them.

Pages inserted at the front of Bella's family bible record her marriage in Melbourne to William George Rainer, the birth dates of their five children and the places in the United Kingdom where they were born. Every address is different. Bella's medical practitioner husband and his family did not stay for long anywhere.

In about 1936, when she was in her early seventies, Bella prepared eighteen pages of 'Recollections' which she sent off for publication under the alternative noms-de-plume of 'Another Mother' or 'Dora Gettings', the name of her grandmother. The names of her husband and father are mentioned nowhere. The recollections were sent back to her, probably unread. She had not taken the trouble to write them out in an easily decipherable hand.

A side note on the first page states her mother 'when a little girl had often seen the blacks in their corroborees opposite the Village Belle Hotel St Kilda ... among the tea tree'. Bella's mother, also named Isabella, died in 1923.

Bella's 'Recollections' begin:

> I was the second of five daughters, my father being a
> pioneer of Victoria, owner and proprietor of 'Cobbs
> Coaches' for the Victoria section travelling to St Kilda ...
> He accumulated a considerable fortune ... My father's name
> will not bear repetition as it is so well-known, his having
> been one of the first councillors ... but is still remembered
> as the originator of the 'Poets' Corner' St Kilda.
>
>   Fortune was cruel to him; his trust in a friend and
> backing of the friend's bills, led to what the papers called
> 'A Wholesale Robbery'. His signature was forged ... He

had a fall from his horse resulting in two broken ribs and a head and leg wound. All of this culminated in his valuable property being sacrificed in a big auction sale ... and the forger getting six years imprisonment in Darlinghurst Gaol – he having absconded dressed as a woman to Sydney.

Her 'dear father' died the day before his case against the bill holders was listed so, as his solicitor told the court, 'he would show cause before a mightier judge than Mr Justice Molesworth'. Bella then has an account of her time as a governess – the only time in her life when she was employed:

I always had a wish to visit a sheep station – now was my chance. I looked out for a position and secured one, as nursery governess, on one of the biggest stations in New South Wales, carrying 120,000 sheep, two out-stations, and two towns on the run. My husband later on when we were in England loved to tell the people whom we met, about the 120,000 sheep – much to their astonishment, they thought it unbelievable.

Bella mentions calling 'at many lovely stations' on the Murrumbidgee and Lachlan Rivers, passing through places such as Hay and One Tree Plain. She reported:

My mistress kept a strict eye on me and would never allow me to go to the country races or dances, she thought they were too rough and the town wicked, but as we had our own race course and tennis court on the station and many callers, travelling from one station to another, I learned to love the life ... There were plenty of wild dingos and dear little wild pigs straying around and also a wild white horse, which could not be captured ... I got to know the names of many of the trees, such as the wilga and quandong, the latter having lovely red and white berries which make very nice jam...

She does not explain how this pastoral interlude ended or her return to Melbourne.

Passing over a few years I met my husband while he was a medical student. He was to go to Edinburgh for his final ... While in Scotland he contracted pneumonia and under doctors' orders he had to take a sea voyage ... so his studies were for the time laid aside. In the meantime he had come in for a considerable fortune only to lose it again on the failure of the banks in 1893.

William and Bella married in Melbourne in 1892. In 1893, the year Conan Doyle killed off Sherlock Homes, they left the colony, so William could resume his studies in Edinburgh. My grandmother kept a newspaper cutting headed 'CLEARED OUT – APRIL 22' listing over 200 passengers, including 'Mr. and Mrs. Rainer', who were leaving on the *Arcadia*.

In London, she writes: 'before proceeding to Scotland we lost no time in "seeing all the sights"'. She also lists the many plays they saw and writes about a Sunday afternoon service at Westminster Abbey where 'I saw dear "Maggie Moore". She looked at me so hard I was sorry I had not spoken to her.'

Maggie Moore was Mrs JC Williamson – hence Bella's inverted commas – and was a famous American-born Australian actress married to an equally well-known theatrical entrepreneur and actor. I wonder if Bella stared so hard at 'Maggie Moore' that 'Maggie Moore' returned the stare.

After the young couple's London interlude, they 'lost no time in getting to know Scotland'. She again lists all the sights and describes going 'to the outskirts of Craigmillar Castle (accompanied by my dear little son) and I would take sewing (mostly darning socks) and lean against those massive walls and think of Mary Queen of Scots, who spent so much of her time there...'

She enjoyed watching 'the Highlanders marching' in Glasgow where they went for William's final examinations, and he 'passed his triple qualification in Edinburgh and Glasgow with flying colours'.

By this time what was left of her husband's fortune after the 1893 bank crash seems to have gone, exhausted by living in style in London and Edinburgh. In 1894 William got his first assistantship near Bolton Abbey in Yorkshire. It was for a single man, and she took lodgings in a room in nearby Bradford – a comedown from the sights and theatres of London and Edinburgh. But for a while Bella's high spirits were not to be dampened.

Her lodgings were next to a theatre, and 'with a wink and a nod to the doorkeeper' she got into the gallery to see 'a capital pantomime' eight times. She became so familiar with the music, she could play the score of the pantomime from beginning to end on the piano 'much to the surprise of our host'. On these visits to the theatre, who cared for Leslie, then aged one, is unclear.

Bella and her husband next went to Cumberland, 'the land of the red man, as the colliers are called – an iron district, the men get covered in red dust'. While they were in the Lake District they witnessed a visit by Kaiser Wilhelm II, and later partook 'of some of the dishes expressly prepared for his ex-Majesty such as the Emperor Soup, William entrée etc. We all took a turn in sitting in the *chair* occupied by his Imperial Highness...'

She goes on to describe how 'my own dear little son' – later killed in World War I – 'waving his hand and joining in the cheering' was among the crowds welcoming the Kaiser, 'little dreaming that in a few years he would be the supreme sacrifice…'

Bella and her husband next spent 'a short time in Hull with its many canals and the ferry trip'. She visited Thornton Abbey where 'we picked some most lovely mushrooms amidst the ruins' and reports my mother's birth while on holiday in Manchester, which was 'followed on the next day by an urgent telegram to accept a locum tenens at Gargrave Yorkshire…'

She often accompanied her husband on his consulting days to see the historical sites. Presumably a servant cared for the two small children. There are detailed discussions of the places she saw:

> Wandering into some private fields and seeing a beautiful residence in the distance I asked a boy to whom it belonged. He replied Earl Manners (Pierrepont), once the home of the famous Lady Mary Wortley Montagu.

At this point she adds:

> I prefer not to say why my husband was continually on-the-move, suffice to say no sooner had I got to know desirable people than my friendship was crushed.

After a short stay they went on to Brixton in Derbyshire 'exceptionally lovely, wild daffodils, blue-bells and snapdragons'; then to Newport in Yorkshire 'purely hunting and shooting country. One week we had continually meals of hares and rabbits… Our conveyance was a dog-cart with coachman in livery.' Then two assistantships in Wales:

My husband had to hold surgery twice a day, attend calls, draw teeth and make up medicines. The calls were down valleys or up mountains (often at night) and across creeks with only the light of a hurricane lamp.

He also had to 'battle with' the Welsh language, buying a Welsh language textbook, and had to contend with opposition from other doctors, as his type of practice, employed by a workers' club or lodge, was looked down upon. William tried to establish roots in the communities where he worked. The Hebburn Colliery Association Football Club published a card for their 1902–1903 season listing 'Dr. Rainor' [sic] as their 'Hon. President'.

By this point it is apparent Bella was becoming increasingly desperate. Early one morning she was woken by a noise of travelling carriages:

> On getting out of bed I surveyed a long procession of elephants' caravans and lions in cages. I longed to join them.

She realised later this was a circus she had attended with the children at Ebbw Vale.

> We eventually reached London, my husband securing two assistantships only to end in disaster; we were living in one room, five children, myself and husband. One day walking through Covent Garden I stooped to pick up some wood (thrown away as waste from boxes) acceptable to me for a fire, when I was approached by a man, saying, 'I saw you pick up something from the ground Madam.'
>
> I did not know what to answer, so was silent. He went on to say, 'Will you come this way.' I became frightened, so I followed to where there was a group of men. Addressing

me, one of them said 'You must be very poor. We have been watching you. We have made up a little collection. Will you accept it?' handing me 15 shillings and sixpence, which I gratefully accepted with tears and joined my husband and children.

I appealed to the Medical Society for help, which was granted without delay or a committee meeting, as the head of the medical profession (a titled man), a name I shall not mention as happily he is still alive (for I read of him presently) granted the application. He said he was astounded at the knowledge that a doctor, his wife and children were practically starving in London.

While there I was not to be cast down however. I used to attend Westminster Abbey services regularly, getting the children off first to St Pancras's Church near where we lived, to Sunday School.

During these months in London she 'would occasionally go to see a society wedding (from the outside)'. She once joined a crowd outside Chesterfield House where the names and titles of arriving guests were called out. She recalled:

a hurried stride from a young man requesting to be announced. 'What name?' the crier queried. 'Lord Hyde' was the answer (the present Earl of Clarendon) ... Such shouts took my thoughts away from home.

She was only briefly bucked up by events such as these. The unhappy months in London came to an end in 1905. Worse was to follow:

> We left London for Australia, the day of the opening of Parliament and viewed the procession with the King and Queen in their glass and gold carriage. We then departed for Tilbury Docks, my husband securing a position as ship's doctor. After a short stay in Melbourne we went to Queensland, my husband dying tragically in his sleep at the age of forty years and I still in my thirties, my eldest boy being a little over thirteen years old. It was a great shock to me as I had just rejoined my husband a few weeks before.

It is typical of her account that viewing 'the King and Queen in their gold and glass carriage' and her husband's death all occur in the same short paragraph.

Bella did not like the Queensland town of Eidsvold (unnamed) where her husband had become the resident doctor. Eidsvold, she recalled, consisted of three stores, several hotels and a disused goldmine, which 'happened to be in the yard of our house'. The mine was flooded – a death trap for small children. Their brief stay began with a 'terrifying experience'.

On the day following her arrival with the children, William had to go to an outlying station 57 miles (90 km) away, a journey of a day and a half. When he got there, the station hand he was to see was already dead, and (my mother told me) he had to dig the grave and bury him. While William was away, Bella wrote:

> I was living alone with the children, and a terrible thunderstorm came on. We had to get rugs, curtains, anything to try and keep the lightning out. There were deluges of rain, and things were not made easier by knowing that blacks haunted the place – one day my eldest boy came running into the house excitedly saying he had seen a nude black girl in the creek.

Bella did not stay long in Eidsvold after William's death. They returned to Melbourne and she explained, 'I took a fairly big house, near church and school and let rooms for 7 flats'. Bella says she was able to furnish this house and received 'a grant from the benevolent medical profession'.

Her eldest son, Leslie, took up rural work in Gippsland. My mother remembered Leslie standing, on the verge of tears, among the giant mountain ashes – *Eucalyptus regnans* which can grow up to 90 metres tall. He was thirteen. He remained in Gippsland, sending money to his mother, and joined a correspondence school with a view to becoming a commercial artist. Then war broke out in 1914 and he enlisted. Bella wrote:

> I had the last tea [the evening meal] with him in his tent out at Broadmeadows and decided that I must see him again on his departure from Port Melbourne. The next day I arrived there and joined the crowd near the embarkment, mostly composed of women. As I stood in the background one of the women (minus hat and [in] rough working clothes) said to me, 'Have you anyone going?' I said, 'Yes, a son.' She had words with her companions, saying make room for her, she has the best right to get in the front. The policeman, seeing what was taking place, addressed me saying, 'When you see your son, you can join him.' So my dear son came swinging along, pleased and surprised to see me. I joined him, catching him by the arm and marched with him to the landing place. That was the last I saw of him.

She relates that he was one of the last to leave Gallipoli and went through many battles in France 'without a scratch' and went missing in action at Flers. She would not give up hope, thinking he might be a prisoner in Germany, until a letter arrived from General Birdwood confirming that he must have been killed. His typed letter, dated 27 May 1917, from 1st Anzac Corps, France, states:

> ... I fear there is nothing but bad news I can give you regarding him ... I find that on the 15th November last he was employed in carrying bombs to the front line in Flers, which he reached safely. He then left to return to our support line, but was not seen again, and it would seem almost certain that he was killed by German snipers who were particularly active in that vicinity ... Movement, as you will realise, is restricted mostly to the night, while the ground, as a result of the continual heavy shelling, is so torn and shattered that very often it is quite impossible to trace our men ... It would be quite wrong of me to attempt to buoy you up with hopes that your son is still alive and a prisoner in the hands of the Germans ... it is, I fear, certain that he was then killed...

The last page of Bella's recollections describes her involvement in ladies' auxiliary committees for the church and she says all her other children are now happily married and doing well, and there are six grandchildren. She concludes: 'And now I am alone'.

※

When she lived in Wales, Bella enjoyed the blue cornflowers growing near the door of her house. But they were the German national flower and after Leslie's death she came to hate them. She was critical of my mother for marrying a man with a German surname, and claimed her own married name of 'Rainer' was Austrian not German – the Austrians in her view having no responsibility for the war.

Her recollections are written in a bold, chaotic nineteenth century hand which, despite its steady slope, is often barely decipherable, with its loops and flourishes. Some sentences took hours to decode. I thought she picked up 'food' scraps in Covent Garden and days later I realised it was 'wood'. There are numerous passages taken up with details about the family relationships of nobility and royalty. Page after page of this trivia made me feel slightly bilious.

The few surviving letters from her husband are written in a small, meticulous and lucid script. He was ambidextrous and, as one hand tired, switched hands when taking lecture notes. William Rainer's elder brother Tom, a bank manager, had similarly neat handwriting, and kept a watchful eye over his brother's family after William's death in Eidsvold. One letter he wrote to Bella criticised her careless use of apostrophes, and warned her my mother's correspondence showed the same failing.

Bella's recollections are evasive. She was not in her thirties when William Rainer died. She was forty, almost forty-one – only a few months younger than her husband. There are two important omissions. One of them is laughable. She did not mention she was the daughter of a well-known publican, Joshua Mooney. That may be why she says 'My father's name will not bear repetition as it is so well known'. She hid the fact that she was a publican's daughter.

Joshua Mooney's Victorian section of the Cobb & Co coach business could not compete with the railways when they were built. In 1866 he became the licensee of a hotel on the corner of Flinders and Swanston Streets Melbourne and renamed it 'Mooney's Prince's Bridge Hotel'. He became well known for lighting the fire for his saloon with the IOUs of poets – literary figures of the era such as Adam Lindsay Gordon and Marcus Clarke used to drink there. Under its current name of Young and Jacksons, it claims to be Australia's most famous hotel.

Unfortunately the jovial publican formed a friendship which was to be his undoing. In Bella's ultramarine blue 'Album' she has cuttings from the year 1883: 'Arrest of the Absconder White', 'The Absconder White' and 'More About White'. They report how not once, but twice over the years Mooney was conned by White, a Quaker. Mooney died before he could set aside bills with his forged signature.

Bella mythologised her father. Shortly before his death Bella said: 'Oh pa, and you never left us any money'. His reply: 'That's what's killin' me Belle, that's what's killin' me'. As he lay down on a couch to die, he announced: 'Bring me me hat an' me stick, for ah'm goin' a long journey'. The family myth is that his dog then jumped to its death in the cellar of the Royal George Hotel.

The death of her 'Dear Father' is recorded in her family bible. But her mother's death is not. Bella preserved little relating directly to her mother. She kept a short newspaper article published after her mother's death. The brief side note in her recollections about corroborees refers to 'my mother' with no adjectival endearment – unlike 'my dear father' and 'my dear husband'. One senses an estrangement between them – two strong-willed women both wanting to be the centre of attention.

Bella's life was coloured by being the daughter of a publican. William Matheson's *billet doux*, which begins 'Je vous aime' has 'I love you' in brackets. He may have doubted she could understand French. My mother recalled that her mother as a child loved to look out of the upstairs windows of Mooney's Princes Bridge Hotel at the passing traffic – horses and carriages crossing the bridge, billows of steam from the trains pulling into Flinders

Street railway station, and portmanteaux carried into the vestibule of the hotel.

There were less savoury aspects of living above a pub – the smell of liquor, the nocturnal comings and goings, the sounds of drunkenness and occasional skirmishes heard up stairways or through windows open on summer nights. A girl who lived in a hotel was not respectable. Bella seems to have been educated in public schools and perhaps by governesses at home – in the hotel.

She is almost a caricature of a woman of the Victorian era. If she were not my own grandmother, I might be able to feel more sympathy for her thwarted life. Bella gazing out of an upstairs window as a child became the woman who kept scrapbooks about other people's lives, and gazed out the window in Wales in the early morning, and longed to join the passing procession of elephants' caravans and lions in cages.

Bella's recollections are surprisingly reticent about her piano playing, referring only to the incident in Bradford. My mother remembered a more striking example of her virtuosity at the piano. When Bella was a governess out in the wilds, she overheard a piece being played on the piano. Later she sat down and began playing it herself. The composer came into the room, exclaiming, 'Where did you hear that?'

(I have two memories of Bella. I had probably just turned three. Bella is seated at a black piano in her flat, her aged fingers travelling across the keyboard. I may have brought her some light blue plumbago flowers, picked from the low hedge at 'Ivanhoe'. A couple of months later we visit her in hospital. She is rapidly fading. I still have her piano stool and reams of her sheet music dating back to the nineteenth century.)

The most important omission in Bella's recollections is her silence about why William had so many medical assistantships: he was an alcoholic and morphine addict. Nor does she explain how he contracted pneumonia in Scotland before their marriage. He had a bet with fellow medical students in Edinburgh he could sleep out in the snow all night. He took along a whisky bottle, won his bet and lost a lung.

The family story is that William would have liked to train as a lawyer. But his parents wanted him to study medicine, as the 'brainy one' of their five children, and have the title 'Dr'. Binge drinking may not have been a problem for a lawyer, but it was for a medical practitioner. William restrained himself for weeks or months, then started drinking and could not stop – running down the street and throwing pennies to the children. A doctor who disgraced himself like this could not be trusted by his patients. The family had to move on.

William was a schoolboy boxer and won prizes at Wesley College. High jinks were reported in an 1889 newspaper, when he was one of a contingent of seven medical students sailing from Melbourne on the *Valetta* for further studies in Edinburgh. William was the social secretary on the ship. He sent out notices for an evening concert and was one of the performers. He sang 'Sailing' and 'Maid of Athens'.

Bella mentions the 'fortune' which he came into and lost. In 1891 he inherited £15 000 from his maternal uncle, Thomas Moubray, a mayor of Melbourne in 1868, and founder of one of Melbourne's largest drapery stores, where my mother became a seamstress at age thirteen in about 1910.

William was not a casual user of drugs. According to my mother his 'normal' dose would have been fatal for most people. She remembered him offering her a teaspoonful of cocaine, saying, 'Here, have this. It's good for you.' His clinical notes mention prescriptions of cocaine for patients.

If William had married Alice Wilson, he may have sobered up. Bella was ill-suited to dealing with William's addictions. There is a story, perhaps told by Bella against herself, or witnessed by the children. When they arrived back in London in 1905, she insisted on buying a copy of the fashion magazine *The Tatler*. This was a time when Bella was seen picking up firewood in Covent Garden. William protested there was not enough money for them to live on. Bella insisted she must have it.

Bella's recollections are evasive about the period when they sailed from England in 1905 and her husband's death in Queensland in a town which she does not name.

Early in 1906 William obtained a position as medico for the town of Oakey, in the Darling Downs area of south Queensland. He set out alone in the steamship *Arrawatta*. There was soon a series of newspaper stories which Bella pasted into her album. She appears to have been a passive spectator as the events unfolded.

Under the heading 'Tragedy Suspected' it was reported that a large carry-all bag with medical textbooks and instruments belonging to Dr W.G. Rainer was found abandoned on the rocks at Bondi beach – the implication: when his ship stopped at Sydney, William went to Bondi and jumped into the sea.

A few days later, a man from Randwick advised there was no tragedy – Dr Rainer had continued sailing north to take up his position at Oakey. Finally Dr Rainer himself confirmed his bag had been stolen from the ship. It had been left on the rocks at Bondi, when it was found to be of no value. The very last newspaper cutting may have been mailed by William to Bella. Referring to the adventure with the carry-all bag, the local newspaper welcomed Dr Rainer to Oakey.

Shortly after these events, there is an entry in his clinical notes:

On 3rd February 1906 was called to examine a man James Noonan aged apparently about 45 years who was found in

> the creek at Oakey. On examination I found that he had incised wound of the front of the neck. Was made obliquely from left to right, higher on left side than on right, and carried downwards, and being deeper on left side. I formed the opinion that the wound was self-inflicted as such a wound is common in suicide cases…

My grandfather then set out further details about the body. On the opposite page there is an entry I assumed at first was inconsequential musings. It took me a while to realise it was an oddly incoherent poem in rhyming couplets he had started, with many crossings-out, but in a more elaborate hand than his clinical notes. It begins:

> There is nothing so pleasant as work that's light too
> Where the ordinary mills are more than busy putting flour thro'

Several almost illegible couplets follow. It was not part of the family myth about William that he wrote poetry. A final incomplete couplet rhymed 'sugar mills' with 'ills'. He may have been trying to say the ordinary mills make you happier than the sugar mills – ordinary pleasures are better than highs from morphine.

Bella and her children did not have 'a short stay' in Melbourne before they went to Queensland, as her recollections suggest. William was away from his family for at least ten months before they were reunited in Queensland. Her claim that his death 'was a great shock to me as I had just rejoined my husband a few weeks before' was also false, as he met up with his family in Queensland just nine days before he died.

William had not stayed for long at Oakey when a lodge of the Manchester Unity International Order of Oddfellows took him on as resident medical officer at Eidsvold, a gold mining town then in decline, and 200 miles (over 300 km) further north – a harsher environment than the Darling Downs.

His elder brother, Tom, the bank manager who cared about the correct use of apostrophes, gave moral and perhaps financial support to William's family in Melbourne over the ten months or so when William was in Queensland. Like many wealthy families who become impoverished, Bella and her children were to become paranoid in later years about where the money had gone. They would not accept it had been in the wrong bank in 1893. They formed the ridiculous belief that Tom had robbed them.

William's last letter was to Bella, dated 16 October 1906, on paper headed 'Eidsvold General Hospital'. It is in his meticulous hand and with no crossings-out. He wrote in the top left hand corner: 'Let Tom see this letter'.

It begins 'My dearest Belle' and gives her detailed instructions about how she and the children were to travel to Brisbane and the boat she should catch. He adds: 'if you miss it, all my arrangements for you are thrown out of gear'. He would meet her in Brisbane after she disembarked, and escort her further north on the last leg of the journey to Eidsvold. But she is to send a telegram 'letting me know you have started. If I do not receive that wire I will not start from Eidsvold as I would presume that you had missed the boat.'

The last paragraph reads:

> I think, after you have settled down here and got used to the quietness of the place, that you will like it. You will never be in want of money, and as regards dress, books and those things can be got up by the parcel post from Anthony Horderns' Sydney. You will be made a lot of here, and we should be happy. I know without being egotistical, that I

am [a] great favourite with all sections, and the Committee would do anything, within reason, to keep me here permanently. They are all looking forward to your coming, and I am sure that when they see we are settled that my salary will be raised to £250. Now dear Belle I will conclude, hoping soon to have you and the children with me and looking forward to a bright future.

Your loving husband

W.G. Rainer

Despite the expression of affection, there is a formality about much of this letter. My grandfather underlines the ship's name (the *Arrawatta*, coincidentally the same ship my German grandfather travelled on from Brisbane to Sydney, to die a day after arrival). The detailed instructions to Belle, as he calls her (rather than the more exotic 'Bella' she called herself), and the warning that he would assume she had missed the boat if he did not get a telegram, sound like a parent writing to an unreliable child.

Nevertheless there is genuine warmth towards the end. Perhaps the letter is simply to a loved wife from a man who has treated her badly and cannot be sure she wishes to join him after ten months apart. No significance attaches to the oddly formal signature 'W.G. Rainer'. This was how he signed letters to his children.

She did send a telegram, and he met her and the children in Brisbane. They probably got to Eidsvold on the 11th of November and he died six days later on the 17th. He came back late and drunk in the afternoon before his death, having gone into town to buy presents for the children. My mother heard them arguing. He is supposed to have said 'Belle, I'm turning over a new leaf' and let

Bella know he had taken morphine – his normal dose – and they slept separately, apparently having reconciled after their quarrel. My memory is that my mother was the first to discover him dead next morning.

The cause of death on the death certificate is 'Poisoning by Morphia'. The inquest was conducted by WW Farquhar JP, the secretary of the Oddfellows Lodge which had employed my grandfather as their local medical officer. By the time of the inquest Bella and her children were back in Melbourne, having received money from a benefit concert organised by William Farquhar.

My mother remembered hearing her parents argue. Their 'reconciliation' sounds like one of Bella's fabrications. Whatever the argument was about, I am inclined to side with William. He had exhausted his chances in more civilised places. He had come to terms with his own unreliability and her flightiness, and felt they could make a go of it in a harsh, tropical mining town. I believe Bella said no.

My mother remembered the hymn at the funeral service was 'Thy will be done'. It stuck in her mind as a child because this line is sung at the end of each verse like a repetitive axe stroke. But it was not the will of the authorities that Bella or her children should attend the burial. He may have been buried in unconsecrated ground.

Copies of some receipts survive. Farquhar paid the undertaker's bill and also the grave digger 'for digging grave no. 70'. There was no headstone when I visited the cemetery more than sixty years later. Also Farquhar, as the secretary of the Cemetery Trustees, issued a receipt for ten shillings cemetery fees to himself as the secretary Eidsvold Hospital.

There is one very odd receipt with a duty stamp dated 20/11/06:

Received from Mrs Rainer the sum of two pounds being amount due to the Eidsvold Hospital on account (Lizzie) aboriginal, from Hawkewood Stn.

W.W. Farquhar
Secretary
Eidsvold Hospital

My grandmother paid for none of the other expenses. Why was she asked to pay to the hospital a not insignificant amount for Lizzie?

My mother's memory of her three weeks stay in Eidsvold played through her mind like a colour film she saw again and again – the blacks in chains at the railway station at Mount Perry, tomatoes ripening quickly to red on a railing, the night of the terrifying thunderstorm, the white silk suits her father and Farquhar wore, a black man rummaging for drugs in her father's surgery after his death, the white girls with her sister Eva, dancing naked around a hose one evening – but my mother would not join them.

Bella's vanity was such she could not live away from the bright lights. Eidsvold was different from the imposing sheep station where she had been a governess. She did not like living next to a disused goldmine. William seems to have been prospering in Eidsvold in his own erratic way – until Bella joined him.

Bella implies in her 'Recollections' that she survived after her husband's death by renting a large house and subletting rooms. My mother's story was that for two or three years they moved from house to house in Melbourne; Bella let the rent mount up and they flitted. My mother went looking for her mother in hotel bars to bring her back home. Relatives became wary of meeting them, expecting requests for a handout.

My mother never outgrew her childhood. Apart from a few notes and letters, she left no written memoir. I have a photocopy of a note on the back of a postcard. The front of the card may have had a photograph of a bridge – a small arched stone bridge over a river running rapidly among jagged rocks. In a quavery but clear hand my mother had written:

> Jesmond Dene near Newcastle on Tyne. Came over the bridge I think and walking along right hand side, my father pretended to throw me in which frightened me. Was about five then I think. I was Iris Rainer then. And what year, well, I'm not sure of that. This is 19/12/68.

My mother often used to say: 'Read Henry Handel Richardson's *The Fortunes of Richard Mahony*. She was writing about her father. That's my father's life too.'

When I eventually read the novel, I was struck by the parallels. Richardson's father had his medical training at Edinburgh and Glasgow Universities, like my grandfather, but twenty years earlier; then went from medical practice to medical practice in England, always failing, like my grandfather. He came back to Australia, made and lost a fortune and died insane. In real life Ethel Richardson was nine when her father, the hero of her trilogy, died. My mother was ten.

Another parallel between the two lives emerged from a strange conversation with my mother. I had just divorced and, as my mother and sister saw it, I had been married for a few years and now that part of my life was over. I was to become theirs again. That I was caring for three small children for half of each week was irrelevant. My feelings about the end of the marriage were irrelevant.

We were sitting around my dining room table. My mother, who was then eighty, announced suddenly, 'Don't go fucking around'. I had never heard her use that word. She was desperate to convey her meaning. She added, 'Your grandfather was a very good man. He got syphilis from a woman in Edinburgh. He cured himself with arsenic and gold injections. He made sure he was cured before he married my mother.' (Richardson's father died of tertiary syphilis.)

My grandfather's teacher at Edinburgh University was Dr Joseph Bell, the model for Sherlock Holmes – something my mother often talked about. Several years after her death I was reading Sherlock Holmes stories to my son Nicholas. We came to a passage about Holmes's use of morphine. I had a shocked intuition. Dr Bell might be linked to my grandfather's habit that ruined his family. I explained to Nicholas why I needed to pause for a few minutes.

More than a hundred years had passed since William's death. I had been married to Gail for thirty years, and we were visiting the old medical faculty at Edinburgh University. We were standing in the quadrangle of nineteenth-century buildings. It was reassuring to be surrounded by this solid stone architecture; we were enclosed, protected from the outside world. I thought how enticing, to lie here one night in the snow, with a whisky bottle for company. Was this where William carried out his wager? One would feel quite safe. Nothing harmful could happen.

SHORE SCHOOL

Despite my mother going through Latin and French exercises with me at home (although she had no knowledge of either language) and the special tutoring I had from Mr Yarnold at Mosman Prep, I did not get a scholarship to Shore.

Somehow my parents managed to afford the fees, and one morning in 1952 I placed on my head the school's distinctive straw boater with the broad diagonal navy blue and white striped band, and caught the train from Gordon station to North Sydney, where Shore (Sydney Church of England Grammar School), with its tower, stood at the top of the hill in landscaped grounds, looking out over Lavender Bay and McMahons Point, where I had grown up. The school was far grander than Mosman Prep. The main buildings faced north into the sun and overlooked a large rectangular playing field.

It was an all-male school with a mysterious group of country boys who boarded at various 'houses' in the school grounds. We dayboys were also allocated to one of these houses. Our headmaster was LC Robson, 'the Chief', who watched from the front door of his dwelling in School House as the boys filed into morning chapel – a tall, dry, thin, imperious figure. He stood gazing out, shading his eyes from the morning sun, with his hand across his brow in a kind of salute. One boy was less in awe of the Chief's icy demeanour, and walked up to him one morning, imitating the salute-like gesture, hand over his brow, and Robson laughed. No other boy dared repeat this extraordinary act.

The Art Master, Ross Doig, who taught at the school from 1954 to 1989, in an interview published in the school magazine, had some recollections of Robson, who, Doig recalled, 'had the status almost of a demi-god':

> I only saw him in his last years and he was unlike anybody I'd met before. He had a habit of grasping at every opportunity pieces of paper between each hand and using his finger-nails to shred them into increasingly smaller pieces. I never did see where he discarded them, but he was always doing it.

Doig mentions that his predecessor as Art Master, John Lipscomb, had persuaded Robson that a bequest left to the school by a doctor should be spent, not on a swimming pool as originally intended – which apparently was not possible – but on an Art School complex. This was unique at that time in New South Wales.

When Doig was first interviewed for the position in 1954, he said:

> I didn't know anything about this type of school or its ethics and Headmaster Robson said to me 'What religion are you?'. So I said quite casually, 'Atheist.' He put up both hands and said 'Don't say that too loudly around here'...

A 'sergeant-major', Mr JH Dixon, patrolled the grounds in a navy blue uniform with silver buttons. He had a pink pugnacious face and short-cropped ginger hair under a military-style cap, and conducted after-school drills. Boys who misbehaved were made to run around for twenty minutes in a pack. The leather baton he carried under his arm was quick to whack the backside of any boy with his hands in his pockets. There was a story that a boy was standing, hands in pockets, gazing at a noticeboard, and the inevitable whack followed. The face that turned around with surprise was that of a rather short schoolmaster. Neither spoke and they walked off in opposite directions.

Apart from Dixon's whackings, I don't remember much corporal punishment at Shore, only drills and Saturday detentions, and writing out 'disobedience' 100 times on a sheet of paper after school had finished.

I was eighteen months below the average age of the class but I was tall for my age, and not at a physical disadvantage. I came about tenth in the top-streamed 'A1' class. But I was immature in other ways. I became friends with a boy in the next year up. Eleven years old, I had not yet reached puberty and had no idea about sex. I made some ignorant remarks. He and his friend decided I needed to be told how babies are made. I was shocked and surprised, but grateful for the knowledge.

A few months later I overheard a dirty joke some boys were telling in class. I began to laugh. 'Look, Boof's laughing', one said in a kindly way. It was assumed I would not understand.

I was well treated by most of my classmates and protected myself by a show of diffidence. One boy found me irritating and used to punch and bully me. I responded by taking no notice – the younger boy's classic method of avoiding conflict. I was Diana's younger brother and the youngest in the class, and became imprinted with the idea that I was younger than other people.

I became an intellectual snob. I was soon to play no sport in a school where sport was supreme, and I had little contact with boys in lower streamed classes. In this way I came to believe that

Shore School

there were two races of human beings: people who were clever and those who were not.

I was one of the poorer boys. Some were second- or third-generation Shore boys. I told myself that perhaps my father had more property than theirs, but I could not convince myself this counted for much. My father was working class and in his sixties. Their fathers were younger, and in the professions, or owned businesses.

Some decent suits from his bachelor days still hung in my father's lowboy, but his everyday wear was second-hand clothes, with frayed collars, picked up at auction. I was catching a train home with other boys and saw my father ahead of me in the carriage. I nodded as discreetly as I could to say hello, but in such a way my friends did not notice. I felt ashamed of myself – I could not say 'That is my father over there'. He was discreet and did not give me away.

I had been wearing the Shore boater for two or three months and was waiting for a train at North Sydney station. One of my new school friends asked, 'Where do you live?' 'Gordon', I replied, pleased I could say I lived in a respectable suburb (although the roof of our house was rusty).

'How long have you lived there?' 'Nine months', I replied. To keep the conversation flowing – I think my friend was just being polite – he asked, 'Where did you live before then?' 'At McMahons Point.' This was still a slum suburb in 1952, and Shore boys were familiar with McMahons Point as the suburb directly adjacent to the school. 'Oh', he said, realising he had made a mistake in asking this. He gallantly tried to retrieve an embarrassing situation. 'It must have been just after you came out from England.' He had assumed this from my posh English accent. I naively believed I always had to tell the truth. 'No I'm not from England. It's where I grew up.'

Walking back to North Sydney station one afternoon, I saw one of my father's tenants passing in the opposite direction: Mrs Humphries, the widow whose white hair had purplish tints. I said hello, but did not raise my boater. Another pupil who was coming abreast turned to me: 'Just because a woman's old and poor doesn't mean you don't raise your hat'.

In the year when the school performed the Gilbert and Sullivan operetta *The Gondoliers* my voice had yet to break and I was cast as a chorus girl. I came with my parents and sister, by tram, to the performance at the Cremorne Orpheum. As I entered the dressing room, a tart voice remarked, 'Here come the boys whose parents don't have cars'.

Mr Yarnold, the headmaster at Mosman Prep, had suggested I learn Greek at Shore. The school told me it was not taught. But German was. My German teacher for the first two years was Daniel Fomenko, a Russian emigré. In the 1930s he walked across Russia with his wife into China, something he mentioned casually to our class. Only six or seven boys were learning German. 'Fom' sometimes closed his eyes as he taught us, already old, thin and with a yellow pallor.

In my five years at the school, I got only one Saturday detention – from 'Fom', for talking in class. I decided I didn't like poetry when our English master, Mr Grigg, tried to get us to learn Shelley's 'Ode to the West Wind' by heart. He was 'Darcy' – with that given name he did not need a nickname. As my class master, Darcy set the assignment for my detention. It was an idyllic Saturday morning. The sun was streaming into the decrepit high-ceilinged nineteenth century classroom. I had to write an appreciation of Coleridge's 'The Rime of the Ancient Mariner' and was entranced, though I did not acknowledge this to myself at the time.

Peter Jenkins ('Tojo') was my German teacher for the next three years. He had a real interest in the literature and language. In 1955 he arranged for me to be awarded the German prize, two 700-page volumes of Goethe's poems and plays in a blue cloth binding. Over the next two years I read the first and second parts of Goethe's Faust in German, something I could not manage now.

Our Latin teacher was Mr IF Jones, an unflappable man who took no notice of the dull rumble of a shot-put ball rolling under the desks across the parquet tiles. We tried this trick sparingly – so it could be explained as an innocent accident. This was a smallish class, about fifteen boys, and he taught us the complex rules for scanning Latin verse. He had a large and beautiful garden on a hillside in Northbridge, looking out over a valley, and his son Alex was the boy who had explained sex to me.

I fell in love with one of the Latin set texts from 1955: the fourth book of Virgil's pastoral *Georgics*: the happy cornfields, the wind in the trees and the evening star; Virgil's precise observation and lyricism that suddenly abandons bees and darkens, like the storm in Beethoven's *Pastoral Symphony*, when Virgil describes Orpheus vainly trying to bring Eurydice back from the underworld. I decided I too would write pastoral poems. How – I was unsure.

In my second-last year our entire grade had a couple of lectures from a local doctor, Dr Dey. He was the general practitioner who had treated my sister as a child and had signed Bella's death certificate. The last of his lectures was eagerly anticipated. He explained the facts of life, causing a few stifled guffaws. Then he announced that, from a medical viewpoint, masturbation was completely harmless. This was greeted with roars of relieved laughter and applause.

I had an intense and unsatisfied curiosity about the female anatomy. For some reason, our home bookcase contained a couple of issues of *Man* magazine, a small Australian 'girlie' magazine. I used to gaze surreptitiously at its demure black-and-white photographs of naked young women. I also found a little pamphlet explaining human reproduction and stared fascinated at a diagram of male and female reproductive organs.

⚜

My father taught me chess. After I joined the school chess club, I studied some small books he had about openings and stratagems. I was soon playing in the chess team. In my second year at Shore, on the afternoon scheduled for our rugby practice I had to play in the inter-school chess competition. I was given a dispensation from rugby – the only boy in the school who played no sport at all. I regarded it as a great accolade. We played chess against a wide range of schools and trekked across Sydney after school in the car of one of the older boys – which was unusual. His family owned a flour mill.

In 1953 when all of my class joined the army or air cadets I was too young to enlist. On Tuesday afternoons when the cadets were training, I sat in a classroom studying with the small group of senior boys who did not enlist. The following year I joined the air training corps or ATC. I'd heard we would get ice cream at training camp and the army cadets only got custard, and I preferred our navy blue uniform to their khaki. A myth was circulated that the army cadets were more manly than us. It conveniently ensured only a few applied for the limited places in the ATC.

In the ATC, I learned how to shoot. I once flew upside down – the earth above us – when a pilot took me up in an old Wirraway and we 'looped the loop'. The sensations were too novel – the huge gravity forces as we banked – to feel alarmed. My confusion about left and right meant my marching and drill skills were poor. When I heard the order 'Left turn!' I sometimes quickly consulted the small piece of graphite lodged in my right hand. In my final year, some external examiners were impressed by my histrionic commands to squads of younger boys and promoted me to flight sergeant. They were unaware of my poor co-ordination.

My specialty was ordering a squad of air cadets to march across an aerodrome. I watched them march to the perimeter and estimated how long my voice would take to reach them. When they could march no further, I shouted 'about turn' in my loudest megaphone-like voice, a fraction early. My command had to arrive when their left feet hit the ground.

The training camps brought together boys from many backgrounds and we slept in long galvanised iron huts. A hand tapping on a metal cupboard in one of these huts was my introduction to rock-and-roll. 'I've just heard this terrific piece,' one of my hut mates said. He sang the lyrics of 'Rock Around the Clock', beating the rhythm out on the top of one of the metal cupboards where we stored our things. It had no resemblance to tin pan alley, which I hated. I was excited. I sensed this was something new and radical.

After the last chapel of my final year at Shore in 1956, as the boys filed out, I saw two small old men waiting on the path outside. At first I did not recognise them. Then I realised the tiniest was Mr Yarnold, now in his eighties. The larger of the two was Mr McDougall. When I was at Mosman Prep I had not realised he was so small. They shook my hand and seemed pleased with me. They would have known I had been a prefect in my final year and done well academically. My two old teachers were gratified with the success of their experiment when they promoted a ten-year-old into a class where he was eighteen months younger than the other boys.

In 1955, when I moved into sixth form, the final year of secondary school, I was fourteen. The tradition was that a few final-year boys would form a team to compete in GPS debates. Although there was a master in charge, my recollection is that I effectively nominated myself as captain of debating. The school allowed boys a free hand to take over leadership roles. The exception was sport, where masters were coaches and the school's reputation was at stake.

In 1955 we chose our own team by consensus. The GPS debating competition was held in second term – in winter. Our first debate was at Riverview, a Jesuit boys' school of sandstone buildings and its own astronomical observatory, set on the banks of the Lane Cove River. Shore was grander than Mosman Prep, and Riverview was grander than Shore.

We walked down a long colonnade to the room where the debate was to be held; through doorways we glimpsed large fustian oil paintings of madonnas and saints. We were given the topic of the debate and a few minutes to prepare. A typical topic was 'The Pen Is Mightier than the Sword'.

The Riverview team was trained by Father Jones, who was said to be a former actor. Robert Hughes, the future writer and art critic, was the captain. He began his speech with a memorised quotation from GK Chesterton or Hilaire Belloc, and ended it with a similar quotation from a Catholic author. He had a suite of gestures. When he had an important point to make, he moved forward a step on the stage and raised his hand. Years later, standing in front of Sydney Harbour and talking about art in a TV program, he employed the same gesture. The two other speakers in the Riverview team had a similar style – although not as polished. We were thrashed.

I resolved our school should emulate Riverview. In more junior years at Shore debating was non-existent. I pinned signs on the notice board to recruit younger pupils, and we soon had several teams. I co-opted the school's tape recorder and recorded the boys so they could listen critically to themselves.

At the end of the year I decided to repeat my final year, rather than start university at the age of fifteen. In 1956 I was made a prefect and continued as captain of debating. But as Protestant boys we never achieved the finesse of the Jesuit-trained Riverview debaters.

My encounter with Robert Hughes in 1955 had a surprising Act II. In 1962 he was already famous as an artistic man-about-town in Sydney. By accident – we had read the same books and international journals – I became aware of three plagiarisms by Hughes in university publications: two poems and a drawing. I asked Bob Ellis, then co-editor of Sydney University's student newspaper *Honi Soit*, if he would like an article about them.

My article, bolstered with quotations from TS Eliot's *Four Quartets*, suggested the plagiarisms were an example of time travel. A Hughes poem published in 1957 and winner of a university poetry prize plagiarised a George Seferis poem written in 1936, and had an echo of a Dylan Thomas poem written in the 1940s. I wrote:

> Mr Hughes in 1957 was moving back to 1936 in order to reply to a poem yet to be written by Thomas. He was thus moving back in time to move forward in time.

The journalist and poet Elizabeth Riddell devoted a page of the *Sunday Mirror* to the controversy with a full-length photograph of Hughes, wearing a dark suit and trilby, posed with a cigarette in one hand, and leaning against a brick wall ('of a nearby box factory' a friend cattily informed me). The photo was captioned:

HUGHES 'Geoffrey Lehmann is a malicious …'

After drinking at the Royal George Hotel (a Sydney hotel with that name, not my grandfather's former hotel in Melbourne), I bought an early edition of the newspaper. It was midnight. I read Riddell's article as I was waiting in the underground station at Wynyard. My shock when I read the caption had gone by the time I was on the train home to Gordon. I could not be sued.

Sitting in Vadim's coffee shop in Potts Point some weeks later, I was approached by 'Chester' (Philip Graham), a fine poet and a friend of Hughes. He complimented me on my article being well written. Bob's mother had been ill, he went on to explain, and Bob himself had been in hospital with a hernia and had a relapse when the article appeared. This was all said lightly and humorously. Chester continued: 'Bob's worried you might sue him for defamation. What he said to Elizabeth Riddell is that you were a malicious little prig. She misheard this as malicious little prick.' I had assumed the word referred to by the dots was 'shit'. I may have laughed. I said I did not believe in people suing each other.

A few days afterwards at Vadim's, as Hughes passed the table where I was sitting, he greeted me cheerfully: 'Bonjour monsieur'.

Hughes gave up writing poems – they had never been more than an occasional exercise – and also painting and sketching, which had been a more serious pursuit. Despite his facility and flair, there was a brittleness about his own work. He became the art critic for *Time* magazine, and was soon the most famous art critic of his generation. We later had a friend in common. She was surprised to find the walls of Hughes's Manhattan apartment had no contemporary art except some works given to him by Bridget Riley. An art critic cannot collect art, he explained to her.

In about 1977 Bob and I were both at an afternoon party at Barry Humphries's flat in the Astor building in Macquarie Street. Our eyes met across the room, we waved to each other but did not speak. The only person who noticed our mutual salute was the art critic and artist Elwyn (Jack) Lynn. He stared fixedly at Bob and me as we greeted each other. I doubt whether Bob even noticed Jack Lynn's fixed gaze. I never saw Bob again.

The teacher who was most influential in my life was a man then in his mid-fifties. He had small brown eyes twinkling with irony, silver hair, purple-red cheeks and a modestly protruding paunch. An excellent cricket coach, he had a dry way of speaking with a nasal country twang – he had been brought up in the Riverina. His name was Pat Eldershaw ('Pat' was how the boys referred to him – no nickname). I was astonished years later to discover his given names were Percy Hopetoun. School boys have an ability to winkle out awkward facts about their teachers. That his given name of Percy was not exploited is proof of the respect we had for Pat.

In 2010 Pat's son, John, published a memoir about him for family and friends: *A Schoolmaster's Life*. Pat was born on 1 January 1901, when the Australian colonies became a federation on the first day of the twentieth century. He acquired his middle name from Lord Hopetoun, the federation's first Governor-General, an imaginative way of celebrating the coincidence of a child's birth on the nation's birth date.

Pat's childhood was spent on 'Mundawadra', a 50 000 acre (20 200 ha) property owned by the Scottish Australian Company and managed by his father. Miles from the nearest town, there was a large weatherboard homestead and other buildings. Clothing and footwear arrived once a year in a large wooden case from Sydney. There was not much money but the children were educated by governesses paid for by the Scottish Australian Company. 'We had riding, tennis, cricket, reading, music, indoor hobbies of all kinds…'

The summers could be stiflingly hot but his mother had a garden 'considered about the best in the district…' There were visitors on Sundays and she went visiting on weekdays in a horse-drawn sulky with a hood.

> When she was at home she would frequently set out on a fishing excursion in the afternoon, walking to one of the deeper waterholes … her favourite fishing spots were at least a mile away. She thought nothing of walking there and back and on the return trip she was usually burdened by the weight of several fish – catfish and a kind of small mountain perch that she called minnows. She kept up a large correspondence with Queensland friends and played the piano every evening after tea for quite a long time.

As a schoolboy I sensed Pat had this (for me) romantic childhood, although he did not talk about it in detail.

At age fourteen, the time had come for Pat to go to secondary school. He travelled in a train for the first time. His father was Church of England and his mother Catholic. Shore was considered, but his mother had visited the newly established St Joseph's College at Hunters Hill a few years earlier. Pat and a brother were sent there. It was 'a sad decision'. Neither of them were as tough as the typical Joey's boarder – mainly sons of country publicans – and the long-term effect was to make it impossible for Pat to become a headmaster. The headmasters of the prestigious Catholic schools were all in religious orders and the headmasters of Protestant schools were all born and bred Protestants. His birth name of Percy, a good if rather silly Protestant name, had not helped either, when it elided into the easy-going 'Pat', which could only belong to a Catholic.

Through this series of accidents, I was to have Pat as my English master for three years. I suspect I first came to his attention one day when he was teaching a soporific class of boys, heads lowered, all working on an assignment he had set. He may also have thought us a very smug group. To wake us up, and perhaps himself also, he asked in his dry, country accent: 'Is there anyone here who is not *absolutely certain* there is a life after death?'

This was a carefully worded, but subversive question to be asking. Pat could ask it – his reputation in the school was rock solid and it was a tolerant institution, like the Anglican Church itself (apart from its evangelical wing).

I was the only boy who put up his hand. If he had inquired further, I would have replied one could not be *absolutely certain* of anything. But he did not wish to expose the sole dissenter in the class to further embarrassment. He mumbled that some people believed in a communal life after death.

Afterwards, a boy accosted me in the lunch hour. Did I believe in God? Several informal lunchtime debates between us began, with three or four boys gathered around to listen. The rest of our class had no interest. Or they may have had religious beliefs but did not wish to debate them. Until then I had never mentioned my atheism to anyone – but I was prepared to argue for my position. (At a sixty-year reunion, my fervent Christian antagonist told me he had become a Catholic. Through Pat's English classes he fell in love with the poetry of Gerard Manley Hopkins. Hopkins had helped lead him to Catholicism.)

Pat handed out copies of poems for us to critique. The first which caught my attention was WR Rodgers's 'Stormy Day'. The poem begins with an overwritten description of the stormy day. But its language is vivid and contemporary. It finishes with a reference to the end of the 'phoney war' in 1940 and 'motionless newsposters announcing/ That now the frozen armies melt and meet…' This was my introduction to modern poetry.

Gerard Manley Hopkins, Robert Graves, John Crowe Ransom, ee cummings, TS Eliot, WH Auden – their poems were about a world I could recognise. Poems might have hidden meanings. Blake's 'The Sick Rose', for example, was not just about a rose. It was about formal religion corrupting innocence and spontaneous sexual desire.

In my two final years, 1955 and 1956, I was a member of Pat's English honours classes. These were held in his study, in one of the school's boarding houses, where he lived as housemaster with his wife Flo. Surrounded by walls of books which we were allowed to borrow – Virginia Woolf, André Gide, James Joyce, Graham Greene, as well as poetry – our late Wednesday afternoons with five or six other boys were a magical time, as we looked from the windows across the harbour to Pyrmont, pennants of steam from the power station's chimneys and the lights coming on in the dusk.

In 1954 I had begun writing poems, in rhyme, in fixed and free forms and different styles: two or three a week. I showed some of these to Pat. He thought I should meet a prastising poet and arranged for his friend RD FitzGerald to give a talk to our group. 'Fitz' as he was familiarly called (although I never called him that) talked about what it was like to be a poet. Gesturing to the radiator – it was a winter's night – he said: 'If you're going through a dry period you have to start again somewhere; you might start by writing a poem about that radiator.'

Another Australian poet I first heard about from Pat was James McAuley. Pat took him on as a housemaster at Barry House in the early days of World War II. McAuley came back at night and played jazz piano after the boys were in bed.

I also found in an old school magazine, dating back to about 1916, a school song written by Kenneth Slessor when he was a pupil at Shore. Its title was, I think, 'The Old Red White and Blue'. Already Slessor was a fluent versifier.

In the thirty years I knew him, Pat never mentioned that he wrote poetry, although I should have guessed. He started in his youth and continued until the night before his death. Some of his poems were in bush ballad style and others were epigrams, such as this lampoon about an early nineteenth century pastoralist and explorer:

x = ck's

> Did Gregory Blaxland's surname ever
> Inspire in him the feeling
> That the acquisition of his land
> Was really a kind of stealing?

Although we never discussed religion, I was conscious of Pat's religious scepticism:

Cogitation at a Cremation

> The 'undiscovered country' which
> Must finally be found for all
> For most of us will be a niche
> Now vacant in a long brick wall.

LEEWARD

Pat never lectured us. He presented things to us and asked what we thought. He was unopinionated; at the most he might gently guide us. He was well aware of what he was doing and wrote these lines on his retirement:

Now departs one
Who taught as unsuccessfully as most others have done.
But he had good books on his shelves
Which did induce a few to find out things for themselves.

During his years of teaching at Shore, from 1924 to 1965, his salary was modest and he and his wife Flo never went overseas. Nor, when he retired, did they travel around Australia as they had planned. Inspirational teachers are rarer than good headmasters. If his mother had not sent him to Joey's he might have been a headmaster of a prestigious Protestant private school by 1954, and my life may have been very different.

When Pat retired, I continued to see him. He and Flo bought a house at Roseville. I had lunch with them and they had lunch with me from time to time. He loved to feed kookaburras. They gathered around him on a rotary clothesline, while he handed them pieces of raw meat, smiling tolerantly as though they were his pupils. The last time I saw Pat, he was in his eighties. He was having difficulty getting a taxi in George Street in the city, and I flagged one down for him.

IRIS

My mother was born in 1896. In the years after her brother Leslie died in World War I, she became critical of organised religion and developed a social conscience. 'All the starving people in the world' was a favourite phrase of hers.

Not all happy families are alike and we were a happy family in our own strange way. We lived together in the Gordon house from 1950 until my father died in 1968. Diana looked back fondly on those years. She still had a father and mother – and loved them both – and a brother living at home, even if he was an unreliable member of the household.

My father Leo wore long singlets under his shirts and never owned underpants. He did not care about external appearances. He was a man of property. His happiness was a simple, mathematical sum.

Iris was the least satisfied of our family quartet. Despite her social conscience, she cared about appearances. She was ashamed that we had no car, that our front fence was falling down and that the house was unpainted. She felt uprooted geographically. When her brother Billy moved from Melbourne to Sydney, Bella had imperiously insisted that she and Iris follow him. Iris hated Sydney. She compared it with Melbourne in predictable comments. People in Sydney were crass, and Melbourne people were gracious. These comparisons prompted my father to sarcasms about 'Smelbourne' – a standard witticism from Sydney-siders dating back to the nineteenth century, when Melbourne's Yarra River ran with sewage overflow.

Apart from a few relatives, my mother had no friends. We were visited every few years by her Melbourne cousin Bell Firth, a jovial, plump, unmarried woman, with pink shiny skin and grey curls. Bell's loud voice cheered my mother up when she came to stay. Two other Melbourne cousins, Molly and Jimmy Blake, a sister and brother who lived together, occasionally visited. Jimmy was a sports journalist with Melbourne's *Herald Sun*, and a jokester. These three cousins were my mother's only real friends later in her life.

Leo badgered Iris about money. He thought matches were an extravagance and brought home flint lighters for the gas stove. Iris could not learn how to flick the small flint wheel with her thumb and persisted with matches. By the 1950s, as the mother of older children, she had leisure time and cheered herself up reading books and newspapers. She railed against 'the Americans' and 'the Catholics' and idolised Bertrand Russell. One day she noticed an iris growing in a bed of onions in our backyard. 'I'm an iris among the onions', she told us.

I was an articled clerk and drinking three glasses of beer with work mates at lunch, and more beers after work. Diana mentioned my bleeding gums. My mother said, 'It serves you right. It's all that staying out at night and getting no exercise.' I replied: 'You've got such a satisfied look. On your mean little face.' 'Mean little face! I shall remember that until I die,' my mother said later at lunch.

Iris was a pretty child, with brown hair and lupin-blue eyes, and throughout her life was proud of her fair 'English' complexion. When they were in England, as children of a doctor, even one as peripatetic as William Rainer, their household usually had servants.

Three years after her father's death, as the second oldest child, at the age of thirteen she left school and went to work as a seamstress in the factory of the Hicks Atkinson department store, founded by her grand-uncle, Thomas Moubray. Her father had been one of the beneficiaries in his estate. Now her family was penniless. She told stories of herself as a school child fetching her mother, smelling of alcohol, from hotels to cook the family dinner and help put the younger children to bed.

Working in a clothing factory was a bitter loss of status. At about the same time, the poet Lesbia Harford, a committed socialist, gave up her middle-class life to become a seamstress in Melbourne. My mother did not have a choice. She told us how she used to jump up on the trestle table in the sewing factory. Swathing herself in a gown, she would call out to the other women and girls: 'Fancy me in fancy dress'. After a forewoman caught her doing this, she did not do it again.

Iris was desperate to escape factory life, and took singing lessons. Her fantasy was to be an opera star with the stage name 'Irisi di Rinia'. Her paternal grandfather John Cragin Rainer (she told me impressively) 'sang before Queen Victoria by special request'.

He was a baritone from New York and a member of the 'Ethiopian Serenaders'. In 1846 they performed for Queen Victoria, their faces painted black and lips white, their jokes toned down for the royal family. While on tour in the United States, Rainer's forehead was grazed by a bullet from a man in the audience – not a story, I suspect, my mother knew about. In 1852 'Rainer's

Original Ethiopian Serenaders' arrived in Australia from the Californian goldfields.

As well as taking singing lessons, Iris also learned typing and shorthand at what was then known as 'night school'. She found she could not afford both classes, so gave up singing – something she regretted for the rest of her life. She got a job in the bankruptcy office and used to stand on the stools and take down the heavy, bound court records and read about her forefathers' bankruptcies.

She went dancing with boyfriends at the St Kilda Palais de Dance and had a lively girlfriend, Bessy Sinnott, whom she likened to Becky Sharp in Thackeray's *Vanity Fair*. At these dances Iris wore a dress she had made of an eye-catching green. A poem I wrote in the 1960s retells one of her stories.

The Australian Summer of 1913–14

My mother, Hugo Wolf and Henry Davis
Paraded on St Kilda Pier, a threesome,
My mother sweet on Henry, not poor Hugo
Who tagged along – until an urchin squawked
'Two into one won't go!' and laughed and ran,
And Hugo never went with them again.
My mother and her sweetheart Henry Davis
Hands linked, strolled past the fish-shops of St Kilda,
Through long suspended pre-war summer dusks.

Iris's elder brother Leslie enlisted, as did the boys she danced with at the Palais de Dance. My mother handed out white feathers to able-bodied men who had not enlisted, a story about herself she later repeated, ashamed. Before he arrived in Gallipoli, Leslie sent a postcard to Iris's younger sister Eva from Heliopolis, Egypt, dated June 1915, telling her about a trip 'with a fellow named Lilly. Mother knows him. We went through the principal pyramid. The passages inside are very steep, we had to take our boots off. Else we could not walk up the slippery marble...'

Leslie was among the Australian troops who survived the torpedoing of the *Southland* on the voyage from Egypt to Gallipoli. One of the last to leave Gallipoli, according to my mother, Leslie survived for almost two years in France.

Before General Birdwood's letter of 27 May 1917 to Bella, advising of Leslie's almost certain death, my mother received a letter from a man signing himself 'Cecil'. Cecil tells Iris not to give up hope. Because of the confusion in the dark, Leslie could have wandered into the German lines and been taken prisoner. That had almost happened to Cecil himself, when he and his mate worked out where to go from the noise of a German gun opening fire. Cecil concluded:

> ... this war has knocked what inclination I had to roam, all out of me and if I do not get bowled over they will have to drive me out of the house if they want me to go anywhere; once I get home I will get you to play to me ... you could always play the piano real well before I left ... P.S... I have still got great hopes of hearing Les sing some of his favourite songs to all of us when this war is over.

I had no idea my mother could 'play the piano real well'. I have no memory of ever seeing her play the piano. This was not for lack of opportunity; our houses and my father's boat all had pianos. Living for many years with the piano virtuoso, Bella, she may have lost confidence – the mother outshining the daughter, which was the pattern of Iris's life.

When the war ended, my mother was a twenty-two-year-old office worker. Many of her pre-war boyfriends did not come back, and those who did were less idealistic. Iris was still inhibited and impractical. Henry Davis came back, but their pre-war romance did not revive as my mother may once have hoped. I do not know if Cecil came back, and if she played the piano and sang for him. Iris and her mother visited hospitalised war veterans in the hope that one of the veterans with memory loss would be Leslie.

My mother went on holidays with Bella to Sorrento, the beach resort close to the entrance of Port Phillip Bay. After days spent on the ocean beach in a discreet bathing costume and rubber bathing cap, there were walks around the foreshores of the bay as the sun went down, and sing-alongs around the piano at night at the guest house. Iris often sang songs from that era to Diana and me: 'How Ya Gonna Keep 'Em Down on the Farm After They've Seen Paree'.

My mother went to mayoral balls in St Kilda and boasted that she had she danced with General Blamey. She and her mother were active in the social life of the Anglican churches they attended, and she saw many films. When I was a child she talked about Charlie Chaplin, Greta Garbo and Rudolph Valentino, and W D Griffiths and his *The Birth of a Nation* and *Intolerance*. In later years she became anti-war and supported the campaign for nuclear disarmament. She talked about Wendell Willkie's book *One World* and became a believer in world government.

Iris's middle brother, a second William George Rainer, Uncle Billy to my sister and me, moved to Sydney. Bella insisted on following him. As Iris lived with her mother, the two women moved to Sydney in about 1930. Iris counted seven bridges and hated them when Billy drove them across Sydney. She was dismayed by the waterways and hills. Melbourne was flat and safe and Sydney had razor gangs in William Street. She began to notice cars backfiring – unburned fumes exploding in the exhaust. It was: 'Another person shot' until she was told it was just a car backfiring.

The two women settled in a rented flat in Rose Bay. My mother got work as a stenographer. She was now unmarried and in her thirties. Although she still had her youthful good looks, she was 'on the shelf'. Billy, as a man, was able to make introductions for Bella and Iris, and at a party at the O'Donnell's – their name is all I remember about them – my mother met my father.

Iris and Leo were such a strangely assorted couple it is hard to imagine what brought them together. Perhaps having been brought up by widows was something they had in common. After a courtship of a couple of years, they married. Although a bit overweight from drinking with the 'Buffs' (or Royal Antediluvian Order of Buffaloes, sometimes known as the 'Poor Man's Freemasons'), he was presentably handsome. She married him, she told me, because he made her feel safe.

When my mother married and moved into 'Leeward' at the head of Lavender Bay, Bella moved to a nearby flat in 'Burundah Hall' in East Crescent Street. My mother visited Bella often with Diana, and then with me when I was born. I have a distant memory of these visits, the dim echoing hallways of 'Burundah Hall', and my grandmother with gold-framed spectacles, dressed in black, opening the door. After Bella's death in 1943, my mother and sister used to point out her former flat from the street when we walked past.

My mother did not note Bella's death in the family bible, but she took Diana and me to visit her metal niche with inscribed plaque in the crematorium's garden of remembrance. Bella's marriage to William in her early twenties was a love match between two glamorous people. My mother lived in her mother's shadow for forty years; then as she was approaching menopause married a working-class man, whom she did not love. But my mother's marriage persisted for more than thirty years, without dramas or incident, until my father died.

My meek mother's boldest act was marrying a man who she felt was beneath her. Bella was possibly even more surprised than her daughter when this working-class man paid cash for three waterfront houses at McMahons Point.

Iris's illusions about marriage to Leo – her leisurely life of reading books – had gone by the time I was born. Her frequent complaint when we were young – it became a family joke – was 'I don't even have time to go to the lav'. I hated it when my mother asked, 'Have you been to the lav?' She did not seem to understand children reach an age when they do not need to be reminded. Although inhibited about certain parts of her body – in the bathroom, she kept the door firmly shut – she had no sense of decorum, filing away the dead skin on her corns in front of the family and pointing to the bunions on her feet when I was a little boy, saying how silly she had been, wearing tight shoes when she was a girl.

This intimacy faded and I became resistant to 'Your father's just a working man' or 'He's not a reader'. I began hinting to my father that I sided with him and made a point of contradicting my mother while he was present. I suspected my father's sceptical detachment was the accumulation of many small rebuffs. Under the layers of habitual disappointment, he might even have still been in love with her.

After I reached puberty, my mother would sometimes say with a worried look: 'There's something I have to tell you some day'. My standard response was a pretended ignorance. This flustered her even more. I eventually gave up teasing and told her there was nothing she needed to tell me. Once she knew I knew, a flood of intimate confessions began that I could not stop, anaesthetising whatever feelings I still had for her.

One of her stories was that on their wedding night, my father explained to her 'he'd done it before'. He was seduced, he said, by his landlady when he was a young man in the country. She used to come to him on the outside veranda where he slept. One night she pointed to a doll: 'Perhaps we shall have one of those'. My father left the next day.

Some other confessions were not as harmless. On their wedding night Leo, she said, was surprised at how hard she was to penetrate. (It may have been her peculiar way of letting me know she was a virgin when she married. It was not something I wanted to hear about.) My mother used to tell me: 'Save yourself for marriage'. What I was saving myself for was unclear, as sex was 'that dirty business'. After sex with Leo (she said): 'I had to wash myself out in the bathroom. Late at night. While your father was asleep.'

I asked my mother why she married, if she found sex so abhorrent – did she ever love him? 'Your father was comfortable', was her reply, or 'safe'. I asked had she ever enjoyed sex, and she once admitted it was 'close to heaven'.

As owner of a passenger boat, my father found it easy to strike up a conversation with strangers, but he did not talk about his feelings. I deduced he had been in love with my mother when they married, and, as far as I know, was faithful to her. He was respectful with women. A physically shy woman such as my mother may have appealed to him. By the time he moved out of the marital bedroom though, he knew he was not loved. He revealed little, only comments such as he was too young (at forty-four) when he got married, and 'Your mother likes the gold braid and brass buttons' (referring to her boast about General Blamey). I came to believe the unreciprocated feelings between my father and mother were normal: there was always a lover and a loved.

As my mother grew older, her tendency to talk *at* rather than *with* increased. I became the target of her diatribes about 'the

Catholics' (often 'the dirty old Catholics'), 'the Americans', the starving Africans and Asians, world peace, and nuclear weapons. My father shrugged his shoulders: 'Why should I worry about the Bomb? I'll be dead and buried by the time they let it off.'

Many of her generalisations began 'They say…' I asked her, 'Mother, who is this "they say" you are always quoting?' One evening I was particularly dismissive of her. After she had gone to bed, my father stood in the doorway of my room. He said, 'Don't be too hard on your mother son. She's…' He pointed at the side of his head and rotated his forefinger.

Bella's 'Recollections' end with the sentence 'And now I am alone'. But she was not alone. She was surrounded by the ghosts of famous people she had caught glimpses of. She wrote a page-long 'After-thought' which begins 'Amongst distinguished people I have seen…' She lists the King and Queen of Portugal, the King and Queen of Italy, King George V with his wife in Edinburgh when they were the Duke and Duchess of York, and she reports attending the funeral of the Duke of Cambridge, who was uncle to Queen Mary, and so on. Compared with Bella's fatuities, Iris's obsessions were generous and humane.

I was hard on my mother, with the intolerance of youth. In many ways I was her embodiment. When I was a child, she encouraged me to read books and listen to music. She once tried to teach me to sing a Nat King Cole song we both liked. There was an extra note I couldn't get, which I stumbled over. She sang the tune for me, but this note still eluded me, even when we sang it together. One day she told me I should become a lawyer and a writer. From the age of twelve I no longer had to think about what I would become.

My mother read Pepys's journal. She suffered with Swann in Proust's *Swann's Way*. Gertrude Bell and Mary Wortley Montague were among her heroines. She loved H V Morton's travel books and Dickens, and above all Boswell's *Life of Samuel Johnson*. But she was married to a man who never read a book after he left school. He spent hours studying form guides for race horses and his only reading matter travelling in the train between his houses was old copies of the *Reader's Digest*.

Perhaps I expected too much of a woman of her age. In the mid-1970s, when I was divorced and looking after three small children half of each week, I was vaguely resentful of her lack of interest. But she was eighty years old, frail and slightly forgetful, although she could always retell, in great detail, what had happened in last night's television show.

A steady decline in her health had begun in her early fifties. Late in 1949 she had a fall in the David Jones Elizabeth Street store and broke her arm. She took herself along to a nearby public hospital. Badly shaken, she arrived home at seven that night. We had been alarmed, wondering where she was.

The Sydney Hospital interns had botched the setting of her arm. A few weeks later the fracture was reset and a steel plate inserted in a private hospital. Her hospital stay was prolonged by pleurisy and a thrombosis in her leg, and she was found to have high blood pressure.

This was the Christmas when Diana and I had no Christmas gifts. With our mother out of the way, my father cooked hearty meals, and invited over to the McMahon's Point house his friends and relations, the people in his life who were unwelcome when my mother was there. He entertained them with sherry and Christmas cake (already made by our mother with an enormously thick white coating of delicious marzipan). Our father enjoyed the bustle he created, but it was a desolate Christmas for us children.

Iris came home and we moved to Gordon. She insisted we go by train to look at the house of the surgeon who had reset her arm. As we walked past, my mother salaciously pointed out his mistress's cottage – in the grounds of the house where he lived with his wife. Iris had heard all about it from her surgeon's irascible old mother, who had an adjoining hospital room.

She was nervous about falls. In winter she could sense the steel plate in her arm. In 1968, after my father's death, she met the parents of my future first wife. Aged seventy-two, Iris was crestfallen when she saw they were in their fifties: 'I'm the only one who's old'.

SYDNEY UNIVERSITY

In 1956, my final year of high school, I was in the refectory of the Sydney University Union. A row of tall French doors had an outlook onto trees. Murals of romanticised figures from Shakespeare to Dickens looked down on the hundred or so young men and women at the tables below. In summer the young women wore nylon stockings and tried to arrest the ladders in their stockings with a spot of nail polish. In winter they wore knee-high woollen stockings, black or with tartan patterns, and tartan skirts, whose folds were held in place by a prominent safety pin or rabbit's foot. The young men wore sports coats and ties – usually wool, cotton or rayon ties, rarely silk. The murmur of young adults coming and going, and the clink of teaspoons stirring sugar in coffee cups, were intoxicating for a sixteen-year-old from a boys' school.

A school friend – I'll call him Robert – who was in first year Architecture, had arranged to meet me there before taking me to a lecture in the Wallace Theatre where the composer Richard Meale was to talk about Webern and Schoenberg – composers I had heard of – and Berio, Boulez, Varèse and Xenakis – four unfamiliar names.

Robert was two years older, and we had become friends at Shore in 1955 when he was repeating his final school year. We got to know each other in the Honours English class Pat Eldershaw held after school. During school holidays Robert invited me to his parents' house where we listened to long-playing records, and I heard for the first time the symphonies of Sibelius, and Bartok's string quartets.

In 1956 Robert asked me to be his witness on a court application for exemption from compulsory military training, or 'Nasho', for males turning eighteen. Robert was not objecting on religious grounds. If he succeeded, this would set a precedent. Vivienne Abraham, the solicitor for a pacifist organisation, was acting for him and briefed a maverick barrister, Peter Clyne, chubby with a goatee and prominent glasses.

At the time, I was a prefect at Shore and a flight sergeant in the Air Training Corps. In my mind neither of these things stood in the way of my being a witness. But I had private qualms. Not understanding I was just a character witness, I naively felt I could not give evidence about another person's beliefs. As we were walking to the District Court, another problem occurred to me. I was an atheist. I turned to Clyne and told him I could not swear on a bible.

I made a statutory affirmation and was in the witness box for only a few minutes. In his final address, Clyne argued that the conscientiousness of his client's belief, not its logic, was what mattered. 'If my client conscientiously believed he was a poached egg' said Clyne, 'that would be his conscientious belief'. Poached eggs did not make it into Judge Holt's judgment, but Robert won his exemption.

Not long before the hearing something happened that exacerbated my squeamishness about giving evidence. On one of our bush walks through Lane Cove National Park, Robert spoke about his horror of war. He looked at me and added, 'Remember I said this'. I realised our conversation had been rehearsed with his lawyers.

A few years later, when I was an articled clerk, I used to see Vivienne Abraham around the courts. 'Robert hasn't paid Peter Clyne's fees. The Society had to pay them,' she told me. I passed this message on. Robert's reply was the pacifists had wanted a precedent for a non-religious objector. In his view, he had done them a favour.

In my final year of school, Robert took me to visit Timothy Suttor, then living, as we both did, in Gordon. Tim and I found a common ground with our shared love for the poet Emily Dickinson. Tim was working for a building supplies company and was married, with a baby. His face was painfully thin, dominated by spectacles. He spoke in a light, quizzical voice, in carefully constructed sentences. Tim was a Catholic convert. While training for the priesthood with the Dominicans, he edited volume 11 of Thomas Aquinas's *Summa Theologiae* (now the standard edition published by Cambridge University Press). He did not take holy orders.

My first exposure to intellectual Catholicism was disturbing. I saw Tim as personifying the Jesuitical Naphta of Thomas Mann's *Magic Mountain*. I kept thinking of young Hans Castorp witnessing Naphta's verbal demolition of Settembrini's liberal humanism – the liberal humanism with which I identified.

We discussed James McAuley, a formalist poet, whose poems I admired, and who, like Tim, was a Catholic convert. One day Tim, with a laugh of evident enjoyment, read out lines from McAuley's 'Celebration of Love' which referred to koalas as 'sober citizens of sweet content' looking down on lovers with 'grave astonishment'. I was unable to laugh. I thought these lines were ghastly.

Encouraged by Tim, who seemed to like my poetry, I applied myself with enthusiasm to writing in rhyme and something resembling regular metre. But my understanding of metre was still wayward, until I met McAuley a couple of years later, and he became a friend.

In 1957 Tim moved with his family to Canberra to undertake a history doctorate at the Australian National University, and I stayed with him from time to time. We called on Alec Hope (an old friend of Tim's) and his wife Penelope. I had a copy of Hope's astonishing first book of poems *The Wandering Islands*, with its red and purple end papers. I was unable to say how much I admired the great man's poetry. He seemed reserved, and I understood he had no reason to be friendly to a stiff and pimply undergraduate.

In 1964 Tim and his family stayed briefly in a Wahroonga flat I was renting before they moved to Canada. He became a professor of Religious Studies at the University of Windsor in Ontario, and stayed at my house on trips back to visit his parents. I still occasionally find pencil notes in my books, written by Tim on his visits back. Some years after his death I found this epigram in my copy of James McAuley's *Under Aldebaran*.

> Jim was no pretty man, no petty man
> But was
> A pretty petty poet –
> After the first scandal
> Never quite scandalous enough again?

The scandal was the 1944 Ern Malley affair, when it was revealed that McAuley and his accomplice Harold Stewart had invented a modernist poet. Like many epigrams, Suttor's oversimplifies. The balanced paradoxes explain why his mind was attractive to an intellectually raw schoolboy in 1956. Classicism and formalism – ways of writing poetry and thinking that did not depend on subjective emotions – were unfamiliar and compelling. Tim did not resolve the conflicts in himself. There was an unsatisfied energy and restlessness about his embrace of orthodoxy.

Sydney University

At the beginning of 1957, I was starting an Arts-Law course at Sydney University. Robert introduced me to Ruth Hansman (later Burgess). She was just back from Paris where she had studied musical composition under Darius Milhaud. (Ruth remembers that she and I played piano duets. I cannot understand why she agreed to this. I could only produce meaningless discords. My piano playing in the Gordon house was a torment to my father.)

Ruth talked nostalgically about Sydney University's Art Group. She had been a member when she was an undergraduate. Robert and I revived this defunct student society and renamed it. We put up posters. Before a first year English lecture in the Wallace Theatre I announced the first meeting of the Writers, Artists and Composers Group. About a dozen turned up. Two admitted to writing poetry: Libby Sweet (who later married my school friend Alex Jones) and a big raw-boned, moon-faced boy from Taree with scabs on his face. Les Murray was about eighteen months older, and, like me, a first year 'fresher'. The three of us agreed to meet later that week and exchange poems.

We met one afternoon on a university college oval. Les and I produced our poems. We asked Libby to show us hers. 'No, no,' she said, 'they're just little things, little things'. That became Libby's standard reply, when I met her again. One of the poems Les showed us was 'Refugees', which described fleeing refugees 'with their faces dusty-white/ Flowing peristalsis in the dirty gut of night'. I was impressed by the easy mastery of rhyme and metre, and the extraordinary peristalsis image, which I thought verged on genius. I said his poems were terrific.

I can't be sure what I'd brought along. One poem may have been about the holidays with my mother and sister. It begins:

> There is always a sense of disappointment
> When you are on holiday,

The final horizon you were hoping for
Is still just as far away…

We published two poems of Les's in a roneoed publication of the Writers and Artists Group, as we now called ourselves. (We gave up on the composers. Robert was our only member who wanted to become a composer.) One of Les's poems was 'The Inquisitor'.

Les was yet to convert to Catholicism, but this early poetic monologue begins with the inquisitor addressing his victims as 'Vile termites in a dried-out well', and ends with the inquisitor saying he is requited if their deaths 'can save the souls to come'. I can almost hear Les's cackle of laughter in the last line: 'Now my brothers, wind the rack'. In this poem, Les's mix of irony and genuine spirituality was even then apparent.

He was already a large-framed, heavy young man when he started at university, but not excessively so. He exploited his body shape for humour. It may have been our first year at university. We were standing in a porch looking out at the rain. Les: 'Well, I think I'll dodge in and out among the rain drops'. Only in later years did he weigh 20 stone (130 kg) or more, and join 'the Stone Age aristocracy' as he calls overweight people in 'Quintets for Robert Morley'.

Early in our friendship Les persuaded me to come with him one night and watch two black-and-white German films in the old Lyric, near Central Station, a rundown cinema in a tatty end of town. Sitting next to him, he was exceptionally rancid. He must have been wearing the same pale moleskin trousers for weeks. I guessed what the problem was. I suggested Les start wearing underpants and washing them. Peter Alexander in his biography of Les states Les 'was enlightened, and grateful'.

Les later reciprocated my advice on matters of dress and I was equally grateful. I used to wear a tweed sports coat, sometimes with a yellow cotton tie, until Les gave me a friendly warning: 'I think I should let you know. Up my way – on the north coast – only shirt lifters wear yellow ties. It's their signal to each other.'

I admired Les's sociability. He hated snobbery, believed generously in his friends and liked anyone who liked him. He used to joke: 'You can buy Murray with a meat pie'. He was welcoming to a wide range of people and not judgmental. Once (probably when we were co-editing the 1961 Faculty of Arts magazine *Arna*), he handed me some poems, saying 'These show real promise'.

The poems were written by a younger student whose name was John Tranter. I read them and made some negative comments. They were apprentice works. Les continued to defend them. This was a surprising start to a celebrated literary feud, with Tranter becoming one of Murray's most persistent critics.

Les often talked about life on his father's farm at Bunyah: how bush objects were sanctified by use. An old tree stump, used as a stool, was polished by years of people sitting on it. I suggested that he write about such things. I still had my long-term ambition of writing Virgilian pastoral poems, but had no idea where my subject matter might come from – unlike Les.

I became his day-to-day critic. When he was at Bunyah during university breaks, he regularly mailed me a sheaf of new poems. I also showed him my own poems in the hope he would make detailed criticisms. In general, he did not. (A few years later he told me he dreaded the moment when I would say after reading a new Murray poem, 'That's bullshit, Murray'.)

One day, having known Les for about six months, I was walking along Parramatta Road with two friends. One of them said, looking behind him, 'Look, there's that awful Les Murray person. Let's *run!*' They were not friends of Les's, but I was. I ran with them.

Les was keen on his middle name – Allan – he first published poems under the name 'Les A Murray'. He later addressed his wife as 'Valerie Gina' and often addressed me as 'Geoffrey John' – perhaps a habit picked up from reading Russian novels. He may have hoped I would address him as 'Leslie Allan'. Despite different temperaments, our friendship lasted for more than twenty-five years. After we had drifted apart, he said to my daughter Julia, 'You know, I have Asperger's syndrome. And your father has too.'

About ten years after this conversation I was visiting Les at his two side-by-side houses at Bunyah. He was then seventy-seven. It was early spring and the grass was still lush. Large citrus trees were loaded with orange and yellow fruit. Lotus plants were at one end a dam and water lilies at the other. 'They're fighting it out' was Les's comment. I pointed to a half-dead vine scrambling up a trellis: 'I see you've got a Dutchman's pipe'. Les had not known its name and responded with a story of how he had rescued it – I think from a school that was closing down. 'Yes', he said conspiratorially, 'we're both autistic'.

As well as three early Les Murray poems, the roneoed publication of the Writers and Artists Group contained a ballad-like poem by Ian Bedford, using half-rhyme. (Ian introduced me to my second wife Gail Pearson more than twenty years later.) Ruth Burgess had a poem 'Paradise Regained' about the bombing of Hannover during World War II. Ruth later abandoned poetry and musical composition and became a leading woodcut artist, making prints of forests and birds.

The first meeting of the Writers and Artists Group was at the waterfront Vaucluse house of Ruth's parents. The house had a grand circular staircase and marble fountain in a large entrance hall. Ruth remembers Les Murray reading to us from C.J. Dennis's *The Sentimental Bloke*, also her kind-hearted mother expostulating with her: 'You haven't told those poor young men where the bathroom is'. One afternoon I was standing with

Mrs Hansman at her front door. She hurried off into the garden and came back with a look of triumph, holding a needle she had found at the foot of a bush: 'I've been wanting one of these'.

We were an earnest and introverted group. Robert Hughes participated in our 1957 group exhibition of paintings in the Sydney University Union, but he came to only one meeting. Les also stopped coming.

Towards the end of 1957 our group spent a weekend in a house in isolated bush at Woy Woy. I had fallen in love with the poetry of Wallace Stevens and also a blonde girl with dazzling white skin. As we rowed across the water one night to the township I recited Wallace Stevens's 'The Plot Against the Giant', one of the few poems I knew by heart. My attempt to impress her was a failure.

I met Brian Jenkins through our group. Brian worked as a salesman, drove a large new Ford car and had a disregard for parking signs. Brian loved Dylan Thomas and wrote poetry with a metaphysical flavour. Through Brian I got to know Lex Banning, a legendary older poet with cerebral palsy. Lex presided over a table of admirers at Repin's coffee shop. Brian told them a story about putting on a cerebral palsy act while trying to cross Parramatta Road, and a police car stopping and halting the traffic. Lex was the only person at the table who laughed.

In the last couple of years of the Writers and Artists I shared the administrative responsibilities with Ian Boden, who started at university in 1958. Ian was a plump young man who wore horn-rimmed glasses and a tweed sports coat. He was not a writer or artist but seemed to find the amateur and ineffectual nature of our group congenial.

Ian worked in a bookshop. He often sat at the table in the university's Manning House where Les Murray presided; and was one of Les's unpaid creditors. Ian was not easily aroused, but one morning he must have felt unusually fed up with Les. Waving a five pound note in front of his debtor, Ian set it on fire and used the burning note to light a cigarette: 'Now I'm enjoying spending *my* money as *I* want to spend it'.

Years later Les wrote a poem 'The Quality of Sprawl', referring to this incident, and the five pound note had become a ten dollar note lighting a cigar, not a cigarette.

Robert often talked about the importance of what he called 'feeling'. Certain lines of Shakespeare and passages in Beethoven's late quartets expressed 'feeling'. Without 'feeling', life was not worthwhile. 'Feeling' was elusive and days might go by without it. The more you thought about it, the harder it was to experience it. Ruth mentioned Robert's obsession about 'feeling' to her mother. Mrs Hansman said to Ruth, 'You can tell Robert not to worry. I'm sixty and I can still feel!'

In 1959 I started at the Law School. By the end of the year the Writers and Artists was defunct. We had all to a greater or lesser extent been obsessed by 'feeling'. Robert was our inspiration. He spoke sombrely and with deliberation. His smiles were ironical. Some friends were laughing about me, he said, and named them. Then he added with a nervous cough, 'I defended you'. I was relieved when Robert dropped out of my life.

Robert died a few years ago. He invented a new musical notation, which he said was simpler. I suspect he pursued the solitary path of 'feeling' for the rest of his life.

⁂

In my first year of university I had another group of friends quite separate from the claustrophobic Writers and Artists. We were an informal group of five from different schools. We sat together in classes, and drank coffee during breaks. I knew John Hamilton from inter-school debating. Colin Mackerras I knew from inter-school chess. He had a friend, John Sheldon, who became a Sanskrit scholar. They both knew Pam Suttor. She had been educated at Rose Bay Convent and was Tim Suttor's cousin. Hamilton and I were Protestant atheists. The other three were linked through the Catholic Church.

We could have been earnest young actors in a Whit Stillman film, with our know-it-all discussions, as we walked along the stone paved paths that intersected at the centre of the lawn of the nineteenth century sandstone quadrangle. They were my first group of close friends. Until then I had been the younger boy in the class, conscious that I had a family that was odd.

John Hamilton knew he would become a barrister. He later became a Supreme Court judge. I was planning to study law and wondered whether a barrister's life would squeeze out poetry. John was certain about his career in a way I wasn't. He had been a 'Quiz Kid' on a well-known radio show. When we met as captains of opposing school debating teams, his distinctive and quietly authoritative voice was already familiar from the radio program.

He was the only one of us who had a car – paid for with Quiz Kid earnings – a small fawn Ford Prefect whose number-plate began with the letters MU. I teased John by calling it the 'Mu-car'. After a couple of years this car got a new number-plate, beginning with the letters 'BUJ'. The 'Mu-car' became the 'Budgeri-car'. He did not complain, but I sensed his irritation.

The Mackerras family were Catholic converts – with a defiant twinkle Colin began many conversations: 'Mother Church says…' Colin's large family of brothers and sisters (one brother was Sir Charles, the conductor) were Wagner fanatics. 'Wagner is the greatest composer', Colin often claimed. 'Well, a lot of people say that of Beethoven', I once argued back. John Sheldon and Colin debated whether I was qualified to have an opinion. They devised a game. Colin's knowledge of Wagner and Beethoven was encyclopaedic and he used to sing a few bars of music, and I had to pick the composer.

John Hamilton and I became regulars at the Sydney University Union's weekly 'Union Night'. An external speaker spoke to a motion and students spoke for or against. John and I joined the Union Night committee. Not long after Sir Garfield Barwick was appointed federal Attorney-General in 1958, the Union invited Barwick to address a dinner. My role was to be his minder. I sat next to him. He was a modest and courteous man, friendly in a reserved way with students, and pleased to be among us.

In 1957 I had a conversation with Clive James in the internal stairway of the old Fisher Library. We were each about three months into our first year of study. We discussed literature. I spoke about some poets I had become keen on at high school, probably Wallace Stevens and Rainer Maria Rilke. Clive replied with bitterness that having gone to Sydney Technical High School, he knew nothing about writers such as those.

A few days later I was talking to John Hamilton. John was at primary school with Clive (and appears in *Unreliable Memoirs*). Clive could have gone to a selective high school, John said, but chose Sydney Tech because his classmates were going there. The products of selective high schools became doctors and lawyers. Sydney Tech made Clive different from the rest of us. In 1957 he regretted the 'bad choice' he made as a primary school child. But it may partly explain why he has become one of Australia's most famous expatriates.

That year there was great excitement when a university film society showed the Swedish feature film *One Summer of Happiness*. It had a long shot of a young woman and a young man swimming naked, and a more intimate shot of her breasts. We had an alternative name for the film: *One Summer of a Penis*. I had to wait another four years before I saw a naked girl. I was sexually frustrated and naive – like most of my friends.

A victim of sexual disquiet and resident ghost of the university's sandstone Victorian Gothic quadrangle, if it had one, would be the son of an Irish brewer, Christopher Brennan. He was a student there and later one of its most celebrated teachers, with a study in the quadrangle. He was a big man, his great hooked nose complemented by a meerschaum pipe. He died in 1932.

When I was a schoolboy I borrowed the HM Green anthology *Modern Australian Poetry* from the Gordon public library and found these lines from Brennan's long poem 'The Wanderer':

> All night I have walk'd and my heart was deep awake,
> remembering ways I dream'd and that I chose,
> remembering lucidly, and was not sad,
> being brimm'd with all the liquid and clear dark
> of the night that was not stirr'd with any tide;
> for leaves were silent and the road gleam'd pale,
> following the ridge, and I was alone with night…

Brennan then speaks of the painful awareness where everything becomes meaningless after the ecstasy of being alone with the night:

> But now I am come among the rougher hills
> and grow aware of the sea that somewhere near
> is restless; and the flood of night is thinn'd
> and stars are whitening. O, what horrible dawn
> will bare me the way and crude lumps of the hills
> and the homeless concave of the day, and bare
> the ever-restless, ever-complaining sea?

Brennan's poem may be the greatest *fin de siècle* poem in our language, richer and more resonant than its contemporary, Oscar Wilde's 'The Ballad of Reading Gaol'. One of the strengths of 'The Wanderer' (like Wordsworth's 'The Prelude') is that it is set in an identifiable landscape – Sydney's northern beaches, then sparsely inhabited. This was where Brennan went to live with his German bride after studying the German Romantics in Berlin. His marriage soon soured and his wanderings at night inspired his poem.

Many from outside the university attended Brennan's erratic lectures. He was scheduled to deliver them early in the day, before he was too drunk. A student introduced into his study was likely to find it in darkness, lit only by the red glow of a beaker of claret over a flame. Eventually the university dismissed him. My German professor Ralph Farrell, when young, was a friend of Brennan's. Unfortunately I was unaware of this in 1957 when I became his student. With Farrell we studied Goethe's *Sturm und Drang* (storm and stress) period and *Die Leiden des jungen Werthers* (The Sorrows of Young Werther). I was also having a love affair with the poetry of Rilke: the *Neue Gedichte* (1907), poems such as 'The Panther', 'The Spanish Dancer' and 'Blue Hydrangeas'.

I sensed Farrell might have encouraged me to become a German academic. But I baulked at the prospect of spending the rest of my life with the claustrophobic German Romantics – the forebears of Robert's obsession with feeling. I began to see Goethe's escape from Romanticism into objective classicism as a way out of my own *Weltschmerz*. Timothy Suttor was also an influence.

Our most colourful German lecturer was a handsome, elderly aristocrat, Dr von Stutterheim. He joked about German pedantry and used English in an interesting way. One of his favourite English words was 'trickish' – the German equivalent is *betrügerisch*.

When we asked him a difficult question, he would say, 'Ah that is very trickish'.

I was younger than most first year students. I painfully asked a couple of girls out and was refused. A girl in the German class told me I gave her the creeps, because of how I stared. I was surprised. I was unaware I stared at her. She was a pleasant looking girl. That was all.

Not long after I started at university I became obsessed with another student. Each morning I woke up, with nothing on my mind, ready to enjoy the day. Then my chest tightened – as though breathing in an iron lung – when I remembered her. I spoke to no-one about my obsession. She was a friend. I was sure she would not reciprocate my feelings. If she had known, she may have been mildly flattered, and treated it as of no concern.

A portly fifty-year-old man in a striped, navy blue suit regularly visited the State Library reading room where I studied. He had soft lips and horn-rimmed glasses. He read at a table in his waistcoat, white shirt sleeves held up by silvery garters. Once, when he had left for the day, I looked at his pile of books. I flipped through them – they were about spiritualism – and I noticed a photographic plate of a woman with a startling resemblance to the girl I was in love with – Mrs Eileen Garrett, an early twentieth century medium. I began ordering up the book from the library stacks, to stare at the photograph. One day I showed it to a friend without commenting. He recognised the resemblance at once, and asked me some pointed questions. A few days later I ordered up the book. The page with the photograph had been removed.

I dramatised my feelings in a poem:

LEEWARD

A Youth

She did not now, she would never like him.
Whining like a mandolin out of tune
The tram rambled inanely through the afternoon,
And he felt all sense forsake him.

There was nothing at all gained by cursing,
There was no use being embittered
And regretting hours of hoping stupidly frittered.
He felt too tired to feel anything.

He felt as though the rickety tram would whine on and on
And never stop and nothing could be done
To make it stop, as though the afternoon sun
For a whole millennium had shone and shone,

And felt like some girl who in harsh sunlight lingers
By a doorway for support, face white and drawn,
And remembers a small back-room and something torn
From her by crude, unsubtle fingers.

The blankness was relieved by writing many poems. In one of them I saw myself as unable to close my eyes and staring at the sun. I knew I was in the grip of a lurid, almost comical madness:

The Seed

For months I was a field where nothing grew,
I hugged my sunlessness with helpless greed.
For months the rain fell and the wind blew
And I nurtured in my brain a monstrous seed.

For months the wind blew on the field in nightmare
And the unsleeping seed swelled in my brain.
I felt the seed grope upward after air,
I tried to strangle it. I tried in vain.

The seed butting with convulsive power
Pushed through my skull as through a stubborn husk,
And shot forth leaves and a lurid orange flower,
Trumpeting insanely in the livid dusk.

Before the end of 1957, the 'iron-lung' sensations I had when I woke up had stopped. I did not fall out of love. But I had exhausted these feelings. They were no longer important. However, the affinity I felt was not completely misplaced. About forty years later I had lunch at her house. Growing by the front door were the pale fern-like leaves of *Rosa moyesii*, a Himalayan species rose I grew myself.

I heard from a friend that Judith Wright was addressing a senior English class. I loved poems such as 'The Company of Lovers' and 'South of My Days'. The class was in a lecture room off the main quadrangle and we pushed the door slightly ajar. Judith was a compact woman, in her early forties then, and dressed in a grey woollen skirt and top. She was speaking in her firm, musical voice and characteristically dry manner. I was very taken with her. We reluctantly shut the door.

In 1958 James McAuley gave a lunch hour talk to the Newman Society. I was one of the few non-Catholics in the packed lecture room and noticed a girl with natural blonde hair to her shoulders and high cheek bones. She was tall for a girl, and I was later to ask her out. I shall call her 'S'.

McAuley was a lean, aesthetic-looking man, with sallow features, and strongly marked lines in his lower cheeks. He was then a lecturer in the Australian School of Pacific Administration. He stated forcefully that poets should have a career unconnected with literature. I had already convinced myself of this. (Two years later he contradicted himself and became a Reader in English at the University of Tasmania.)

McAuley's explanation of what scansion in English verse really did, its true function, changed how I wrote poetry. He chalked up a line on the blackboard to illustrate his point. I'll use a line of iambic pentameter from his poem 'Because' (which he was yet to write). I have italicised the five syllables that are stressed if the rules of scansion are applied strictly.

Why *should* this *mat*ter *to* me *now* so *much*?

As spoken naturally, the stresses might fall in the following way:

Why should this *mat*ter to *me now* so *much*?

You will notice there is a tension in the line – a quarrel between the syllables that are stressed as spoken, and those stressed under a strict application of the rules of scansion. 'Why' is given extra emphasis, because the normal scansion has to be reversed to pronounce the line in a natural way. When you come to 'to me now', you have to slow down as it becomes unclear where the stresses fall. You speed up again with 'so much'. What might be a fairly uninteresting line in free verse is given life by the form. Free verse has no rules you can break. Fixed forms allow greater variety than free verse.

A few weeks later I posted some poems to McAuley for *Quadrant*, the literary and conservative policy magazine he edited. They were written before his university talk. I placed my telephone number in the top right-hand corner of the covering letter.

I received a phone call from him a couple of days later. He did not want to use the poems but wanted to meet me.

I went to the *Quadrant* office in a tall, narrow building in Albert Street, near Circular Quay. I travelled slowly up several floors in an antiquated lift. It was late afternoon. McAuley was sitting at a desk in a large, almost empty office, which was dimly lit by the fading daylight. For twenty minutes he gave me an exposition of the rules of scansion. It was identical to his Newman Society talk. Our meeting had a surrealistic quality, of time replayed. As he spoke, I could almost predict what he was about to say next.

I was beginning to realise McAuley's theory of prosody had a larger context. When I was writing a poem within prescribed rules, I had to think about the form rather than my emotions. Adherence to conventions freed me from solipsism. It can liberate emotions in a way formlessness cannot. Perhaps this is what Yeats meant by 'the ceremony of innocence' – if you are intent on the ceremony you regain your innocence.

I admired McAuley's first book of poetry *Under Aldebaran* for its ideas and brilliant language. I sensed he had experienced German Romanticism, as Brennan had. But his way out of the Romantic dilemma – formalising the Romantic impulse in the rituals of an established religion – for me was an evasion, although an improvement on Brennan's rhetorical mysticism.

In 1958 I was still writing a couple of poems each week and I studied just enough not to fail my three courses – German, History and English. Now I knew how to scan, I wrote 'A Dark Sea-view of Cats' subtitled 'A Georgic on the Care of Cats' – more than a thousand lines of blank verse about cats. Faber & Faber rejected it. I was still not ready to write a *true* Georgic on a pastoral subject.

I sat in the State Library studying overseas literary magazines, then purchased international reply-paid coupons and mailed out around fifty poems to twenty or so international journals. I sent 'An Image', a poem about lions on a beach at dusk, to *The London Magazine*. I was unaware Charles Osborne was preparing a small selection of Australian poetry. In January 1959 he published my poem alongside poets such as Judith Wright, Douglas Stewart and John Blight. The editorial note said: 'Geoffrey Lehmann is 18 and is in his second year at Sydney University. He has been writing poems since he was 14 and has had some of them published.' I received fan mail from Britain and felt my career as a poet had taken off.

Not all tables in a student canteen are equal. There was one fashionable table in Manning House – where students sat who were involved in the weekly student paper *Honi Soit* and satirical stage revues. Clive James and Robert Hughes were among the habitués of this table. But not Les or I. Chester (Phillip Graham) presided. Like Hughes, he was an old boy of the Jesuit school, Riverview. He was the author of some remarkable revue scripts and poems. I was dazzled by a Chester skit in which the Oedipus story was parodied to the tune of the nursery rhyme 'This old man comes rolling home'. When the skit came to its inevitable climax, a curtain opened, showing Jocasta – Libby Sweet – hanging from a rope.

I had some small roles in this revue. At a post-revue party, standing in a garden, I impulsively kissed a girl. She opened her mouth so that it was almost a kiss with her teeth. I was shocked. I had not realised people kissed like that.

I was having coffee with Donald Kirby in Manning House. He had been at high school with Ian Boden and was occasionally dating S, the girl with long blonde hair I had noticed at the

McAuley lecture. Several other boys were also seeing her. I should feel free to ask her out, he suggested.

On our first night out, in the back seat of a taxi, she leaned her head on my shoulder. I was surprised. We kissed. I had not tasted lipstick before. I began seeing her regularly. I was grateful for the freedoms she allowed with her body – very big freedoms they seemed to me. But as my hands became bolder she made it clear there were strict boundaries. She still went out with Donald and other boyfriends. Some young men came and went.

We saw films, ate out and went to the beach. I studied with her and Donald at the State Library, or the 'lipe-ry' as she jokingly called it – why I do not know. It was one of her mannerisms. She and I got out of a bus at St Leonards Park one night and went on the swings among the white trunks of lemon-scented gums.

I did my best to keep her amused. Sometimes before catching the Manly ferry at night we strolled around Circular Quay. The Opera House was then under construction. If we were passing a young couple I used to toss a few copper coins over my shoulder. The young man (thinking the coins were his) would bend down looking for them, while his girlfriend stood by. A freak throw caused a halfpenny to lodge in a young man's trouser cuff.

I quickly realised our relationship was unequal. I was in love with an enigma. She was slightly short-sighted and walked along with her head down so she did not have to recognise people. I was in love with that. The lipstick on her cigarette butts, and the way she arched her neck to draw back the smoke (the dizziness was why she smoked, she said) were all irresistibly attractive. I was enthralled by her short love affairs with particular words. As well as 'lipe-ry', a favourite word for a while was 'rich'. I'd tell her a person had said something or done something and she would say, 'That's rich'. I had no idea how I could escape from this unequal relationship. When I did escape, I was shocked by how easy it was.

By 1961 my social circle was widening, I was becoming more confident and I was in my second year of articles with a law firm. *Hermes*, the university magazine for 1961, had poems by Les Murray, Ron Blair (the future playwright), 'Tempest Teacup', Clive James, Chester, Richard Appleton (one of the few literary members of the Sydney Push) and me.

My own over-long poem in *Hermes 1961* was portentous. Murray's sonnet, 'Personality', nominated Sorrow as the Self (out of his collection of Selves) that would determine his fate. Les, the genial wit and raconteur who presided at the less fashionable Manning House coffee table, was already aware of something his friends were unaware of – he would wrestle with life-long depression. 'Blue Glass' by Clive James was a series of imagistic poems influenced by Chester.

The outstanding poem (and a big influence on my own poetry) was Chester's 'Provincial Report'. It is a report from a Roman provincial governor (Pontius Pilate) asking Caesar (the Emperor Tiberius) what he is to do with this Jew (Jesus Christ).

My life was about to change. I was having coffee in the Union refectory. A couple – a tall blond man older than his tall blonde girlfriend – sat down at a nearby table. Both looked as though they had stepped from a Swedish film set. He was rugged, she was statuesque. A few months later I found out he was Darcy Waters, a wharf labourer and philosophy student, and she was Gill Burnett, both members of the Sydney Push.

I had been seeing S for about two years when I lost my virginity elsewhere. I took her out one last time, and explained our relationship would have to change if it was to continue. She said, 'This happens to all my men. I'm surprised it did not happen with you earlier.' We shook hands outside her mother's house and said good-bye.

I was in the backroom of the Royal George Hotel, sitting with the girl who had seduced me, and with Donald Kirby. Darcy Waters entered the room, with his lumbering walk. Turning to Jan Miller, my seductress, Darcy said in a genial voice the whole room was meant to hear: 'Hi, virgin-fucker'.

JOHANN

When she died in 1974, my aunt Agnes Lehmann had lived almost all of her ninety years in a wooden cottage in Walker Street, North Sydney, now the site of an apartment building. The house was elevated and had a sunken garden in front, with bamboo, a spreading poplar, mulberry and fig trees, and wine-grape vines. A small wooden bridge crossed a small stream. As a child, Agnes had picked pink boronia growing wild on the next door land.

When I was a child it was a magical place, and stayed so, even after the council encased the stream in a concrete pipe. The house was an old Queenslander, on high wooden poles enclosed underneath by wooden latticework. Agnes's father Johann bought the land in the 1880s and the architecture reflected his year in Queensland.

Johann used the large basement area as a workshop for his building business and it was later used by his sons Carl, Otto and Leo (my father). Years after Johann's death, the three boys trained as carpenters. Johann, my father said, reached the second highest of the five rankings in the carpenters' guild. He was a staircase maker. The highest rank was die-maker. I have a small cabinet with tiny drawers and small metal handles, made by my father when he was sixteen, in which he kept watchmaking tools and hairsprings. The cabinetry of his brothers was as fine. Otto was

Johann

still working in the 1970s on an intricately carved table top begun by Johann almost a hundred years earlier.

By the 1960s the Walker Street house was slowly falling down – thanks to my aunt having three brothers who were carpenters. No one else was allowed to work on the house. On many visits I was asked into only one room, a cosy kitchen-cum-dining room where my aunt listened to the radio of an evening, sitting at a table where guests also sat. Somewhere in the dim interior of the house she had a bedroom, and there were other derelict rooms where her brothers once slept. Late one afternoon in the mid 1960s Agnes, my father and I were sitting outside on a brick-paved area that overlooked her garden. A blue-flowered water hyacinth, a noxious weed she admired, floated on the surface of a glass fish tank. Small goldfish were occasional flashes of orange in green murk. My father walked down the steps into her garden, rummaged in bushes and came up the steps again, clutching a copper kettle. 'Leo, how did you know that was there?' Agnes squawked. He had just remembered hiding it there as a child.

Johann Ernst Lehmann was born in 1854 at Grosswelka, a village in Saxony which is about a half hour walk from Bautzen, later the site of the notorious Stasi political prison. Johann's father was Peter, a farmer, and his mother Agnes, her surname possibly Dutchsmann.

In 2004 I drove across a fertile green plain to Bautzen. I wondered why anyone would wish to leave such a beautiful hilltop town with mediaeval towers and a cathedral. Dom St Petri is shared by Lutherans and Catholics, its two halves divided by a knee-high fence. I noticed a Lehmann on an honour roll, killed at the Battle of Sedan in 1870. The story handed down in my family says Johann left Germany because of religious scruples about military conscription.

Among many Johann Lehmanns who sailed out of Hamburg for New York at about that time, one broadly matches my grandfather. This Johann Lehmann sailed in November 1873. If he is my grandfather, he may have disembarked at Southampton. My grandfather's surviving draft letters indicate he worked in London before going on to America. He wrote in English, spiced with strange Germanic syntax and spellings (which I have corrected when quoting him).

Young carpenters of that era roamed the world with their cumbersome toolboxes and often a mate. In the spring of 1877 Johann wrote from the United States to a friend in England. Work prospects were good, but negroes were undercutting carpenters' wages 'so it is hard for a good workman to get anything like a fair price for his work. Of course the negroes as a class are very poor and of course have to work for anything rather than starve.'

The next draft letters are from Australia where he continued to wander, working along the way. He practised his signature, sometimes 'John Lehmann' and at other times 'Johann Lehmann', in the exercise book where he kept his drafts.

His letters are not unlike those a young European on a working visa might send from Australia in the twenty-first century. His first Australian port was Sydney. Sydney, he says, has the handsomest bay in the world, and very nice parks and museums like the old ('alt' in his spelling) country. Other references to the 'old country' in his correspondence make it clear he refers to England not Germany.

In 1879, he writes from Sydney telling of his travels around Queensland. He spent Christmas eve 'under a big tree in the wilderness' with twelve men, two women, children and dogs, one goat, about 100 horses and many mosquitoes and ants. It was very hot and the worst of it was they had no plums ('blams' in his spelling) for a pudding, but overall 'I enjoy myself very much'.

Johann

Another letter, written to a fellow German – but the draft is in English – says he got the gold fever 'again' and travelled to Charters Towers with a companion, who got cold feet when Johann decided to walk 275 miles (440 km) further west to the Gilbert River diggings. Johann was alone on the road for thirteen days:

> This long journey through the bush was an interesting one. I was free like a bird in the air, especially in the morning when day was breaking. I travelled sometimes for a few days without seeing a single person, but [saw] plenty of beautiful birds and kangaroos and many other beautiful things. I always was accompanied by a very nice concert all day and night ... of beautiful birds and [in] the night from thousands of mosquitoes around my body.

After three weeks on the diggings, he had panned two and a half pennyweight of gold, worth eight shillings (a day's wages as a carpenter). He says he lost the gold fever ('golt fiver') and instead got a fever from an 'ague'. Back in Townsville he did some horse breaking, then carpentry.

In 1882 he married the Welsh daughter of a paper maker, Annie Jones, in St Philip's Anglican church, York Street, just south of the Sydney Harbour Bridge, which was yet to be built. He was twenty-eight and she was twenty-six.

There is an absence of letters to family members in Germany – they may not have survived – nor does he mention them. Johann is like a man who has no family, apart from the statement on his marriage certificate that his father was Peter and his mother Agnes, her maiden name undisclosed.

I am unable to form a clear picture of Annie Jones. Before her marriage she was a 'general servant' and described in a reference as 'honest, sober and steady' and able to wash, iron and cook. A letter from a sister, Mary, gives Annie a week's notice of Mary's wedding in Ipswich in Queensland in 1879 and invites her to attend. A sister in Wales wrote several letters; in February 1886 the sister laments that Mary last wrote back to Wales seven years ago, and says of their father: 'I have seen the tears running down his cheeks when he would be talking about you'. This letter mentions another sister Catherine, married to a goldminer in Charters Towers called Aldridge.

In the following year the sister in Wales wrote again. She laments that both Mary and Catherine have died. Their parents, she says, 'do vex a good deal about our two sisters that is gone I hope to the land of Bliss where God will wipe away all our tears'. William Aldridge had a child by Catherine, remarried and continued to write to Annie every few years.

My aunt Agnes, an enthusiastic talker, rarely spoke about her mother, except to say she nursed her during the last week of her life. My father, when he read aloud, spoke in a singsong voice, with a trace of Welsh. This singsong voice and a letter Annie wrote to Johann when he went to New Guinea are as close as I can get to her.

Annie and Johann were still living in Phillip Street, Sydney, when their first child Agnes Annie was born in November 1883. My father once pointed out where his father had his Phillip Street workshop, among some yellow-painted corrugated iron buildings which survived until the 1950s.

It is likely Annie and Johann had moved to his North Sydney house by the time the next children, May, Carl and Otto were born. Johann prospered. No letters to America or England survive in which he asks about possibilities for work. The family story is that he became a spec builder, and built one or two stone houses in Mosman.

Johann

Then one Sunday in 1891, Alfred Yarnold, rector of Christ Church, North Sydney called for volunteers for the first Anglican mission to New Guinea. There was a recession in the building industry and Johann may have had an attack of his old wanderlust. He agreed to be head carpenter. A neighbour wrote advising against going to 'New Guinea to do manual work in that hot and unhealthy climate'. A letter from Frederick Felton, Sydney's leading hardware store proprietor, reached Johann in New Guinea. Trade is quiet, Felton says and asks: 'Whatever possessed you ... to go so far ... May God in His Great Mercy ... bring you back.'

Johann engaged two carpenters as assistants. He listed his purchases of building materials in a black-covered diary with gilt-edged pages. This diary was small enough to fit in a shirt pocket and became stained with water or sweat.

After a farewell service at St Andrews Cathedral in July 1891, the carpenters and their building materials set out from Double Bay, Sydney in an old collier schooner, the *Grace Lynn*. The two missionaries, Albert Maclaren and Copland King, were to join the ship in Cooktown, where they also took on a horse. Johann sent a letter from Cooktown to his wife towards the end of July:

My Dear Wife,

We arrived here this morning in this beautiful place of the far north of Queensland among the high mountains where the black natives are at home. I had a stroll through the town this afternoon. It looks rather pitiful to see the poor Black Gins playing about the street half naked with their little ones on their backs naked as they were born. In particular I could not help taking notice of a three months old, sitting on its mother's neck, holding itself on to its mother's curly hair...

His diary records that when they set out again, they were immediately becalmed. The Reverend Chalmers visited their ship while they were at anchor that night. (Chalmers was known as the Dr Livingstone of Melanesia and was later eaten by cannibals.) Next day at noon, they passed the Barrier Reef, and it was 'very rough' until the New Guinea coast was sighted.

They were again becalmed and finally towed in by the Governor's steamship *Merrie England* to Samarai ('this beautiful island' he calls it). In a letter to Annie he says that while waiting off Samarai:

> we were visited by the black natives. They came to us in little boats (or canoes) and brought us some coconuts, shells, yams, and grass for our horse and we paid them back with some tobacco and bread. They were very jolly fellows, they did sing and dance for us very near all naked.

Like many of his letters to Annie, this was signed 'I remain yours truly husband John E Lehmann'.

After leaving Samarai they ran aground at East Cape. A letter described a 'near wreck … we ran onto a reef in the middle of the day and after being on it 10 hours, we accidentally floated off. She bumped very heavily several times and I thought she was going to break up…' They reached Chad's Bay and were becalmed for two days in stifling heat. Their dog became sun struck and a carpenter shot it with a revolver.

They sailed the final 25 miles (40 km) and anchored within rowing distance of the future site for the mission station. Johann started work on a punt. When the horse swam up onto the beach, the natives ran away in terror calling out 'Big pig!' – a detail I heard from Archbishop Hand (ninety-nine years later). Johann 'witnessed the purchase of about 25 acres of land for

30 or 40 pounds of tobacco, tomahawks, shirts, flax etc'. This was the grassy plateau of Dogura. It was considered healthier than low ground with its 'bad air' (the Italian *mal'aria*) associated with malaria. (When I visited there, I discovered 'Dogura' meant 'cannibal battle ground'. This was why it was unoccupied land available for the missionaries.)

A letter to his wife, dated August 23 and not in his handwriting, may have been written for him by one of the other carpenters:

> We are anchored about 400 yards from the shore where the native village is situated… We have to pull across every morning to work in a boat. The natives are very friendly. We get plenty of coconuts from them. We drink the milk from them and it is better than water. We built a large punt to unload the vessel. We started to build the church last week. It is a very large building … with a verandah 12 feet wide all around, and a tower and cross and belfry … is to be built on the top of a very high hill which is nice and level as a bowling green … We have over a hundred naked savages both men, women and boys digging the holes and clearing the grass … there is one large river of splendid fresh water. We have a swim in it every evening … We are all in good health … one of the sailors is laid up with fever, he got it the first day. The weather is very hot here. I can only wear my flannel shirt on in the day and we can't bear the blanket on at night…
> yours truly J. E. Lehmann.

The 'good health' mentioned in the letter was short-lived. The elevation of the site did not protect the missionaries (or my grandfather) from malaria. Malaria was to cause the death of dozens of missionaries across New Guinea.

Johann's diary records that on August 24 for the 'first time' he visited a 'native built house'. Johann was a meticulous craftsman and would have admired the neat lines and tightly woven palm leaf walls of the native house, several of which I saw more than 100 years later.

On August 30 Johann wrote again to 'My Dear Wife'. This letter is in his hand writing with his Germanic spelling. The difficulties of building on the site are becoming apparent:

> We commenced to build the house last week, but we have not been able to do much as we are waiting for the materials … it is rather difficult to bring the materials to the site where the building is to be built. It is about 15 minutes walk down to the sea shore and in one part of it very steep …
> The place is surrounded by high mountains .,. There is but very little timber about here. We scarcely have enough wood to cook our meals. We are staying in a house which we had built by the natives of young timber and grass, and is large enough for 3 carpenters, one cook and 2 missionaries …
> We commence to work at half past five in the morning and [have] one hour at 8 for breakfast. From 12 to 2 is dinner time and then we leave off work at 5…
>
> The natives are helping us carry the timber etc. both men and women. But the men are working by themselves and the women work by themselves and in every way they are very decent in their clothing and behaviour.

The stereotype of 'the hundred naked savages' in the letter written for Johann contrasts with his own observation of segregated and decently clothed native workers.

His diary records removing timber from the seashore and unpacking galvanized iron. On September 1 the horse was unable

Johann

to carry lumber up the steep slope ('Horse not ben strong enough'). The following week Carroll, one of the assistant carpenters, used obscene language ('upseen languige') and struck Johann in the face. Carroll left the job and went away on the *Grace Lynn*. (Years later when he passed Annie in the street, he stared in the gutter.)

There are the last two pages of a letter from Annie, probably received by Johann on 17 September. Her letter is in a confident hand with a few minor spelling mistakes, which I have corrected:

> ... It is a great pity as you did not join the Lodge before you went away. It takes all that I can save to pay doctor and medicine. May is getting better. Her nose and mouth is very sore yet she had to have all hair cut off. There is lots people sick ... Same as May. I am not all right as I thought you may expect something next year [a very matter-of-fact announcement she was pregnant with my father] ... It was flower service today. I sent Annie [Annie called her daughter Agnes 'Annie' – this was a surprise to me] with a bunch of roses and other flowers ... Otto say[s] you are gone, he sometimes point[s] down the street. No more at present.
>
> I remain your affectionate
>
> Annie Lehmann
>
> Hoping to hear from you soon.

A British naval steamship, the *Royalist*, visited and probably delivered this letter. A barely legible letter of Johann's dated September 18 mentions that electric lights from the *Royalist* were used to illuminate the village and twelve natives went on board.

He wrote (much more graciously than she had): 'I am very glad you with child'. (My father was to be born nine months and two days after the farewell service at St Andrews Cathedral.) This is his last letter that survives.

Next day he was 'taken sick with bronchitis'. Three days later he started work again 'but very weak and unwell'. Successive diary entries record his work, with 'unwell' circled on several days.

Desperate about the lack of progress, the head missionary Maclaren lost his temper with my grandfather, then apologised. Johann's diary records that he began work on the 'native chapel' on November 2. The 'native chapel' was an unplanned attempt to get something built quickly before the wet season began. An old photograph shows a thatched roof, logs laid end to end for walls, no windows and an open gap at the front for a doorway – in effect a Melanesian roof on top of an American log-cabin. Perched on the edge of the escarpment, it had magical views across the Coral Sea. On November 10 Johann and the main body of the mission left. Copland King had malaria and went with them. Maclaren remained and celebrated matins and evensong in his chapel until he died of malaria a couple of months later.

A sick carpenter at Samarai, whom my grandfather helped, paid him with native 'curiosities' (grass skirts and an intricately carved oar inlaid with mother-of-pearl). He sailed for Cooktown on the schooner *Myrtle*. His last diary entry – in pencil like all his diary entries – states 'Friday 19th', but records nothing else. He now had malaria. He was briefly hospitalised in Brisbane, then continued on to Sydney by the steamship *Aramac*. An account by Arthur Kent Chignell *Twenty-One Years in Papua* states:

> one of the carpenters was carried unconscious from the ship to his home in North Sydney, and there next evening he died.

Johann

My family's account is slightly different. When he arrived in Sydney, Annie had no idea he was coming back. She imagined he was still in New Guinea. When he disembarked from the *Aramac*, a stranger noticed him sitting on the wharf at Circular Quay, surrounded by his curiosities and toolbox, apparently helpless. The stranger arranged for a dray to take him across the harbour.

My aunt Agnes, aged eight, was playing in the sunken front garden of the house in Walker Street, when she saw a dray pulling up. Her first reaction was to wonder why this black man had come to visit. His face, she said, 'was brown as a penny'. Then she recognised her father's toolbox. As he mounted the front steps of the house, he greeted all the children by name, as if to show he still remembered who they were; but he stumbled on Agnes's name. He died the following day, 8 December.

Frederick Felton, the hardware store owner who deplored his going on the mission, and the Reverend Alfred Yarnold who recruited him were the witnesses on the death certificate. This stated he was aged thirty-seven, and listed his mother as Agnes, 'maiden surname not known to Informant', who was Annie.

I have a clear picture in my mind of Johann, a wanderer and idealist, full of curiosity, and open-minded. In a photograph he is a small man in a bowler hat, standing with three of his children outside his house, a black shovel beard almost down to his waist.

My impression of Annie is less clear. I have seen no photograph of her. Her letter to Johann in New Guinea scolds him for not joining a lodge for medical insurance, the complaint of a romantic wanderer's wife. When he died, she had to struggle with four young children, and a child about to be born. Working as a servant in a nearby house, she was given bread and a bucket of dripping, her family's main sustenance for some years. As a young child, Agnes once had to beg at the railway station for matches to light the stove.

In 1893 Annie arranged for a 'KJ Read' – the signature is unclear – to draft a letter asking for help from the Australian Board of Mission to clear the debt on the land. After Annie copied this letter in her own hand and sent it, she received a prompt reply from Alfred Yarnold, secretary of the Board, who two years earlier preached the sermon persuading my grandfather to go on the mission:

Dear Mrs Lehmann

I received your letter this morning and I regret very much that you were so unwise as to write it. Your husband was well paid for his work in New Guinea, and after his death you received a large sum as the balance of wages due to him…

The letter went on to explain how a collection had already been raised to help reduce her mortgage. Yarnold was the father of AH (Tibby) Yarnold, the much-loved headmaster of Mosman Prep, who tutored me, aged eleven, in Latin and gave me two small books on archaeology. He awarded me as a prize Guerber's *Myths of Greece and Rome*, which later inspired many teenage poems. I do not know if he knew I was the carpenter's grandson.

As well as annoying Alfred Yarnold with her demands, Annie upset the doctor who certified her husband's death, BJ Newmarch. He reprimanded her for tenaciously holding on to her husband as he died, prolonging his life. She should have let him die in peace, he said.

There was no widow's pension in 1891. Annie had to get her children into jobs as soon as they were old enough. Agnes went to work at a young age in a steam laundry. The next daughter, May, started out as a domestic servant, became one of Canberra's first tailors and had two daughters by different husbands. The three boys all trained as carpenters. My father's first job was in an iron foundry, perhaps at about the age of twelve. This job lasted a week.

Annie had paid off the mortgage on the Walker Street house by the time she died of kidney disease in 1918, aged sixty-one. No will was found and the three boys – Carl, Otto and Leo – continued living with their elder sister for some years. One day someone lifted up the linoleum on the kitchen floor and there was Annie's will, leaving the house to Agnes. Agnes regretted this – 'all the trouble it caused'. Otto and Leo married and only Carl continued living with her for the rest of his life.

Agnes continued to work in a steam laundry until her late seventies. If her father had lived, she would have become a doctor, she said. In her early eighties, her old boss dropped in and asked her to come back to the steam laundry. She said no: 'I'm an old age pensioner now'. She was a short woman, stooped and with a prominent nose, a long face and a small growth on her cheek, like a pink dewdrop sprouting two or three wisps of hair. She had a low widow's peak that started only a few centimetres above her eyebrows. Her hangdog face lighted up with a smile as she let out a squawky laugh, which was often.

North Sydney was becoming a second urban centre. Agnes was nostalgic for the brilliant night skies of her childhood. 'Where has the Milky Way gone?' she sometimes asked in her raucous voice.

In one of her stories, Agnes, as a young woman, was picking a bunch of flowers in a field in North Sydney, and came across some boys tormenting a horse: 'I let those rascals have it'. That evening she presented her bunch of flowers at a clairvoyant show, and the clairvoyant (closing her eyes and stroking the flowers) announced: 'This one sure can rouse!'

The oldest son, Carl, engaged in spec building, in which he involved his younger brother Otto. Carl died in his early seventies of septicaemia, when he cut his foot, dragging an old sheet of galvanised iron through the streets of North Sydney. None of the brothers read books and all spoke with broad Australian accents. Although the neighbourhood thought they were 'strange', all Annie's children had regular features except Agnes. Agnes was the ugly duckling of the family.

Annie and her children harboured a grudge against the Anglican church. She sent my father to a Plymouth Brethren Sunday school where he was awarded a large red-bound, illustrated copy of Bunyan's *Pilgrim's Progress* for finding a record number of references to the coming of Christ in the Old Testament. How such a reluctant reader of books won this prize has been a source of puzzlement to me.

One afternoon Agnes was describing how she was sticking pamphlets under front doors for the Rationalists' Association – a group of freethinkers and atheists. 'You mean the Irrationals', my father kept interrupting her. When Agnes fell ill and we visited her in the Mater Misericordiae, a hospital run by nuns, she told us: 'They kept asking what my religion is. I kept telling them 'eathen. Now look at this,' she said, displaying a wristband on which a nun had neatly written 'Heathen'.

How can we judge grandparents? Johann, who became John, I admire for his open mind and love of nature, practical and impractical at the same time. Annie, the least sympathetic of the four, was dealt the worst hand at birth, coming from a poor family in Wales. Then as a widow with small children she had no family to fall back upon. She and her five fatherless children were 'strange'. But she succeeded in a way my more cultivated maternal grandparents did not. William and Bella were spendthrifts from a privileged background and ruined their lives for no good purpose.

Johann

Annie may not have been greatly loved by her children – it is unclear what their feelings for her were – but they did not have to fetch her from hotels, as my mother had to fetch Bella. Annie was living in a house she owned, free of debt, when she died, and left a will protecting her most vulnerable elder child – Agnes with her long face – who was unlikely ever to marry.

Neither Annie nor her five children ever knew that the corner post of the 'native chapel' built by Johann miraculously sprouted after the missionaries left in 1891. It grew into a modawa or rosewood tree, and its leaf became the emblem of the Anglican Church in Papua New Guinea.

Dogura is a 160 acre (65 ha) grassy plateau, backed by jagged mountains, and more than 60 metres above a black pebble beach fringed by coconut palms. The 1891 chapel survives only in old photographs. There is now a white-painted concrete cathedral nearby, completed in 1939. The cathedral of St Peter and St Paul is a simple Norman-Romanesque building with a red galvanised iron roof and two square towers – one tower is St Peter's and the other St Paul's. It is 52 metres long – longer than St Andrew's Anglican cathedral in Sydney. There is also a large school.

In 2014 I went on the annual Modawa Pilgrimage to Dogura – the only atheist pilgrim. Dogura has no running water or electricity (except at dusk when a generator is switched on for a few hours). There is no road in, and we set out for Dogura from Awaiama in the morning, in a dinghy powered by an outboard motor, a three-hour trip past denuded grass-covered mountains towering above beaches of black pebbles and basalt rock shelves at the water's edge. Waterfalls glinted on mountainsides. Every mile or so a small canoe, carved from a tree trunk and with a flimsy outrigger, could be seen riding precariously on the swell.

We lunched after arriving and walked up a dirt road to the escarpment where my grandfather had struggled with his 'not ben strong enough' horse. The modawa tree had a lush canopy of leaves. I stood beside it – a large spreading tree, about 12 metres high, surrounded by a circle of stones – as a pilgrim took photographs with my phone.

THE SYDNEY PUSH

I started at the Law School in 1959, in a building since demolished. It was in the city, 'downtown' from the university campus. Law was a new discipline and way of thinking. I had no ambition to excel. All I wanted was an interesting livelihood, paying me enough to have a family and write poetry.

Although I coasted through my four years at Law School, I always went to classes. Examinations were closed book, and held on the main campus. My favourite examination room was in the medical faculty, where we entered through a foyer with glass cabinets displaying pickled heads and diseased body parts in jars of formaldehyde. I sometimes stayed up at night before an exam without going to sleep, memorising lengthy written lists of case names. I was always afraid I might forget critical names during the ten minute reading time before an exam, when putting pen to paper was not allowed. So I waited outside, reading my list. When the ten minutes expired, I entered the examination room, hundreds of case names fluttering through my mind, and hurriedly wrote down those that were relevant to the exam.

The Law School had several outstanding teachers. A shy, slightly built man, Pat Lane, described by Michael Kirby (brother of my friend Donald) as 'brilliant and cerebral', taught us constitutional law from a black letter, literalist view point. At the start of a lecture he would chalk up on the blackboard a little cartoon head and pair of hands, staring over a wall at the class. For me, constitutional law was the most intellectually challenging area of the law.

I was not as impressed by Julius Stone as some were. His lengthy, self-published texts were turgidly written. In lectures he boasted how he had originated the concept of a Washington to Moscow hot-line.

Ross Parsons was the professor I admired most. (I got to know him well thirty years later.) He distributed fifty or so pages of material for commercial law where he had cleverly chosen pairs of court decisions with similar facts but in which the courts had come to opposite decisions. The students had to work out why there was a different outcome. Parsons, unlike Stone, was self-effacing. Many of us underestimated him because of his quiet and studious manner.

In about my final year of law, Parsons conducted a two-month pilot course on tax law. It was the first time this subject was taught at Sydney University's Law School, perhaps the first time in an Australian law faculty. Many keener students enrolled. I thought it was irrelevant for my future career.

My first day at Law School felt like a return to an all-boys high school. There were no female lecturers and only four or five female students in a class of about 100. I made frequent trips to the Sydney University campus to have coffee with friends in student refectories where there were as many girls as boys.

In 1960 I became an articled clerk with a law firm. With my modest wage, I had begun taking girls out (in addition to S), although I was still lacking in confidence. I was given a small desk in an office with an employed solicitor in his late fifties – a quiet and courteous man. His very pretty young secretary, who wore an engagement ring, sat in the room with us. One day she surprised me, saying, 'You seem very unsure of yourself with girls. You shouldn't feel that way ... I can say this because I'm engaged. *I* would be attracted to you.'

In June 1961 Brian Jenkins, the friend who introduced me to Lex Banning, suggested I drink with him one Friday night at the Royal George Hotel (now the Slip Inn). The George was a workman's pub, smelling of tobacco and spilled beer, where fights might break out. The walls of the backroom were hot pink with a Robert Hughes mural of expressionist figures blocked out in black. It was there that members of the Sydney Push drank.

Push members were known for hard drinking, methedrine use (an early amphetamine) and free love (as it was then called), and were intolerant of outsiders or 'Alfs'. The nucleus of the Push was the Sydney Libertarians, who began as followers of John Anderson, a professor of philosophy at Sydney University. Unusually for such a group, the Push was sceptical about all political positions, left and right. Despite the Robert Hughes mural, Push members were not interested in art, literature or music, except folk singing – Muddy Waters and Woody Guthrie rather than Joan Baez, who was suspiciously glamorous.

My first Friday night at the George was daunting. I was an 'Alf'. I was relieved to be under the protection of Brian, who had been drinking there for some months. That night I noticed a girl with a pale, translucent face, high cheek bones and dark lustrous eyes. Her hair was pulled back in a plait, and was densely black, unusually so for a Caucasian woman – her face like a Noh mask. I do not remember Brian's reply when I asked who she was. I would have liked to become her friend and suspected I would have to be a distant admirer.

I arranged with Brian to go back to the George the following Friday, being two days after I had turned twenty-one (not a birthday I celebrated). That week my mother and Diana went on their annual holiday to Melbourne, leaving my father and me in the Gordon house. That night I met the girl with a face like a Noh mask. Her name was Jan Miller. (Jan spelled her name in various ways – sometimes Janne and sometimes Millar – she later told me her actual name was Janet Campbell Muirhead.)

When the hotel shut at ten we went back with a group to the student house where she lived, a narrow two-storey workman's terrace in Forbes Street, Woolloomooloo. We were soon alone together in the sparsely furnished downstairs living room, lit by a single bare light bulb. I told her I was an articled clerk with a law firm and wrote poetry. She was from Melbourne, she said. She had a child and it had been adopted out 'to good parents'. She had come to Sydney several months ago and had had an affair with one of the students who lived in the house. That was over now, and they were letting her stay on.

She pointed to scars on her wrists. 'The cuts are across my wrists. It's what I do. If I were trying to commit suicide I'd slit the veins lengthwise. Then they couldn't bind them up … Tell me one of your poems.' I recited a poem from a cycle about Adam and Eve:

> Adam spat out a pip.
> The bright red apples which
> Had trembled in the tree
> Were gone.
> A small bird sang
> Cheep-cheep and whirred and flew
> Down upon Adam's shoulder,
> Bubbling and talkative,
> And Adam smiled and took
> The bird and quietly crushed it…

And so on. I was busily rewriting much of the Old Testament and Greek mythology into poem cycles. Being so prolific, I could rarely remember any of my poems, but I could recall this, because I had written it just a few days earlier. Perhaps when recited slowly by a boy twenty-one years old – taking time to recall each line – to a twenty-year-old girl at one o'clock in the morning, the poem was not as excruciating as I find it now.

I offered to leave. She left the room and came back in a red nightdress and said, 'Tuck me into bed'. I explained I had never slept with anyone before, and followed her into her small bedroom at the back of the house. She pointed with embarrassment to the scar on her abdomen from the caesarean.

We had unprotected sex in her narrow single bed and fell asleep with the light on. Near dawn I woke, hearing strange noises, like bird calls, that seemed to come from her throat. Some hours later we both woke up. She asked me if I had heard her grinding her teeth while she was asleep – that was the strange sound I had heard.

Children were playing in the back lane outside. It was a sunny day and they were calling out in Italian. I suggested we go out and spend the morning together. She said no, and we kissed good-bye. (Jan often did not go out until late in the day. It was one of the reasons why she was so pale.) I found a public phone booth and telephoned my father. 'It doesn't worry me, son', he replied. 'You do what you like.'

I walked to the Botanic Gardens. I was in a state of shock and confusion. I drank a glass of lemonade, to calm myself down, sitting at an outdoor table in the winter sunlight. My painfully unreciprocated relationship with S, the blonde Catholic girl, would have to end. I was free from her, and free from my mother. I would come and go as I liked – I did not have to come home every night. It was like the moment of freedom when I was seven years old and swam in deep water in the Manly baths. The irony of reciting a poem called 'The Fall of Man' to Jan when I was about to be seduced did not occur to me.

The following weekend I slept with her in a double bed upstairs in the Forbes Street house. 'You're quite good', she told me with an encouraging laugh. This was our second time. It was also the last.

Push women were not supposed to have sex outside the Push, although this was acceptable for Push men (particularly if the non-Push women or 'Daphnes' or 'Daphs' were inducted into the Push and became available to other Push members). I was still an 'Alf'. There was the incident when Darcy Walters called out to Jan 'Hi virgin-fucker' a few days after our first night together. There was a later incident when Kathy McMullen called out to me, as I was entering the backroom of the George to wait for Jan, 'Go home to ya mother!' Kathy had married the man who was the father of Jan's child.

Anne Coombs's 1996 book about the Push, *Sex and Anarchy*, says Jan 'took up with' me soon after she 'left Paddy [McGuinness]'. Paddy confessed to Coombs that the reason Jan left him was that he 'was getting heavy' with her. He told Coombs:

> She was very independent and the men classically used to get possessive and Janne classically used to reject the possessiveness. It's a very interesting theme in literature. It's a kind of female type that crops up in literature a lot: she was very beautiful, very attractive and very independent.

Paddy also told Coombs:

> Janne was one of those figures that was briefly on the scene but had a big impact. She was just a character of

considerable importance, not intellectual significance – she pissed off from school when she was about fifteen – but she was important.

When she was in Melbourne Jan was a friend of Barry Humphries and Germaine Greer. She probably got to know Humphries when she played a lead role in Arthur Miller's *The Crucible*. (She called herself Millar or Miller after the playwright and to avoid embarrassing her mother.) Greer was yet to be famous, but Jan was an admirer and often spoke about her.

In her short life Jan may have had twenty or thirty sexual partners – I am only guessing – but she said she never achieved orgasm. I suspect this was not unusual among Push women. This was ironical given that the Push regarded itself as a pioneer of sexual enlightenment. The men who dominated the Push were not interested in human emotions (as distinct from Freudian theory and Reich). Greer had been a member of the Push when she lived in Sydney. When her book *The Female Eunuch* was published some Libertarians were 'upset', according to Coombs, by Greer's criticism of Freud, and her reference to the Freudians' 'proscription' of the clitoris.

In 1972 there were two articles in the Libertarians' *Broadsheet* magazine criticising Greer. One was headed 'Germaine Greer's Misinterpretation of Freud':

> It is not that one must get rid of clitoral sensitivity, but rather that one must get rid of vaginal anaesthesia...
> vaginal eroticism is an essential part, even the major part of full adult sexual gratification...

The other article was headed 'Women's Lib and the Vaginal Orgasm'. Both articles were written by men, in effect telling women they had to become aroused through their vagina, rather than their clitoris.

Greer did not advocate a simple-minded focus on the clitoris, but suggested that male virility without emotional involvement is 'profoundly desolating' and 'sex becomes masturbation in the vagina'.

I did not become possessive about Jan after our brief sexual liaison, which ended when she became pregnant, and the hat was passed around in the backroom of the George to pay for her abortion. I was not told about this at the time, and still do not know if I was the father, but this may have contributed to the vehemence of Kathy McMullen's 'Go home to ya mother'.

Jan had lost two molar teeth on the left side of her mouth. This gave her a rabbit-like look, startled, beautiful and comical at the same time. The missing molars may have contributed to her slight lisp, which made her small jokes and witty sayings so captivating for a naive young male.

I continued to see Jan often and brought friends to meet her at the George. We would sit at a small table by the window in the backroom, looking out over the wharves and across the street at a roaring lion about to jump out of a fading blue mural on a brick wall – an advertisement for 'Richmond Lager', a long defunct label. Jan adopted the nickname I gave to the spot where we sat – 'Tiny Tots Corner'. I was still in love with her but had come to realise I did not want a sexual relationship either. I was hoping to find a girlfriend outside the Push.

I did not have another sexual involvement until more than a year after Jan. I passed my third year law exam at the end of 1961 – only just. I was employed five days a week as an articled clerk with one of the larger law firms and living at home in the Gordon house with my family. Les Murray and I co-edited the 1961 edition of *Arna*, the annual literary magazine of the Arts Faculty, and began co-editing the 1962 edition of *Hermes*, Sydney University's annual literary magazine.

When I came to the Royal George to see Jan, I formed friendships among the less dialectical Push members, such as Kathy McMullen's brother Terry, a psychology academic. I was no longer an Alf. In August 1962, with the publication of my Robert Hughes exposé, I was unconditionally accepted into the Push – even briefly popular. But I remained celibate, although I was surrounded by casual sex.

At the time of the Cuban Missile Crisis, in October 1962, I was with a group of students drinking one night in the beer garden of the Forest Lodge Hotel, not far from Sydney University. I was only mildly interested in the crisis. My attention was focused on a girl in a silvery grey jacket and skirt. I had seen her before, a friend of friends. But we had not spoken until that night.

At closing time our group drove off to her flat in the northern suburbs. When the party at her flat was breaking up, I was walking to the door, and she reached up and spoke in my ear, 'Please stay'. Within minutes we were in bed together. She had contraceptives. We had coffee afterwards. I had no change of clothing for work next day and could not stay. Our relationship must be a secret, she told me. I stood on the Pacific Highway, staring at a red and yellow neon sign for 'Mortein' insecticide, and flagged down a taxi.

Twice in the following week I phoned – but there were always unspecified things she had to do. I realised it was hopeless. I saw her again once, when we met by chance at a party some weeks later. 'Let's be friends', she said.

For years afterwards when I drove down the highway past her block of flats, I asked myself if I failed by not staying the night – or if she had an involvement that was not going well and I was just an experiment.

Jan Miller's father died when she was a baby. She greeted men she liked by touching them lightly on the crotch – this was unusual, even for Push women. At a party one night – I had known her for just a few days – she took me with her into an outdoor toilet while she peed. I was surprised and flattered. One night she decided we would hitchhike to get to the address of a party – I was still a student without a car. The houses she took me to had no curtains or carpets, often just a bare light globe hanging from the ceiling, walls grey and damp, mattresses on the floor and kitchen sinks stacked with unwashed dishes.

Jan was still living in the Forbes Street house (known as 'PP' or 'Paranoia Palace') when she died in May 1963. The two men who were the tenants treated her with an avuncular kindness. She had no money to help with their rent and did some housekeeping and washing. It was not always easy sharing a house with an ex-lover, whom she still loved, and particularly hard (she told me) washing semen stains from his sheets.

Jan sometimes went without food, surviving on beer and pills. During the two years I knew her, I usually saw her once or twice a week, if she was not seeing a lover. By some strange chance, one of these young men was my father's solicitor when my father administered Carl's estate. Some action may have been needed with one of Carl's tenants, and my father told me his solicitor was 'a smart young rooster'.

'You're a smart young rooster!' Jan called out, when her lover joined us at the Royal George.

When she was by herself, I took her to dinner, usually at the Athenian Club up a steep flight of stairs. We must have eaten there together almost fifty times. I was always keen to make sure she had food. After one of these meals – Donald Kirby was with us – we were walking down Castlereagh Street and she asked me to give her a piggyback. As she was clambering onto my crouching shoulders, she overbalanced and hit her head on the pavement.

Jan considered seducing another of my friends (she told me later) when I left them together at the Forbes Street house. Instead they talked, and when he left, he shook her hand, saying: 'You're the finest human being I've ever met.'

The implicit hierarchy of the Push was congenial for her. 'My mum was an old Com', she used to say. When Jan was young she was a member of the Communist Party's Eureka Youth League. Coming to Sydney and joining the Push was just swapping hierarchies. I am not sure how Jan's 'old mum', as she called her, became alarmed about her morals. Jan went on a trip with people she knew, I think an older couple and a younger man – they may have been friends from the Eureka Youth League. Jan was only thirteen and insisted nothing had happened on the trip. It had been innocent.

Surprisingly for an 'old Com', her mother had sent Jan to a Catholic 'reform school' for wayward girls next to St Kilda Beach. Every day the girls went to early-morning mass. When Jan fainted one morning, she was dragged outside and hit in the face by older girls. She developed callouses on her knees, working nine hours a day in a steam laundry. The girls slept in a large dormitory and at night heard people on the beach, laughing, talking and drinking. Jan's mother was on a widow's pension and sent the nuns a pound every week for her board. She once sent two extra pounds for shoes. The nuns gave Jan second-hand men's shoes. Months later, her mother found out what was happening and took Jan away.

By chance Jan met one of her fellow graduates of the 'reform school' outside Flinders Street railway station. Her friend had become a prostitute. 'Most of us', Jan said, 'landed up on the streets. I'm the only old girl who made good.'

Although Jan assented to the hierarchy of the Push, in practice she ignored it, unconcerned at what would be said when she seduced a 'private school boy', and uninterested in the theoretical discussions in the Libertarian *Broadsheet*. I was with her one afternoon in the Forbes Street house. Nestor Grivas, the burly Greek printer of the *Broadsheet*, called in. She delighted in Nestor's company and his burliness. She showed us a sheet of paper that was completely black. She had spent the previous night inscribing circles on it with a ballpoint pen. To prove she had not eaten for a couple of days she squeezed her stomach and made it rumble and croak – alarmingly. She announced she would boil an egg, and turned the cooking and eating of the egg into a comedy.

Despite its hierarchical nature, the Push was socially porous. The Libertarians were critical of everything (except being critical, as Professor Anderson remarked to the poet Lex Banning). This included being critical of political activism (until the 1970s). If nothing was sacrosanct, everything was tolerated. People with an eclectic range of views were accepted. One of these was 'Della', his *nom de plume* for satirical pieces in the *Broadsheet* and which Anne Coombs used for him in *Sex and Anarchy*.

Della wore glasses, carefully chosen silk ties and a cream linen suit. When I started going to the Royal George, Della was one of the first Push members to welcome me, as I was young and male. He had an often-discussed fantasy: when he reached his hundredth boy, he would take a group of them out one night on Sydney Harbour in a rowing boat and set the boat alight. Hundreds of candles would be burning and rockets exploding. He would have 'a Viking's funeral'. Each week he reported on how the tally was going. Then he got into the high nineties and I heard no more about the Viking's funeral.

Della was a master of self-parody. More than once I was standing near a doorway in the Royal George and his arm would shoot out in front of me: 'You are standing in my line of sight. A most beautiful young man has just come in.'

He was unusual in having a flat in the central business district. After a party at Bondi he offered a friend of mine a lift back to the city. As he was being dropped off, my friend said he was 'busting for a piss'. Della suggested using the toilet in his flat. As my friend was relieving himself, Della came in holding a ruler and measured his penis. What would have been offensive from anyone else, Della was able to turn into a comic performance.

One evening I was talking to Della and a Push academic (a psychologist) at the Newcastle Hotel. Peering around speculatively, Della remarked: 'There's nothing much going on tonight. I think I'll go home, and watch TV and eat a biscuit in bed.'

The academic, a kind man, enjoyed making carefully phrased jokes: 'Well, Della, be careful not to get a crumb in your bum'. Della: 'I've had plenty of crumbs in my bum and I could even tolerate you!'

Jan loved the down-and-outs. She was keen for me to meet the poet Bob Cumming, who gave up the trombone (from which he earned a little money) to be a full-time poet (from which he earned nothing). Eventually she introduced us. He was barely coherent and died not long afterwards.

One afternoon at the pub it occurred to Jan and some of her girlfriends to have a night out at Luna Park – a forbidden place in my childhood. I found myself next to Jan in a roller-coaster seat, clattering up the first steep ascent of the Big Dipper. We paused at the top and suddenly descended – surrounded by the stereophonic amplification of screams I used to hear as a child in bed at night across the bay.

Jan had a small plump friend, a prostitute called Chrissy. I was with Jan in the Royal George and she persuaded me to walk with her down Sussex Street to the 'Bunch o' Cunts' – the

Maitland and Morpeth Hotel, a waterfront pub then popular with prostitutes. We began drinking with Chrissy and her friends. It was close to dusk and hot. The girls decided to go for a swim. The harbour is a short walk down from the hotel and they stripped to their bras and panties, wading in as the sun set across Darling Harbour. Jan was wearing a black bra. I stood and watched. I did not want to get wet.

Another evening I had arranged to meet a Canberra diplomat friend at the Royal George. Jan came with us to the Veneziana in Stanley Street. This was a favourite restaurant of mine, with a singing waiter. (I ate there usually with non-Push friends and always ordered bocconcini veneziana with a bottle of riesling.) Before I could stop her, Jan began playing noughts and crosses with a black ball point on the white starched table cloth. In a few seconds it was ruined. Aghast, my friend and I cast sidelong glances at her and continued talking. The management politely ignored what was happening.

Jan hid her black moods, only occasionally mentioning her hallucinations – petrol bowsers by the side of the road becoming people – brought on by alcohol, pills and foodlessness. I did not criticise her. I hoped one day she would learn some modest selfishness – some part of her enthusiasm for other people might focus on herself.

In the first part of 1963 Paddy McGuinness began making plans to go to Europe. Jan wanted to go with him and tried to raise money for the fare with raffles in the pub. I was only vaguely aware of these arrangements. I had just started a new job, working as an employed solicitor with the Government Insurance Office.

Jan's raffles were unsuccessful. In May 1963 I attended the circuit hearings of the District Court in Cessnock. I was standing on Maitland railway station one night, waiting for a train to Cessnock as Jan, with a group of Push friends, was farewelling

Paddy's ship from the Circular Quay overseas terminal. Jan may not have eaten for some days, or may have been drunk. She stood up on the railing, perhaps to get a better view, and fell through perhaps 9 metres of air onto the concrete wharf.

I was told of her death when I came back to Sydney later in the week. She survived for a day or so after the fall, but she did not regain consciousness. I did not go to her funeral.

If I had been with her when she saw Paddy off, I hope I would have watched her every move. We would have eaten together, and a meal might have made her less reckless.

Jan never saw her child. A white pillow was put over her face at the moment of birth. She had been my closest friend for almost two years. In our conversations, she sometimes referred to herself in the third person as 'yer old mum', as though I was her child. Yet she was a few months younger than me. When she died, she was twenty-two.

I do not know whether I could have stayed her friend, when my life and hers inevitably diverged. I have no photograph of her or even a memento such as her cream fountain pen. Before Jan's death, Kathy McMullen died of a ruptured uterus in the eighth month of pregnancy. The rebuke Kathy flung at me was just. I was happy to enjoy the entertainments offered by the Push, but not the hardships the core members endured.

I met Della by chance at a business function more than forty years after the 'crumb in the bum' exchange of witticisms. He did not remember his riposte when I repeated it: 'Did I say *that*?'

Della (January 2016 at a Push reunion): 'Everybody who was in the Push seems to be writing a book about it. There are too many of them. I shall buy each of their books and select a page at random and read it, and I shall be able to say, "I have read your book".'

LEEWARD

Towards the end of his life, Darcy Waters had emphysema and needed help from oxygen, but he was still tall and handsome in a grey and frail sort of way. He was a genial man, greatly loved by members of the Push. He telephoned me a couple of times in later years and said he was 'working on Hughes'. I did not ask what this 'work' was, and tried to dissuade him. I said I liked Robert Hughes and respected his success.

Coombs has an account of Darcy in the 1960s bringing home a young woman for the night. Gill Burnett was sleeping in the next room and heard everything they said and did through a thin partition wall. The woman (later prominent as a feminist) was horrified and angry when she found out.

Darcy may not have regarded himself as a victim of the Push, but anthropological studies confirm that hunter-gatherer males bond with just one female at a time (although they may engage in serial monogamy). Although the Push advocated sexual freedom, we did not evolve as members of polyamorous groups (according to Alan F Dixson's *Primate Sexuality*). Chimpanzees have relatively much bigger testes – to make large volumes of sperm to swamp the sperm of other males. Our small testes indicate we evolved as a monogamous species.

As well as getting the physiology of sexual stimulation wrong, the Push was unaware of evolutionary history when it rejected our basic social unit: a man taking responsibility for a woman and their children. After Jan's death I yearned for marriage. It was still some years away.

STUDEBAKER YEARS

My articles had been served with a prestigious law firm. Although my work there was of a humble and junior nature, it was for well-known corporations. I was used to briefing barristers who were future Supreme Court and High Court justices – one of them became a Governor-General. In my last year there I sat in an office with another articled clerk and a secretary we shared. The partners, descendants of two long established legal families, arrived and left in chauffeured hire cars, and went sailing on Wednesday afternoons.

Because of outstanding examination results as a schoolboy and a letter of recommendation from a solicitor who was my sister's boss, I had been given an entrée to this world of privilege. It did not occur to me that it could all disappear. When I was effectively sacked, the economy was in recession – that was the reason given for letting me go, but my notoriety after the Robert Hughes article may also have helped, and I was now an unemployed young solicitor with an indifferent law degree.

I was lucky to start my working career during an era of almost full employment. Even in the middle of a recession I was able to get work again in a matter of weeks. I became an employed solicitor with the Government Insurance Office – a job I would have once turned my nose up at.

On my first day there (in the old *Sun* newspaper building, built in 1929 in 'skyscraper Gothic' style, embellished with rising sun motifs) I was escorted to the back of a large room where fifty employees sat at fifty desks. I was shown my desk. On it there was a neat pile of fifteen or so files in manilla folders. They were the matters I was responsible for and I had a couple of days to read them all – not a very onerous task.

I was in the District Court personal injuries section. We only acted for defendants. I was introduced to an older lady who kept a record of who had which files. She also had to write down when each employee arrived in the morning and left in the afternoon. That was all she did. Miss F. was devoted to her job and the high point of her day was when the file of a plaintiff or defendant with an unusual name crossed her desk. 'Abramovich', she might say, 'Isn't that an interesting name?'

When a letter arrived, the man distributing mail would ask her who had the related file. He would collect the file and secure the letter to the outside, then return it to the *bottom* of the pile on the desk from which it came. (This often happened when we were away in court.) We read our files from the top down. It might be a day or two before we came to the file which had a new letter. We would remark to ourselves: 'Ah, a letter has just come in'. There was an office myth about a plaintiff's solicitor who sent increasingly urgent letters. Each time he sent a letter, his client's file went to the bottom of the pile and he could not understand why it was several weeks before anyone read his letters.

As I placed my briefcase (with my mother's cut lunch and a book inside it) beside my desk on my first day, a man sitting behind me greeted me with a booming, strongly accented voice. His name was Dusan Grcic or 'Dan'. He was balding, swarthy and powerful – over 6 feet (1.8 m) tall – and reading Baudelaire in French under his desk. A Serb, he had studied law in

Yugoslavia before World War II and not requalified when he migrated to Australia.

He had a story about standing in a Berlin doorway at the end of World War II. Two heavily armed Germans with steel helmets were running past, pursued by a lightly armed Russian. The Russian could not catch them, flung his cloth cap on the pavement and swore 'Yop tvai mat'. 'Fuck my mother', Dan explained. The Russian was a Slav, like him. The Germans were a race of weaklings. Years later I discovered Dan swam at the 1936 Berlin Olympics.

The GIO's District Court section dealt with smaller accident claims, such as whiplash and broken limbs. Ian Sharp, an excellent administrator and a man whose honesty I admired, was in charge. He later gave me good references. We established a rapport, and he delegated some of the more interesting assignments to me. One was to the hearings at Broken Hill, although it was not my circuit. Sharp had become concerned about a spate of claims from a law firm and reports from a particular medical practitioner. My brief was to speak to the other Broken Hill doctors.

Cessnock was my actual circuit. Years earlier Clive Evatt Senior regularly appeared for plaintiffs at the Cessnock sittings, even when he was a state government minister. (Circuit pickings could be very lucrative for a barrister.) According to legend, at the end of one sittings, he did not wait for the train back to Sydney as the other barristers did. Tall with silver hair, he strode out onto the road and hailed a passing car. Getting into the front seat, he told the driver: 'I'm your Minister for Housing'. He got a lift all the way to the front door of his Wahroonga (Sydney) house.

Stories about Clive Evatt are legion, although many have probably been forgotten by now. For example, he liked addressing the jury at close quarters, in a soft voice inaudible to the court. His nemesis, Justice Jock McClemens: 'Would you mind speaking up a bit Mr Evatt, so the rest of the court can hear!' Evatt, cupping his hand to his ear: 'What was that, your Honour?' Another time, jumping up to make a pointless objection while an opposing counsel was reading out a complicated submission, he knocked over an inkwell and the opposing counsel abandoned his submission – he could not read his own writing.

I was given a file that had been troubling the GIO for a year or so – involving a plaintiff called Scrimshaw. His chest had hit the steering wheel when his Plymouth collided with our insured's vehicle. Scrimshaw had been incapacitated by his injury for much longer than would be expected, and he had as his specialist Dr Brian Haynes.

Dr Haynes was a notorious plaintiff's doctor. Haynes once explained to a court that being hit by a tram gave a plaintiff cancer: the cancer was triggered by 'autonomic dyspraxia'. Fact-checking for this memoir, I found a review by 'SC' in the journal *Psychosomatic Medicine* of Haynes's 1958 book *Autonomic Dyspraxia*. 'SC' was concerned that Haynes's book made 'psychosomatic medicine look ridiculous'. Haynes had a paragraph linking autonomic dyspraxia to a wide range of complaints, from chorea to rheumatic fever. 'SC' commented: 'This paragraph is really unbelievable!'

There was no internet then and we were unaware of SC's review. But our specialist physician, a Dr Anderson, filed lucidly funny reports with us. Mr Scrimshaw told Drs Anderson and Haynes at their joint examination how he walked despondently around Botany Bay on cold winter days: 'I have my ups and downs'. When Dr Anderson asked why Scrimshaw had grease under his fingernails yet was unfit for work, Dr Haynes interposed, 'That's all part of the autonomic dyspraxia'. One day Scrimshaw hallucinated while watching TV. He saw his TV set catch on fire.

It was not our usual practice but I wrote to other compensation insurers to see if they had similar claims from Scrimshaw.

I first obtained Ian Sharp's approval. Two wrote back stating they did – injuries similar to those sustained in our motor vehicle accident. He was making multiple claims for the same set of symptoms.

I usually lunched with Ian Fincham, who was an articled clerk in the firm that was acting for Scrimshaw. Sometimes Donald Kirby joined us in his small office. When I finished eating my mother's cut lunch, I would aim the scrunched-up brown paper bag at Ian's waste paper basket. A ritual developed where he tried to intercept the bag. I tried to distract him and – while he was not looking – threw it at his basket. These games became more elaborate. I would aim the bag at the ceiling so that it bounced down into his basket as he jumped up to field it. One lunchtime I miscalculated my throw. The bag sailed over Ian's glass partition, dropped through a void and landed on the desk of an employee of Vanguard Insurance, who was out to lunch.

During one of these lunch sessions of paper bag basketball I advised Ian that Mr Scrimshaw had made two other almost identical claims through other firms, and Ian's firm should consider whether they would continue acting in the matter.

Mr Scrimshaw died many years later, in his seventies. The name in his funeral notice – 'Henry Burton Peace Scrimshaw' – would have delighted Miss F, our guardian of the files, except that none of the court documents mentioned he had 'Peace' as a middle name.

The GIO story was that Haynes made so much money from his favourite disease that he could afford a house on Sydney Harbour, where he sat with Mrs Haynes in a love seat on the waterfront watching the sun go down – bright red from autonomic dyspraxia.

Notwithstanding the strange system for attaching letters to files, the GIO was an efficient and good employer. But after eighteen months the work had become monotonous. One of the reasons I had gone to the GIO was to get experience in personal injuries work, then a lucrative field for barristers. I came to dislike this area of the law intensely and decided the bar was not for me.

⨯

In 1963 I briefly rented a terrace house in Short Street, Balmain with Ian Fincham and Rod Madgwick. The front door opened onto my bedroom (like the Sutherland Street house I later rented). My bedroom was a horrible bright pink and I stayed there only once or twice. But I was able to put my share of the house to good use. Brian Jenkins and Sue McGrath, a girl I knew from the Newman Society, had a baby together. Sue's father, a prominent Catholic solicitor, arranged for the police to pursue them. The Short Street house provided them and their baby with a temporary refuge. Eventually Sue, on her parents' insistence, gave up her child for adoption and went back home to live with them. She became a chronic smoker and died young of emphysema.

Ian Fincham drove a pale blue Morris Cowley from the 1920s with a loud klaxon, usually driven with the hood down. In 1963 he persuaded me to buy a six-cylinder sedan, which we believed was a 1927 Studebaker 'World Commander'. I paid £17 for it. I had not learned to drive. Ian used to take me in the car to an uninhabited promontory of Homebush Bay so I could practise driving my heavyweight monster up and down an abandoned strip of road. Friends of Ian's sometimes came on these expeditions. Everything became a party with the Studebaker. On one side of the road there was an electrified fence outside a disused factory. We piled out of our assembled cars, linked hands, one of us touched the fence, and we fell about laughing as the electric current ran through us. (I say 'we', but I think I stood by as an observer.)

Unfortunately I was not present when Ian was driving the Studebaker with friends down a steep road in a national park. The wind lifted the roof off like an enormous hat, and deposited it in the valley below. The felt ceiling and interior light were still intact and I had the roof recovered with green canvas.

I learned to double declutch with my left foot, accelerate with my right foot if I was changing from third to second gear, or let the motor slow if I was changing from second to third. I had to listen and empathise. If my timing was wrong the gears clashed. The brakes were slow at decelerating such a heavy vehicle and I learned to change down to help them. With my left hand pushing the gear stick through its various positions, my right hand on the steering wheel and both feet in motion on the accelerator and clutch, it was like playing a pedal organ. I took care to leave a large expanse of road between me and the car ahead.

I let the car get bogged in puddles on dirt roads in the bush. I backed into a wooden garage door at Potts Point and drove away without leaving a note. I parked on the edge of a road at the back of my Wahroonga flat, and the car slid sideways into a ditch and had to be winched out. I was stopped by a police car near Crows Nest. It was a Saturday afternoon and a pub crowd emptied out onto the opposite footpath and began booing the policemen.

There were few cars of that vintage still on the road in 1963. Driving along, we were stared at like royalty. Christopher Koch was intrigued by the blinds on the rear seat windows. When people stared at us, Chris pulled down his blind with a look of pretended petulance.

On hot days the petrol vaporised inside the long fuel line from the petrol tank to the engine. When an air lock happened in this way, the engine would let out an immense sigh and stop. I would have to wait twenty minutes for the petrol to recondense.

Once I was driving up a steep Harbour Bridge approach

(reconfigured since then) on a hot day. My girlfriend Livija was with me. There was an air lock and the engine cut out, and traffic began banking up behind us. I had to hold the enormous weight at a 20 degrees upward tilt with one foot (shaking) on the brake, another on the clutch, my left hand (also shaking) pulling at the handbrake, and my right hand flicking a manual accelerator on the steering wheel every few minutes, trying to restart the car. We were causing a small traffic jam. Livija's white skin perspired wonderfully in the heat and her cheeks flushed red.

On cold days I had to make obeisance in front of the radiator and pull at the crank shaft, while hopefully someone was in the driver's seat, ready to hit the accelerator, if the engine showed signs of life. Hill starts were a way of dealing with this problem. I would park on a hill with the handbrake on and gears in reverse. (The gears and not the handbrake stopped the car from rolling down the hill.)

The running boards could be a problem. I was driving a girl home through Kings Cross. John Quinlem spotted my car, jumped on the running board and climbed in. I was desperate to get to know this girl and take her somewhere for coffee. John was happily chattering away; it was clear he was now a fixture in the back seat, and I had to let her out where she lived. Over time I began to understand there was a pattern in John's actions. They were not random.

I was having the Studebaker serviced and a mechanic pointed to oil pools on top of the cylinder heads. He told me there was a problem with the piston rings, implying this was a fatal defect. I wrote an elegy 'To My 1927 Studebaker Sedan' with lines such as 'Rusting queen of the road, queen of my nightmares too…' I do not remember if I had the piston rings fixed.

Months later I was still driving the Studebaker and became concerned I had nowhere to park it under cover. I sold it to Brian

Jenkins for the same price I had paid. Many years later he gave it a coat of burgundy duco, a colour which must have pleased the old goddess. Fact-checking, I found on Wikipedia a photograph Brian had posted of her. The caption states:

> 1928 GB Studebaker Regal Commander, photographed near Murray Bridge, South Australia in March 1975, en route from Sydney to Perth, a distance of some 4100 km.

Not only was my poem about the car's imminent death wrong, I was mistaken about the marque and year of manufacture.

We often find our friends through long chains of people. Through the person I have called 'Robert', I got to know Ruth Hansman. She introduced me to Robin Pratt (daughter of Pixie O'Harris) and Robin introduced me to John Quinlem at the State Library. I habitually studied in the main public reading room that later became the Mitchell Reading Room. John was about twenty-nine and I was about twenty. He was often at the library – he read widely – and sometimes researched material for the handful of articles he wrote for *The Observer*, a monthly intellectual magazine edited by Donald Horne.

Hundreds of novel readers and movie goers who have never met him love John Quinlem. He is Billy Kwan in Christopher Koch's novel *The Year of Living Dangerously*, and the subsequent film. The book is set in Indonesia at the time of the fall of Sukarno in 1965. Anthony Burgess wrote: 'In Billy Kwan, Mr Koch has produced one of the most memorable characters of recent fiction'.

When I got to know John in about 1960 he was yet to become Billy Kwan. His father, whose original surname was Chong, acquired his strange Irish/Chinese sounding surname because an Australian customs officer could not quite understand what John's father was saying and put down this name on a form. John dismissed his Thursday Island childhood as men on a jetty shooting sharks – a typical Quinlem aphorism.

Billy Kwan, in *The Year of Living Dangerously*, wanted to become a secondary school teacher but could not because of his 'appearance'. Early in his life John Quinlem suffered similar discrimination. When he was only seventeen the Brisbane *Courier Mail* took up his cause to report his claim he had been excluded from an arts teacher fellowship because of his Chinese ethnicity. At age seventeen John was already a provocateur. The *Courier Mail* reported:

> Quinlem last night removed his slippers to demonstrate he was 5ft. 4in. His speech is typically Australian, even to accent and colloquialisms. He challenged Mr. Edwards to prove that he suffered any speech impediment.

Billy Kwan was 4 feet 6 inches (1.4 m) tall. He was an achondroplastic dwarf, which John wasn't.

John was already inhabiting his past, often talking about his 1951 editorship of the Queensland University student newspaper *Semper Floreat* when he castigated the establishment (including the *Courier Mail* which had championed him) and mentored students who later became well-known names: Zell Rabin, Lillian Roxon and David Malouf.

John and I often met at the NSW State Library. He introduced me to the poetry of Peter Porter, who later played a fateful role in my life. John was interested in Porter as they were both refugees from Brisbane – John a refugee in many places and Peter in London. Another poet we ordered up from the stacks at John's suggestion was Constantine Cavafy, who became a particular influence for me.

One day John came to me with a fistful of printed rejection slips. He had taken these from a desk at *Weekend Magazine*, which was a girlie, titties and beer weekly edited by Donald Horne (along with *The Observer*, for which John wrote). The rejection slips had a cheerful red banner with a message to the effect: 'The editor of *Weekend Magazine* thanks you for your contribution and regrets it does not suit our current needs'.

'Lehmann,' Quinlem announced 'you should write a parody of Vincent Buckley. We'll post it to him, with one of these rejection slips.' Vincent Buckley was a Melbourne poet we sometimes discussed. Almost every poem in his first book *The World's Flesh* had a reference to either 'black', 'dark', or 'wind', including a poem which had a fortuitous last line: 'To hold the escaping dark continuous wind'. I wrote a poetic raspberry, stringing together phrases from Buckley's book. We sent it to Buckley, in an anonymous envelope with the *Weekend Magazine* rejection slip.

In late December 1962, in the dead, hot days between Christmas and New Year, Quinlem took me to visit Christopher Koch. Christopher was a workmate of John's at the Commonwealth Office of Education at North Sydney. I knew of him as the author of a novel, *The Boys in the Island*, published in 1958. He and his wife Irene, and their baby son, were staying in the Sydenham house of Irene's Lithuanian parents.

As Chris ushered us into the Vilnonis household, he turned to John and said, 'Well, what notable things have happened this year? There is the Robert Hughes affair...' He stopped in mid-sentence and gazed strangely at me. 'Well, of course...'

Chris and Irene were a glamorous couple. If I had not read *The Boys in the Island* at that stage, I read it soon after. Quinlem suggested the three of us play squash. We first had to find out what the rules were. We began playing inexpertly in the North Sydney squash courts not far from their workplace. John Hamilton later joined our group.

My friendship with Chris continued until his death more than fifty years later. Like Mr Scrimshaw, we had our ups and downs. Koch, like Quinlem, was obsessed with climate. Cold climates were virtuous and productive. Warm climates such as Sydney were enervating and decadent. All his life Chris longed to get back to Tasmania, when he was away from there. There was one problem. Tasmania was an intellectual backwater and had too few people. As a result, Chris bought and sold six houses, oscillating between Sydney and Tasmania. His seventh house was at Richmond just out of Hobart, more than an acre of English-style garden by a river – his perfect climate, but friends had to fly down to visit. A year or so before he died, aged eighty, he was considering moving back to New South Wales.

In about 1964 Chris and Irene moved briefly to Melbourne. He had rejoined the Australian Broadcasting Commission. Melbourne was a recurring mirage in Chris's mind. The climate was cold enough and it was large enough to be his perfect city. But I suspect the bohemian in Koch was not drawn to Melbourne's earnest flatness, and it depressed him.

Knowing how conflicted Koch was about climate and Melbourne, Quinlem decided we should send him a telegram. Quinlem was laughing as I wrote it out and handed it across the counter of the General Post Office: 'COME UP TO SYDNEY TO THE LIGHT OF A MILLION SUNS'.

Chris and Irene came back to Sydney not long after our telegram and rented an upstairs flat in Challis Avenue, Kings Cross. Chris held a salon every weekend, finished writing *Across the Sea Wall* and always spoke about this time with nostalgia, notwithstanding the humid frangipani-scented Sydney nights.

Studebaker years

In August 1963 I received a letter from John Quinlem, then living in his mother's Brisbane house. It begins:

Dear Geoffrey,

Nothing will surprise you now. I may have an imbalance of blood corpuscles, and ought to keep out of the cold for a while. Also bronchitis. Sydney doctors are careless!

The opening captures John: his hypochondria, a dash of medical science followed by the bald generalisation about Sydney doctors. These generalisations were thrilling for young people getting to know him.

John was sceptical of the medical profession, but he needed doctors to get prescribed pharmaceuticals. He could stand in front of an open medicine cabinet in a friend's bathroom and recite the names on the bottles and what they were for, with barely a glance at the labels, diagnosing the household's diseases. He later became, he told me, disastrously addicted to Mogadon (nitrazepam). As well as chemical compounds, he sought relief from his angst in religion. He collected religions as some collect stamps, with sojourns in Zen Buddhism, Roman Catholicism, Anglo-Catholicism and becoming a Jew.

John was yet to introduce me to Livija when he sent the 1963 letter. It refers to a girlfriend I had then, as 'beautiful, proud, and terrifying'. He had lent her Kawabata's novel of wasted love, *Snow Country*, and his letter asked what she thought about it.

John romanticised the people he knew; they became 'proud and terrifying' – just as Billy Kwan befriended an Indonesian girl, Ibu, referred to in Kwan's files as:

Ibu is Durga incarnate: she is life

As friends of John's, we became part of an Ibsen or Chekov play. He exercised a spell over us. I became the heir of the Sydney Vitalist tradition. He addressed his male friends at times by their surname, their first name, or often simply as 'old man' as Kwan addresses the journalist Hamilton in *The Year of Living Dangerously*. For a while it was enjoyable for Chris and me to be actors in a play scripted by Quinlem but eventually we both opted out.

In October 1990 I received an unexpected final letter from John, who was now living in what had been his mother's Brisbane house. It began:

> Dear Lehmann,
>
> As you see I've returned to my place of origin. Koch is *right* about climate…

The letter was written on the back of a photocopy of an interview with an Australian author. The author suggested that in Sydney 'the sea, sex, physical love, might develop an almost sacramental status … Maybe we are developing a genuine paganism here.' Quinlem had been this author's friend and made disparaging comments in the margin:

> You are more likely to be sympathetic to this sort of argument than quasi Christians like Koch and I or Christians like [Les] Murray.

When Quinlem sent his 1990 letter he assumed that, having no religion, I would be attracted to paganism as a substitute. I had long ago stopped having any resemblance to the person Quinlem imagined me to be. I did not reply.

Studebaker years

In *The Year of Living Dangerously* Billy Kwan hangs an anti-Sukarno banner from a window in the Hotel Indonesia and is murdered by secret police. Unlike Kwan, Quinlem miraculously survived to old age, despite his pharmaceutical addictions and epiphanies, which were more punishing for him than his friends.

He was living in Melbourne when he died in 2010, one year short of his eightieth birthday. On the internet I found a late photograph: John is reclining in an easy chair beside a grandchild in a bouncinette. The blog of John's son Daniel Bowen has an affectionate memoir, 'Things I discovered when picking up my father's ashes from the crematorium'. Daniel had doubted his father's stories that he was Billy Kwan in the novel until he read it and discovered Kwan had all of his father's idiosyncrasies of speech: starting a conversation in mid-sentence and addressing his friends as 'old man' – that was how John often addressed Daniel.

The family had John's measure and the death notices in Brisbane, Sydney and Melbourne newspapers described him as 'Scourge of the 1950s establishment'.

⚜

After Jan, I had two relationships which were more than casual. I should have learned from them. I did not.

I can put rough dates around my three- or four-month affair with Livija Strauts (pronounced 'Livia Strouts'). I had flown into Canberra airport on 23 November 1963. It was a hot Saturday morning. I was stepping down the metal passenger stairs from the plane. She was waiting at the bottom, straw-gold hair down to her waist, statuesque, with green eyes. Her white linen dress had the simplicity of a Roman toga. Her armpits were sweating and her pulpy, dazzling white skin was radiant in the heat. She told me President Kennedy had just been assassinated.

I first heard about Livija from John Quinlem when he was living in Canberra. She made it clear, I think, she was interested only in a friendship with him. He decided to introduce us (as Kwan introduced Jillie to Hamilton after she refused to marry Kwan – the model for Hamilton was Chris's brother Phillip, who was in Indonesia at that time, and also Chris himself). Livija and I met a few weeks before the Kennedy assassination. I began visiting her in Canberra and stayed with Les and Valerie Murray.

Livija lived with her parents. She was a female embodiment of her father, a tall, strong, good natured man who worked in the Radiata pine forests around Canberra. We went for chaste walks in Canberra at night, with breezes rustling in the birch trees. English (she said with vexation) had only two or three words to describe the sound of wind in trees. Latvian had twelve. It was an ancient language, with more complex conjugations and tenses than Latin.

Livija had a spare bicycle and we went bike riding at dusk through the deserted streets of her Canberra suburb. I had never ridden a bicycle and was unsteady sitting on top of just two wheels as I rode down a gentle slope.

Her family came to Australia on a refugee ship. At Port Said they swapped their woollen pullovers for oranges, haggling with local people on the wharf. They believed Australia would be as hot as Port Said. Sailing into Sydney Harbour, the little girl Livulji (as she was then) burst into tears. She thought the enormous laughing face that was the entrance to Luna Park *was laughing at her*.

She had a ponderous shyness. At the Canberra railway station, as I stepped forward to kiss her goodbye, she hid in the railway shed, and came out waving only when the train was leaving. She showed me the spot in the Cotter River where she lost a gold necklace and cross in the water. Following her through the bushes and willows on the river bank I felt she was running away. But she began addressing me as 'dear', which no other woman had called me.

She agreed to spend some weekends in Sydney and we became lovers – once at a hotel in Manly and the second time at a motel in Auburn. (These were places a friend had used for assignations. He was irritated when I told him. I had no wish to innovate and did not want embarrassing questions at the front desk.)

When I picked her up at Sydney airport in my 1928 Studebaker, she persuaded me to drive to a Castlecrag house where she had met a man at a party who 'would climb walls' for her. We wandered around in the garden for a while. Neither of us knew the owners. This type of consideration did not worry her. (I later got to know the Buhrich family well.)

She had heard about a party that night on the northern beaches. It was my first experience of the Beatles, their banal 'I Wanna Hold Your Hand' blasting us as the front door was opened. We did not stay long and checked in at the Manly Pacific on the front beach. Afterwards she explained her experience of sex. It was different from a man's. She had never had an orgasm. When she made love, she could see right into the man: 'I have a splinter of glass in my heart'.

I took her rowing next day in Lane Cove National Park. That weekend, as we drove around Sydney, she was disheartened by the untidiness and humidity, the crowds on city footpaths and the traffic jams. Despite this, after our second weekend together she applied for a transfer from her government job in Canberra to an administrative job in Sydney with the navy at Garden Island.

I rented a flat with high ceilings at the back of a Federation-era house in Wahroonga. Furnished by the owner in a bohemian style, it looked out onto a lawn and tall trees. I thought it would be good for Livija to have a cat as company. We wandered one night around the deserted city markets and found a scrawny black and white cat. We called him 'Oliver' after the Dickens hero.

Livija had surprised herself by moving to Sydney. She and Oliver moved into the flat but I did not. She made it clear she wanted time by herself. I imagined if I was patient, I could make our relationship work, and I let a few days go past. She had started her new job. I suggested we spend the night together. She shrank back and burst into tears. I did not press her and drove away to my parents' house.

Two incidents hastened the break-up.

At a gathering in the Short Street, Balmain house, John Quinlem turned to Livija and me and said in his loud voice – he intended the whole room to hear – 'You two should get married'. I could not say anything. John knew he was meddling and I was angry.

Another friend (who had a fiancée) used to tell me to get rid of Livija: 'She's no good for you'. One morning he telephoned: 'I've done you a good turn. I slept with Livija last night. I can tell you, for her it was just like having a cigarette.'

Livija moved out of the Wahroonga flat and I saw her one last time in a room she rented, looking down William Street, near the naval dockyards where she worked. She had a water lily floating in a glass. She had left her parents to be with me. She was a stranger in an unfamiliar city, in a new workplace. I should have stayed in contact.

The Wahroonga flat became my occasional residence. It had a white Bendix front-loading washing machine, far more efficient than my parents' primitive arrangements. My mother still washed my clothes but I began washing my Wahroonga sheets.

I held after-the-pub parties, cooking up a large pot of borscht, a dish I copied from Irene Koch, Chris's wife. I do not remember what happened to Oliver. Ten years later I received a phone call from Rod Madgwick in Port Moresby. Livija had been killed in a car accident in New Guinea – she was with her husband and their car had collided with a tree.

♛

There was no chain of friends who introduced me to Stephen Wilson. 'Robert' pointed him out to me as a person one should know. But they were not friends. Stephen and I saw each other around the university and lived in adjoining suburbs. In about 1960 we probably introduced ourselves – perhaps on the train.

Tall and fair haired, with hazel eyes – an odd colour combination – he was a few years older and active in university politics (not something I cared about greatly). He had a shy manner, and many women (and men) were in love with him. He was aloof, yet popular. To be his friend made one a member of a charmed circle. We may have known each other for a year or so when I invited Stephen to join the John Quinlem squash group. He and I became its nucleus.

His father was a Freemason and partner in a small, old established law firm that had specialised in admiralty law. Stephen was articled to a larger firm that acted for the Masons – their reception room displayed a print showing the burning of Sydney's St Marys Catholic cathedral. It was always the plan that Stephen would join his father's firm at the end of his articles. Unlike my own bizarre mixture of backgrounds, he was solidly upper middle class.

The Wilsons' single storey Federation house in Orinoco Street, Pymble was palatial (to my way of thinking), with a wide veranda, and had the Catholic name 'Loyola'. Stephen's father Cecil may have chosen the name as a joke, or it may have been inherited from a previous owner. Either way, Mr Wilson apparently enjoyed the perversity of a leading Mason living at such a Catholic address.

While Stephen was willowy in build, and tactful and gracious, Mr Wilson was stumpy, gruff and practical. Mr Wilson's old gardener had an ex-wife who kept on turning up at the gardener's house to shout abuse. 'Turn the hose on her' was Cecil Wilson's advice. Technically an assault and battery, the advice put a permanent stop to her visits.

Mr Wilson erected two heavy front gate posts, as sturdy as small telegraph poles – probably with help from his old gardener. Stephen was amused that his father dug the post holes so deep that, if you could stand in them, they would be up to your waist – deep enough to survive an earthquake. Everything about Mr Wilson was solid and robust. I sensed he was disappointed in his son.

Stephen reminded me of Ralph Touchett, Isabel Archer's self-effacing cousin in Henry James's *Portrait of a Lady*; but Stephen was strikingly good looking and not ugly or sickly as James describes Touchett. With his devotion to his parents, his politeness and instinctive conservatism Stephen was like a survivor from the Edwardian era. He spent much of his childhood in his grandmother's mansion in the industrial suburb of Botany. A railway line ran through a garden of several acres. The ceilings were 15 feet (4.5 m) high and a stick was placed at the door of each room to strike down any snakes that might find their way inside. The house was demolished in his late childhood to make way for a large chemical works.

Stephen's undiscussed childhood illnesses (asthma in my recollection) meant he was slightly older than his classmates when he left school. An air of knowledgeability and this age difference gave him an edge over his peers and younger friends like me.

He used to collect me from my parents' Gordon house in his family's large grey Vauxhall. We would drive down the final steep hill of Mona Vale Road and head for the beach. Stephen seemed more interested in getting a tan than swimming. Both of us had pale skins, and I tried to cover up under my beach towel. I once fell asleep and woke with a badly sunburnt leg. Stephen welcomed this punishment from the sun. He would regret it.

On Saturdays Stephen and I played squash in the late morning, usually at the Kings Cross squash courts – others often joining us – and had lunch at the Chuck Wagon Bistro in William Street, a steak with a cream and cracked black pepper sauce, always finished off with lemon meringue pie and ice cream. After this I would feel ill. It would be another four or more hours before I was able to eat again at the Veneziana in Stanley Street or at the Athenian Club.

In late 1964 or early 1965, Ian Fincham, Stephen Wilson and I rented a terrace house in Sutherland Street, Paddington from Diana Dupain, wife of the photographer Max Dupain. The terrace she owned was one in a row of three, it was newly painted pale grey inside, had a basic kitchen and an outdoor toilet and shower. The tenants of the other two houses moved in at the same time and were the cinematographer Mike Molloy (Les Murray's friend), and Raina Campbell, the daughter of David Campbell the poet. Despite our common links and affinities the three sets of neighbours did little more than nod to each other.

There were no carpets and I stained the floors with a mulberry-coloured stain. Stephen had large black-and-white linoleum tiles laid on the kitchen floor and furnished the house with nineteenth century mahogany items his parents had in storage. He also installed silver mounted emu eggs in the small dining room. I planted three roses in the cindery backyard. They did not do well.

Ian was the only full-time resident and had the large upstairs front bedroom. Apart from being in the law, he and Stephen had little in common. Ian had a bushy, brown beard and was a passionate spear fisherman (and still is in his mid-seventies). He had a testosterone-fuelled suite of standard epithets and witticisms. One of them – 'very superior', his adjective of approbation – he said came from me. We both enjoyed a dish called cauliflower au gratin at Lorenzini's wine bar. 'Well, I think I'll have some cauliflower au gratification', Ian would announce. Unknown to him, he was a leading character in my notes for a novel about an all-night bonfire on a beach, a great deal of hetero-sex and a possible murder.

My two house mates regarded each other with amused tolerance, and Stephen was able to retreat from Ian's jovial wisecracks into his small upstairs back bedroom. I had the front downstairs room, which opened onto a small concrete veranda with five steps down to the street. It lacked privacy but was large enough to fit a double bed.

On our second weekend at Sutherland Street I set about cooking *duck à l'orange*, a dish I had always aspired to, and believed was the ultimate in *haute cuisine*. I kept opening the oven door to see if anything was happening. By about midnight the duck was only slightly warm and we realised the oven was at fault, not the duck. We must have chopped it up and braised it. 'Rubber duck', Stephen's name for my dish, became one of his favourite jests.

Paddington had only just become a hub for artists and bohemians. One night a group of ten or eleven of us was trying to ride in a small white VW beetle, some sitting on the bonnet. It was travelling at about 6 kilometres per hour as we scrambled around it. I had sold my Studebaker and was now driving a 1963 anthracite grey VW beetle. I used to call it the 'Dodgem Car' after its DOJ 896 numberplate. At about eleven one evening I was driving my VW past the foot of Cascade Street, a long sloping street that cuts Paddington in two. I saw an unruly group of people and did not stop. They were pushing a piano down the hill. It heeled over and smashed.

Richard Meale was one of Stephen's musical friends. Meale's compositions were then fiercely atonal, but he was a fan of Virgil Thomson's tuneful short opera *Four Saints in Three Acts*. Stephen and I each bought a recording from Edel's music store where Meale worked. Stephen collected people, introducing himself to Alfred Brendel when Brendel was spending hours tuning his piano for a performance. He befriended Alicia de Larrocha after a concert. On her tours of Australia each year he organised a motor launch party for her on the harbour. His friendship was why she kept coming to Australia (she told me). A concert pianist's life is very isolating.

He collected information, as well as people, giving me, for example, a detailed account of the Mongol siege of Kiev. This became a poem I wrote which in turn prompted Robert Gray to become my friend.

Stephen had many girlfriends and sometimes told me of their attempts to seduce him. 'Of course I couldn't', he would say. I was envious, and at first amazed by his ability to resist these advances. X 'is a terrible old queer' was a typical comment he made. I did not try to clarify where his true sexual interests lay. Once or twice he took me to 'camp' parties – effeminate men with a sprinkling of women. 'Some interesting people will be there', he would say. I thought these invitations odd. By then I knew I was limiting his ability to mix freely. We continued with this charade for years. I was a 'straight' friend he could show his family. Our pact of silence allowed us to continue sharing the Sutherland Street house. Ian and I would have been uncomfortable if Stephen had begun taking back male lovers.

My second serious relationship after Jan occurred a year after my breakup with Livija. Again I learned nothing from it.

I had been seeing a very pretty girl. Not much was happening between us. At her twenty-first birthday party I was to come as 'her boyfriend', which I was not. She warned me I would be very attracted to her best friend, when I met her at the party. She insisted I should not start taking her out. A few days after the birthday party I had dinner with the best friend and we spent the night together. She reminded me of Jane Fonda and I'll call her by that name. I was twenty-four or -five and she was three years younger.

She had a natural innocence and called me 'James' after James Bond because of some fanciful physical resemblance she saw between me and the actors who played Bond. Every week we spent three or four nights together in the Sutherland Street house.

It was summer and we went swimming on the weekends. I remember lying with her in the sand hills by a beach in our swimming costumes, tormenting ourselves, other people nearby. One night we went swimming naked in Parsley Bay, inside the shark-net. We were alone and swam out into the middle of the bay, and made love treading water.

Our bedroom door opened onto steps leading down to the footpath and there was an old quarry on the other side of the street. To give the room some pretence of privacy I put up a bamboo blind across the window. As we lay in bed I found myself tapping out the beat of a poem with my fingers on her shoulder (as in one of Goethe's *Roman Elegies*), and hoped she didn't notice.

One night I was at a Christmas party held by some art students in the top storey of a building in Taylor Square, a former sewing factory. An old bearded tramp, who used to sleep on the landing, had been adopted by the students as a sort of mascot.

Wearing a decaying singlet, like Spanish moss, he was dancing with them and boasting he was 'no mug'. He had snaffled a couple of chooks and a bottle of champagne from office parties raided earlier in the day. Ferdie – I think that was his name – began drunkenly sweeping small cakes off a table with his arm. Then he picked them up off the floor and pocketed them.

I was used to being anxious at such parties, the young man with no girlfriend, wondering if there was some girl I could find. But not that night, or during my months with 'Jane Fonda'. I left the party. She was working late. I did not have an arrangement to pick her up. As she came out of the building and walked towards me her face lit up.

I was faithful, but unsure of myself. Although I was on the letterhead of a firm of solicitors as a partner (a salaried, not equity partner), I spent what I earned on rent, my car, and eating out with her and friends. My father was not well. I was preoccupied with selling his properties.

Once we were at a beach. For no particular reason – so it seemed to me – she said, 'You will remember this moment for the rest of your life'. Afterwards we went back as usual to Sutherland Street.

She sometimes spoke of another person. The other person eventually married her – he was someone I immediately liked, when I met them together years later.

I did not sufficiently appreciate our equal relationship. It was too novel.

LEO

Unlike my mother, my father avoided explicit statements. When he ceremoniously planted in the garden at Gordon a cutting from his father's fig tree in Walker Street, there was an implication. I should continue this tradition. There should be an apostolic succession with the same fig clone passing down the male line, like the male chromosome I inherited from him and passed down to my sons and grandsons.

As well as not taking a cutting from his fig in the Gordon garden, in other ways I was a disappointment, although it was not in my father's nature to complain. He was keen to transmit his expertise with tools and his interest in horse racing, things which were quite foreign to me. I tried to show my affection in my own way.

Old people seeing a photograph of themselves as a child or young adult may feel they are looking at a stranger. We are multicellular organisms. We are each a living bundle of attributes. We are different beings when we are awake and asleep, and as we age. Our fluid selves change into what we think observers think we are.

It was hard for me to have a normal conversation with my mother. I became the target of her diatribes. But my mother was a different person with my sister. They talked together as a mother and daughter, and as two adults. The mother my sister genuinely loved was not the mother I found so hard to love.

Our father chatted to strangers he met in the street, but with us was not a talkative man. As well as not revealing his age to his children, he would not tell us his religious beliefs or how he voted. Yet Diana and I could both have normal conversations with him. We were living at Gordon; he was excited by an unusually active aurora australis. He walked with me, and probably Diana, to a high point in our street one night where we could see more of the sky and the flickering red and green veils as they formed and dissolved. He said very little. It was a conversation without words I could not have had with my mother.

He recommended eating bananas that were almost rotten. I do not know whether this was because he hated waste – an example of his penny pinching – or whether he really liked them that way. He also had a genuine love of fatty meat.

When we were children he cut Diana's and my hair. He clipped my hair at the back and sides with a polished metal clipper that was manual, not electric. Tapering the cut was not a detail that interested him. He stood between two battered mirrors to cut his own hair. By his fifties, his brown hair was turning grey and his head was almost bald on top, although not quite a monk's tonsure. I still have the small white canvas bag in which he kept his collection of clippers and the steel scissors with which he accidentally cut my sister's ear when she was eight.

My father was born not quite four months after his father's death. Annie had only a day to discuss the unborn child's name with her husband on his return. But it is unlikely she discussed anything like that with a dying man. My father's elder brothers were given Germanic names, Carl and Otto; when she found she had given birth to another boy, she also gave this child a Germanic name. To make sure she got it right, she gave him three.

It was a joke among his friends and family that my father had been named after the kings of Europe: 'Leopold' after the notorious king of the Belgians; 'George' after the German kings of England; and 'Peter' after the Russian czar, Peter the Great.

My father had been named by his mother, and he happily ceded to Iris the right to name their children. She called me 'Geoffrey', she told me, after Geoffrey Fairbairn, the fifteen-year-old son of James Fairbairn, the Minister for Air. Bella's scrapbook has a newspaper photograph of Geoffrey Fairbairn as a baby. His mother and Bella were distant cousins – a relationship of which I'm sure the Fairbairns would have had no inkling, but Bella boasted about it, as the Fairbairns were 'squattocracy'.

We were unaware that my father spelled my given name 'Geoffray' when he registered my birth. Twenty-two years later I applied to be admitted as a solicitor. I was mortified to discover his mistake. I made a joke to the Registrar that my father was not a good speller. With a flick of his pen, he altered the twenty-two-year-old registration to read 'Geoffrey' and initialled the change, which then became retrospective. I have never been 'Geoffray' – the only retrospective name change I've come across.

My father was embarrassed when we laughed about his mistake. I can imagine how in 1940 he was in a puzzled frame of mind on his way to the Registrar General. As a man who worked Sydney Harbour, there was a Jeffrey Street wharf he knew well. If the spelling of the first half of my name was exotically different, the last part should have a highfalutin spelling too – 'ray' sounded grander than 'rey'.

Three small china toddlers that I have tell me something about his childhood. When he was a small child wandering with his mother through the city markets, young Leo insisted she buy the three little figurines. Cheap and simple and with no markings, they are in white children's smocks and have pink faces. One of them has orange boots. Two of the toddlers are lying on their side. One is sitting up with legs spread out. There are various ways to arrange them. They are gazing out, and yet seem to be communicating with each other.

*

Leo and his two brothers were skilled tradesmen. In their late teens and early twenties they rode motorcycles to building sites across New South Wales, staying with landladies in country towns. I knew the brothers only as cautious old men. I imagine as they rode their motorcycles, jolting over rough country roads – all dirt then, none were paved – they sometimes overtook each other with a burst of extra power and a jeering comment. Or they stopped, when one called out he had a 'flat', or paused for a leak, standing together and jibing each other.

I know my father stayed with a Mrs Cranfield in Wombat Street, Young. Leo heard so much about her absent daughter, Emma, that one night coming back from his evening stroll, he tapped on Mrs Cranfield's bedroom window and said: 'I've just seen Emma. Waving a hurricane lantern from the window of the train.' Mrs Cranfield was aware of his practical jokes and told him he was just kidding. Ten minutes later there was a knock on the door. It was Emma with casks of wine from the vineyard where she lived. 'But where's your hurricane lantern?' said Mrs Cranfield. She became convinced my father was clairvoyant.

Otto was the only brother who continued as a tradesman. He married young and had no head for business. He said he liked to set up a line of nails on a rafter above his head – standing on a trestle – then drive them in, one after another, a single hammer blow for each nail.

I do not know how my father became a contract boat driver

for the Adelaide Steamship Company. His boyhood friend Archie Bryant worked for the company, but did not own his boat. Archie may have given my father the necessary introductions. In 1921, when he bought the *Liberty*, Leo was just short of thirty.

Unlike Carl and Otto, my father did not became a Mason. He had a good-humoured contempt for the hocus pocus of their rituals. He picked up some passwords and signs from his brothers and enjoyed mystifying any Mason he came across by employing the handshake and exchanging some signs, then playing dumb. This was not un-Masonic, my father explained. Some Masons liked being a bit mysterious.

As well as being spiritualistic mediums, my father's second eldest sister May and her daughter Ursula Gwynne were Rosicrucians. May joined an exclusive female lodge, becoming a Master. The brothers ridiculed their long white robes. May was one of Canberra's first tailors. My father was visiting her, when one afternoon a group went bathing in the Cotter River – a typical Australian river, short of water. May was sunbaking on the bank and furious when my father called out 'May, come on in. Help the tide to rise.'

'Otto's the natty dresser', my father would say, 'and he doesn't even own the roof over his head'. I suspect Otto was the family member who was most upset when the brothers found Annie's will leaving the Walker Street house to Agnes. For forty years Otto lived in a rented flat in Walker Street, several doors down from Agnes, and reared a family there: a son and two daughters (all with dark-eyed good looks inherited from their mother, Winnie). He finally bought his own house in his mid-eighties with his share of Agnes's estate, in a neighbourhood where his children already had houses.

By the time I knew them Carl and Otto were two silver-haired, pink-faced old men with broad working-class Australian accents, both slightly built, like two peas from a pod – Carl with a bit more hair than Otto. Like them, my father was on the low side of medium height, his build a bit broader, more black in his hair and more tanned.

Carl's career as a spec builder petered out when he had enough money to stop working. He kept one of his spec houses and rented it out. He bought a narrow nineteenth century shop, three storeys high, on the Pacific Highway and set up the ground floor as a combination junk and antique shop. He rented out the two upper storeys to a widow. Carl sat in his shop all day, talking at length to anyone who called in – my mother called him a 'gas bagger' – and rarely sold anything. Late in the afternoon he would go home to Agnes, who cooked their dinner. His junk shop is now 'The Cloisters', an antique shop heritage-listed as: 'A very unusual example of a three storey brick commercial in the Victorian Free Gothic style with decorative coloured brickwork…'

Before his marriage, Leo went to horseraces on Saturdays and drank with the Buffaloes: a fraternal organisation originating in England. In 1932 the 'Buffs' or Royal Antediluvian Order of Buffaloes presented him with a medal in a plush jewel box – a gilt horned buffalo's head with red jewel eyes hanging from a pale blue ribbon. The medal was inscribed on the back: 'Bro. L. Lehman For Services Rendered'.

Before his marriage to my mother, my father may have had a friendship with a married woman – a story my sister heard from family members – but he apparently avoided entanglements until he began courting Iris, at about the time he was awarded the medal. The first years of the courtship were leisurely.

When I mentioned this courtship in a poem about him, and

quoted his statement that he was 'waiting until she'd got some sense', his reaction was: 'Son, that's dirt'. I did not publish the poem while he was alive.

When he married he gave up drinking with the Buffs and lost a couple of stone in weight. He continued wearing suit trousers bought in his bachelor days, now much too wide around the waist.

My father idolised Diana when she was born. At the christening, the wife of his friend Archie Bryant was my sister's godmother and gave Diana her 1300-page nineteenth century edition of Mrs Beeton's cookery book. Mrs Bryant was good-hearted — my childhood memory is of a robust woman who laughed a lot — but she was not a person who could be my mother's friend.

In my last year at Mosman Prep our art teacher took us on weekends to paint landscapes *en plein air* and encouraged us to paint in oils. He introduced us to modern art and I felt free to give green faces to portraits of imaginary people. A black metal Winsor & Newton paintbox with gilt decorations had sat in my father's main workshop for years. It came with brushes, tubes of oil paint and a wooden artist's palette which slid in and out. My father gave me this coveted box. We bought more tubes of oil colours. I was intoxicated by the scent of linseed oil and Payne's grey becoming translucent as it was spread across a white ground. The density of oil paints fascinated me: ultramarine blue, alizarin crimson, and best of all, viridian. I loved the sable brush — how it soaked up the paint — and the fine brush that could delineate an eyelash (not something I ever achieved).

My father seemed to have known a painter called Mr Bray for a long time, perhaps from the artists' picnics on the *Liberty*, and took me to his house. Mr Bray painted gumtrees and paddocks in bland colours and gave me a lightly sketched landscape on Masonite I was to complete, as an exercise. I thought it had no feeling and did nothing to it.

We also visited an Italian lady my father knew from the auctions. She had a backyard orchard and rooms full of oil paintings of flowers and fruit, some her own, and other paintings she had restored, all very stereotyped. I was a critical eleven-year-old, and began to realise I could not draw well enough. There were many bad artists and I did not want to become one of them.

I loved the dust and clutter of auction rooms when we went there, father and son, in the school holidays. There was a call for bids on an old chaise longue, with carved oak feet, broken springs and torn faux leather fabric. For me, it was love at first sight. 'Dad, get that.' 'Sold to Leo', Mr Ellis called out. For years it stood, unloved in the upstairs hall of Number Fifty-three. But it had a secret admirer. I knew one day it would be mine.

An assortment of characters known by their initials and nicknames frequented Mr Ellis's auction room in Bridge Street. 'Dee Why', a swarthy shifty-looking man in his mid-fifties, had a furniture and junk shop at Dee Why, now a charity op-shop. My father was bidding for a large red Cassell's German dictionary I wanted. 'Dee Why' began bidding against my father, and forced the price up to thirty-one shillings. I touched my father's arm. I whispered this was more than the new price. 'Sold to Dee Why', Mr Ellis announced as he brought down the hammer.

In the morning we shaved together, using his collection of cut-throat razors, dating back to the nineteenth century, and a leather strop which rolled up into a decorated silver-plated scroll. Every few days we nicked ourselves. Blood showed through the lather and we applied styptic pencil to the cut.

Leo loved collecting. He taught Diana and me to play the old-fashioned card game cribbage. We kept the score using an antique cribbage board with tiny ivory pegs. He had an early twentieth century stereoscope with more than fifty stereoscopic views, and a nineteenth century 'therapeutic' electric shock machine with a steel and brass mechanism in a wooden case. I later entertained friends at dinner parties with both devices.

He was not fussed about having a poet as a son and often left books of poetry from the auction room on my bed, nineteenth century editions of Ella Wheeler Wilcox, W Mackworth Praed and Thomas Hood. I once heard Bill Hart-Smith read a surprisingly frank poem by the New Zealander James K Baxter about his father. I began writing poems about Leo and he began telling me stories, opening with a comment such as: 'Son, here's something you can use…'

A developer made an offer for his McMahons Point properties in the late 1950s – enough to buy thirty terrace houses. This may have been conditional on development approvals, and my father would have had to pay out his protected tenants. Becoming very rich was something abstract, and his three houses were tangible wealth. He stalled. When his land was rezoned as harbour foreshore, its value halved. He was cash-poor for the rest of his life and entering into a slow decline.

When I started at university, we stopped our weekend expeditions to Sydney's beaches. My father went back to his old love, the racetrack. He sat for hours reading newspaper form guides with his second-hand glasses, his brow furrowed and a pencil in his hand underlining likely winners. At the end of each Saturday he came home, clutching his form guide, usually rueful. 'Here', he would say, showing me the underlined names of winning horses he had not backed. Either he wrote the wrong number on the betting paper or overheard the bet of someone in the queue ahead of him. My father urged me to come with him to the races. I didn't.

Leo's love of horse racing once inspired Iris to a rhetorical outburst at the kitchen table: 'Our life would make a book. Look at your father. He spends hours writing down the names of horses. He thinks he's going to make a packet. Money's no use to him.

He'd be happier with scythes and oxen. He should have been a nomad. Or an Arab camel driver. I was born in the wrong place.'

I had been ashamed for friends to meet my father when I was at school. This changed when I began writing poems about him. My father seemed to have a soft spot for Les Murray when they met, and later asked me if Les wanted to become a dairy farmer like his father. I said he did not. 'I don't blame the coot for that', my father replied. The dairy farmer's life was 'no good', their work never stopped from dawn to dusk 'three hundred and sixty five days a year, and three hundred and sixty six days every leap year'. Only one job was worse – being a sanitary carter. My father could not abide 'Robert', and coined a pejorative nickname for him. Stephen Wilson was too exotic for Leo to classify.

In the early 1960s he unexpectedly produced some bottles of 'Great Western Champagne' he had bought in the mid-1920s. This was a time when Australian wine companies could still call their wines 'burgundy' or 'champagne'. He had been under the mistaken impression that wines such as this improved with age. We chilled the bottles. Uncorked, the wine was an unpromising brown-gold liquid with a faint bubble. Some of it had evaporated. I suspected it would taste like vinegar. By some quirk he had bought a sweet 'champagne', and the sugar acted as a preservative. These bottles were my first taste of an aged white. We drank this strange and beautiful wine in small incised crystal glasses.

After he was banned from sleeping in the marital bedroom, Leo began sleeping during the week in the old marital bedroom of the skinny house. He came back to Gordon for the evening meal then set out in the train to sleep at McMahons Point. I was with him one night in the train.

Leo: Where are you going son?
Me: The Royal George Hotel.
Leo: Where's that?

Me: Sussex Street. (Then a rough part of town.)

Leo (in his mock pompous voice): Why don't you drink at the Hotel Australia? (Then Sydney's grandest hotel.)

Me: A lot of poofs drink there, Dad.

Leo (pausing to consider this): I never could work out why they were interested in the tan track.

The 'tan track' became one of Les Murray's favourite phrases when I reported this conversation.

Carl's shop was the destination for some of the items my father picked up at auctions. One of these was a large ice-making machine which sat in the shop window for years. Carl had a small cedar coffee table he was carving by hand, with elaborate curved legs. It seemed to be permanently unfinished. In many visits with my father over a decade, I did not notice any change in its appearance. The transactions between the two brothers were more an excuse to 'gas bag'.

Carl was diabetic. One day he was dragging a sheet of galvanised iron through the streets of North Sydney to his sister's Walker Street house. He gashed his heel on the iron, contracted gangrene and some weeks later died, intestate. As the businessman of the family, my father took out letters of administration, sold Carl's two properties and distributed the estate among the next of kin.

My father once brought home from the Bridge Street auction rooms some false breasts, wrapped in cellophane. He thought I might be amused. I put them in my briefcase to show friends. A few days went past and I had not shown them to anyone. I placed them in a rubbish bin – discreetly, out of sight of my mother and sister. In the back of my mind I had intended to show them to Jan Miller. She loved hearing about my father's eccentricities. But she was dead.

The false breasts were an aberration. He and I never talked

about women or sex. The closest we came to it was a story from when he was a young man. He was drinking in a country pub and a dairy farmer asked him back to his farm for the weekend. When my father got there, the reason for the invitation became clear – the man had four daughters. One morning my father was watching through a window as one of the girls was milking a cow. Suddenly she stopped, caught a cow pat with a shovel, then resumed milking. 'Now how did she know that was coming?' my father asked. The real story was not the cow pat and shovel, but my father watching the girl through a window.

In about 1965 Leo went to hospital with appendicitis. This hospitalisation was the prelude to his falling out with Archie Bryant, his friend since boyhood. Archie was a slightly built man with a bulbous purple nose and a humorous, 'chirpy' manner. While my father was hospitalised Archie visited twice a day.

Not long after this, Archie was in hospital for several weeks with an eye illness. Leo visited him only twice. When Archie recovered, he complained, adding, 'What's more your brother died of malnutrition'.

My father visited me one evening in my bedroom. He told me about Archie's insult and said darkly: 'Archie has been the trouble all my life'. My father recited a list of instances where an unknown person had dobbed him in. North Sydney Council had got the strange idea his flats were an illegal boarding house. The Adelaide Steamship Company somehow heard my father had used some of their paint on a roof. Then there was the big income tax assessment, when the Tax Office was told about my father's watch repairs. Archie was a gossip, he was jealous. He knew all my father's little secrets and he was the unknown dobber.

I did not know what to say. A week or so later I was present at the denouement. My father and I were at Number Fifty-three. Archie turned up, wanting help with a little job.

'Get out you mongrel', my father said. Archie asked what was wrong. My father said Archie knew, and Archie said he did not. 'The thing you said about my brother', my father said. 'I'm almost blind. I can't help what I say,' Archie pleaded. 'Oh yes, you can', my father snarled. 'Get out.' My father rushed at Archie, pushing him back up the stone steps. 'Watch out, my glasses', Archie called out, retreating up the backyard. My father was panting: 'What about how Harry Edmonds killed his wife?' This was one of Archie's choicer speculations.

Once he was safely on the street, Archie shouted back: 'Your brother did die of malnutrition. And what's more you went and burned his will.'

I had not been my father's solicitor when he administered Carl's estate, but I now began looking after his affairs, negotiating with estate agents and developers. Gradually his protected tenants died or left, and were replaced by tenants who signed what were known as 5A leases that did not give protection. The buildings were becoming run down and many flatettes were empty.

Old man Leitner had moved out from 'Ivanhoe' with his daughter and grandson. He was a protected tenant but did not ask my father for any money. His son Freddie, also a protected tenant, with a wife and child, stayed on in their half of the cottage, paying rent, I believed, in the hope of getting a payment from my father. I suspected they owned another house. One day I arrived at 'Ivanhoe' with a friend and a locksmith, to seal off old Leitner's part of the house. Juliana, whom I had admired when I was a child, was working at a sewing machine, in the hallway in old Leitner's section of the house. I asked her to move the machine, which she did. We then bolted the door which separated the two halves of the house – this door had not existed when I lived there as a child, and the Leitners themselves had installed it. My friend and his girlfriend moved into old Leitner's part of the house and within days Freddie and his family had gone.

They still continued paying rent. I carried out a purchasers index search and found the address of the house Freddie had bought. Accompanied by a process server, I personally served a notice to quit on him at his new address. We issued ejectment proceedings for the other half of 'Ivanhoe'. I had subpoenaed the Registrar General's volume and folio to establish that Freddie owned another house. I also had to prove he lived there.

On the morning of the hearing, Freddie's solicitor was delayed. The magistrate asked if Freddie wanted to proceed in his absence. Freddie worked for a debt collection agency and was not shy about being in court. He was incensed with me. He said, 'Yes'. He wanted to go straight into the witness box. After being sworn in, he turned angrily to me and asked why I had insulted him by serving proceedings on him in his house, before his family. The magistrate and I exchanged glances. In his first sentence Freddie had made all the necessary admissions. When the solicitor arrived shortly afterwards, the magistrate advised him the case was already over.

My father sat quietly at the back of the court. He did not express any emotion after the hearing had ended. I drove him down to his houses and went into the city where I worked. He now had prostate cancer. When my mother told Diana and me about the cancer, she implied he did not know. I cannot imagine his doctors did not tell him. But the secrecy meant we did not talk about it.

A nerve in my father's left arm became infected in 1966, and he was back in hospital, or 'the betting agency' as he called it in his delirium. This time Archie was not a visitor. The problem was, my father explained, Iris gave him two pills, there were lottery numbers on the wrappings, he reversed the numbers, 'then I saw these two things and knew I was done for'. There were three big discs beneath his back, long-playing records, 'everything here just goes around and around. I've got to get out of here.' He was seeing 'black molecules' and they were putting his knees in refrigerators. When he came home, he went back to his routine of visiting the McMahons Point houses.

The houses were almost empty. He was in the cellar of the skinny house when I called on him one weekend. He took hold of a length of rubber hose with his right hand and indicated I was to follow. A pack of dogs had taken up residence in Number Fifty-three's hallway. Holding up his left arm as though in benediction, he cracked the hose on the tiled floor and we ran at the dogs. One pounded up the stairs and jumped across the back balcony railing into the garden. I tried to slam the front door shut, so they could not get back in. The tongue of the lock jammed against the edge of the door frame. My father licked his finger, wetted the tongue of the lock and the door shut easily.

He needed physical activity. He had recovered most of the strength in his left arm when he hauled a refrigerator up the hill from 'Ivanhoe'. Then he cleared the growth on this lower level and burned a pile of brushwood. A neighbour was painting the hull of an upturned boat white as ash from my father's fire blew across. 'You silly old fool!' the neighbour called out. Recounting the story my father said, 'He sold his parents' flats for just four thousand quid! Who's the silly old fool?'

A year before his death heavy winter rains were making a roaring sound on the iron roof of the Gordon house, and the lawns were lakes pricked by grass blades. Hunched by a radiator in the dining room, he joked: 'I'll have to get on the roof of the boat and bail the tubs out'.

My father lost his last friend when he despatched Archie from his life. An old drunk living in a room in the skinny house fell to his death over the high stone embankment between the upper and lower sides of East Crescent Street. Now my father had lost his last tenant. I doubt it occurred to him that his marriage had made him as isolated as Iris.

In August 1968 the grey plastic phone on the floor of the Sutherland Street house began ringing. It was my mother. She was barely coherent. 'There are two policemen at the door…' She kept on repeating this. I could not work out whether the two policemen were still at the door or whether they had come and gone, but she kept on talking about two policemen.

I said, 'Mother I'm about to serve dinner to some friends. Could you please tell me what you are phoning about?' I was starting to become angry with her.

'Your father is dead.'

I asked to speak to Diana. It had been agreed between them my mother should make the phone call. Diana told me his body was at a police station at Millers Point near the south end of the Harbour Bridge. It had been found in the street outside the skinny house, slumped on the footpath.

Later we discovered his glasses sitting on top of an open newspaper in the room where he stayed during the day. This was the upstairs bedroom which my parents and I had shared. It was now full of junk. His heart attack must have begun while he was reading. He took off his glasses, hurried down into the street and collapsed. No-one was with him when he died.

I told my sister I would take my car to the police station and identify the body. I had prepared veal viscayenne and I told my friends and Sally (whom I was yet to marry) to have it without me. After identifying my father, I drove to the Gordon house. My mother became worried, as I had not eaten: 'There's a chop here, that was for Leo. Here, you have it.' I was upset with my mother yet again. It was indecent to eat my father's chop.

When I saw my father stretched out on a bench in the police station, he was dressed in his brown suit of Harris tweed with a herringbone pattern, something picked up at auction three or four years earlier. It had become a bit worn. He must have put on the coat before he went down into the street.

We are more than a bundle of attributes in the minds of observers. We have a strong and continuing sense of our own identity, even if it is just an illusion from cells signalling to each other. My father's was the first dead body I had seen. His strong sense of identity had gone. It was an assembly of dead chemicals. It was not my father.

CONCRETE NYMPHS

Until the 1970s Australia's writers and artists saw themselves as an embattled, enthusiastic minority. Gregarious and appreciative, many worked outside their chosen art form to survive – as teachers, housewives, booksellers, stenographers, journalists, public servants. They were not competing financially. They wrote or made art for its own sake and welcomed those of us starting out.

Founded in Chicago in 1912 the monthly magazine *Poetry* once published 'Portrait of a Lady' by TS Eliot, then a banker, 'The River-Merchant's Wife: A Letter' by Ezra Pound, a professional bohemian and provocateur, and 'Apology' by WC Williams, a medical doctor. If you visit the magazine's website, you will find most contemporary American poets now survive on grants, teaching creative writing and rotating through academic positions. Poets once used to have *jobs*.

During the 1960s about five or six volumes of poetry appeared each year in Australia. More novels were published, but not so many that a new novelist was overlooked. I read the reviews of Christopher Koch's and Randolph Stow's first novels, both published in 1958. They were greeted with excitement as new 'poetic' novels.

Of the few commercial galleries, Sydney's oldest was the Macquarie Galleries. As a young law clerk I peered through the glass door at dusk, after the gallery was closed, and in the half-light saw some luminous Lloyd Rees landscapes. (Rees was once a guest at a Writers and Artists meeting and was quizzed relentlessly by a young art dealer about his views on Australian artists. Rees was invariably complimentary about other artists, except for a comment that 'Norman Lindsay's oils are too oily'.)

The Hungry Horse Gallery was above a restaurant of the same name in a modest white-painted Victorian-era building on a Paddington street corner. There is a photograph of the Hungry Horse artists, a flamboyant group of abstract expressionists and figurative painters, looking down from the long cast iron balcony railing above the restaurant. One of them is Robert Hughes.

Older writers were generous. I was eighteen or nineteen when a poet I had never met and whose work I admired phoned my parents' house and invited me to dinner. Rosemary Dobson and her husband Alec Bolton also lived at Gordon. While we had our meal, her children played or read picture books nearby.

In my early twenties I became a regular book reviewer for *The Bulletin*. Every couple of weeks the literary editor Charles Higham posted me a book or two, and I sent my review back within the next fortnight. I was not fussy. I read every page of every book. Most were by overseas authors and few were worth keeping. I usually sold my review copies to second-hand booksellers.

Although I received dozens of rejection slips I had no difficulty in getting poems published. It was closing time at the Royal George, we were exiting onto the footpath. Among the stream of faces I was introduced to a girl who said, 'You must be the poet's son'. She looked at me, slightly incredulous, when I corrected her.

Concrete nymphs

Ruth Hansman introduced me to Pixie O'Harris, the children's artist and author. During my late teens I regularly went by train and bus to her house at Parsley Bay, a trip of about ninety minutes, bringing a swimming costume and perhaps some new poems to leave with her. I always phoned before I set out. I once made my phone call when I was at a public phone box a block away from her house. I arrived five minutes later, much to her surprise. I was childishly delighted with my trick.

Pixie had become a celebrity. On weekends her house was filled with artists and friends. As I came down the front path past garden beds decorated with brightly coloured plastic flowers – Pixie liked colour but could not be bothered growing real flowers – I used to think, 'Ah, one of her actor friends is here' when I heard an unusually resonant male or female voice booming across the garden.

At Christmas the Pratts' house (her husband was Bruce Pratt) overflowed with Christmas cards on mantelpieces, the tops of cupboards, picture rails, any unoccupied surface. There were literally hundreds of cards, far too many to reply to. So she had a rule which she let all her friends and well-wishers know about: she sent no Christmas cards to anyone.

I came into Pixie's life as her intense friendship with the Australian poet Ray Mathew was coming to an end, and he was about to leave Australia permanently. She had three daughters and talked about Ray often, like a long-lost son. Fairies had been the stock-in-trade of her illustrated books and hospital murals. They were becoming passé and she was trying her hand at painting landscapes. We had been friends for just a few months when she did a portrait of me in oils. It has a strained, posed look. Neither of us liked it. Much later she did a much freer, small watercolour sketch.

Born Rona Olive Harris, the daughter of a Welsh artist,

her parents were always calling out 'Behave yourself, Rona! ... Come here, Rona!' and she came to detest her given name. She became 'Pixie' because of her pranks on the ship when the family migrated to Australia in 1920. Hearing this story, I formed a picture of a young child skylarking with passengers and sailors. She was then an attractive, solidly-built late teenager who had already exhibited drawings in Wales, aged fourteen. In Australia she began signing herself Pixie O. Harris. One day through a printer's error this became 'Pixie O'Harris'. This preposterous mix of Irish and Welsh caught her fancy. Her sister, also an artist, became O'Harris as well.

Pixie was once a household name rivalling May Gibbs. She had only a brief stint at the Julian Ashton Art School and was largely self-taught. Before they could graduate to live models, the Ashton students had to draw skulls for an entire term. Pausing to examine one of Pixie's skulls – it had a fairy flying out of the eye socket – the elderly Julian Ashton was dismissive. 'Mr Ashton', Pixie replied, 'Just because you don't see fairies, doesn't mean other people don't see them'.

If she had been exposed to a few years of rigorous criticism in an art school she may have become more self-critical. She has been criticised for garish colours and too much detail. In one of her large colour illustrations of marine objects, an exquisitely drawn spider shell is lost in the clutter. Her true métier was pen-and-ink drawings. She gave me some of these when she and Bruce moved from the Parsley Bay house to a flat: a weeping hippopotamus, and a Chinese girl with sharp fingernails riding on the back of a swimming turtle.

But she could not restrain her ebullience. As a child she frightened her parents by painting eyes on her eyelids and pretending to sleep with her eyes open. She had a life-long leg injury from trying to climb on a horse in the surf; and she and her husband Bruce were awarded medals for diving off a ferry one night to save a drowning man. They saw his face lit up by the lights of the ferry and she hit the water first (being heavier than Bruce, she claimed). As she swam towards the drowning man she was disgusted when he breathed whisky on her.

Publicity was her lifeblood. She needed frequent newspaper mentions to keep her name before the public. I used to phone her to read my many poems. I was straining her generosity and we agreed some would have a dedication to her. I affixed the dedication to lighter, shorter pieces, but had no luck getting these published.

Eventually, I published a poem dedicated to her. A young Irishman was one of her regular visitors. After he had left one afternoon, she laughed about how he used to take his sandals off, stretch out in an armchair and say: 'Don't you think I have beautiful feet?' A few weeks later I showed her a poem about two swans at sunset floating in a windless moat, unable to touch, and 'haunted/ By their image in the other's eye'. I said it was about this young man. To my surprise, Pixie exclaimed, 'That's me! That's my poem.' I was embarrassed by her 'That's me!' The poem was not about an ebullient person like Pixie. But she understood herself better than I did. Her ebullience was narcissistic. When I published 'The Two Swans' some years later in a book of my poems, it had a dedication: 'For Pixie O'Harris'.

I introduced Pixie to my friends. She became particularly fond of Stephen Wilson. She opened my friend Paul Delprat's first exhibition. After her launch speech, she was reciting Longfellow's 'The Village Blacksmith' to a small group clustered around her. 'Under a spreading chestnut tree/ The village smithy stands...' she began, then stumbled at the second verse: 'His something something is long and black...' and gave up as I started laughing. She had a streak of ladylike ribaldry. I forgot about her gaffe, but years later she reminded me: 'Now don't you go telling people how I muddled up the Longfellow poem'.

At the Chuck Wagon Bistro after Paul's exhibition, I suggested Pixie try frogs' legs as an appetiser. She had just eaten her frogs' legs with evident pleasure when she turned pale. She had just overheard *they were frogs' legs*. 'Oh dear, I feel ill', she turned to me with a look of horror. 'I thought you were joking.'

In the 1970s I used to visit Pixie with my young children. Julia, as a child, loved her warmth, the pretence there were fairies in the garden, the nooks and crannies of the house: 'there were so many things to interest a child, the wooden staircase, shells on boxes, she was so welcoming to us'.

When Pixie said of 'The Two Swans', 'That's me!' she may have been thinking of her marriage. She married when people married young and did not necessarily know much about the other person. Marriage was final. They were trapped like the two swans. When Pixie and Bruce sat down for their first evening meal on their honeymoon, she was twenty-four. They discussed the menu. Each announced broadly similar choices. But Pixie was worried about being a burden on Bruce. So she suggested something a little less expensive for herself. She was surprised when Bruce said he would order something more expensive. She suggested something even less expensive for herself. Bruce announced a yet more expensive choice for himself. Eventually Pixie chose the cheapest item, probably sandwiches. She wondered who this man was. 'It poisoned our marriage', she told me. She did not understand their meal was a line in a budget Bruce was determined to spend.

I was a teenager. We were playing a group ball game on the beach at Camp Cove. Bruce, who was approaching sixty and silver-haired, threw a tennis ball to me, straight and hard. It almost hurt. It felt like a message. Although Pixie was my friend, I wanted to be his friend also. Bruce's income from full-time work sustained the family. The honeymoon meal, where Pixie had been provocateur and victim, was an ambiguous story. When they rescued the drowning man together, she felt – more intensely than she had ever felt – that she and Bruce were man and wife. She would have drowned happily with him. As she swam towards the drunken man, she heard imaginary voices cry out not to touch him. Then Bruce came swimming towards them, bringing a life-belt. That was why she hit the water first. Before diving in, Bruce had the good sense to get a life-belt.

Not many living people have been portrayed on screen by Hugh Grant, as Richard Neville was in the 1991 television film *The Trials of Oz*, which dealt with the obscenity trials surrounding Oz, the satirical magazine he edited with Richard Walsh and Martin Sharp. I first met Richard in Lorenzini's bar and coffee shop in 1962 when he was editor of the University of New South Wales student newspaper *Tharunka*. He was sunny, optimistic and without malice: unusual traits for someone planning to start a satirical magazine.

The first Australian issue of *Oz* appeared on April Fools' Day 1963. Its second issue a month later had Robert Hughes satirising Campaign for Nuclear Disarmament marchers ('Bob Hughes Covers the Big Campaign') and my critique, 'Harry Seidler's Functional Ugliness'. It began:

> Like an upended hammer-head shark against the horizon at dusk, the Blues Point Tower hits the northward bound commuter in the eyes after a busy day at the office.

As soon as I saw Seidler's later office towers I changed my mind. My daughter Julia, an architect, admires the geometrical simplicity of his forms.

I did not publish in *Oz* again but I enjoyed Richard Neville's parties. Unlike Push parties, there was always dancing. Side 1 of the *Ray Charles in Person* album was played, and played again and again. To my surprise I found I could dance the twist. Disjointed pivoting, shifting from foot to foot, where frenzy counted more than finesse, suited my temperament. (Despite my sister's encouragement I was never able to learn the jazz waltz, quickstep or foxtrot.)

A house on Sydney's northern peninsula looking out over a surf beach was a venue for some of these parties. The owner, a small, pretty woman, was a few years older than us and had a son at primary school. She once stood at the door and greeted us, wearing her son's school tie and white shirt hanging loose over his school shorts.

I imagined Christopher Brennan's ghost stepping out of his poem 'The Wanderer' (where he roamed the Newport coastline sixty years earlier) and stumbling upon one of these parties:

Chris Brennan at Newport 1965

>Battered sou-wester streaming rain, legs aching
>From tramping lonely roads by echoing beaches,
>Half-blind from the smudged countryside of night
>Your ghost with soggy shoes comes stumbling towards
>Loudspeakers, floodlit lawns and smoking flambeaux.
>Your meerschaum's glow announces you are here.
>Your great alcoholic bulk with bloodshot eyes
>Surveys the couples necking in the grass,
>Food scraps on paper plates, young people dancing,

> Their reflections moving in a plate-glass window,
> Sucks on your pipe and vanishes leaving
> A layer of smoke among the oleanders.

In 1963 my win in a poetry competition was written up by the *Daily Mirror* in a small story. The headline was 'POETRY WITH A TWIST' and was followed by a subheading 'Dancer in a poet's corner'. I was photographed with a wholesome smile, dark suit and spotted tie, holding a briefcase and doing the twist on my parents' front garden path, on the way to work. I was cashing in on the dancing skills I had learned at Richard Neville's parties.

Roland Robinson, then in his fifties, was the senior poet at a reading in Hyde Park associated with the prize. He complained to me he was just a simple man and not a smooth talker like people with university degrees (such as mine). But I observed that when we were interviewed for radio, Roland had a ready answer for every question and took hold of the microphone like a media professional. I floundered when asked, 'Why do you write poetry?'

Roland had swept-back black hair (turning grey) and a leonine bearing, reciting his poems in an incantatory voice – like plainsong. He knew them by heart. If he had been a lesser poet, the performance would have been slightly absurd.

His initially abrasive manner was calculated (perhaps unconsciously) to attract young people. He was childless. He used to tell me it was un-Australian to write poems (as I did) with Roman settings. With a lofty inconsistency, he named his large Alsatian dog Caesar. He came to one of the many parties I held in the Sutherland Street house. There were no chairs. Roland and I were sitting on floorboards I had only recently soaked with the mulberry-coloured stain. He was saying Edward Thomas was the greatest poet (after Shakespeare) in the English language. We should become blood brothers, he suggested, producing a pen-knife and offering to cut his arm and mine, and mingle our blood.

Roland liked playing tricks on young friends. A few years earlier he took Christopher Koch and Vivian Smith on a hiking trip. The three writers were walking along high cliffs by the sea. Roland was leading the way and suddenly jumped off the cliff. His two young companions edged forward, imagining they had just witnessed the suicide of the leading Jindyworobak poet. Roland was looking up from a lower ledge, and laughing. It was a spot where he had done this before.

David Campbell and his first wife Bonnie owned a house in Sutherland Street opposite the house I rented. Roland came to a party there with Joan Mas, a tiny, pretty poet with round cheeks and black hair. Joan was putting her arms around Roland's waist and looking up and saying, 'You are so beautiful'. Roland tried to disengage, saying, 'Stop, Joan. Stop.'

When the party at the Campbells' broke up, I was standing in the street as Raina Campbell said good night to her father. She lived in the house next to mine. She stared challengingly at her father and slowly said 'Good night – *David*'. I like to think this was the moment encapsulated in a poem of Campbell's: 'Mothers and Daughters', about the subtle daughters who steal their mothers' beauty and their 'blue stare/ Of cool surprise'.

Joan Mas some years later walked into the sea and suicided. Roland was a vain, but decent man. He was grief-stricken and wrote a book, castigating himself, his histrionic *Letter to Joan*.

Concrete nymphs

In 1962 I was at a Bayview party not far from the Newport Arms, the hotel of Martin Sharp's 'obscene' poem in *Oz*: 'The word flashed round the Arms'. I had worked out a special way of drinking beer from a 750 ml bottle. By not touching the bottle with my lips I could pour the beer into my mouth in an uninterrupted flow. A young painter noticed my bizarre habit and came across the room and introduced himself. He was to be best man at my second wedding, and I was to be his best man twice. He said he would like to paint my portrait.

When I called on him a few days later, to my surprise it was an address I knew well. A few months earlier I used to park my Studebaker in the evening in Burran Avenue, Balmoral and wait for the girl John Quinlem described as 'beautiful, proud, and terrifying'. At the end of a painting class, she came up from a studio halfway down a bushy gully. She modelled for classes conducted by 'an older man, Paul Delprat', 'not the whole body, just a hand or a leg'. I had always regarded 'just a hand or leg' as a harmless fiction she repeated to her parents. My bigger surprise was that this 'older man, Paul Delprat' who I thought must be at least thirty-five, was aged just twenty, two years younger than me. But he was older than her. She had been seventeen.

Paul lived with his two sisters and his mother Rosalind in a grand Federation house owned by her father, Howard Ashton, artist, entomologist, musician and newspaper editor, who was effectively Paul's father. The elevated bushland at the northern end of Balmoral Beach where Howard Ashton had his house had been a bohemian haunt nicknamed 'Poison Point'.

Like Pixie, Paul did not have much luck painting my portrait. As he painted, he played LPs belonging to his grandfather – the unaccompanied Bach cello suites, performed by Pablo Casals – in the studio of the house where his mother lived. This had a raised ceiling with skylights around the perimeter. We talked while he laboured to depict his strained and self-conscious subject on a much bigger canvas than Pixie's. By the time he abandoned it, we had become friends. That was the main point of the exercise on both our parts. I began calling on Paul.

His family and wide circle of friends became my friends (and clients when I acquired a small law firm). I have a small stack of letterheads Paul printed up when he had just left school: 'J Snevets Tweeds Gardenologists'. He and his school mates thought they might make extra money doing odd gardening jobs.

Helped by his architect friend Harold Johnston, Paul began building a two-storey house halfway down his mother's hillside in a rude Palladian style with windows set between square columns of sandstock brick. With a view across the gully, it looked like a toy Greek temple. The smell of linseed oil and turps was irresistible to Paul's constant visitors. His nudes tantalised the young men and encouraged the young women to compete with the girls on his walls.

Paul and I decided to combine our skills. I would write a poem and he would do some linked drawings. The first of our subjects was Norman Lindsay.

Paul Delprat's great-grandfather, Julian Ashton, introduced Norman Lindsay to Rose, who became Lindsay's second wife. Through his grandfather, Howard Ashton, Paul had become a friend of Lindsay's. Both old men, Howard Ashton and Lindsay, despite their different painting styles, were united in their hatred of modern art, an *idée fixe* Paul handled with amused tolerance. In 1967 Paul suggested we drive up to visit Lindsay, then in his late eighties, at Springwood in the Blue Mountains.

At the end of a road, set in landscaped grounds, Lindsay's single-storey stone house had wide verandas and white Ionic columns as veranda posts. In the gardens there were concrete statues of naked nymphs and a fountain. Lindsay was already getting

Concrete nymphs

his house ready to turn into a museum. He was standing on the veranda in white shirt and baggy cotton trousers to welcome us, alone in the large deserted house, like a stage set:

> Smiling and frail as balsa, nose light as a wing,
> Expectant in the shadow of the veranda, gentle
> As watercolour or some summer ghost who mocks
> The sunlight, frisking airily under boiling noons,
> We saw you, sniffing shade from pines and coral-trees…

This was how I described him in a poem published in the *Sydney Morning Herald* a fortnight later, with drawings by Paul.

Norman invited us to have afternoon tea at a table in the spacious white kitchen. He was pottering about, boiling the kettle and fetching cups and saucers. He found out I was a poet and became excited when I mentioned Douglas Stewart.

'When the Asiatics were about to invade Australia', he told us, 'Robert Menzies held a meeting of prominent Australians. We had to decide what to do. He didn't want to leave it just to the politicians. I was representing the arts. They were talking about the Brisbane line. [The proposal was to sacrifice northern Australia to the Japanese above a line running through Brisbane.] I told them the Japs would never be able to invade Australia. The Gods wouldn't allow it. We had a secret weapon, a Shakespeare in our midst. Douglas Stewart. While we had Douglas Stewart, the Gods would protect Australia.'

Not long afterwards I began to tell Stewart about this conversation. 'Not that again', he said and shook his head, visibly upset.

My poem in the *SMH* had a line:

'He's making skin out of paint,' a small boy once exclaimed.

Norman Lindsay wrote a letter of appreciation and added a PS.

> This afterthought arrived to me just as I was about to close this letter. What the small boy of five said was 'He's making skin out of paint'. Flesh is a word beyond the vocabulary of a small boy … Transferred to the act of oil painting, making skin out of paint, especially the skin of a girl's body, is a technical profundity which leaves the artist muttering 'It can't be done.' I've never convinced myself yet that I have caught the silvery shimmer of high light on a young girl's breast. Ask Paul what he thinks about this infernal test of virtuosity the Gods have imposed on a few pigments extracted from coloured earths.

I included 'The Journey to Springwood' in a volume I brought out the following year. I have not included it in any later selection. A mixture of genius and ratbag, Norman was an almost impossible subject for a serious poem – like the light on a girl's breast. I was unable to get the balance right.

In 1969 I was quickly reading through every issue of *The Bulletin* from its first publication date in 1880. This was for a collection of Australian comic verse I was preparing. I came across a story about Lindsay which prompted me to write a piece of light verse, which I don't think I got around to typing up:

Norman Lindsay and the 1924 Bushfire

When the bush at Springwood crackles like gunfire
And the scrub is burning with relish and zest,
Norman Lindsay doesn't twitch a muscle
And orders a cask or two of the best.

Concrete nymphs

Cinders are falling on the statues,
Smoke drifts across the curving drive.
Norman quietly pulls out some brushes,
As the casks, the icy casks arrive.

The casks, the icy casks roll up
To the broad, low sandstone house on the rise,
The concrete nymphs and satyrs snicker
As thirsting firefighters swarm like flies.

Pub are deserted, school is empty.
It's a race to Norman's to splutter and choke.
Drinkers with keen noses smell
The beer from miles off through the smoke.

The ladies in their flappers' dresses
Form bees to fetch the fighters beer.
With bags and sticks the heroes fight
While Bacchus smiles with a ghostly leer.

Outside the burning logs are crashing,
But Norman fiddles with some paint
Sketches a wave in water-colour
And sea-nymphs calling green and faint.

Paul's and my second poem and drawings project was 'The Pearl King'. I was intrigued by Colin Wall, a man with a long ginger beard who styled himself 'The Pearl King'. He sat behind the counter of his small shop in the city, wearing a white shirt and tie, thickset and with a shiny pate. Rethreading some beads or pearls, he sometimes looked up at the passers-by, his kind blue eyes enlarged by his glasses. I introduced myself and presented a poem I had written about him.

He sat for a drawing by Paul and the poem and drawing were printed again in the Saturday *Herald*. Colin was delighted with the publicity and became a friend. My sister gave him one or two small jewellery repair jobs.

He had a weekend shop in an underground mall at Manly, the southernmost of Sydney's northern beaches. The local lads there tried to play practical jokes on him, but Colin was watchful and quick on his feet. This region is often referred to as Manly Warringah and he styled himself as 'Colin *M*alcolm *W*all of *M*anly *W*arringah'. He loved the initials 'MW'.

He sponsored a '*M*otor *W*isely' campaign. He insisted: 'It's not just a publicity stunt – that's what people accuse me of – it's a *genu-ine* ['genu-ine' to rhyme with 'wine'] safety campaign.' He loved all word games and could talk word games in his quiet, persistent and pedantic voice for at least 15 minutes. (I always excused myself after 15 minutes.)

Colin had been a wrestler in the Australian Navy. In Japan with the occupation forces after World War II he became interested in cultured pearls. He patented a device (he said) which irradiated live pearl shells with multiple infrared rays from different angles creating a small grain of charcoal at a focal point in the shell. This could become a pearl – a natural pearl formed by the bivalve itself (if the radiation had not killed it) and not a cultured pearl formed around a foreign object artificially inserted. Colin delighted in fine distinctions like this.

He had a friend who owned a barber's shop. One day a colour photograph appeared in the friend's shop window: Colin wearing a golden MW crown, with a caption, 'King Colin Barbarossa with his famous 18" growth of natural wavy beard'.

Concrete nymphs

Before I knew him, he had a substantial jewellery business with employees. One of his main customers failed, bankrupting Colin as well. He allowed his 'famous' long ginger beard to be shaved off for money at a country show. This was not Colin's first experience of hardship. Growing up in the Great Depression he used to watch his father eating a boiled egg at breakfast, while Colin ate the egg white in the small cap from the top of his father's egg when it was cracked open. The man of the house needed calories to go out and earn the family's bread. One morning Colin was given a whole boiled egg in an egg cup. When he cracked it open, it was hollow. His father had tipped his own egg upside down.

Colin was devoted to his short plump wife Elaine and their children. They were church-goers. I did some small legal jobs for him and drafted his will. I sometimes talked to him at the end of the day when he locked up his little shop. Before he left, he put on his suit coat and a black felt hat – by then wearing hats was old-fashioned and unusual. I was catching a train to Lindfield, and Colin a bus to Forestville where he lived. As we briefly walked along Wynyard concourse, Colin with his black hat, dark suit and expansive ginger beard could have been mistaken for a rabbi.

My third poem and drawings project with Paul was the 'Witches' Houses'. I was fascinated by the eight 'Witches' Houses' at the eastern end of Johnston Street, Annandale, a group of large houses built in a variety of styles, some of them twins with steeples like witches' hats, dating back to the nineteenth century. One or two had become derelict. I found they were built by John Young, a speculator and builder who was a pioneer in the use of concrete. Paul and I did another poem and drawings for the *Herald*. It was a rough-and-ready piece:

In Johnston Street the mighty derelict ghosts of your dream
still linger
On concrete foundations like marzipan that will rub away
with a finger.
Eight elephantine sisters looming grey against the sky.
Curtains stream from an open window like a shattered eye,
Pigeons like messengers of death roost on a cold damp sill,
Newspapers rot in basement rooms, palm trees are never
still… .

I used one of the 'Witches' Houses' to play a practical joke on Shelley Rose, Paul's girlfriend and the muse for his paintings at that time. An animated and generous girl, Shelley had to tolerate (with good humour and some frustration) competition from his other models.

One night after a dinner party at Paul's Mosman house, I suggested we go later that night to a party at one of the witches' houses. The address I wrote down was a derelict house. I had already placed a series of candles on each landing. As soon as the meal was over, I went ahead to Johnston Street and lit the candles. I welcomed the dinner party guests at the front door, and we began climbing the stairs. The railing had gone and the ghostly light of the candles on each landing ensured no-one fell down the central stairwell. Shelley was becoming increasingly apprehensive and sceptical. As we climbed the stairs, there was no sound of music or voices, just eerie silence. We reached the top landing. There was a candle on the floor in a cavernous emptiness, its flame flickering in wind blowing through a smashed window.

Shelley said 'So, where's this party Geoffrey?' I lit up my face from below with an electric torch, contorting it in a ghastly grin. Shelley screamed.

Concrete nymphs

Paul often praised a younger artist friend who worked as a labourer during the day and painted at night. Salvatore Zofrea grew up in a house with an earth floor in the Calabrian town of Borgia. The baby of the family, he became the only migrant child in Balgowlah Primary School. His parents, neither of whom could read or write, encouraged him to become an artist. When we eventually met in 1967, Salvatore was twenty-one, and invited me to call on him at his parents' Seaforth house. He began painting my portrait in his tiny studio, a dark lean-to at the back of the house. He did two very quick, large portraits with Prussian blue backgrounds in the style of Chaim Soutine.

I was now used to having my portrait painted. By the time Salvatore had finished his two portraits we had become friends. As usual, this was the point of the exercise for both of us. He later discarded these two early works. Salvatore was painting his drunken bride series from his Calabrian childhood, bravura expressionist works with inky blues and brilliant primary colours. He was someone I often turned to when my marriage with Sally broke up.

I was dissatisfied with my poem-portrait of Norman Lindsay, but I had written a more satisfactory poem-portrait about Maurice O'Shea, the famous vigneron who was Garry Shead's uncle. (I wrote the poem after hearing Garry's recording of a broadcast in which John Thompson interviewed O'Shea's friends after his death.)

I admired the work of Lloyd Rees more than any other Australian artist. I found Rees's number in the telephone book and called him, saying I would like to write a poem about him. I told

Charlie Willcox, the solicitor I was working for. Charlie was Rees's solicitor and slightly apprehensive about my project.

I went about my Rees poem like a portrait painter, interviewing him in his studio one evening, and taking notes as we talked. Many of the works he was exhibiting then were sketches of San Gimignano. We discussed his work methods there: sketching in the olive groves in the morning, lunch, then a doze on the terrace of his hotel. San Gimignano became the locus of the poem.

There is a risk a 'poem-portrait' will become hagiography. I had a sudden intuition – the doze on the terrace after lunch. This allowed a tone shift from a major to a minor key – with a dream-interlude and hints of San Gimignano's violent past as Rees is dozing – then a return to a major key at the end when he wakes up. The descent into the underworld in Virgil's Georgic on bees was my model. (The O'Shea poem has a not dissimilar structure, with O'Shea's lung cancer being introduced halfway through the poem. Wikipedia claims O'Shea did not smoke. The O'Shea of my poems smokes and Garry Shead has a photograph of his uncle with a cigarette trailing from the side of his mouth. He assures me it has not been Photoshopped.)

I sent Rees my poem-portrait of him not long after it was written. I received this reply:

Dear Geoffrey Lehmann

Just a simple 'thank you' is all I can send in acknowledgment of your wonderful tribute. The poem deeply moved my wife and myself.

As to the publication – of course you must go ahead – but you may not want to wait until the 'Retrospective', which won't be until August next year.

Your visit to us with your charming friend Sally gave us
much pleasure and we hope we will meet again before long.

Sincerely, Lloyd Rees

'The Painter in Italy: For Lloyd Rees' was published across two pages in *The Bulletin*. When Sally McInerney and I married the following year, Rees and his wife Marjory were guests and they gave us a drawing of the walls of San Gimignano.

The poem's dream interlude and descent into darkness were apt in a way I did not appreciate at the time. Charlie Willcox had told me that when Lloyd was courting Marjory after his first wife's death, he was on anti-depressants. Marjory used to swap the anti-depressants in his pocket for placebos as they went on walks. Very late in his life, when Marjory began suffering from dementia, Lloyd went into another deep depression.

In 1961 Les Murray and I co-edited *Arna*, the annual journal of Sydney University's Arts Faculty. In 1962 we co-edited *Hermes*, the annual Sydney University journal. Les arranged both editorships. Like many editors of university magazines, we essentially printed whatever came our way. We had no disagreements. I commissioned the artwork for both magazines.

I admired the left wing printers and publishers Edwards & Shaw. I had been impressed by their production (with red and purple end papers) of A. D. Hope's sexually explicit first book of poems *The Wandering Islands* (his best and most remarkable book). This was an era when printers and publishers had to worry about obscenity. Their printing works, in a small nineteenth century sandstone building, one of a row in Sussex Street, occupied a basement at the bottom of a staircase, that was more like a ladder. I called in and introduced myself.

Dick Edwards, a tall serious man, agreed to print *Arna*. He was the printer (also a poet, although I discovered this only many years later). Not long afterwards, I met Rod Shaw. He was the artist and designer. A more ebullient man, with a slapdash air, he had merry pink cheeks and silvery curly hair. Dick and Rod began working together in 1939. In 1983 they held a closing-down party at their printing works and I stepped down the ladder-like staircase for the last time.

I proofread the galleys for *Arna* and cut and pasted them up into pages. I later arranged for Edwards & Shaw to print *Hermes* and again did the proofreading and pasting up. This association continued when Edwards & Shaw printed Les's and my first book of poetry *The Ilex Tree* in 1965. With both magazines and the book, I made the final choices, with Les's agreement.

One Friday afternoon in about 1961, I headed north with Les and his friend Greg O'Hara in Greg's Land Rover. At Hexham Les insisted we stop at the Oak Milk Bar, a large establishment with uniformed female employees. Just back from the milk bar there was a white-painted dairy factory and a red neon sign, OAK, above the three-storey tower. Oak was owned by a co-operative of dairy farmers. We were there not just for a milkshake.

At about midnight we arrived at Bunyah and his father's unpainted, rough-hewn shack in a valley, perched on the edge of a small slope. Cecil Murray, a short barrel-chested, red-cheeked man, greeted us warmly with his megaphone voice. He may have brewed us a pot of tea. Les and I later remarked on how similar our fathers were. Bigger in the chest than my father, Cecil was about the same build. Both viewed their sons with a laissez-faire scepticism.

Lighting was from kerosene lamps. Cecil insisted we boys bed down promptly and get to sleep before him. His snoring could be heard half a mile away down the valley, he said, and told the story of the man who came to build his new milking shed and was kept awake all night by Cecil's snoring.

Next day Les led us across paddocks that had been the Murrays' for generations, (but not Cecil's, who had been dispossessed by family machinations and was his brother's tenant, Les told us). At the top of a hill we looked across the landscape from a summit spattered with brown-yellow cow pats. Parcel after parcel of the Murrays' land, Les explained, had been lost through gambling and alcohol. Les was descended from the Murrays of Atholl, he told us. He used to muse about how many family members stood between him and the dukedom.

Les took delight in setting the bark of paperbark trees on fire. Burning off was good for the health of the land, he insisted. On one of our walks he took a rifle. He fired at a couple of brown hawks riding a thermal, high up. He fired a second time and missed again. Back at his father's house he shot a parrot – at short range, I noticed. (I was a city boy, busily making silent judgments about a country boy who had lived here all his life.)

Les's speech became self-consciously Australian when speaking to petrol station attendants – he dropped his g's and called them 'mate'. (When I visited Les in his two side-by-side houses in Bunyah in 2015 – our friendship had been in abeyance for about thirty years – I heard him speaking in this countrified way again. It had become his normal speech.)

Les (and I) never joined the table of intellectuals at Manning House where Bob Hughes, Chester and Clive James sat. Clive James was an early fan of Murray's poetry. But Les knew he was not one of them. Les was unusual at that time in detecting a tension between the educated left and working-class people, people from the bush like him. More than fifty years later his resentment of the Manning House intellectuals still lingered. On my 2015 visit to Bunyah the late Robert Hughes, without being named, was briefly alluded to. Speaking to his wife Valerie, Les said, 'What's-his-name, that fellow who used to ignore you? What *was* his name?'

Surrounded by students at a table in the Manning House cafeteria, Les assumed the laughing and cackling role of court jester. Most of us were undergoing male adolescent depression. For Les this was more than a phase. Even the farm at Bunyah became unwelcoming when he failed Arts I. But his father was a forgiving man. On one of his trips home, Les was sitting alone in a paddock when he saw his father advancing across the grass, with an impish grin and playing a fiddle: 'Cheer up, Leslie, my boy'.

Members of the Newman Society outnumbered Protestants two to one at the Manning House table where Les presided. They were welcoming, and interested in logical argument. My friendships with them continued. In 1960, my first year as an articled clerk, I did not finish my rounds (filing documents in courts and at the Land Titles Office) until well after 2 pm. I then joined a group of slightly older Catholic (or ex-Catholic) intellectuals who met for lunch in a bar at the Hotel Metropole. By the time I got there everyone had eaten, but many lingered on: the journalist Dick Hall, Father Ed Campion, Bob Vermeesch (a solicitor) and Brian Johns. In 1976 two of these friendships were to play a fateful role in my life.

I was among the large number of friends attending the 1962 wedding of Les and Valerie at Our Lady of Dolours, Chatswood, but not one of a much smaller contingent attending the wedding reception. I was not one of Les's boon companions, the Army of Four Colonels.

'Halt and Turn', a poem about his marriage to Valerie, does not appear in Les's *Collected Poems*, but it is one of his finest. We included it in our 1962 issue of *Hermes*. Les describes himself as a wanderer 'driven … past house and light' until the snow stops. It is a way 'beyond weariness' that brings him 'home to your hearth'. Valerie literally saved Les's life. Without her, he may not have survived very far into his forties.

Not long after their marriage I called in on them in their few rooms in a large dilapidated Glebe Point house. They were desperately poor but Les was optimistic. He suggested we walk down to the waterfront. We found a rowing boat tied up to the shore. With an insouciance I could not match, Les stepped in and I followed.

He took hold of the oars, assuming I was a city boy who knew nothing about boats. As he clumsily pulled, jerking the boat this way and that, he accepted my suggestion that I take over. We rowed out to a deserted hulk and climbed up the side. We roamed the decks peering in through portholes and exploring dank corridors, watched over by curved ventilator heads. The ship was suffused with a peach-coloured rust that matched the late afternoon sky reflected in Rozelle Bay. Les was in his most companionable guise, the informative host.

In 1963 Les and Valerie moved to Canberra, where Les took up a position as translator with the Australian National University. A few weeks later their first child was born. I stayed with them on weekends when courting Livija Strauts.

I juggled my duties as an articled clerk with joining some early morning coffee drinkers who met near Circular Quay. Our convener was Geoff Mill, who had a public relations firm, and was author of *The Malady of Creeping Flowers and Other Poems*. The patriarch of our half dozen coffee drinkers was Walter Stone, the founder of Wentworth Press and a strong Labor man like Geoff. In late 1962 I approached Walter to publish a book of the poetry of Murray, Brian Jenkins and myself – our provisional title *A Hatching of Goslings*. When Walter could not get a grant from the Commonwealth Literature Fund, Les approached his employer, the Australian National University, to publish our book. In the meantime Les had devised a new title, *The Ilex Tree*, and Brian had withdrawn from the book.

In September 1965 Les was a delegate at a Commonwealth poetry festival in Cardiff. Just before he left, he told me, Valerie used to gaze up and say: '*My* Leslie is going overseas'.

When it was published towards the end of 1965, *The Ilex Tree* received a long, favourable review from the English poet and solicitor Roy Fuller in *The London Magazine*. In his *Canberra Times* review the poet Ronald McCuaig said he was tempted to compare our book with the *Lyrical Ballads* of Coleridge and Wordsworth. Kenneth Slessor's review in the *Daily Telegraph* described us as 'two young men whose writing is so brilliant that it offers an exciting promise for the future…'

Not along after we published *The Ilex Tree* Les suggested we bring out another joint book. I thought we each had enough material for an individual collection. We were the youngest poets in the new edition of Judith Wright's *A Book of Australian Verse*. The goslings had hatched!

—

The *Bulletin* commissioned Garry Shead to draw a laurel-wreathed cartoon figure of me to accompany my report on a 'Writers' Retreat' at the University of New England at the start of 1967 organised by Derek Whitelock, an English academic. Les and I were among the fifteen younger writers invited. The faculty of older writers included Frank Hardy, Thomas Keneally, Kenneth Slessor, Judith Wright, John Manifold and John Thompson. My friendship with the poet John Thompson was to

Concrete nymphs

be brief. He died a year and a half later of a ruptured duodenal ulcer, aged sixty-one.

John had put together the collection of live interviews of friends of Maurice O'Shea on which I based my poem. He initiated *The Penguin Book of Australian Verse* (1958) that later sold 10 000 copies and was the first book to bring modern Australian poetry to public attention. After he got Sir Allen Lane on side, John (an ex-Communist and a man of the left) brought in his right wing friend Kenneth Slessor and the academic RG Howarth as co-editors. John (I think) told me how they went about compiling it. Each editor worked alone and collected the poems he admired, then they met in a large room laying out their favoured poems on the floor. After a debate (or perhaps a couple of debates), that was their selection. This was very different from the long series of discussions Robert Gray and I were to have co-editing our three anthologies.

On one of the nights of the Retreat Les Murray and I were pacing the university cloisters with the Communist novelist Frank Hardy. I had an unreliable baritone voice. I could also sing three or four or even more unreliable notes of countertenor. I began singing the opening bars of the Purcell aria 'Come, ye sons of art' in my countertenor, and Les joined me in his countertenor. Frank seemed shocked that young men should sing in soprano voices, but was delighted, and egged us on to sing for Ken Slessor, which we later did.

Frank Hardy had a story about Ken. Frank was having a drink with one of Ken's drinking mates at the Journalists' Club. Ken was the club's president. The man was not surprised when Frank mentioned he was going to a Writer's Retreat: Frank's *roman à clef Power Without Glory* had by then achieved notoriety. Frank added, 'By the way, Ken'll be going too'. The man, whom Ken drank with two or three nights a week, had no idea Ken was

Australia's leading poet, and was genuinely surprised. 'Old Ken, eh? What'll he be doing there?' Frank laughed.

My Sydney Harbour childhood was full of Slessorian imagery, without my knowing it. Ever on the prowl for odds and ends, one of the places my father used to take me to was a marine junkyard in either Balmain or Glebe. We would moor at the bottom of a hillside strewn with old anchors, masts, ship's lights, engines, capstans and bits of brass cascading down to the water's edge. The owner lived on the site in a large, decrepit Victorian-era house. At high school Slessor's poem 'Captain Dobbin' reminded me of this junkyard of old sea-things – so much so that the owner and Captain Dobbin (who was based on Slessor's father-in-law) became fused in my mind. Years later I realised there was no marine junkyard around Captain Dobbin's residence and no connection between the poem and the place of my childhood memory.

My first 'brush' with Slessor was when I was an articled clerk. One of the solicitors came back from a day in court. 'We have been cross-examining one of the most arrogant and cold-blooded men I have ever come across – Kenneth Slessor', he said. Our client was Slessor's ex-wife, Pauline, in a custody battle over their son, Paul. Despite his 'arrogance', more probably reticence, Slessor obtained custody of Paul, which was unusual for a man in that era.

At the Writers' Retreat, a year or so after his review of *The Ilex Tree*, I set eyes on Ken for the first time. I'm not sure if he was wearing his green tweed coat and red bow tie with white polka dots, but this is the picture in my mind, his face pearly pink, with a high-domed shiny forehead. Economical as ever with effort, his talk on the Australian poets Kendall and Gordon was recycled from a lecture given to the University of Sydney eleven years earlier – something I realised when I read his prose collection *Bread and Wine*.

Judith Wright was still recovering from the death of her husband Jack McKinney and it had been rumoured she would not be coming. Finally to meet Wright was a thrilling experience. Talking to a group of young writers in her room, her hand shook as she poured herself a small glass of whisky. She had a hearing aid and spoke with a loud musical voice, clearing her throat from time to time. Her thick-lensed spectacles gave her eyes a fish-tank look. Poor vision at a young age meant 'I broke just about every bone in my body. Horse riding. I couldn't see what I was riding into.' She demonstrated one remarkable knack. She could wriggle her ears up and down in an amazing way.

I was bowled over by Judith. A friend later reported back to me that Judith thought I was 'an odd sort of person, but you get used to him'.

The night Les and I strolled through the cloisters with Ken, doing our countertenor rendition of the Purcell aria, Ken sheepishly made a joking reference to 'the widow McKinney' and laughed at his own crassness.

As part of the Retreat, Derek Whitelock organised a visit to an old goldmine. As Les and I were walking up out of the abandoned valley beside Ken, he turned to us: 'I think I may write a poem about that one day'. Ken had maintained a stoic and notorious poetic silence for almost thirty years. Les and I exchanged significant glances. Forty years later, preparing *Australian Poetry Since 1788* with Robert Gray, I realised why this poem was never written. Slessor's father was a German mining engineer. A poem about an old goldmine would involve Slessor writing about his father and himself. The Slessor who did not tell a frequent drinking companion he was a poet may have hesitated about discarding the anonymous voice that was one of his strengths.

At a poetry reading towards the end of the Retreat, Slessor announced he was amazed by the quality and range of the work:

'This should not be called a Writers' Retreat, but a Writers' Advance'. John Manifold jumped up: 'I hereby nominate Ken for the first ambassadorial post of a free, republican Australia'. I was yet to become friendly with Manifold, a Communist who remained loyal to the Moscow line all his life, and later stayed at my house once in the early 1970s.

⚜

I next met Ken at an afternoon party in a house Christopher and Irene Koch were renting in Woolloomooloo. Afterwards I gave Ken a lift home and he waited patiently in the passenger seat of my VW beetle as I changed a flat tyre on the approach to the Harbour Bridge. In the last few years of his life Slessor went back to live in his mother's old house at Chatswood, an ugly liver-coloured brick two-storey house with a pocket-handkerchief front lawn and hundreds of cars passing every hour on the Pacific Highway. The site is now a Toyota car yard. Ken is remembered by a half-acre park, 'Kenneth Slessor Park', with hoop pines and date palms, just down from where his house stood. At the park's opening, the state member for the electorate, a local councillor and I spoke to about fifteen local people.

My first visit to Ken's house was in the early evening. We parked off the highway in his small front garden, lit by sodium street lights. He was living in the downstairs flat. The walls were pale green, the carpet was green and the fabric of the lounge suite was green. There were one or two splendid glass ash trays which may have been a different colour. I doubt he had a particular fondness for antiseptic green – making everything green was the easy way out. But he was particular about books, wine and his dinner parties. Ken used to light the candles of a fine silver candelabrum in the middle of an elegant table, and with modest pride would present a saddle of roast beef, rare in the centre. He offered horseradish sauce as a garnish.

I could not match Ken's courtly decorum when I returned his hospitality at the Sutherland Street house. At that time I was cooking my way through Robert Carrier's *Great Dishes of the World*. The spine of my Robert Carrier had split and the pages were splotched with food stains. Ken must have tolerated my cooking, because he used to invite me back.

When Douglas Stewart and his wife Margaret Cohen were at Ken's dinner parties, the conversation always included talk of Norman Lindsay. Were Lindsay's oils too oily? I ventured this opinion, which I had heard from Lloyd Rees. Anything that remotely smacked of criticism of Lindsay did not go down well with Stewart. Slessor was more open to a variety of opinions. 'Ah, yes', Slessor responded, 'but he was a master water colourist!' He showed us a deft small Lindsay watercolour in his bedroom – a nude with turquoise glass slippers poised on a glassy floor. I noticed Ken's bed (probably it had a coverlet which was his trademark antiseptic green) near the doorway. The bed was the narrow bed of a monk or schoolboy (perhaps Ken's childhood bed). Ken had given up.

When he came to dinner at Paddington, I sometimes played Kurt Weill's *Threepenny Opera* with Lotte Lenya singing the Bertolt Brecht libretto. Ken bought himself this recording and began playing it at his own dinner parties. Douglas Stewart recounts in *A Man of Sydney: An appreciation of Kenneth Slessor* (1977) the silent tortures Stewart endured listening to this music at Slessor's house, referring to its words as 'largely incomprehensible' and the music as 'fearful sounds'.

Stewart failed to mention that Slessor himself was sometimes subjected to 'fearful sounds' at his own dinner parties – I recall Doug and his wife Margaret were both present – when his son

Paul insisted on playing Bob Dylan. Ken hated Bob Dylan. He complained bitterly while the music was playing. But he did allow the record to play right through – such was his affection for Paul.

One evening we came to dinner and there was a woman in the flat. She was introduced as Pauline, his ex-wife. I had not met her when she was a client of the firm where I was articled. She was blonde, and still attractive, but nervously unsure, perhaps feeling out of her depth. While she was out of the room, busy in the kitchen, Ken came back and whispered to apologise for her presence. 'I have her here for Paul's sake. He needs to see a bit of his mother.'

We said, 'Don't worry, Ken. Pauline's fine. We were all just saying how we like her.' This remark seemed to dismay Ken and he whispered more apologies for inflicting Pauline on us. At the dinner table she took an active role in the conversation and this caused Ken to become agitated and withdrawn.

Ken was impressed by the large black-and-white linoleum tiles Stephen Wilson had laid out in a chess board pattern on the kitchen floor at Sutherland Street. A couple of years later he moved into the top storey of the Chatswood house and his brother Robin (I think) took over the bottom half. When I went to dinner there and Ken opened the door, I noticed the interior was Ken's trademark antiseptic green. He whisked me through the rooms and proudly displayed the floor of his new kitchen: black-and-white linoleum like a chessboard!

In 1968 I was standing in the corridor of Angus & Robertson's editorial offices in lower George Street talking to Stewart. I asked how I could make money from writing. 'Publish a lot of books', was his reply. He added as an afterthought, 'Would you like to edit an anthology of Australian comic verse?' I did not know much about Australian comic verse or any comic verse, but immediately agreed.

Concrete nymphs

At Slessor's dinner parties we often discussed the anthology. Ken was devoted to John Farrell's almost forgotten, macabre 512-line 'My Sundowner', which I included in full. Ken also loved the nineteenth century Australian light verse writer, WT Goodge. 'As good as WS Gilbert' was Ken's verdict.

The three short pieces of George Wallace which I anthologised were as Slessor recollected them. My favourite is:

Rhapsody Over Ben Hur

O to be in ancient Rome
Watching the gladioli galloping their carrots around the aroma!

This 'poem' was probably never set down on paper and may have been merely something Slessor remembered from a radio show. Another of the George Wallace 'poems' recollected by Slessor was:

The Waiter

'What will you have?' asked the waiter, reflectively picking his nose.
'Two boiled eggs, you bastard. You can't put your fingers in those.'

Stewart discussed this piece in his Slessor book and related his argument with Slessor about what the diner said to the waiter. Stewart preferred 'Two hard boiled eggs, you bastard!', for metrical reasons and because this made them 'more impenetrable'. Slessor preferred 'Two boiled eggs' as this was enough.

I plumped for Slessor's preference for two reasons: less is best, and it would be unusual to order hard-boiled eggs. This difference of opinion illustrates why one of them was a great poet, and the other was not, although a very good poet.

Ken sometimes fondly mentioned the memoirs of William Hickey, the subject of his poem 'The Nabob'. On the strength of Slessor's recommendation I bought this book. When I finally read it, long after his death, it was a shock. The drunken promiscuity of eighteenth century gentry, most of them teenagers, and their women, who had only just reached puberty, made the Push seem like a Sunday School picnic. Stewart refers to Hickey with distaste as 'that scapegrace attorney of India', but Ken revelled in the memoirs, as (I am afraid) I did.

After the dessert he would make coffee in an electric percolator. This had two almost spherical glass bowls, one on top of the other. An electric coil glowed bright red in the softly lit room and heated the water in the bottom bowl. Ken used to hover about it while it took an age before the water started bubbling and coughing up through the coffee grounds, and a dense black pool formed in the top bowl. Only then were Ken and his guests able to relax. The red glow of Ken's coffee percolator reminded me of the red glow of Christopher Brennan's beaker of claret over a flame. The young Slessor met the older poet at least once.

After a night on the town, Ken was too late for the North Shore ferry across the harbour, so he stayed overnight in a Woolloomooloo boarding house run by Christopher Brennan's daughter. This was probably Anne, a prostitute of whom Jack Lindsay (Norman's son) wrote, 'Everybody was in love with her'. Coming downstairs for breakfast, Ken found Brennan's daughter cooking breakfast. The kitchen window was open. A light sprinkle of rain was falling on a courtyard where two drunken figures were sprawled on an iron double bed. The two men were her father (the great poet) and his brother. 'I'll wake those bastards up!' she announced to young Ken and sent a fried egg flying through the window in the direction of the drunkards.

In 'My Kings Cross' (his prose collection), Ken painted a verbal picture of another bohemian poet of that era, Geoffrey Cumine 'with his blue beret, pea-green shirt and brass ear-rings and a butterfly tattooed on his face'. Slessor said Cumine was one of the few in Australia who shared his enthusiasm for the Pound–Eliot poetic revolution. He also told me the story of Cumine's love affair with a married woman, which was cut short when the husband castrated Cumine.

Ken recited a quatrain of Cumine's. I wrote it down and included it in *Comic Australian Verse*.

Elegy for Dame Nellie Melba

> Melba stormed up to Heaven. What d'you think she said?
> 'How very droll, to think that I am dead:
> Remove the fishermen about the throne –
> I wish to see the Manager, *alone*.'

I am unaware of any published source. The quatrain Ken happened to remember is now Cumine's most frequently cited poem on the internet.

Ken once explained why he had not become a novelist. 'I gave it a go once. I had got to about page fifty describing the hair in people's nostrils and the shine on pores of skin and details like that, but I'd got nowhere with the plot. So I decided I was not cut out to be a novelist and gave it away.'

Ken departed one evening from his customary roast beef. He announced he had brought in Chinese takeaway (such as duck in black bean sauce). We all agreed this was an inspired idea and congratulated him at the end of the meal. He served the pre-cooked Chinese meats with gusto, and was very pleased with himself – particularly that he had so cleverly avoided the chores of the kitchen. As we said goodbye I wondered whether I was the only guest disappointed by the lukewarm food.

This may have been the last time I ate at his Chatswood house. I somehow assumed Ken had another ten years of dinner parties left in him. The silver candelabrum would always light up the mahogany table, the smiling pink face would appear with the saddle of beef and Douglas Stewart would continue to be silently tortured by *The Threepenny Opera* (unknown to Ken and his other guests) – a martyrdom of good manners.

Slessor's death seemed premature, unfair to the one or two people who were dependent on him – his son Paul had only recently left school. When Ken died, as I entered the crematorium chapel, I had a premonition I would see him standing there, watching his own funeral service. Instead, I saw his facsimile, his younger brother Robin quietly watching at the back of the chapel.

A bizarre enclave of streets in Glenmore Park near Regentville Public School may be continuing these dinner table conversations. Kenneth Slessor Drive is joined by Harwood Circuit to Lehmann Avenue and within shouting distance are FitzGerald Place – incorrectly spelled 'Fitzgerald' on Google maps – Stewart Place, Richardson Place, Banjo Paterson Close, Manifold Crescent and Harpur Close. Does the talk between the streets become more animated when one of their writers dies? Only one is still alive.

In 1940 a New Zealander in his mid-twenties, too unfit to be drafted into the army, became the editor of the *Bulletin*'s literary pages (they began on the weekly's pink inside cover and were known as the 'Red Page'). With Douglas Stewart as literary editor for twenty years the *Bulletin* regained its status as Australia's most important literary publication.

Stewart himself wrote in rhyming verses, but he published Bill Hart-Smith's free verse. He was the earliest champion of Francis Webb's knotty, violent language, which was a long way from Stewart's own practice. Judith Wright, David Campbell and John Blight were among the many poets whose work he promoted in the *Bulletin*. He regularly published the naive or 'primitive' poet 'Bellerive' in the 'Answers to Correspondents' column and ensured he was paid.

As a fifteen- and sixteen-year-old I was put off by the fustian appearance of the *Bulletin*. It looked (and smelled) like the 1920s. But it was the first place I sent my poems to.

In 1961 Stewart's reign at the 'Red Page' ended after Frank Packer's Australian Consolidated Press bought the *Bulletin* and Vincent Buckley became the poetry editor. Buckley wrote poetry of high seriousness and a seigneurial detachment as a committed Catholic, such as his 'Eleven Political Poems'. (When his Catholicism later lapsed it was replaced by a passionate involvement in Ireland and a barely disguised admiration for IRA terrorists.)

Stewart recovered from this palace revolution and became a 'literary adviser' to the most significant locally owned publisher, Angus & Robertson. He published editions of many of his *Bulletin* poets, consolidating his achievement at the *Bulletin*. In 1964 he edited the Angus & Robertson *Modern Australian Verse*. He wrote to me saying he would include 'The Last Campaign', if I removed a line where the horsemen 'wiped snot on their saddles'. I changed this to 'stared hard through the twilight haze', and was the youngest poet in the book.

Stewart's detestation of Kurt Weill's music was comical, but his limitations were his strength. His poems had a purity of language missing in the type of poetry Buckley promoted, which ran the risk of becoming self-righteous. Stewart's benign scepticism about religion and politics may have seemed shallow to poets of a committed generation, but the three decades from 1940 to 1970 when Stewart was Australia's literary arbiter were relatively faction-free.

David Campbell was one of Stewart's closest friends. I first met Campbell one evening in the bar of the Newcastle Hotel. He was a tall handsome man with a broken nose and golden hair. He was wearing a striped, vivid green silk tie. Stewart wrote a sonnet for David Campbell, 'Familiars', in which he likens himself to a 'humble ant-eater ... clumsy and prickly' and Campbell to the 'biggest reddest fox I ever saw'. These were two animals the friends encountered on one of their fishing trips along small rivers on the western edge of the Great Dividing Range.

At about the time he wrote this sonnet I was talking to Doug – that was what we called him. A glazed expression on his face, he told me of Campbell hosting a dinner for friends in Canberra, and his misgivings as David (at his own cost) insisted on ordering the most expensive wines, bottle after bottle.

When David's marriage to Bonnie broke up, he lost his grazing property. He became a Vietnam War opponent and reinvented his poetic style. Unlike his friend Campbell, Stewart was unable to reinvent himself. After publishing his *Collected Poems 1936–1967* at age fifty-four, Stewart lost his characteristic assurance and ability to surprise. Doug once asked me if I would like some of his Australian orchids: 'I've written all the poems I want to write about them'.

When he died in 1985, his wife Margaret still retained her allegiance to Catholicism. Although Doug was an agnostic, his funeral was at an Anglican church in St Ives, the suburb where the Stewarts lived. It was a disappointing farewell. Not much was said about Douglas Stewart, the fine poet, and friend and benefactor of so many writers. Instead there was a long evangelical harangue. Doug would have hated it.

※

The 1969 edition of Francis Webb's *Collected Poems* has an introduction by Sir Herbert Read, the English literary critic, where he includes Webb in the front rank of twentieth century poets, at the level of Rilke, Eliot and Pasternak. This assessment contrasted with Webb's demeaning personal circumstances, as an inmate of mental hospitals for most of his adult life.

Lyn Riddett, whom I knew at university through Les Murray's Newman Society friends, knew two nuns who used to see Webb at Sydney's Callan Park Mental Hospital. In about 1966 she suggested we visit him. I went with the two nuns and Lyn, and also our mutual friend Robyn Read (who had married John Hamilton, after I introduced her to John at Les Murray's wedding). As we were ushered into the visitors' room, we were met by a shambling, disoriented man, who looked twenty years older than he was.

I could hardly believe this was the well-known poet. I had imagined someone who was neatly dressed, a bit depressed, and sat in a hospital room writing poems – not this wild and disorderly man with a face disfigured by eczema, which he continually rubbed, and carrying a string bag, where he kept his few possessions. Confused and barely able to maintain a coherent conversation, he rambled from anti-communism to Catholic piety, with frequent references to 'Our Lady' – perhaps to show respect for the nuns.

He seemed unsure who we were. After about half an hour he turned to me with a baleful look and asked, 'Are you Geoffrey Lehmann?' He then recited a couple of lines of my poetry, which he thought 'very beautiful':

> ... all through your verse there blows
> A gracious, clean, colonial innocence.

These were some lines I had written about the poetry of JAR McKellar. After that, I was a fan of Webb's for life. As we were leaving, the nuns produced some bananas from a bag. They handed them to him. With enormous courtesy – he was always very courteous – Frank said: 'Thank you kindly, sisters. I much appreciate it. Like the animals at the zoo.'

This first meeting was followed by other visits in the Kafkaesque visitors' room. At these later meetings Webb's condition was hardly improved, except that he now recognised us. There was activity among the patients – what Webb described in a poem about Parramatta Psychiatric Hospital as 'our droll old men ... darting constantly'. When there was a scuffle, Webb jumped up and separated the antagonists. Inmates in an adjoining room, locked away from the visitors, hoisted their heads above a high wooden partition, and peered in through the glass divider. Our little group bought a transistor radio for Frank, so he could listen to classical music. He was devoted to Bruckner's symphonies. The radio did not last long in his string bag, and was stolen.

Webb wrote some of his best poems in mental hospitals in England. A grant from the Commonwealth Literary Fund in 1958 brought him back to Australia and he wrote much less. The conditions in Australian mental institutions were such that there were periods when he was unable to write anything at all.

The visits with my friends and the nuns ceased. A year or so later I called on Webb by myself. I knocked apprehensively on the door of his ward and asked to see him. Frank appeared. His eczema had disappeared. Even more surprising, he said to the male nurse, 'I'd like to go for a walk outside with my friend'. For an hour or so we walked in the grounds, talking about poetry. He referred to a recent book of a young Australian poet and asked what I thought about it. 'He is a much better poet than me', Frank said with characteristic humility.

It was an awkward question. The book had a poem about a poet in a mental hospital. The poem presented the poet as a heroic figure. But it had a phrase 'the defeated poet' and mentioned the poet's string bag. I replied to Frank's question evasively. Realising my embarrassment, Frank quickly said, 'Of course I have not read all the poems in the book'.

Standing under some trees, there was a sprinkle of rain. Webb reached out his hand to feel the rain-drops: 'I'll record this in my memoir, if I ever write one'.

A year or so later I heard he was at a mental hospital in Orange. I drove to Orange and called in at the hospital. I found he had transferred to yet another institution in Victoria. This may be when he was befriended by the poet and doctor Kel Semmens. The hospital authorities had been surprised when Semmens proposed a visit. Webb is a hopeless case, they said: he just sits in a rocking chair on the veranda, rocking and talking to himself all day. Frank later told Semmens: 'The only way I can stay sane in this awful place is in this chair, reciting all the poetry I know'. (My informant: Jamie Grant.)

Frank died at Rydalmere Psychiatric Hospital in Sydney in 1973, of a coronary occlusion. He was aged forty-eight, four years younger than his pianist father Clarence was, when he died as an inmate of Callan Park in 1945. Frank was then twenty-one.

In *The Gene: An Intimate History* Siddhartha Mukherjee has written of the genomic origin of schizophrenia. The immune response region of the genome (the MHC region, 'a gene mapper's nightmare') is involved in coding a protein that clears up cellular debris. This protein also edits and trims synapses in the brain. 'Good' editing during adolescence is necessary, but 'overpruning' in one's twenties leads to schizophrenia.

Francis Webb's personal history follows Mukherjee's account exactly. Frank was an outstanding school athlete, came second in English in the state-wide New South Wales Leaving Certificate, was a flight sergeant in the Royal Australian Air Force when he was demobilised at age twenty-one, and became engaged to a young woman in Canada. His delusions and episodes, such as breaking a shop window, then began. The Frank I knew in his lucid intervals was protective (towards other patients), friendly, discreet, loyal and ironic. He had a nobility of character. This was the real Frank.

♛

A profile of the seventy-two-year-old Robert Graves, with his unruly mane of silver hair, like a Roman emperor on a medallion, appeared on the front page of the *Sydney Morning Herald* in October 1967, on the day of his arrival in Australia. He was in Australia to promote his translation of the *Rubaiyat* and to read his translation the following night to a large audience at the Sydney Town Hall. A couple of days later there was a short news story about the disappearance of his briefcase at a party after the reading, and its recovery. The disappearing briefcase was also news on the morning radio.

I had given Graves's *Collected Poems* to Les Murray for his twenty-first birthday. I was part of a small group — Geoff Mill, Sally McInerney and Stephen Wilson — sitting near the front at the Town Hall, looking up at Graves, tall and craggy, clothed in black and purple, reading from his translation. Geoff Mill proposed we throw a party for Graves in the Sutherland Street house.

Geoff was an imposing, handsome man, and after the reading we went backstage and he quickly convinced Graves a party with some poets was a good idea. Within half an hour fifty or more young people were crammed into the small terrace house – we must have made phone calls to round them up – and I had brought in a supply of cheap wine and beer. Not long afterwards the great poet arrived with his Sydney relatives.

Graves was anxious about his briefcase. It contained drafts of his translations he was planning to sell to academic institutions. The party was crowded, there were people we did not know, and Geoff offered to mind the briefcase. He stowed it in the back of his car. About forty minutes later, he told me he had to leave. It was an hour or so before we realised the briefcase had vanished with Geoff in his car.

Graves was thunderstruck. I took him up to Paddington police station at about midnight. Graves and I sat before a police desk and I told them this was 'an international incident'. Before we put the matter in their hands, I asked would they give me Geoff's address. It was in Collaroy and they could find it by telephoning the motor vehicle drivers' registry. When we had the address, Graves and I drove out in my grey VW beetle and woke Geoff's family up at about 2 am. There was no Geoff. His wife Sarah did not know where he was.

Graves and I drove down to Collaroy beach and found a public phone booth on the main road. I rang the police and told them the matter was now in their hands, and I put Graves on the phone, so he could satisfy himself I was speaking to police. It was now about 3 am. White rollers could be seen in the light of the street lamps, breaking coldly on the beach. Graves asked, 'How about a swim?'

Early next morning Geoff discovered his mistake. As he advanced across the living room of the Roseville house where

Graves was staying, Graves stood, glowering, and obsessively searched the briefcase when Geoff handed it to him. Geoff had a moment of nervousness. He had not checked the contents.

A few days later in the rain on the tarmac of the Oodnadatta airport in Central Australia, Geoff again met Graves, by a strange coincidence: 'He must have thought I was stalking him'.

⁂

After our meeting in the dimly lit Albert Street offices of *Quadrant* in 1958 I remained in touch with Jim McAuley. He took up a readership with the University of Tasmania in 1960. On one of his sporadic forays to Sydney in the 1960s Jim phoned and we had dinner at the Sutherland Street house. I decorated the table with a bowl of wisteria and azaleas from my parents' garden. In 1969 he sent me a thank you letter after I reviewed his *Surprises of the Sun* favourably in the *Bulletin*. He asked in his letter whether an author should thank a reviewer.

He was subject to bouts of an almost disabling pessimism. Writing in his poem 'Explicit', not long before his death in 1976, Jim said of the twentieth century, 'No worse age has ever been', and described it as 'Murderous, lying and obscene'.

I last saw McAuley in 1976, a few months before his death. I was aware he had terminal cancer. There was an afternoon reading of his poems to a small group at the NSW State Library. I may not have been invited, or may have been unable to come because I was caring for children. Quite by chance after the reading had finished, I was driving my Kombi Van past the library with my three children in the back. I saw Jim with Alec Hope, Leonie Kramer and Peter Coleman, walking slowly down Macquarie Street. I was unable to stop.

Concrete nymphs

♛

We did not realise it was the start of the 'poetry wars' when Robert Adamson replaced Roland Robinson as president of the Poetry Society of Australia in 1968. (The 'poetry wars' were to run intermittently for a couple of decades, with Les Murray leading the poets labelled as 'conservative', and opposed by John Tranter leading the 'generation of '68'.) I voted for Roland at the angry Poetry Society meeting on the evening when he was stripped of the presidency. Roland and JM Couper had staged a putsch against Grace Perry a year or so earlier, and at the end of the meeting I was indifferent about what had happened.

As I was walking out into lower George Street, a fair-haired young man on the footpath stepped forward and introduced himself. Robert Gray was in his early twenties. He called me 'Mr Lehmann'. I was only five years older than Bob. I insisted I was Geoff.

We began meeting, eating meals together and occasionally going to films. Bob was always well informed about films. We have maintained these habits now for fifty years. When we were younger, walking through the city – on our way to a restaurant or to call in at a bookshop – young women's eyes fixed themselves on us as we walked past. It was Bob they were looking at. Not only his Nordic looks, but an instinctive reticence attracted their glances. They knew they could look at him and he would take no notice. Bob was unaware of their attention.

Peter Alexander's biography of Les Murray says Murray 'greatly admired' Gray's 'lapidary poems', 'but he found Gray the most elusive of men' with last-minute dinner cancellations and mysterious absences from places where he had promised he would be. After a couple of years I realised this elusiveness was not intended personally – it was a fear of being confined. I started letting Bob initiate arrangements for a meeting. If he phoned and suggested we meet, he was punctual and reliable. Living with Dee, now his partner of forty years, has also changed Bob. For more than half a lifetime he has proved to be the most steadfast of friends.

When we first met, he regarded himself as still an apprentice poet. He had been attending Poetry Society meetings, where Bill Hart-Smith was inscrutably neutral and Roland Robinson clashed with JM Couper, the poet and academic, who later returned to Scotland.

Gray's poetic interests were already strongly formed and changed mine: his insistence on the primacy of the image and his love for the work of Marianne Moore and William Carlos Williams. I had been aware of Hart-Smith's Williams-influenced poems – Williams with sweeteners. Williams taken straight had been too bare and unadorned. I looked at Williams again and found a classical plainness and freedom to say almost anything. He was a liberating influence on the poems I wrote over forty years called *Ross' Poems* and later *Spring Forest*.

I became friendly with Robert Adamson (I think) through Bob. Many years later Adamson told me he had found himself on the wrong side in the poetry wars. He was shocked by the belligerence of his allies; for example, he was told off for having a Les Murray volume on his desk.

⁂

In about 1971 David Malouf suggested we organise some poetry evenings at the Cell Block theatre at East Sydney Art School (the site of the old Darlinghurst gaol that once held Henry Lawson for drunkenness and not paying child support). We held two readings.

Concrete nymphs

At the first reading, Bruce Beaver arrived early with his wife Brenda. They hid in two large cardboard boxes set up for them at the back of the theatre. Bruce was suffering from agoraphobia, and could not read. Someone installing sound equipment had cut himself. Roland Robinson's large Alsatian dog Caesar lapped up the blood on the steps to the podium as the audience was drifting in.

Our plan at the end of the reading was for the Beavers to climb out after the audience had dispersed. But before they could make their escape, Caesar came bounding up and sniffing at their boxes.

Leonie Kramer (she was David's professor) held a post-reading party at her Vaucluse house. She had a slipper orchid on a small table in the middle of her drawing room. Roland (now minus Caesar) was pointing at his feet and bending down to take off a shoe. He was telling a group of younger people he had webbed toes. Leonie was anxiously hovering nearby, out of hearing range. When Roland changed his mind and straightened up, she moved on with a look of relief.

Michael Dransfield, already famous as a young drug poet, read at the second Cell Block evening. A few months earlier Michael had collared me and said, 'Man … you've got a lot of property'. He explained how as a Tax Office employee he had ordered up my tax return to see what property I owned. Michael had misunderstood the information on the return. I did not try to disabuse him.

The party after the second reading was at my Lindfield house. I was driving there with John Manifold and Dransfield. Michael may have been excited that John was a Manifold, from one of the great grazing families of Victoria's Western Districts. That he was also a Communist was probably of little interest. We were at the midpoint point of the Cahill Expressway, halfway between the Opera House and the Harbour Bridge. Michael asked John: 'Where's your property, man?'

John replied in his posh accent, a mixture of Geelong Grammar and Cambridge, 'I don't think poets should have property'. As Michael kept pressing him, John finally surrendered: 'Well, I've got a modest house in Brisbane. At Wynnum. That's all.'

Biographies of Dransfield and Manifold were later written by Rodney Hall. Although they were to share a common biographer, I suspect neither had read a word of the other's poetry.

'The sonnet is a house that's been destroyed', David Campbell remarked later that evening as we were talking at the post-reading party. I memorised and used his sentence in a poem. David had just come through a painful divorce and had to sell a grazing property, 'Palerang', with a historic stone homestead. Michael Dransfield joined us. He immediately asked: 'Where's your property, man?'

David knew and liked Michael's poetry and was not at all taken aback: 'Well, I've just sold my old property for a large profit and I've got a new place, quite small, a few hundred acres with a lemon orchard, and I must say I'm very happy.'

John Manifold was one of the Cell Block readers who stayed at the Lindfield house. A tall, handsome man, he had been in the British Army's Intelligence Corps and sprinkled his upper-class English with numerous 'dinkums' to remind the listener he was Australian. (I particularly like his sonnet 'Death of Stalin', which invokes the vastness of the Soviet Union and imagines Stalin as a fighter pilot, flying a crippled plane to a friendly aerodrome, 'his petrol spent', his victories blazing in the air. Wisely, Robert Gray resisted my suggestion to include this poem in *Australian Poetry Since 1788*. Such a blatantly *Sovok* piece would have done a disservice to Manifold.)

I took Manifold on an inspection tour of my antique roses in the former tennis court. I had also planted a young pine I could not identify. Manifold said, 'I've seen that growing in China'.

(I later saw forests of it in China. By that time I knew its name: *Cunninghamia sinensis*.)

I was aware that John, like many Communist writers, had travelled widely in Eastern Bloc countries. This led to a conversation about the Communist Party. I said, 'John, what about Hungary?' (referring to the 1956 Soviet suppression of the Hungarian uprising). Manifold answered, 'I was in Hungary six weeks after that. I can tell you they were counter-revolutionaries.'

Bruce Dawe and John Blight (or 'Jack' as he was usually called) were other Cell Block readers who stayed in the Lindfield house. Bruce was an exemplary guest. I later included in *Australian Poetry Since 1788* his story of watching students arrive when he was working as a young man on a university building site, and remarking to a fellow worker: 'What lucky bastards, I wish I was one of them'.

Jack Blight's life history was unusual for a poet: he was an accountant at a sawmill where he was a part owner, then a purchasing officer for a hospital. Jack became a regular at my house on visits to his Sydney publisher Beatrice Davis (or 'Beetriss' as he always called her). We would have breakfast, then catch the train: Jack to see 'Beetriss' and I to work at my small law firm.

Jack, who was pink-faced with silver hair, chubby but trim, was in awe of Beatrice, and also half in love, I suspect. Still beautiful in her sixties, Beatrice was dainty and small, and may not have been aware of her nickname 'the pocket Venus'. She was as tough as she was small. Her greeting for friends at parties in her double-decker cream house in the P & O style at Folly Point was to blow a kiss and say 'Consider yourself kissed'. I doubt whether Jack was given this flirtatious greeting when he called at her home office.

Douglas Stewart (at Angus & Robertson) had published Jack's two extraordinary volumes of sea-sonnets. There are only so many sea-sonnets a poet can write. In his late fifties Jack decided to make a change. He told me: 'You should end a line with words like "the" or "a" … That's what poets are doing now.' Rhyme and metre were old hat. Unlike David Campbell, Jack's attempt to renovate his style was not a success, as he began writing poems that were obscure and inconsequential.

Beatrice published Jack's later poetry. If she ever sat down and read these books with any degree of attention, she would have hated them. She relied on Douglas Stewart for advice. Stewart almost certainly did not like them, but must have championed Jack out of loyalty. Stewart would no doubt have been of the view that Jack had an outstanding body of work and it was not his role to tell Jack how to write. (Les Murray did not feel constrained in this way when, as poetry editor for Angus & Robertson, he rejected Stewart's final book of verse.)

'You and I should have a joint book launch', Jack suggested to me one day. 'I know a very good-looking young man. We could invite him along. Good-looking people at a book launch mean the newspapers will to take photographs. We might get into the social pages.'

Jack was a delightful house guest, scrupulously clean, and always keen to do the washing up. Perhaps because he had lived much of his life in Maryborough, a country town, with his wife and daughters, Jack liked visiting Kings Cross when he was in Sydney, vicariously enjoying its bohemian wickedness. He had some tangled story about the police at Kings Cross. It made no sense. 'You know', Jack said, 'There's all this skin flying around in the air up at the Cross. You can see it!' Every day, he explained, we are each losing thousands of skin cells and they are in the air – particularly at Kings Cross.

Jack was convinced he had been identified as a national security risk because he was a campaigning conservationist (like his friend Judith Wright, with whom he used to speak on the phone). There was a cylindrical junction box for telephone lines on the corner of his street. He once saw technicians crouching and adjusting wires and was sure this was to tap his phone.

The secret ballot or 'Australian ballot' originated in South Australia in 1856. Many older Australians took pride in concealing their political allegiances. As a child, when I asked my father how he voted, he used to say, 'Son, it's a secret ballot. I don't tell anyone who I vote for.'

This attitude may have affected our poets. Apart from a burst of political poetry in the 1890s, for much of the nineteenth century and the first half of the twentieth there was not much political poetry written in Australia. Coming to terms with the strange Australian landscape – so different from the cultivated landscape of their European ancestors – preoccupied our poets, as it did our painters, from Streeton and Roberts to Nolan and Arthur Boyd, and after them William Robinson. Reacting against this in the 1960s, Vincent Buckley railed against landscape poets and what he called 'wattle-gilding', and introduced religion and politics into his poetry.

'Emperor Mao and the Sparrows', written when I was eighteen, is the only political poem I have cared to preserve. Through poor judgment I let myself to be lured into writing political poems. I had a poetic exchange with Bruce Dawe about the Vietnam War, which was written up in the *Australian*. I was probably the only Australian poet supporting Australian involvement. Dawe was in the Royal Australian Air Force at the time and published anti-war poems; two of them, 'Homecoming' and 'Phantasms of Evening', have become classics. Dawe's poems were beyond politics; mine were tendentious.

When Jørn Utzon was famously sacked as architect of the Sydney Opera House in February 1966, I was reading about it on my way to work and had composed a poem by the time I got off at Wynyard station. It appeared a few days later in the *Sydney Morning Herald*:

Opera House Blues

'I'll build you a white roof, my daughter,
A flight of sails across the water.'

'Mother, oh mother, alack, alack;
The roof I see is not white but black.'

'Child, it's a sight that's hard to bear.
A hundred crows have settled there.'

It has since emerged that Utzon's dismissal was not just a simple dispute between a creative artist and philistine politician.

A year or so later the *Australian* published a ballad I wrote which suggested Harold Holt was a failure as the new Liberal Party prime minister. In this banal piece, which was similar in style to 'Opera House Blues', I had him addressing his mother as he was drowning in the ocean at Portsea. Frank Hardy congratulated me when he read it. I was having a drink later that year in an apartment at Woolloomooloo. The news came over the radio that Holt had just drowned at Cheviot Beach, near Portsea. My friends stared at me.

Concrete nymphs

I was uncomfortable when John Quinlem used to tell me I was the heir of the Sydney Vitalists, the tradition of Norman Lindsay and his short-lived magazine *Vision*. I enjoyed Lindsay's concrete nymphs, but there was something preposterous about them.

Adelaide Writers' Week, held once every two years, was once Australia's premier – perhaps only – literary event. I was invited for the first time in 1974. Towards the end of a session, a now forgotten poet came up onstage and told a large audience she had been married to a masturbator. For a moment she misunderstood the roars of laughter and had a look of gratified surprise. The poetry world was becoming factionalised. At an open-air reading I read a poem 'Five Days Late', about a girl worrying when she had a late period. There was a loud jeer. It felt like an assault.

My literary world was becoming a museum – not somewhere I could live. In other ways also, my life was heading towards a crisis. This unravelling began in Adelaide.

TEN YEARS

My marriage to Sally was happy – for me. Despite awkward silences between us I was optimistic. I believed in unreciprocated love – I imagined this was how men and women were. I was prepared to try what had failed before in my life, hoping we would succeed, if we were patient.

⁂

I met Sally McInerney at a party in the Carslaw Building at Sydney University soon after the building was completed in 1965. Slightly apprehensive that I would know no-one apart from Ted, the acquaintance who had invited me, I stepped out from the lift into a room of young strangers. A girl introduced herself as Liz Buttsworth and explained we had met at Paul Delprat's. She led me across the room to meet her friend – she said this girl and I shared an interest in literature. When the party ended, I drove Sally back to Women's College. She was eighteen years old; six years and six months younger than me. We talked briefly at the main door of the college. We were awkward and distant with each other. I did not make an arrangement to see her again. But I asked for her college telephone number as we said goodnight.

Ten years

I telephoned the number a week or so later. The girl who picked up the phone called out Sally's name. The Women's College is a large brick building of long verandas with tiled floors. There was a delay of several minutes. I heard footsteps coming back to the phone. Sally was not there. I gave the girl details of a party I was holding at Sutherland Street and I asked her to pass them on. I did not really expect Sally to come, or ever to see her again.

I was wearing a Thai silk tie with black and green stripes. Guests were arriving. I opened the door. Sally looked as surprised as I was, and she gave the tie a friendly tug. In the years ahead I looked back on this as a sign. Whenever I wavered, I remembered her hand touching my tie. It was why I married her.

It was like a happier rerun of an odd encounter in 1960, my first year as an articled clerk. I was intrigued by two elegant, olive-skinned young women, registration clerks. They were almost always together, filing documents in government offices, and wore tailored silk clothes, dark blue or dark violet. Late one afternoon I found myself alone with one of them, going down in a lift in barristers' chambers. I spoke to her. She reached out and touched my tie. I was dumbfounded. The lift door opened and we walked out, embarrassed, not looking at each other.

But I misunderstood the meaning of Sally's gesture. She had been given my telephone message. She was an eighteen-year-old country girl finding her way across the city at night. It took two bus trips to get to Paddington from Sydney University. Then she had to find her way to a steep street of 200 almost identical terrace houses. At last she came to the house number noted on her piece of paper. She knocked, a door opened, and there were lights and a person she recognised. As she touched my tie, she let out a small laugh of relief. I was someone welcoming her in from the dark.

We began seeing each other several times each week. We sat chatting with Salvatore Zofrea on the front veranda of his parents' house at Seaforth. He made us strong black coffee. In a small back shed he was preparing his 'Drunken Bride' exhibition. We called on Paul Delprat in his house and studio of glass and sandstock brick columns near Balmoral beach. We went to dinner parties given by John Buttsworth, Liz's brother, in his large old house in Balmain, nicknamed the 'Balmain Embassy', with its large untidy garden. John shared the house with friends – they were the 'ambassadors' – and in winter there were fires in an old fireplace and we played ridiculous word games.

Sally talked about her childhood: growing up on a farm in the central west. At first there was just a tent, then a house of three rooms, no kitchen or bathroom, and no running water or electricity. She used to climb a silver poplar to watch for her mother's return from toilet trips among the bushes. She lay in bed at night listening to her mother move about the house. Until she was ten or twelve years old she had not seen herself in a mirror.

We were walking along a street. I had a camera and suggested we stop so I could take her photograph. Each time as I brought her into focus, she moved away. Eventually she stopped, half-hiding in a climbing fig with fleshy fruit and leaves. In the photograph she is camouflaged by the leaves and smiling.

Sally and I had been seeing each other for some months when we set out after work from the Domain parking station in my grey VW. We had packed a few clothes and my sleeping bag for a weekend at her parents' farm.

It was the first of many 4-hour journeys I came to dread and love with a kind of heartburn: the wastelands beside the Windsor road, the sign 'Adult Dolls $34' on the veranda of a rundown fibro house on a large bare block, the giant rearing fibreglass horse outside a hotel, the airport at Richmond (lit up at night with lines of blue lights for landing planes), the ascent up Kurrajong Hill in second gear, the relief when we reached the plateau of apple orchards and forests. The views across the uninhabited valleys of the Blue Mountains, the winding descent down the Great Dividing Range; the sulphur smell of coal fires from miners' houses as we passed through cold Lithgow; then the power station at Wallerawang, lit up at night and emitting steam, like Blake's satanic mills; the stop at the midpoint of the journey for coffee dissolved in scalding milk at Mt Lambie's isolated hilltop service station; then Bathurst (populous and genteel), Blayney (railway lines and meat works), Carcoar (a quaint nineteenth century jewel), red-brick Mandurama (tenuously prosperous), Lyndhurst (a scattering of dilapidated shacks) and finally Cowra.

One morning we drove along a byway out of Bathurst, curious where it might take us, and passed a white nineteenth century cottage set back among a multi-coloured army of velvety hollyhocks. Just outside Bathurst we used to pass a grand, secluded house in a valley, from where Sally's ancestress eloped during Queen Victoria's reign. Driving back from Cowra and approaching Lithgow one afternoon we noticed a large drift of snow some distance from the road, the first ever sighting of snow for both of us. 'Let's stop', she said. We would have had to walk across a couple of paddocks and I kept on driving.

Our first journey had an expectation not yet dulled by later repetitions. We observed the ritual coffee stop at Mt Lambie, stepping into the cold night air from the car, tramping across the forecourt and through a swing door into the heated air of the dining area. As we drove into Cowra a light rain was falling. The windscreen wipers were working rapidly, and the headlights were lighting up the black mirror of the road and a landscape of incandescent green grass. I have an image of an older man in a yellow raincoat at the edge of the town, waving at the traffic, instructing us where to go. I could not understand why he was there – a momentary phantom as we drove on.

I was feeling unreal and elated. Cowra was behind us, we were across the Lachlan River, and had turned off the highway onto the Boorowa road. Our destination was close, but still another 25 kilometres. We drove down a row of tall eucalypts, each commemorating a local soldier, then past the obscure bulk of a feed mill looming in the night, and paddock after paddock, and patches of scrub, and a tiny hamlet, Morongla, then more paddocks and trees and fences. My foot left the accelerator as we came to the final turn-off from tar onto a road of red clay, ruts glistening from rain, and banked-up soil on both sides; phalaris grass, seed heads bending with drops of water. We were driving through optical illusions, the two headlight beams and shadows in constant motion. I was wondering how I would locate this turn-off if I drove up here alone. There was a small bush school on the left just beyond the turn-off, Sally told me. If I saw that, I would know I had gone too far.

It was around midnight. The gate to 'Spring Forest' may have been open. I was about to learn about farm gates and their etiquette – shut gates must be re-shut, open gates stay open. The gates were of metal piping and wire, and closed with a wire loop that snugged onto a large iron hook on the gatepost. When a gate sagged with age, some loops became necklaces of wire. As we drove up the slope of compacted clay and small stones to the farm house hidden behind silver poplars, blank headlights of derelict vehicles, driven by Sally's father until they were beyond repair, stared back. A black and yellow dog, Joe, was barking and running about on the veranda, where Ross, Sally's father slept.

As we parked near an athel tree he came out carrying a hurricane lantern. Ross McInerney was a tall, handsome man with a pencil moustache, who spoke in a muffled voice. Sally's mother, Olive Cotton, seven years older than Ross, was anxiously offering hot drinks.

My first impression, beyond a screen of silver poplars, was the wide front veranda with a curved galvanised iron roof running the full width of the weatherboard house's two rooms, cane chairs and farm implements scattered along the veranda, and the narrow bed where Ross slept.

I had been warned there was no running water, electricity, sewerage, bathroom or kitchen, and no outside toilet, though there was a telephone. Washing up was done in the main room in a plastic dish with hot water boiled in a kettle that hung over the fire in the brick fireplace. This room was lit by a pressure lamp and had a small Lance Solomon harbour scene in oils on one of the cream weatherboard walls – acquired, I assumed, by Olive when she shared a photographic studio in the late 1930s with her first husband Max Dupain. The surface craquelure of the painting had become encrusted with smoke from the fire. The room had a warm, lived-in feel, with a bookcase and books about birds – Ross was a keen bird watcher – a settee, a small table and a car seat from an old Morris with a sheepskin draped over it – Ross's favourite armchair.

A doorway from the main room opened into the second room, Olive's bedroom (and also Sally's when she stayed), which visitors rarely entered. Olive's black upright piano with elaborately carved decorations stood by the door in this room and was never played. A kerosene refrigerator glowed in a friendly way through the night on a small back veranda, which led to an added-on galvanised iron room for Peter, Sally's brother.

Balanced on his haunches, Ross liked to squat on the edge of the front veranda in riding boots, drawing on his pipe and staring into the night. A white Cherokee rose climbed against the old brick chimney. It was a house a poet could love and a housewife hate.

'Spring Forest' was not much more than 500 acres (200 ha), some paddocks and a lot of rocky, bushy scrub. Ross's choicest land was a lush paddock across the public road from the house, next to a creek that had permanent water. He ran a few retired horses on it. The land was there for the horses, not people. Olive, unlike Ross, rarely expressed her opinion. When she expressed warmth, it was through placatory gestures such as 'Rossie ... a cup of tea?'

I slept on the settee. Next morning, Joe started barking, surprised by a man-monster as I stood up in my sleeping bag. We drove into Cowra and walked down a long echoing corridor of a 1920s building, deserted on a Saturday morning. We were hit by the smell of chemicals as we opened the door into Olive's small studio. I noticed a few photographs from earlier decades, such as 'Tea cup ballet', but Olive was then unknown as an 'art' photographer. I was depressed by the display of weddings and children – girls with ribbons in their hair, bright-eyed toddlers – so much effort for such meagre rewards.

Sally was completing a liberal arts course. During term, we ate with friends at the Sunah Restaurant and the Athenian and Veneziana, and I drove Sally back to the Women's College. As we climbed up the steps to the front veranda we were greeted by a neutered tabby cat, a large handsome creature with a white bib. He had a trick: he would throw his front paws around your neck when you picked him up.

A rumour went around the college that stray cats were to be rounded up. One night we bundled this tabby into my grey VW, and drove him back to the Sutherland Street house. I confined him for a couple of days, prowling from room to room, and christened him with the absurd name 'The Sun King'.

During university vacations, Sally stayed with her parents. Her letters were written in a small, distinctive, elegant script and full of incidents and natural feeling. I felt almost embarrassed by how they usually began: 'Dearest Geoff ...' I wished there was the same spontaneous affection when we were together. There was an awkwardness between us. I was the driver who would not stop for the snow.

※

I was at that time a non-equity partner in an old established firm. The work for my main client, a Catholic building society, was conveyancing, and although this was repetitive, I enjoyed it. I had at last escaped motor vehicle insurance litigation. My senior partner, the owner of the firm, known by his initials 'KD', was a benign, silver-haired man, whose spacious office was decorated with large sepia photographs of the Roman forum and Hadrian's palace circa 1900.

KD was executor of the will of an elderly estate agent and took out probate when she died. Although Mrs England was a Protestant, her beneficiaries were the Little Sisters of the Poor and other Catholic charities. To KD's surprise, an old tramp called Edward Edwards, together with a tenant of a house she had owned, challenged our grant of probate. They were executors of a later will. However, we believed she lacked testamentary capacity by the time that will was made. We produced earlier wills, made over many years, consistent with our will. I conducted the case for KD. We lost. The later will was upheld.

When I had been seeing Sally for a few months, KD took on one of his partners as an equity partner. The new equity partner would eventually own the firm and did not want me. KD told me the news and said it would not have been his choice. I did not express disappointment. I knew I was not a good long-term fit. KD had been a great benefactor to me. I had little conveyancing experience when he took me on and gave me the firm's largest client, a Catholic building society.

I told KD I wanted to write a novel about Mrs England and he agreed to my taking the file. He was chuffed several years later when I gave him a copy of *A Spring Day in Autumn*, published by Thomas Nelson. My not very good novel makes it clear the court's decision was right. The printed dedication page reads 'For K.D.M.' His full name was Keith Dennis Manion.

Within a week of leaving KD's firm, I found myself back with my former employer Charlie Willcox and doing insurance work again. Mr Willcox had been contacted for a reference when I applied for some jobs. He promptly telephoned me. His practice was not glamorous or innovative, but his clients were prosperous and dependable, like him. After a trial I was to become his partner.

Mr Willcox was short and wore leg braces – perhaps the result of childhood polio. An old-style solicitor, frugal and tough-minded, he reminded me of my sister. He was someone I could work with. He sat, surrounded by several hundred active files in manilla folders, in a large dimly lit room. His day was made up of regular events. Early each morning he went through every file, setting aside those where action was needed, and tossing the other files to a girl who had the job of replacing them on a table, in a pile with no order, several tiers high. When the files cascaded onto the floor, he would announce, 'Lass, you haven't built the foundations right'. While impaling yesterday's letters on the double prong which held the correspondence together, he sometimes stabbed his finger. Waving his wounded hand about, he would use his uninjured hand to press the button on the intercom for the switchboard girl: 'Lass, get the Dettol please'. During the day as I walked past his office and he sat at his battered antique desk, I would hear him happily singing a tuneless song with the words 'Kadink, kadink, kadink'. He always had a simple lunch, reading a novel at his desk; he got through two novels a week, 'lending library books, nothing literary' he once explained, apologetically.

He was devoted to his wife Mary, a former teacher, a fine looking woman, taller than Charlie. They had honeymooned on Turtle Island, Fiji. When their wedding anniversary approached his secretary had to find a gift with a turtle theme, such as a turtle brooch. After twenty years of marriage, finding new turtle gifts was not becoming any easier.

Mr Willcox was tolerant with his young adult children. If I phoned his home I might hear a good natured call: 'Hey old baldy, they want you on the phone'. But his abrupt ways intimidated younger staff. He had an army of white and green intercom handsets – the Gecophone Junior – that barked like geese around the office. Young clerks almost fell off their chairs when he called them on their Gecophone. When I moved back with Charlie I noticed the legs of my predecessor's chair had worn two rips in the office carpet.

One morning Charlie called on my Gecophone. He wanted to know what was happening in a particular matter. I opened the file and told him. 'Are you checking in the file itself?' he asked. I realised he could not understand how I had been able to get the file so easily. 'Yes, Mr Willcox. I'm looking at the file. I keep them in alphabetical order.'

I was having lunch in my office with my squash partner Stephen Wilson. We sometimes shared a slice of pie my father had baked – 'citronella pie' was Stephen's name for it. Each slice was a dense, highly spiced wedge of dates and dried fruit with a crust of sugary pastry like hardened concrete. We were talking. With an apology, Mr Willcox popped his head in the door to ask about a matter. I introduced them: Stephen, willowy and artistic, and Mr Willcox, short, brusque and Dickensian. After Charlie left the room, there was a look of gullible astonishment on Stephen's face.

So I invented a suitable story: 'Mr Willcox keeps a blue cattle dog under his desk. The dog is shooed from his office when he sees clients.'

Mr Willcox's stringent honesty and economical ways were reassuring. One of his favourite sayings was 'Little fish are sweet', when we collected a mere $7 on a discharge of mortgage. I liked the fact that he wrote up his own trust account, which was audited every month by Mr Brown, a chartered accountant and friend of Charlie's. By keeping an eye on the movement of funds through the trust account, Charlie had an overview of every matter. I followed this practice myself, when he retired. Mr Brown, a gentle and sceptical man, continued with the monthly audit.

As well as his insurance companies (one of them the Hartford of which the American poet Wallace Stevens had been a vice president), Charlie acted for Australia's leading garage door manufacturer, largest poultry grower, and many families and small businesses. I imagined this would be my firm for life and was thrilled by my obscure Wallace Stevens link. I also hoped to marry Sally.

The *Sydney Morning Herald* published her poem 'Cattle Incident', about a herd of wild cattle her mother had encountered as a child on holidays at Pretty Beach. The poem describes:

> Nights of driftwood fires,
> sparks crackling like salty stars,
> and the constant sound of the cattle, distant, invisible,
> among the shadows of the trees, camouflaged
> against grey lichened boulders, dappled trees…

I was happy to spend the rest of my life with the person who wrote this poem.

Sally had moved into the Sutherland Street house and was majoring in English literature. She talked about one of her tutors; she used to have coffee with him. David Malouf had recently come back from England, where he had taught in secondary schools. When Sally arranged for us to meet, we found we had a troublesome friend in common – John Quinlem.

John and Lyssa Hagan were ash blond and shared their blondness with their Samoyed dog. Frank Zappa's *Freak Out*, which I did not like at the time, was a favourite album they played at dinner parties. One night Sally and I had to park away from their house in Kirribilli. We took a shortcut across Anderson Park. Men were pacing backwards and forwards among the trees, snapping their fingers, and going in and out of a public toilet. We began walking quickly, looking straight ahead. The Hagans later told us how a man, covered in blood, having been bashed up in the park, came knocking on their door a few days earlier. This story became 'On the Beat' in *Nero's Poems* when I had Nero write about his bisexuality.

In the winter of 1968 Sally and I decided to drive to Broken Hill. We wanted a congenial relief driver and asked a friend – Ross Grainger, a sailmaker with wild sandy hair like that of his great uncle, the composer Percy Grainger – to come with us. On our first night we slept in sleeping bags halfway up Mount Arthur just outside Wellington, NSW. At sunrise we boiled a billy and looked out across the mists rising from the plain. It was cold. We gave up our Broken Hill plan and decided to go north for the warmth. A couple of days later we got to Townsville. We found a row of small tourist shacks by the ocean and stayed overnight. I bought a postcard of a chimpanzee in an artist's smock, with palette and brush, painting a canvas. I wrote a note in a disguised handwriting on the back:

LEEWARD

Dear Mr Delprat

You may not remember me, but I remember you. I was one of the ladies you sketched at David Jones earlier this year. I live in Townsville and would be thrilled if you could come up here and paint my portrait. Would $850 be a suitable fee? I would of course reimburse all expenses. I do think the chimpanzee in the photograph is so cute, don't you?

Yours sincerely, Fiona Bloomfield

I supplied a Townsville address and mailed the postcard with a Townsville post mark to Paul, who was under the impression we were in Broken Hill.

(Earlier in the year Paul had been an artist in residence at the David Jones department store. Seated beside a giant replica of Michelangelo's 'David' and wearing an artist's smock Monsieur Delprat, as he was styled, did quick sketches of the female shoppers for Lancôme cosmetics. A retired colonel-type with white moustache walked past and said to his wife, 'We used to see fellows like him in Cairo'. Paul laughed and the man harrumphed, 'Oh, he speaks English'.)

We drove further north, past hillsides of burning sugar cane, through a fragrant, smoky dusk. In Cairns we stayed at a large, late nineteenth century hotel on the esplanade, one of those tropical hotels with wide verandas and rooms with high ceilings and white mosquito nets draped over the double bed like the ghost of Miss Havisham.

About 30 kilometres south of Cooktown we passed Kalkajaka (Black Mountain, or 'Death Mountain'), composed of large rectangular blocks of black granite piled one above the other. In the afternoon we got to Cooktown. It was a ghost of the town my German grandfather visited in 1891 – just a few old men haunting the hotel bar. I was worried Paul would be hatching plans for spending his $850, while Shelley Rose would be telling him not to be a fool. We began our drive back to Sydney that afternoon, the three of us taking turns at the steering wheel, thirty hours without a stop except for food and petrol.

❦

I did not realise the countdown for our marriage began when the phone rang in the Sutherland Street house and I heard that my father had died. A logical sequence of events had begun. My father had signed a contract for the sale of the McMahons Point houses. When the sale completed later in the year the houses would be sold and new houses bought. I decided to disband Sutherland Street.

I drove my mother and Diana to Paddington to meet the Sun King. He embraced my mother and she screamed and dropped him. A few days later I took him to Gordon, a subdued passenger in my car.

My sister agreed Les Murray and his family (just back from Europe) could stay in the red-roofed cottage until the sale was completed. Diana, my mother and I began weekly visits to the houses. Diana took a colour photograph of Iris in a derelict hallway wearing a prim straw hat and spotted dress. I rescued the broken-down chaise longue I had insisted my father buy when I was a child. We made a bonfire in the garden of old furnishings, rotted wicker chairs and cheap gloomy nineteenth century oil paintings on cardboard that had hung in the hall of 'Leddicott'.

The purchaser's solicitor telephoned: the iron dolphins from Ben Boyd's yacht had just been stolen from Number 51. We completed the sale next day and twenty-four hours later bulldozers moved in and the houses were demolished. The grand staircase of Fifty-three was carted away in one piece on a truck.

For several years the land was an excavation site. One afternoon I looked through a gap in the fence. I saw a deep rectangular pit with patches of water at the bottom and plumes of pampas grass – a plant that had never grown there. That night I dreamt an apartment tower had been built on the site, and strangers were sitting under beach umbrellas around a swimming pool filled with blood.

To avoid double death duty if my mother's fragile health failed, my father made Diana and me the beneficiaries under his will, with a cash legacy to our mother. There was a family understanding that my sister and I were to hold assets purchased out of estate monies for Iris. We decided on shared ownership and began looking for a large house suitable for dual occupancy.

We looked at several large houses. One of them was owned by a client of Stephen Wilson's, an old builder, 'Big Phil' as Stephen called him. At Stephen's suggestion, my mother, Diana and I called on Big Phil in his house in the bushy outskirts of Hornsby, a long way from anywhere. Phil had built himself a two-storey cream-painted extravaganza of fibro-cement, with many rooms and long verandas. It was now too big. It had probably always been too big – a typical builder's own house folly. He may have noticed me looking doubtfully at masses of Crofton weed infesting his land. 'Those plants are a fire-break', he told us. 'If a bushfire came roaring up the valley, they'd stop it in its tracks.'

He soon realised we were not buyers and decided to entertain us. 'I love Fiji', he told us. 'Their national drink is kava, you know. They drink kava until the early hours of the morning – big bowls of it. When I go there, they get me to dance with them – women and men all together with no clothes on, pouring kava all over themselves.'

When my mother and sister failed to express shock, he began talking about a cousin, 'quite a girl' or some similar description. Some person they knew 'was bitten on the bottom by a brown snake. So she pulls his pants down, takes a big bite out of his bottom and spits out the poison.'

Diana and my mother were quietly happy when I drove them home. It had been an interesting afternoon. Stephen laughed incredulously when I told him about our visit. I was met with a similar defensiveness years later when a partnership he recommended did not work out.

We eventually found a house at Lindfield. It had a modern 1950s back flat where my mother and sister went to live, and Sally and I moved into the original house, built in 1907 – the date on a garden tap. It had high ornate ceilings, and a hall with arches and the remains of gaslight fittings. Sally and I held a large party. 'We were worried a group of Beatniks had moved in', our neighbours told us later.

Two people warned me against marrying Sally. After my father's death I had driven up to the Gordon house with her. My mother and I were standing outside in the street and she was twisting her hands together (as I sometimes do now): 'She's too beautiful, like a madonna in a painting'.

The other warning came from Sally. We were shopping in the city. Somehow we lost each other, going off in different directions. About fifteen minutes later we came face to face outside a department store. I was pleased at our reunion. She may have seen our short separation as an omen: 'Are you sure we should stay together? I may be cruel to you.' I was obstinately deaf to what she was saying. I tried to be reassuring. I told her this was a risk I was happy to take.

Shortly after moving into the Lindfield house we went down onto the tennis court, each with a racquet. I patted a ball to her. I was hoping to teach Sally how to play. With a look of distaste, she drove the ball into the back fence and dropped her racket. A few months later, I sent off a lengthy order to an Adelaide rose nursery. The court was an eyesore of yellow clay. My plan was to transform it into a garden of antique and species roses.

Liz Buttsworth, who had introduced us, had a gentle Methodist clergyman as a father. Charl, as his wife called him, lived in a house high up on Bilgola point. Sitting in his living room he used to scan the beach through binoculars and phone the surf life saving club if he spotted a swimmer in trouble. We called on him to discuss wedding arrangements.

Sally began sewing a wedding dress out of a length of white cotton, a garment that began to look like a toga. I became concerned and we found a short white Mexican dress with appliqué flowers. It was a light-hearted parody of a wedding dress. But I sensed even this was a uniform I was imposing on her.

I thought briefly about getting Sally a wedding ring. I had a horror of something metallic around my finger but if I was without a wedding ring, I could not expect her to wear one. I had noticed an antique jeweller, Maurice Mandelberg in the Imperial Arcade. His advertisements stated 'Prices are not astronomical and the quality is the finest'. He worked with two delicate and talkative women in his small shop – his mother and sister. He showed me a nineteenth century half-hoop of Kashmiri sapphires (now rarely found outside museums). There was no exchange of rings at the wedding but Sally wore this ring when we were married.

We ordered a wedding cake from the Bar Roma, the café near Central Station where we had coffee and pastries most Saturday mornings, after our trips to the city markets and to Ashwoods' long, narrow second-hand book and record shop.

A few days before we were due to be married Sally told me her name was not Sally – it was Seirian. If Seirian was the name on the marriage certificate, her doppelgänger Seirian would be marrying, and not her. It was a desperate last-minute message. I was nonplussed.

On the day my mother turned seventy-three and Sally's mother turned fifty-eight, we were married by Charl Buttsworth in the Lindfield house, late in the afternoon. I was in a dark lounge suit and Seirian had become Sally again, and wore the white Mexican dress for the first and last time – after that it became a tainted garment. We did the catering ourselves. Eighty or so guests overflowed from our main living room, all our family members, aunts and uncles, Stephen Wilson as best man, my senior partner Charlie Willcox and his wife Mary, Paul Delprat, Charles and Barbara Blackman, and the painter John Firth-Smith, who volunteered to walk among the guests taking photographs. Several guests quietly remarked to each other that this was a marriage that was not going to last.

Les Murray later wrote a seven-part poem for us: 'Toward the Imminent Days':

> ... And I think of your wedding, I make it shine among trees ...
> ... an incredibly high
> hymeneal piping makes my wineglass sing –
> ... recalling your abundant house, the dancing,
> your shovelled cake rich as the history of Calabria.

The singing wine glass may have been a reference to a dinner party where Les saw Adrian Heber do his imitation of a glass harmonica with a wineglass. The poem's last line is:

> For your wedding, I wish you the frequent image of farms.

Within a couple of years of the marriage, farms became a frequent image in my poetry. Dating back to my schoolboy love affair with Virgil's *Georgics* I had an incoherent plan to write pastoral poems. Hearing Ross McInerney's observations and stories, I decided to write poems through his voice. These turned out to be very different from monologues I had written in the voices of historical figures. I had to keep my language plain. The words appearing on the page were disconcerting – more laconic than I had imagined. But this new, dry voice was liberating. 'Unpoetical' subjects could be made into poetry.

I saved up my first dozen typed poems in Ross's voice for a couple of months before I gave them to him (through Sally). I felt they were an intrusion into his life. I half expected a negative response. But he seemed happy (Sally told me) to have become my muse.

In 1978 when I published *Ross' Poems*, by then seventy-five poems, Sally and I were divorced. The cover illustration was an etching by Sally: 'Peter's Land'. Photographs of people from Ross's life were interspersed through the text – Mr Long seated at a camp fire, hand resting on a rifle, and later as an older man squatting and holding up a cycad by the round ball of its root, like a large pineapple. I did not anticipate then I would be writing poems through Ross's voice until his death in 2010, adding, deleting and revising.

Ten years

There were more than 100 poems when the final selection, now named *Spring Forest*, was published in 2014. Ross continued to see batches of these poems not long after they were written. Not all the stories in the poems were his. He never commented except to say they 'bring back old times'. As a teller of stories himself, I believe he appreciated that a poem could be 'true' although not literally true. He never pointed out inaccuracies.

The first *Spring Forest* poem has a line: 'And I chose the name "Spring Forest".' In the mid-1990s Ross and I were interviewed at 'Spring Forest' for a *Poetica* radio program. To my surprise Ross told the ABC's Mike Ladd that he had always been embarrassed by the name of his property. 'Spring Forest' was the name chosen by the previous owner, a schoolmaster called Hickey. I am relieved I did not know this. Ross cared about loss of biodiversity as much as he cared about people. The vanishing 'Spring Forest' of the poems became a metaphor for that loss.

Ross was a practical conservationist. He had 'Spring Forest' declared a wildlife reserve. At night he went out shooting the feral cats that decimated wildlife. He had killed hundreds of them, he said. I started a poem about this catalogue of dead cats and realised real facts did not always translate into poems.

A couple of weeks before his death I visited Ross at 'Weeroona' the hospice in Cowra where he was ill with lung cancer. It took a while for our conversation to get started. Ross had become quite animated by the time his next-door neighbour, a farmer, arrived. 'I want to introduce you to Geoff', he told his visitor. Referring to his daughter, he said: 'When Sally was at university, she rang up one day and said is it all right if I bring up a friend next week end. I thought it would be another girl friend, but it was Geoff. I was really surprised. (Laughter.) He and David Campbell were my favourite Australian poets.'

This was an astonishing piece of information – he had read

my poetry before we met. This was why he had been so tolerant about the *Spring Forest* poems.

After our wedding, Sally and I drove north for a second time in the grey VW beetle to escape the Sydney winter. In Brisbane we stayed with David Malouf at his parents' house in Hamilton, a two-storey brick house looking out over the Brisbane River, lyrically recalled in his poem 'An Ordinary Evening at Hamilton'.

After Brisbane we drove further north. It was about three in the morning, I was asleep in the front seat of the car and Sally was driving. We were passing through desolate country, yellow clay on either side of the road. I woke up just as a gigantic bird rose up in front of the car and seemed to fly away – an emu. This bird became the title of my second anthology of Australian comic verse, *The Flight of the Emu*.

On our drive back to Sydney we stayed overnight with Judith Wright at 'Calanthe' on Mount Tamborine. Her house sat on an acre, young macrozamias with cones like pineapples growing next to the front veranda, and a large field of jonquils in her back garden.

Judith took us on a tour of the plateau. Speaking in the parade-ground voice of the partly deaf she pointed to the erect and blackened trunks of macrozamias scattered along an escarpment, recording scorch marks from ancient fires. They could be thousands of years old, she said. (I suspect she was showing us the group of plants that inspired her poem 'The Cycads'.) She led us into the rainforest and identified strangler figs and giant stinging trees. A strange booming call echoed through the forest, like a man shouting through his hands from far away. The wompoo fruit dove, Judith explained in her voice that was also like a shout.

Judith told us at dinner that night that she had decided to have no more children after the birth of her daughter Meredith. She felt it was wrong to bring children into a world that had the atom bomb.

It was a sobering thought to accompany us as we drove away next morning. Judith's pessimism was different from James McAuley's, which differed again from Slessor's – but all three suffered from an almost disabling pessimism.

After not much longer than a week in Queensland, Sally and I were back in Sydney, in a marriage only one of us wanted. We had a large group of friends. We rarely quarrelled. We shared many things: when I was looking for material for *Comic Australian Verse* we sat together at night in the State Library; she also photographed many of the paintings for *Australian Primitive Painters*, the book I wrote with Charles Blackman.

Sally painted small, playful designs on old bits of furniture. At first I did not realise she was a gifted draftsman. She began making etchings. Bruce Beaver wrote a poem for her, 'Three Etchings by Sally McInerney', which ends: 'Vista of Mt Morris ... the distance softened hill/ visionary available./ There your spirit found its home,/ reachable, unreachable.'

There was a girl I had gone out with a couple of times, not long before I met Sally. I witnessed her passport application. She returned to Australia a few months after I married Sally, and sent a Christmas card. She may not have been unreachable. I realised I had made a mistake.

Our friends had graduated from the large anonymous after-the-Pub parties of our early twenties. As soon as we moved into the Lindfield house, Sally and I began holding dinner parties. One of our frequent guests was Adrian Heber. Adrian was in the tradition of Baron Münchhausen, composing his fantasies like musical compositions. Some imaginary events occurred to him and he constructed a narrative to tell to his friends. Or some real events were embroidered and became so bizarre he could have had little intention to deceive. He might occasionally ask for small amounts of money. But he did not invent elaborate explanations to obtain a loan.

I got to know Adrian through the Push. In the early days of our friendship I gave him a lift after a night at the pub. He was living in an upstairs flat in Louisa Road, Balmain and invited me in for a drink. When he unlocked the door, the room was bare even by Push standards: a bed, a table and one chair. That was all: no books, just bare walls and floorboards and a few implements to eat and drink with. Adrian possibly offered me the chair and sat on the bed and we drank some Scotch. The empty room reverberated as we spoke. I did not stay long.

When Sally and I married, Adrian and the painter Salvatore Zofrea were among the guests. Afterwards accounts drifted back about 'what an objectionable person that Salvatore Zofrea is'. I discovered Adrian had introduced himself to the guests as Salvatore (whom he did not know and while Salvatore was in the room) and told them what a marvellous artist he was. He carried this impersonation off with my secretary (who was Italian). Salvatore was born in Calabria, and Adrian sang 'Il Calabrese' along with Pina, although he was not a student of Italian, as far as I am aware.

Mostly he was harmless. In about 1970 he said to me 'I went to a marvellous party at Meredith Burgmann's last weekend. I enjoyed myself so much, I tried to set the house on fire.' I said in a reproving tone of voice, 'Adrian, my mother owns that house'.

In appearance Adrian was not unlike the British actor

Kenneth More: wholesome and slightly plump, usually wearing a tweed sports coat and tweed cap. Robert Gray remembers him holding his cap and wringing it, while he talked, as though it was a wet swimming costume.

Adrian sometimes used me as a referee for jobs. I was uneasy during these phone calls. One was from an Anglican boys' school asking if he was a suitable night watchman. I was able to say he had worked for some years as a security guard. That seemed to satisfy the school bursar and much to my relief he hung up. Adrian had also worked in a brewery and at the Glebe morgue. For many years he was a proofreader with the Government Printing Office.

One day he phoned me when he was the voice on the public address system at Grace Bros department store on Broadway. In the middle of our conversation he put down the phone. I heard his voice echoing back from several loudspeakers: 'Little Margaret has lost her mother. She is here at the desk on the ground floor. Will little Margaret's mother please come and get her. She is waiting for you.' If Adrian is to be believed, on his last day as the voice of Grace Bros, ten minutes before the store was due to close, he announced over the public address system: 'Ladies and gentlemen, there is absolutely no need to panic. A lion has escaped in the store. There is no need to panic. Yes, a lion has escaped in the store. Please proceed through the doors onto the street in an orderly manner. A lion has escaped in the store...'

In retrospect Adrian's long history of employment seems remarkable. His younger clone would now be unemployable.

A group of us agreed to meet for dinner at Chez Napoleon, a restaurant in Oxford Street. We had to wait outside in a queue. When we sat down and the order was being taken, Adrian announced he was going to eat two meals as he had two jobs. The waiter was nonplussed when Adrian ordered two entrées that were to be served at the same time, followed by two main courses also to be served at the same time. Eventually the waiter understood. When his two entrées arrived, Adrian folded his linen napkin up under his chin like a bib and tucked in. He started off in the same way when his two main courses arrived, but about halfway through his second main course he asked could anyone help him out. I accepted.

When the waiter came to our table to get the order for dessert, Adrian shook his head: 'No dessert for me. I'm on a diet.'

Adrian paid for his four courses and contributed generously to the tip. As we left the restaurant he turned to us with a happy smile: 'I think they like me there.'

He claimed to be an old boy of St Peter's College Adelaide, an exclusive Anglican school. One of his carefully memorised set pieces was 'the Defenestration of St Peter's'. All I can remember is the portentous title, borrowed from 'the Defenestration of Prague' in 1618. I sometimes invited a friend who was an actual St Peter's old boy to dinner parties when I invited Adrian. I'd meanly say to Adrian, 'You remember Colin, he's also an old boy of St Peter's.'

I often played a recording of Mozart's adagio and rondo for glass harmonica at dinner parties. To show how a glass harmonica was played, Adrian was in the habit of running his finger along the edge of his wine glass to make it sing.

Adrian claimed to be related to Bishop Heber, author of the hymn 'From Greenland's icy mountains…' At one of these singing wine glass dinners, Adrian announced to the seated guests: 'Theology is the queen of the sciences.' Me: 'What sort of queen, Adrian?'

My remark was quite unfair. Adrian was rarely seen with a girlfriend, but was attracted to women – *too attracted* when he lost control of himself. A leering, sideways look as he narrowed his eyes was unnerving for women. Even his male friends sometimes found him unnerving. At a large evening party at my Lindfield house, I stepped into the small front sunroom. Adrian was sitting by himself on a couch, rocking back and forth with silent laughter. For almost ten minutes I stood watching him with alarm. Should I get a doctor? He suddenly stopped, his face relaxed, and he stood up, saying, 'Ah that's better'.

Adrian had many dinner party stories, some of them oft repeated. Sometimes I would start telling one of Adrian's stories for him, and when I had a detail wrong he quickly corrected me and continued the story himself. I do not think I ever met the mysterious Hill, who was his accomplice in many of these stories, though I knew Hill's two sisters. I always imagined Hill as solidly built like Adrian. Perhaps he was quite different. I remember one of Adrian's dinner table stories almost verbatim:

> Hill and I were invited to a retreat in a Catholic monastery. You know what these retreats are like – enormous quantities of food. [Adrian laughs gently and leers around the table at the prospect of all this food.] The monks eat like sparrows when they're by themselves, and they really put on a feast when they've guests, and it gives them a good excuse to eat a lot as well.
>
> So Hill and I had just completed this enormous lunch and decided to go for a stroll. To recover from the meal. We were walking along a railway line. And it occurred to us to test an old saying. If you put your ear to the line, you can hear a train coming from a long way off. So Hill and I did just that. We both bent over and put an ear to the line. And we did hear a train. In fact it was right on top of us! We were almost killed! [Adrian throws his head back open-mouthed, then wipes the sweat off his forehead. He sweated a lot.]

We jumped back and rolled down the embankment. When we got to the bottom, we were all covered in grass. We had to pick ourselves up and get rid of all the grass.

Now after an experience like that, what do you feel like? [He sits up straight with a serious, questioning look.] A cup of tea. *And a cup of tea there was!* [A triumphant smile at all the dinner guests]

Adrian once held a party for forty or so people at the Mosman house where he was staying with a friend. A woman in her late twenties innocently told us she and Adrian had been at school together – *at Lithgow State High School!* We were all childishly delighted that Adrian had been found out. How could he have made such a blunder, inviting an old school friend? We did not let on to Adrian that we knew. I think we underestimated him. He did not care if we knew he was not a St Peter's old boy. His stories were just entertainments.

Thirty years later I saw Adrian from a car window. He did not see me, as I pointed him out to my daughter-in-law Manami. Hunched over and dour, he had on his standard tweed sports coat, and was walking along Ross Street, Glebe away from the university. He was then on an invalid pension and living in a Housing Commission flat.

He died in his flat a few weeks later. No-one was in the habit of visiting him. As the rent was debited automatically against his bank account, and this was refreshed every fortnight by his pension, several months went by before his body was discovered. By this time he was unrecognisable. The body remained for weeks in the morgue, awaiting formal identification – the same morgue where he had been an attendant. He was eventually identified from dental records.

Twenty years earlier in his Balmain days Adrian arrived at his local pub dressed as a nun, in full regalia. The husband and wife proprietors were good Catholics and banned Adrian from the premises for life. Adrian had become more subdued in later life. His wake was held at his usual watering hole in Glebe – the publican providing free drink and food in honour of Adrian's memory.

Few women (apart from Sally) were at the wake. A friend mentioned to me regretfully he believed Adrian may have died a virgin. I assured him this was not so. Adrian was too much of a gentleman to talk about his relationships with women. I knew of a woman who had been his lover once or twice and told her female friends: 'He's quite a doer'.

Around the time of our marriage, we became part of Charles and Barbara Blackman's circle of friends and I later became their solicitor. Charles and Barbara (in particular Barbara) created a Parisian-style salon: there were painters (John Coburn and his wife Barbara); a composer (Peter Sculthorpe); broadcasters and journalists (Gerry Stone and the tall, aristocratic Guy Morrison); a builder (Halifax Hayes, who renovated the many Blackman houses); a quietly-spoken physicist (Ian Bassett, and his wife Janet); and writers (Judith Wright, who would not have enjoyed Sydney's party-going, but corresponded with Barbara and was a thunderous offstage presence in Barbara's conversation).

There were dozens of improvised weekend lunches at the Blackmans' Paddington Street house, extending into the early evening with twenty or so of us sitting around a long table. A high point would be a voice calling out, 'The Wildgeese have arrived!' as a veterinarian, named Wildgoose, and his wife, appeared in the doorway. I don't remember who it was – perhaps Barbara – delighted in making this announcement.

Barbara's blindness was like a theme in a minor key we were conscious of during these lunches. It was present in Charles's paintings of female figures, and his intense awareness of light and darkness. Barbara had strong views about particular paintings, standing very close and scrutinising the work minutely.

It was a complicated household for the children – Auguste, Christabel and Barnaby. At one large party Christabel danced protectively with her mother. The Blackmans went to an afternoon gathering at the Hunter's Hill house of my friends Tony and Anne Gallagher. Barnaby, then about six years old, ran down the hallway calling out, 'Mummy and Daddy, the taxi man's here', worried perhaps that his parents were never going to leave.

Auguste and Christabel were students at a matriculation school which was closing down. The head teacher and his partner – another teacher – had become friends of the Blackmans and often read to Barbara. They were keen for the school to continue. Charles and Barbara found a large nineteenth century stone house on a hill in Balmain, overlooking Snails Bay as a possible site. They were ready to exchange contracts when I was phoned by the estate agent and told the house was being taken off the market for a couple of days to allow someone else to buy it.

The school did not yet have a name. I was concerned about the economics. It would be a continuing source of stress and would distract Charles from his art. I telephoned Charles: 'I think I can get this house for you, but do you *really* want to buy it?' After a moment's pause, he replied, 'Yes'. We both knew Barbara had her heart set on it. Charles was being very selfless.

I knew the other buyer. I phoned the agent: 'The Blackmans are cash buyers and I don't think you can be sure your other buyer will get finance. The Blackmans are interested in another property and will go ahead with your vendor *only if contracts are exchanged today!*' A few minutes later I received a surprised phone call from the vendor's solicitor and within half an hour was exchanging contracts at his office. He was tapping his fingers on his thigh. The new school got a new name: Chiron College.

Each year was touch and go financially. Eventually the school closed down when our chairman, James Murdoch, who headed the Australian Music Centre, warned us we ran the risk of trading while insolvent. We had about eighty enrolments at the start of the academic year, and were seven or eight students short of breaking even.

One of our board meetings at the Australian Music Centre's Circular Quay premises coincided with the afternoon the Whitlam government was dismissed. We listened to the radio news with excited disbelief as across the water the sun faded on the sails of the Opera House. During the election, Charles did not participate in 'Artists for Labor' and cut one of his paintings into two equal sections, which he donated to each of the parties.

My poem 'Roses' was 'commissioned' by Barbara for a 'Rose Evening'. I remembered my schoolboy obsession and set the poem in a landscape devastated by war. The draft I read out that night was very second-rate. It was just a poem for a party. Over the next forty years I expanded and revised it.

When I wrote a book with Charles about Australian primitive painters, we went in his chauffeured Mercedes for our interview with Irvine Homer, one of our artists. This was my first time in such a car. Charles apologised for the air-conditioning. He couldn't travel with the windows open, he said. It affected his ears. I was touched by Charles's apologetic explanation. His parents were working class. In the early 1970s Australians were still egalitarian. It was embarrassing to have air-conditioning in one's car. Ten years later such displays of affluence had stopped being embarrassing.

⚜

The Harbour Bridge has a high barrier where there was once just a low steel balustrade separating the two railway lines from the road traffic lanes. I had a recurrent dream that I was standing on this balustrade at night, the trains passing within inches of my back as cars were speeding past my feet.

My grey VW beetle had several design faults: tubeless tyres (a tyre went flat about every six months); the rear engine (the extra weight in the back made the car spin around when braking abruptly); and the lack of a fuel gauge. One winter night Sally and I were driving over the Harbour Bridge with a friend in the back. Halfway across, the car stopped. We were out of petrol. After a minute or so our friend got out of the car, hailed a taxi and waved goodbye with an apologetic shrug.

We were now alone in the car, surrounded by streams of speeding traffic. The protocol was to stay with the car until a tow-truck came, usually after about thirty minutes. Headlights came up behind us; cars braked and swerved and accelerated past. We sat tensely in the car, buffeted by the slipstream of passing traffic, with no hazard lights, and worried a vehicle would crash into the back. We waited for a break in the traffic, raced across the roadway and climbed onto the low iron lattice fence beside the railway line – perhaps prompted by my recurring dream.

We were now standing on the balustrade, suspended between passing cars and the rail track. Sally was wearing a winter coat and a long white scarf of heavy knitted silk around her neck. As we balanced on the top rail and waited, a train went past, a massive onslaught of steel and wind, just a few feet away. While the succession of carriages thundered past, Sally's scarf billowed gently towards them. I said nothing to Sally. It happened so suddenly, but I was reminded of Isadora Duncan, the dancer who died in 1927, when her long silk scarf became entangled in the wheels of an open-topped car in which she was riding. I regretted my stupidity. It was a metaphor for our marriage.

My mother's and Diana's back flat was smaller than the original house. To equalise the floor space, they had a locked room in our front section, which they used for storage. They had no privacy, with my friends coming and going, and were uncomfortable with Sally. For two years there was an uneasy peace.

We had inherited a small, balding Sicilian gardener from the previous owner. He stood – Sally noticed – with a rubber boot firmly flattening an iris, as I conversed with him in his limited Italian-inflected English. (When I called at his house, his front garden was paved with concrete.) I did the lawns and much of the garden maintenance and I felt entitled to make changes in the garden. The previous owner, June Read, had a row of small dahlias growing in a long, shaded rockery. I replaced them with cinerarias, which I thought were better suited for the filtered sunlight. At first things grew well under my tutelage, in soils June had nourished meticulously. I scattered seeds. Great drifts of cosmos plants sprang up: cerise, pink and white flowers. I grew hollyhocks and an annual sunflower taller than a man. It had one huge flower like a lugubrious clock face.

But as June Read's presence in the garden faded and her soil nutrients leached away, my cosmos and hollyhocks died and would not come back. Weeds infiltrated lawns and garden beds. I replaced my cinerarias – they were just annuals – with kurume azaleas. Then I dosed the azaleas with chicken manure and they went yellow and died.

My sense of proprietorship was misplaced. One day I planted a frangipani near the front gate. Diana was indignant. I had not consulted her. It would grow and obstruct the path. My erratic gardening style was just one item in a catalogue of incompatibilities. After a couple of years of shared ownership, Diana and I decided to split our jointly owned assets. She and my mother went to live in a house they had found in the next street. We sold the Gordon house and I bought Diana's half-share in the Lindfield house. We would still regard ourselves as holding everything in trust for our mother, but would have no assets in common.

Charlie still came in several days a week and had his own office, but was not active in the practice. I had also moved the firm into a smaller and cheaper suite of rooms in the same building, Boomerang House. 'Suite' was too grand a word for my new shoebox offices which never saw daylight and had windows near the bottom of a light well. Charlie's old offices were airy and sunlit, with worn, but acceptable carpet. There had been a couple of spare rooms, which I abhorred as wasteful. My move, however, was a false economy. I was winning extra clients and extra rooms would have allowed flexibility.

One of the clients I gained was one Charlie had lost. Nearing sixty, my new client spoke in a megaphone voice that made a private conversation difficult. After he got to know me better, we would chat. His first visit to my office had been on a pretext, he told me, supposedly to pick up a document. His real purpose had been to 'have a scout around' – to see if he liked me. He had spent his younger days working in his father's well-known ocean baths, making sure toddlers didn't drown, running up and down and shouting to young lads, 'You can't jump off there', 'Put that down', and so on. 'That's how I've got my loud voice.'

'Not a patch on his old man' was Charlie's verdict when he noticed I had regained a client he had lost. That may have been why Charlie lost him as a client.

Charlie told me a story. As well as the baths, the father owned a cake icing business. He decided to set up his son (my new client) in this business and gave him a strict schedule to follow. Every Friday when he took the orders for the week, he was to go to the Protestant shops first and leave the Catholics to the end of the day. At the Catholic shop, they would want to share a drink with him. He couldn't go to the Protestant shops smelling of alcohol. Perhaps he was tired of his father's bossiness and the Catholic shop was the logical starting point. That was where the son began his first Friday round of the shops – and it was the end of the cake icing business.

The son survived the cake icing disaster. He was appreciated by his mother and daughter whom he also sent to me as clients. I learned that intelligence comes in many shapes. I stopped believing in the intelligentsia. My clients' clarity and eloquence were surprising. A young man getting a divorce said with some vehemence, 'I can't see the point of sex'. Then added, 'I haven't a live sperm in my body'.

Charlie was pernickety and demanding when he was active in the firm. In retirement he was patient and uncritical throughout all my mistakes. Not long after we moved to our new office his beloved wife Mary died of a brain tumour. Its progress was swift. When he was not with her, he sat in his small office talking to doctors and nurses on the phone, tears in his eyes, his voice breaking. After her death, he did not know how to go about simple household tasks. His children had to tell him: 'Dad, you don't iron socks'.

I enjoyed my work. We all worked hard and got on well. But once my regular secretary was on holiday and I had a temporary secretary. I was eating a cut lunch in my small office during the lunch hour, and I heard her telephoning her husband – a solicitor: 'This place is a little sweat shop!', she said.

My real existence, I believed, was in the Lindfield house, writing poetry and being a husband and father. My legal work in the city was a pastime. I was about to discover that this cavalier approach was a mistake.

♛

When two people marry, there is often a realignment of friendships, and a new person becomes a particular friend of the marriage. This was so for us with David Malouf. We sometimes had dinner at his apartment in Abbotsford, looking out over the Parramatta River. The smell of chocolate wafted at night across the bay from a nearby Nestlé factory and I envied his ability to cook crème caramels.

David's fiction reflects a personal empathy and selflessness. Once I was acting for him on the purchase of part of an old orange orchard. An adjoining block, I thought, was a better buy. I pointed this out to him. He may have sensed I was interested in this block and insisted on staying with the land he had chosen. I bought the other block for Sally.

As well as new friendships, the marriage brought new responsibilities. Towards the end of 1970, when we had been married for more than a year, Sally told me she was pregnant. She became defensive. Didn't I want a child? I denied this. I said I was glad. Whatever emotion I felt, I knew our actions now had consequences.

When Julia was a baby, I replaced the VW beetle (the 'Dodgem Car') with a pale green Kombi Van that I called 'Bulk' after the BLK of its numberplate. It had only a driver's seat and front passenger's seat and for the back I bought some second-hand bench seats advertised in a newspaper. I must have been preparing for an influx of children. In a short time we had three.

My plant-collector daemon may also have wanted a van to pick up trees from plant nurseries. Some banana palms were on sale. I planted them along the front fence and in a year or so the whole front garden was becoming a banana palm jungle. I toyed with a new name for the house: 'Banana Castle' – we had been considering 'Wombat'. I had to axe the banana palms back over a year of weekends, sectioning the oozing trunks into chunks for the garbage bin, and gouging out suckers with a mattock.

I fell in love with our first-born, Julia, when she was a few weeks old. I was surprised at the intensity of my feeling. Baby car seats were not yet standard and I placed her, about three months old, wrapped in a pale woollen blanket in a white plastic wicker basket at the rear of the van. I was driving down the Pacific Highway, when the Kombi Van's rear hatch door flew up. In the rear vision mirror I saw a line of traffic banked up and Julia's basket poised at the back, perilously, so a jolt or sudden acceleration might dislodge it onto the road. I stopped slowly. I got out, pushed the basket well forward against the back bench and firmly shut the rear door.

We were wheeling her (about four months old) in a pram through a large discount store, buying cheap baby clothes. Each time we passed under a fluorescent light, her eyes followed the light.

Another small child, a few months older, was at Pixie O'Harris's house. I noticed a look of enormous relief on Julia's face – relief, I sensed, to discover another person almost as small as herself in a world where adults were giants.

When she was a bit more than six months old, I was carrying her in my arms at a party. She reached out to touch a small stuffed bird on a perch. Her look of expectation changed to shock. Her face screwed up and between sobs I heard her say, 'Deadie birdie' – her first words, if she did actually say this. 'Deadie birdie' became a family legend. A few years later she was in tears when she found a dead bird in the garden. Her younger brother and sister mocked her, calling out: 'Deadie birdie, deadie birdie.'

She had started crawling and was sitting in plastic pilchers. We were looking at a picture book. I turned over a page. She flinched with horror and burst out crying when she saw a picture of a giant rainbow snake.

She could now totter down the hall on two legs. Standing at the front door and looking out at the rain, she sighed: 'Obab'.

A year later her mother was in the final weeks of the next pregnancy. Julia and I were in a doctor's reception room and Sally was with the doctor. Julia stepped up to the receptionist's desk. Using her newly acquired skill of speaking in a sentence, she conveyed an urgent message: 'I-want-to-see-the-doc-tor'. She coined her own term for farts: 'bottom puffs'.

Julia was a 'horizon-hunter'. I imagined taking her to a disused aerodrome, where she could run as far as she liked and come running back when she felt like it. I was on the veranda of the Blackmans' St Albans house, at an afternoon party. Julia took off and had gone a long way off through long grass. I had to interrupt a conversation with Charles and take off after her. I noticed the dismay on Charles's face, mixed with relief: this was not something he would have to worry about again. (He didn't know it but he was to have three more children with two more wives.)

There is a photograph of my second child, John, six months old, lying in an oval rattan washing basket and looking up with wistful contentment. One day he disappeared from the house. He had crawled around to the front garden and was gazing up at a 'Titian' pillar rose, covered with dozens of raspberry pink flowers.

Ten years

We had a wire fence built to stop this happening again.

I became adept at changing babies' nappies, feeding them from bottles and burping them against my shoulder. I carried them out into the night air when they could not sleep, rocking them in my arms under a large jacaranda tree. Once or twice I allowed exasperation to get the better of me, and I angrily shook Julia. Sally's going away was merely a theoretical possibility, not something I worried about, but I sensed an urgent need to be involved in my children's lives.

Agnes's Walker Street house was zoned as a commercial site. Late in the afternoon, and now without Leo, I used to call in to see her. I sat with her on her raised brick paved terrace, looking down at her trees and bamboo gone wild, and her lawn where the stream had been filled in. Otto, she said, had been pressing her to give him a power of attorney and make a will. Her brother Carl had died intestate. That had worked out well, she pointed out: 'Wills cause problems'. (Meaning her mother's will). One day she told me, 'The title deed has gone'. I explained I would obtain a replacement.

In winter we sat around a table in her kitchen, a comfortable warm room with an old Bakelite radio – the only room of her house I ever saw. She had a table lamp with a wooden base and a white ceramic shade with a blue landscape of hills, pines and a windmill by a lake. I knew she slept somewhere in her semi-derelict house, but was unsure where.

Agnes had turned ninety and was too frail to live alone. After phone calls between family members, Agnes moved in with Ursula, May's eldest daughter, in Ben Boyd Road, Neutral Bay. Ursula was my first cousin and in her late sixties. She had been caring for her oldest son since infancy. Billy had 'water on the brain' from childhood meningitis, could drool just a few words, and was completely dependent on his mother for everything When she was bringing up her three sons, Ursula fossicked for food after dark in the large bins outside supermarkets.

Ursula was also looking after her invalid landlady, a Miss Harte, who was in her eighties, had the best bedroom at the front and was constantly ringing the bell, calling for attention. For one whole hectic year Ursula looked after Agnes, Miss Harte and Billy in one small semi-detached cottage, with little help. (Miss Harte was a retired estate agent. By a bizarre coincidence I had already given the retired estate agent heroine of my novel – in real life Mrs England – the same surname.)

Throughout her life Ursula had earned small amounts as a medium. Once I was chatting with her and one of her grown sons. She stopped in mid-sentence: 'A spirit just flew past the window!' 'MUM!' her son shouted, the blood rushing to his face. (I was reminded of my problems with my mother.) Apart from this, Ursula never mentioned spirits to me. We talked like brother and sister, despite the age gap.

I had a reliable agent (Pax Lambert) acting for my aunt. One day he met one of North Sydney's largest developers in the street and reminded him about my aunt's property. A few days later we had an unconditional sale. Otto, now eighty-seven, called in at my office. He produced the lost certificate of title and explained he had taken it to make sure it was safe. I handed it back. It was a nice piece of old parchment. 'Otto, you keep it. We have a replacement.' He came to the real point of his visit. He had obtained 'a very good offer. Eighty-eight thousand.' 'Don't worry,' I said. 'We're selling for a hundred and fifty thousand.'

A friend on the local council phoned to say that the zoning was changing from commercial to residential. The purchaser would want to get out of the contract. I issued a notice to complete and kept Ursula informed. We completed on the day when the notice expired. Agnes died next day. If she had died before then, we could not have complied with our own notice.

Agnes, the 'heathen', was ever a romantic. As Ursula accompanied her in the ambulance on her last day, Agnes said, 'Now I'm going on my journey to the stars'.

Otto, as the main beneficiary, was able to buy the first house he had ever owned. He turned up at my office and gave me Agnes's kitchen lamp with the blue and white ceramic shade. It had a new base of nicely turned, oiled timber he made himself. As well as her share of the estate, Ursula was paid for looking after Agnes. She already had some blue agapanthus plants and I gave her a white agapanthus to take to Melbourne, when she moved there to live with her son Robert.

My sister had a sign made, 'Agnes Cottage', with gilt lettering on black glass, for a rental house in Glebe she bought with her share of the estate. I used part of my share to buy Sally's parents a dam builders' house that was transported from Carcoar dam to 'Spring Forest'.

♛

I dug up some of June Read's lawn and made a large square bed next to the tennis court for half a dozen Iceberg roses. I was with Sally at a window by the kitchen sink: 'You'll be able to look down and see the roses from here'. I immediately regretted my remark.

I sometimes imagined my father walking up the hill towards the house, in the brown tweed suit he was wearing when he died. I felt that none of what I owned was mine – I was an imposter. Our best wine glasses, a wedding gift, were crystal with a dense glass bulb in the stem. At dinner parties Adrian Heber would run his finger along their rims and made them sing. They were broken one by one when my children drank milk out of them and I washed them in the dishwasher.

I was less cavalier with my clients' affairs. One of the pleasures of owning a small law firm was advising others more constructively than I could advise myself. I twice refused to act for a young man who wanted to buy acres of romantic bushland. Keeping them weed-free would cost hundreds of dollars every year, I said; buy an uninteresting quarter-acre block in Liverpool, and it will increase in value. He eventually did.

A widow told me there was something she could not discuss with her doctor. Her only child had confessed he was homosexual. Her sister wanted her to disinherit him and leave everything to the sister's children. I said she should feel proud of her son. Telling her must have been difficult, I said, and was the right thing to do. I arranged that when she signed her new will (keeping the son as sole beneficiary) he would also be present. When they came in, I congratulated them on the respect they had shown each other. My intention had been to stage a small ceremony, giving a legal imprimatur to her new relationship with her son. She could also tell her sister all about it.

My intervention did not work out well when I was acting on a purchase for a young woman I knew. I prided myself on being an expert at old system conveyancing, which was then a dying art. I noticed an error in a thirty-year-old conveyance by a group of vendors. A name was missing in the conveying words. Solicitors acting in later conveyances had not picked up the error – understandably, as the person whose name was missing had signed the deed. Fortunately she was still alive and we obtained a confirmatory conveyance.

I kept my client informed about the reason for the delay. I made sure she and her mother realised my cleverness. But she was living in a rented house while waiting for the title to be fixed, and was stabbed to death there by a person unknown. If I had not detected the flaw in title, she would not have been in the house where she was murdered. A neighbour heard two female voices arguing just before the death. Her lover had a light voice and became a suspect. He was cleared at the inquest. Years later he had a messy and protracted suicide. A female friend of my murdered client was charged in a foreign country with an assault on another woman.

⁂

My cat followed me down onto the yellow clay tennis court and I dropped him in one of the waterlogged holes I had dug to receive a score of roses. These arrived at Lindfield railway station in the depth of winter, bare roots tightly wrapped to stay damp, and I carried them home. I was intoxicated by their names: *Rosa mutabilis* or the Changing Rose with pale yellow petals that age to pink; and 'Nuits de Young', a moss rose with small red flowers, almost black, named after Edward Young's poem *Night-Thoughts*.

One day I heard a loud noise from my mother's upright Lipp. When I entered the room Puss had jumped down from the piano. I placed some cut-up liver in a small plate at one end of the keyboard. He jumped up again, treading uneasily on the keys, and ate a piece. I moved the plate to the other end. He ran along the keys for more. By snapping my fingers and gesturing at the piano, I trained him to run up and down on the keyboard without liver. Puss performed for friends. Stephen Wilson almost fell off a couch laughing.

Stephen had become a junior partner in his father's law firm, with his father and another older man. Then his father succumbed rapidly to cancer. Stephen and I had an understanding that his law firm and mine would merge when his senior partner retired.

One of his friends had acquired a small, established law firm. She was a few years older than me. Stephen suggested her law firm and mine should merge. She was a likeable and intelligent woman. I asked would he want her as a partner, when his firm and mine merged. He said yes. I said if that was so, I was happy to have her as a partner now. An office suite with wood panelling, far more palatial than my 'little sweat shop', had just been vacated next to Stephen's law firm. It was ready to move into, which my new partner and I did, a few weeks after my conversation with Stephen.

I did not examine her client base or her firm's income and expenses. Nor did she examine my firm's books. I ignored some early impressions. My first memory of her – I was a young student, studying in the State Library – was of her walking into the reading room waving a daffodil. A year or so later she was working in a government office with Chris Koch and John Quinlem. Quinlem claimed to have calculated her weekly taxi fares to and from work each day; it was more than her salary.

Our partnership did not go well. My clientele was different from hers. Our temperaments were different. I was more risk averse. The numbers did not add up. I had already started the demerging of our firms when a mutual friend, a barrister whom she often briefed, accosted me in the street and warned me against remaining in partnership with her.

Untangling the two practices took some months. My firm eventually moved to different premises, leaving her with the offices next to Stephen. She was exceptionally co-operative when all this happened, and I was not upset with her. But I was upset with Stephen. When I first told him about our difficulties, he stared up at the ceiling and said nothing. Our friendship never recovered.

Stephen's friends loved him for his altruism. When I jammed my hand closing a car door, he was more agitated than I was myself. After one of his overseas trips he came back with an antique creamer, a white ceramic cow with black spots and floral base, which he gave me. The partnership with his friend was one of his gifts.

⁂

The venture into partnership was not helped by a six-month recession in conveyancing work when the Whitlam government engineered a credit squeeze – with the bizarre intention, it was rumoured, of freeing up money for public housing. Even worse, the Whitlam government's 20 per cent increase in public servants' pay (intended to put the squeeze on private employers) was the start of fifteen years of runaway inflation.

I survived the credit squeeze and my failed partnership. I had become the secretary of a small listed company, with a finance company subsidiary. I held dinner parties for friends who were clients, and for clients who became friends. My bouillabaisse was written up in the *National Times*. We went to many dinner parties. Judith Wright invited a group of younger people to dinner when she was staying in a flat at Rushcutters Bay. When we sat down at the dining table, she announced with aplomb, as she served reheated meat pies, 'Well, I think it's the company that counts, not the food'.

We were having dinner at the Hunters Hill apartment of Elizabeth Harrower not long after the dismissal of Gough Whitlam's government. Elizabeth confessed she had Gough's photograph in the back of her wardrobe. I said I was not unhappy to see Whitlam go. This was greeted with a shocked silence – Patrick White's face froze. White's partner Manoly Lascaris came to my defence.

Manoly and I used to talk about plants at Elizabeth's dinner parties. I once mentioned driving through Castle Hill past a cottage that had roses climbing over a veranda, a red rambling rose with a white eye, 'Bloomfield Courage', and a yellow Banks rose. 'That was our house', Manoly said (referring to the house where Patrick White wrote *The Tree of Man*). 'I planted those roses!'

(Elizabeth later inherited a house on the hillside above Balmoral Beach, and Christina Stead stayed with her. I met Stead there. Her presence was like that of a large, aged camellia flower, blotched and falling apart – she did not have long to live – but somehow still splendid. Unfortunately I had not read any of her novels and I could not query her about the trip up the Lane Cove River, which may have been in my father's boat the *Liberty*. I now regard her, along with Henry Handel Richardson, as one of the greatest Australian novelists.)

Sally and I were at a party held by the Sea Horse Club, a group of heterosexual transvestites, at the Castlecrag house of a friend, Neil Buhrich. Neil was investigating bloodstream hormone levels and sexual orientation. (The house, regarded as a modernist masterpiece, was designed by Neil's father Hugh. Long before I knew Neil, I had been embarrassed to stand in its grounds with Livija.)

Men in dresses, top-heavy wigs and high-heeled shoes, were clattering up and down a perilous spiral staircase without a railing – Hugh Buhrich was aesthetically opposed to railings. The men – or girls – had stored their dress collections on the ground floor: cocktail frocks with sequins or lurex such as middle-aged women might wear. After a quick bathroom change, they paraded upstairs in their new outfits, sometimes several outfits in a night. A club rule was they all spoke in normal male voices. Some brought their wives and children.

'Constance' – I have changed her assumed name – came without her disapproving girlfriend. Blood was showing through heavy face cream from a shaving nick, and her bra was askew: 'Y'know, I love mixing with women when I have all my gear on

– they think I'm one of them – and I find out all their secret likes and dislikes. If you go into a room and see a really, *really* expensively dressed woman, you can bet she's *one of us*! We spend all this money. And you know what? *We look bloody awful!* All a girl has to do is put on a sweater and pair of jeans and she looks fantastic ... You learn so much watching women. I'm always learning. The way they smoke a cigarette, for instance...'

Constance said she was a storeman and packer. A few days later I saw a man with dark hair and a blond streak striding up from a city basement with a cigarette stuck to his lips, and he *spat* the butt into the gutter. It was Constance, who loved watching women smoke cigarettes.

I still regretted my remark to Sally when we looked down from the kitchen window at the newly planted 'Iceberg' rose bed. This grew into a mass of bright green leaves with clusters of white flowers as though it was a single gigantic plant. It was an optical illusion, like our marriage.

Only a few of my friends who married in the 1960s and 1970s are still together. Yet for much of the duration of the failed marriages, one spouse and perhaps both imagined they were in marriages that would last. When I acted for friends in their divorces, I imagined I was immune. Divorces happened to other people.

When Sally and I went to the 1974 Adelaide Writers' Week, Sally's mother (or perhaps her aunt Joyce) looked after Julia, aged three, and John, aged one. We drove down to South Australia in 'Bulk', the pale green Kombi Van. Sally was pregnant with Lucy. There had been an outbreak of Ross River fever and we crossed the flat plains of the Riverina late in the afternoon with haste and unease, past a long, twisting line of tall trees on the horizon marking the course of the Murrumbidgee. I was seeing for the first time a large wheat growing property, 'Wahwoon', where I had acted on the purchase. 'Wahwoon' was so flat, my client said, 'You can stand on a beer can and see another ten miles'.

At the opening of Writers' Week in the grand nineteenth century central room of Ayers House, Peter Porter was the person I was interested to meet. He was a tall, good-looking man in his mid-forties. Sally and I headed across and spoke to him. Much of the next week in Adelaide we spent with Peter. When he came to Sydney I invited him to stay in the Lindfield house.

We stayed up each night talking after dinner. We would open a bottle and then another bottle. I was shocked at how much Peter drank. He would blink behind his glasses and laugh and the conversation did not stop. I had to go to my law firm next day.

I remember two of his stories. He was to read to the Oxford University Poetry Society. They did not want to miss out on free food and several young Oxford poets attended the dinner before the reading. Then they excused themselves, except one, who led Peter down long corridors, muttering 'We're expecting a good turn-out tonight'. As Peter was ushered into the hall for the reading it was empty – he was the only person there – and his guide had vanished.

In the second story Peter was one of the poets at a reading given by some of the great luminaries. There was an arrangement to eat afterwards. As they were leaving, Auden (the most important influence on Peter's poetry) turned anxiously to Stephen Spender and said, indicating Peter, 'Stephen, are you inviting *him*? There won't be enough food.'

Peter interrupted his stay at our house to visit his father in an old people's home in Brisbane. On his return, on the last night of his stay, Peter took Sally and me to Verdi's *Othello* at the Opera House – a generous way of thanking us, I thought. I had no idea I was at the opera *with them*. My presence was an intrusion.

During the course of a marriage spouses may become aware of the other's small, innocent crushes. At a Chiron College party I had a long conversation with a teacher I liked. I am sure Sally noticed me talking to her. On one of our long car trips Sally playfully mused 'I wonder what ... is doing now' (... being a new friend). I assumed she had a mild attraction to him. (This was a variation of a formulaic exchange we had on long car trips. 'I wonder what Puss is doing now', we would say to ease the monotony of the passing landscape.)

I became aware in a ludicrous way of her feelings for Peter. She did the household washing. 'Peter is offering to wash his underpants separately', Sally told me one day. It was apparent she was surprised and impressed by his delicacy about this matter. I may not have thought much about her remark – apart from the implication that I was too coarse to care about washing underwear separately – but a seed had been planted in my mind.

When Sally and Peter met, and he was staying in our house in 1974, she was pregnant with Lucy. But she felt a spiritual compatibility with Peter, which she did not feel with me, and they began what I understand was a lengthy exchange of letters. I am unaware of the details.

When Lucy was about a year old, Sally and Peter travelled in Europe. While she was away, Sally's aunt Joyce looked after the three children and taught them to speak in Bunkum. In Bunkum or 'Bgunkgum' a hard 'g' is inserted before every vowel. While the children were speaking non-stop Bunkum, I began to realise Peter's relationship with Sally was not just a friendship. I had a sinking feeling as I picked her up from the airport.

A plum tree beside the drive had white flowers in mid-winter, at the time of Julia's birthday. A plum next to it had pink flowers a month later on Lucy's birthday. (There was no tree in the garden whose flowering coincided with John's birthday.) I began telling the children these flowering plums were their birthday trees. Sally responded with irritation. She did not want them to become attached to the Lindfield house.

I was working in the garden one weekend when I noticed a young fair-haired woman in the grounds of the next door house. Ros was married to Steven, who was the son of the previous owner, Maurice Jeffery. They had bought the house from Maurice. They had two small girls. We began having neighbourly dinners together – the four young parents.

Sally had been saying she wanted me to give up legal practice. My working hours (which I thought were quite short) she thought were too long. My failed partnership with Stephen's friend had exacted a toll on both of us. We were at a book launch for Father Edmund Campion's *Lord Acton and the First Vatican Council* at St Patrick's Seminary, a vast stone edifice on the cliffs at the end of Manly beach. As the waves were breaking on the rocks below, I was standing on a stone balcony and talking to Bob Vermeesch. 'Life is very civilised in the School of Accountancy', he said. 'Why don't you come and join us?'

Bob and Ed were two people I used to drink with at the Metropole when I was an articled clerk. Bob was a few years older and understood my situation. He once had a partnership in a small law firm, like mine, and became a legal academic. He was now at the University of New South Wales.

I may have replied, 'Yes, Bob, I will'. Whatever my reply was, within a few weeks I had sold my practice and become a tutor in the School of Accountancy. I was a public servant for the second time in my life. One morning I was hurrying across a university quadrangle. A man I did not know called out: 'There's no need to hurry. You're a public servant now.'

Ten years

I had no personal regret about selling my firm. My one regret was I had let go something Mr Willcox had built up over many years. I had not consulted him during my impulsive moves and at no time did he criticise me. The new owners – another small, old-established law firm – gave him an office, but his name would not appear on their letterhead.

I had no illusions about the marriage I was trying to save. The first instalment of my *Nero's Poems* – a dozen or so pieces – was published by Les Murray in *Poetry Australia*. The magazine's cover reproduced an etching by Sally. Two depressed people – they seemed to be lovers – were wandering through a marsh-like landscape and holding a string attached to a large balloon in the shape of a person. The man-balloon was looking down and following them. I sensed it was me.

Her feelings for Peter were as impossible and desperate as my feelings for her. Marriage vows and our children were not the only practical impediments. Peter was almost twenty years older, he had two daughters entering adolescence and lived on the other side of the world. His life as a London literary figure could not easily transplant to Australia.

We were walking across a university quadrangle – I may have been showing Sally my new office. Young people were all around us, mingling and talking, heading to and from lectures. Sally seemed to be absorbing the excitement around us – the student life she had lost when she met me.

At the end of the year I knew Peter Porter was serious about

Sally. He arrived in Sydney with his two daughters. He and his daughters stayed briefly in the back flat at Lindfield until he found accommodation elsewhere. Sally wanted the back flat herself, so we could live separately in the same house.

There was a sixty-year-old woman who minded the children when Sally and I went out at night. One of her group of parents knew me, she said. This was the girl whose passport application I had witnessed and who sent a Christmas card when she came back to Australia. I felt doubly cheated.

We had two weeks of strenuous debate. It became a theatre of the absurd – accusation and counter-accusation, who was open and sensitive to the other and who was not, who wanted to leave whom. I was uncommunicative, Sally said. She recalled how I said nothing for half an hour when we went with the children to the Botanic Gardens.

Julia, aged five, called out several times a day: 'Cuppa tea mama'. A cup of tea did not stop her parents arguing. Lucy, aged two, called out: 'Get another mama'. Her brother and sister laughed wildly and desperately when she said this. I asked Lucy did she want another mama. She said, 'No, *you* get another mama!'

I had been faithful for more than ten years. Sally was upset when I went out with an old girlfriend.

In mid-December, we were in a bookshop buying Christmas gifts for the children. I was looking at a small replica of the nineteenth century *Kate Greenaway's Book of Games* and thinking I could use it as a source for a poem. Sally noticed and said, 'I'll get it for you' and inscribed it 'Dear Geoffrey love from Sally low-ebb year 1976'.

On New Year's Eve we had our next-door neighbours Steven and Ros for dinner. The four of us sat around a cedar table I had bought from the Salvation Army a couple of years before our marriage. At about midnight Steven announced, 'I feel a prophecy coming on. One of us – I don't know who – will have a serious illness and may even die. And one of us will have an affair, and there may be a marriage breakup.' Sally and I exchanged the ghost of a complicit smile.

I did not want to live separately with Sally in the same house. Early in the new year I arranged for Peter Read, the son of the former owner, and his wife Jay, Ros Jeffery's sister, to have the back flat while one of them was recovering from an illness. Our neighbours were told about the coming separation. Steven was full of apologies for his night of prophecies.

We began looking for a house where Sally could live. We agreed the children would stay for an equal number of days with each parent. I arranged my schedule to teach early in the week when they would be with Sally. I would pick them up on Wednesday afternoon. The weekend handover alternated between late Saturday afternoon and Sunday morning. Over a fourteen-day cycle each parent had the children for seven nights.

When we went looking for houses, our eldest child Julia made hopeful comments: 'That's a nice house, mama'. We inspected an old cottage with a large mango tree. The sixty-year-old owner shook his head and said he did not want to be involved in the break-up of a marriage.

Sally signed a lease for a house in Pymble. I went looking for an antique ring, but not from Maurice Mandelberg. His shop had disappeared. I gave Sally a gold nineteenth century ring with an amethyst set between two green garnets – subject to a condition. She was to come back in six months. Six months later, as one of us was picking up the children, she handed it back, and I consigned 'the poison ring' to a drawer.

When we separated, Lucy had just given up nappies. She has no memory of ever living in a house where Sally and I lived together. But she remembers walking up the front path on the day all four of them left, and in particular her mother putting a wicker basket down on the path. This basket is also imprinted in my memory. It had a cylindrical section that could hold a child's drink bottle.

Puss ('The Sun King') stayed with me.

GAIL

In Errol Morris's documentary *The Unknown Known* Donald Rumsfeld repeats his aphorism about the 'known unknowns' and the 'unknown unknowns' and proposes a third category of unappreciated facts: 'unknown knowns' or 'the things you think you know, that it turns out you did not'. As the documentary is about to end, he corrects himself. 'Unknown knowns', he says, are 'things that you know, that you don't know you know'. I had married and entered a legal partnership knowing they could not succeed, and did not know I knew.

The previous fifteen years of my life had been an elaborate costume party, as in Alain-Fournier's *Le Grand Meaulnes* where a wandering peasant boy stumbles upon people wearing clothes from a previous century in a mysterious chateau.

I was now an accidental legal academic and for half of each week a thirty-six-year-old single parent, looking after three children aged two, three and five. Sally and my former law partner had been generous. There were no disputes when the marriage and the partnership were dissolved. I survived as a whole person. Unlike the hero of Alain-Fournier's short novel, who spent years trying to find the chateau of the costume party, I did not want to go back.

I started reading Andrew Lang's coloured volumes of fairy stories to the children, as much for myself as them. Julia was a consoling five-year-old voice. She used to tell me: 'One day your princess will come'.

⛉

Diana and Iris lived down the road from my Lindfield house for only a couple of years. They loved inspecting apartments on weekends and called in at the office of an estate agent called Douglas Uzell (pronounced You-zell); Iris's nickname for him was Uzzle Duzzle. Eventually they bought an apartment at Lindfield through him, but stayed there for only another couple of years.

While Diana was at work, my mother liked catching the train to Chatswood where she could sit in a coffee shop, or buy crockery ornaments or cloth to sew into a skirt. But when she caught a train, the gap between the carriage and platform was a crevasse. My sister sold the Lindfield apartment and bought an apartment in Chatswood.

My mother and Diana seemed to regard my single parenthood as a punishment for neglecting them. They counselled me to stay single and wanted to get back the twenty-year-old son and brother I had been. Our misunderstandings were mutual. I did not understand my mother was eighty, and living in her past.

Diana and Iris went on a trip to Eidsvold several years before Sally and I separated. I do not know whose idea it was to visit the town where Iris's father had died of a morphine overdose. The few weeks Iris was there in 1906 replayed in her mind – her father's white silk suit, tomatoes ripening in a few hours on a fence, the falling stars and dog whimpering as the white girls (but not my mother) danced naked around a hose.

I recorded my mother's account of their 1971 Eidsvold visit on a cassette tape – my mother speaking with hardly a pause, except for questions from me and interruptions from children's voices. When she had finished, I stopped the machine and said, 'Mum, I recorded all of that'. She pretended to be surprised. Diana remained resolutely silent during the recording session.

The two women arrived at Brisbane's Central Station an hour before their train for Eidsvold was due to leave. When it pulled in, they were the first to board and take up their seats. The train trip involved a confusing cast of characters: a reassuring and talkative Irish policeman (or ex-policeman); a group of rowdy young men drinking; my sister throwing a whiskey bottle out of the train window while its owner had gone to the toilet; a woman joining them in their compartment ('Weren't we glad when she got in') – the woman owned a home for destitute girls that her husband did not know about, and my mother suspected it was a brothel – and at the end of the journey in their Eidsvold motel, my sister standing on a chair and chasing away a gecko on the bedroom wall.

In Eidsvold Iris and Diana introduced themselves to some old men who seemed to recall a 'Dr Rainer from 1905' – my mother had confused the date. But the old men could not remember anything specific. These two strange ladies from Sydney soon became well known. ('We heard them talking about us afterwards. "Fancy that, 1905", they were saying.') They refused a trip to the cemetery in a horse and cart – Iris checked this bizarre detail with Diana, who would not answer while the recording machine was switched on. My mother was worried about how they would get back to their motel, and they did not know the driver of the cart.

On the return train journey to Brisbane they had an overnight stay in Maryborough, opposite the railway at an old hotel (recommended by the Irish policeman). They arrived after midnight. An old man answered the door in his night gown, 'holding a lantern'. My voice interposes 'A hurricane lantern, Mum?', but my mother does not say. And he led them along a veranda, past open doorways and the alarming sound of men snoring, and showed them to a bedroom with mosquito nets. After they unpacked, they had to go to a common bathroom and repeat the alarming trip along the veranda, back and forth, past open doorways and snoring.

The recording reminded me: all her life my mother was afraid. Diana grew up surrounded by those fears, yet did not grow up to be a frightened person. She threw the whiskey bottle from the train and chased away the gecko. But she was infected by Iris's shame about her unusual physiology.

When Iris said she married my father because he was 'safe', she convinced me men and women want different things when they marry. But this was not a disparagement. Hearing her after forty years – talking in an Australian, not English, voice as I had imagined – I realised for a woman who saw fear everywhere, a man who was 'safe' was as close as she could get to love. We blame the dead for sins they did not commit.

I was cured of the costume party, but in a state of shock. The early years of the separation were a time of improvisation, finding false 'bargains', making mistakes that multiplied into more mistakes, hurrying from one emergency to another, and looking for a new partner. Sally was searching also. She did not continue with Peter.

As the house and garden slowly deteriorated, I was teaching law to commerce students in the first half of the week and looking after children in the second half. There were clothes to wash – the children's and mine. I mowed the lawns once a month – but irregularly, so my front garden became an embarrassment to neighbours. Once in a while I vacuumed the rooms, a beer glass in one hand (as I put it in a poem, although that may have happened only once). I did not concern myself about the back garden – it was invisible from the street – as the wooden poles of the tennis court began tilting and falling down.

I held occasional dinner parties and maintained some rituals from my old married life: on Saturday mornings going to Paddy's Markets in the city with the children – Saturday was one of my days – and dragging a trolley along with Lucy, aged two, standing in it and peering out. She had to get out as I began piling in fruit and vegetables. I bought a painted dragonfly mobile and hung it from an Indian lamp in the drawing room. There was a vegetable stall run by a Chinese man, an Aboriginal and a red-haired Anglo-Celt. All three stood on fruit boxes calling out to buyers like a team of actors.

After the markets we had cakes and gelati at the Bar Roma. When Lucy was about to wet her pants, I had to jump up from my coffee and suspend her above the gutter in the street outside.

On Friday nights I took the children to eat satay chicken at the Nanyang near Central Station. I had to get food into them within ten minutes or they would crawl under the table and start bickering. As soon as we sat down, I asked for prawn crisps. If I was lucky, friends without children – Paul Delprat and others – would be there, and we would sit at a large table. I did not wish to inflict my single parenthood on friends and did not phone to check if they were coming. On winter nights, coming home from meals in the city, I corralled the children up the back steps of the Lindfield house, carrying those who were asleep.

I started drinking with the Push again. After a night at the pub I would let myself in and hear the crash of discords. Puss was playing the piano, wanting to be fed.

My son John was subdued and had a male distaste for vegetables. I blended broccoli with meat in a food processor and cooked children's meatloaf and bolognese spaghetti sauce that were green.

When his mother's car arrived in the paved back area for hand-over, John would run down the steps with sudden animation.

I bought children's clothes at Paddy's Markets: for Julia a blue and grey corduroy dress, and for Lucy a smaller matching red and grey dress. Lucy and I loved the white-dotted red and blue pinafore dress for a three-year-old, which I had bought second-hand. She was six, and the seams were falling apart, when she finally gave it up.

Plastic bottles of warmed milk were something she refused to give up. At age eight her last bottle, coated with dust and half-filled with fossilised milk, was found under her bed. With Julia I staged a 'Goodbye Dummy' ceremony outside a toyshop. We agreed she would drop her dummy in a council bin with John and Lucy as witnesses, and I would then buy each child a toy.

I had a reconditioned engine installed in the green van, 'Bulk'. One hot morning two weeks later I was taking the children to school and we had driven 100 metres or so when the van died. My cheap reconditioned engine had just cracked. There was no warranty. Engine oil was ebbing down the hill, wet and dark like my own blood (I thought). We began the 4 kilometre walk to school.

The tennis court poles dragged down the wire netting as they collapsed. Fleabane and pungent vines (German ivy and climbing dock) grew through the wire, mixed with climbing roses and the silken tents of large spider webs at the end of summer. This became a wall of shimmering green I had to attack, with spider spray, secateurs for the branches, tin snips for the wire, a bow saw for the square wooden poles and last of all a mattock for the roots, lifting up clods of yellow tennis court clay mixed with civilising carbon from the plants.

I advanced, armed with my tools and wearing old shirts that were soon ripped, and a hat to keep the sun off my face. Covered with leaf-dust and sweating, I piled up the rubbish in the middle of the court and lit a succession of bonfires.

I was a single parent for three years. As well as the back flat, the main part of the house had several bedrooms and veranda rooms, and I filled the house with young people, by advertising on university notice boards. I fell in love with a younger woman, and when that relationship failed, with another young woman. They became Poppaea in *Nero's Poems*. These relationships could not survive the strenuous untidiness of my life.

I was learning about the methods of the social sciences, test groups and control groups. I began writing academic articles and started a book I called *Dividing the Child*, about joint custody of children. I became a joint custody advocate – if women were to be men's equals in the workplace, fathers should be their equals with children.

During my breakup with Sally I played Janis Joplin; the relentless sexuality of Janis's voice paralleled my excitement as everything familiar was falling apart. I was now the only inhabitant of my bedroom and could turn off the light whenever I liked. Because I felt I needed a respectable higher degree, I was studying until 2.30 in the morning. The bay window was open after a hot day, and baby green grasshoppers with red eyes were jumping about on the desk. I heard a voice on the radio, Frank Zappa singing: 'Honey, Don't You Want A Man Like Me?'. Zappa was the return of structure after the free form of Joplin. I still loved Janis, but she became the past.

In summer I went to the beach with the children, sat on the sand and watched them calling and splashing as the waves rolled in. I kept track of their silhouettes in the glare, making sure I could distinguish them from other children in the water, and every few minutes counted: One, Two, Three. Everywhere I took them I had to count: One, Two, Three. Then I could slam the door of the van.

When they quarrelled I had a simple way of establishing order. If they were in a ruck on the floor, I pulled them apart, held up my hand and shouted, 'Smack wall'. Each child was then surrounded by an invisible wall. If they breached it, they would be smacked. My hand hovered in the air for a few seconds, but I never had to use it.

Teaching at university and looking after small children were not all that different. In my first term I taught the same tutorial twelve times each week to twelve different classes. The dangerous time was at three in the afternoon. I sometimes fell asleep as I stood before a class. The words I had to repeat passed before my closed eyes like hallucinatory words on a teleprompter. I knew I had to ask a question from time to time. Having commented on the answer, I closed my eyes again and continued repeating what the teleprompter told me.

I was appointed a lecturer. My class was now 400 students in a steeply banked lecture hall. Paper darts began to rain down on my dais at the bottom, when I turned my back to chalk up points of interest on the board. By the end of each lecture up to fifty paper darts were scattered about. The next term I began wearing a coat and tie to all lectures, and never turning my back. I stared at the 400 students for the entire fifty-five minutes. One day at the end of my class, another lecturer, about to take a class, asked why there were no paper darts. I explained my method.

The Blackmans' marriage fell apart. Les Murray and I drifted away from each other. He told me he found my poems about the marital breakup too painful to read. The Push, with whom I occasionally drank, were becoming middle-aged. I was immersed in the lives of small children growing up and the unfamiliar world of academe.

Four friends made a particular effort to stay in my life. I drove over to Salvatore Zofrea's house every week. We listened to music and I watched Salvatore's painting style change to intricate and glazed tableaux. He was counsellor, friend and psychotherapist as we discussed my marriage over and over again; the small, painful details. I was able to reward him for his patience. I had a platonic friend, Stephanie Clare, to whom I introduced him. Salvatore and Steph have now been together for almost four decades. Paul Delprat kept me in touch with a wider circle of people, while Robert Gray (now more in touch with other poets than I was) and Christopher Koch gave me emotional support to keep writing.

I still saw Stephen Wilson as we had friends in common. He was diagnosed as having a malignant melanoma. I thought about our days on Mona Vale beach and how many more days he had spent, burning his skin for an elusive tan. A girl at the university often asked about him. He had been ill for a couple of years and his condition was terminal. I thought she should be told certain facts. She answered, almost angrily, 'I know for a fact he's not!'

In his last few months he travelled to Europe with his male friend, and they accompanied Melina Mercouri on tour and were at every concert. A few weeks before he died we had lunch, and that was the last time I was with him. He insisted on my coming back to his house and showing me a painting he had just bought. He was still collecting objects.

His funeral was at St John's Anglican church in Darlinghurst, where a few years earlier I had watched Stephen as a stunned mourner at his father's funeral. There was confusion about the service. A week before Stephen died, he had converted to Catholicism and his family did not know. A Catholic and an Anglican priest agreed to officiate together. Stephen was buried in the family vault in Waverley cemetery. At the cemetery one of his oldest friends suggested I write a poem about Stephen. I was not a good mourner. We had no family vault and I was not born into a law firm.

I was still bitter about his role in my failed partnership. I felt that Stephen did not see my former partner and me as real people. He had been nostalgic about a prominent Roman nose she had – before cosmetic surgery. Her old nose, he often said, had 'character'. That appeared to matter more than her personal happiness.

But when Gail and I met several months after his death, I regretted she had not known him.

My mother and sister wanted to see the Japanese Gardens which had opened in Sydney's west. I took them there with the children. It was early spring, there was not much foliage, and I could look in any direction and see the children running among the newly planted beds. My mother drew me aside: 'I want you to promise to look after Diana when I'm gone'.

If I was to find a wife, I thought a good place to start was fixing the bathroom. It had a claustrophobic brick shower cubicle, faced with large pale green tiles. Diana and Iris were horrified when I said I was replacing this with clear glass shower screens: 'People will be able to look at you when you shower!' I found some white Spanish floor tiles with a hand painted blue daisy in the centre and became an owner-builder, arranging for tradesmen to come in the correct sequence. The Italian tiler thought it odd my children called me by my Christian name.

The year 1979 was the year of the triple birthday party at Ian Bedford's house for three Push friends: Ian turning forty, Doug

Nicholson turning fifty, and Bill Lindbergh turning sixty. Ian introduced me to Gail Pearson, saying I was the author of a book, *Ross' Poems*. We talked for a few minutes. I assumed she was his girlfriend. Bill Lindbergh was a guest at a dinner party I held a few weeks later, and he brought Gail. I still assumed she was Ian's girlfriend.

We both taught at the University of New South Wales – she was teaching Indian history – and one day near the start of term in 1980 we met by chance on the library steps and agreed to have lunch at the University Staff Club. Gail talked about Indian arranged marriages and made it clear she was not Ian's girlfriend. I was nervously sure she was the girl I would marry.

We arranged to meet one night. She was surprised when I picked her up in 'Bulk', my green Kombi Van, to be driven to a restaurant – not a very good restaurant near where she lived, but neither of us were connoisseurs. We saw each other a second time. The next morning she was moving into a flat in Woollahra, and I came along with my children to her new apartment, so she could meet them. If they were to be an impediment, I wanted to find this out quickly. As her possessions were carried in, they played, running up and down the stairs and calling out.

A few weeks later Ian said: 'When I introduced you, I thought you'd suit each other. *You're both such difficult people.*'

Robert Frost's poem 'Meeting and Passing' is about an unidentified 'I' meeting an unidentified 'you' and they walk together. Afterwards each retraces the path which the other took to get to where they met. I wanted to retrace Gail's life to the point where we met: her childhood in Maryborough, schooldays as a boarder at Somerville House, her first boyfriends, her love affair with India, four years studying for her PhD at the Jawaharlal Nehru University in New Delhi, and most of all her mother, who had recently died – the innocent fresh-faced mother of family photographs. 'She would have warned me against you!' She was still grieving and would wake up at night in tears.

Although I was in a hurry to introduce Gail to all my friends, I did not talk about our future. I was ten years older and had children. A couple of months after we started seeing each other, I was swatting mosquitoes on her bedroom wall. Next morning she spoke about our relationship: 'As Lenin said, "What is to be done?"' We decided to marry within a year. She thought I was a little mad when we met, but I had renovated the bathroom – I had shown I was 'practical'.

As a prelude to marrying, Gail moved her antique chests of drawers into the Lindfield house, also a glass-fronted book cabinet with drawers she had bought with her mother, a white nineteenth century cast-iron bed, Indian *objets d'art* and books about India. Three decades later, my daughter Julia remembers being entranced by Gail, her waist-length black hair, her voice and the whiteness of her skin. Gail began to create order in the house and teach my children table manners.

I once came along as Gail's accompanying spouse when she gave a speech at the opening of a Sikh temple. As she spoke from a lectern on the history of Sikhism to several hundred Indian Australians, dressed in a decorous salwar kameez, the twenty-nine-year-old Australian girl I had fallen in love with transformed herself into an Indian girl with choreographed smiles and glances. I was astonished.

We were married the following year on St Valentine's Day after a prenuptial honeymoon with the children at a beach house at Gerroa. The children could not swim properly. I stood in the ocean with them, counting them as I always did, and they splashed and called out, and hermit crabs in small seashells rolled in with the waves. At night in the beach house I was writing a set of sestinas about a single father with three children. Gail was upset because I was not helping with the wedding invitations.

One day I was reading my sestinas to Pixie O'Harris over the phone. I had given the children in the poems pseudonyms, but Julia called out: 'He's written a poem about *us!*'

Keith Looby and Kerry Gregan were the first guests to arrive at our wedding reception. They turned up at our house a week early. We were married the following Saturday morning at the city registry office. Gail was wearing a red and yellow wedding sari sent from India by the wife of her PhD supervisor at Jawaharlal Nehru University. Paul Delprat was best man and Gail's sister Deborah was bridesmaid. After coffee and cakes at the Bar Roma – our Saturday morning routine – we drove back to Lindfield. The paint was peeling on the wall by the stone terrace where speeches were to be made. I changed out of my suit, opened a pot of white paint, and repainted the wall. This was still wet when guests began arriving. We had to warn them: 'Stay away from the wet paint'.

We served wine in plastic cups and our few glasses, and chicken and salad on paper plates. Gail's sister Deborah had made the cake. The three children jumped up and down and called out during the speeches. I made a children's alcohol-free fruit punch in a large brass Chinese bowl of my father's. Later that evening they suggested I taste it. The fruit punch had an awful metallic taste. I had almost poisoned my children. The last guests had left by midnight.

True happiness is not elusive. When I married Gail, I became truly happy for the first time in my life. I was forty years old.

At the end of the year we holidayed with the children in a flat her family owned that looked out over the khaki tidal waters of the Brisbane River. In the morning we went to the Corinda swimming pool and Gail taught the children to swim: 'Face under and blow'. I discovered why I had not been able to swim a convincing freestyle.

Back in Sydney we had to find a spot for a red-flowered frangipani bought in Brisbane. Mrs Read had planted a *Hibiscus rosa-sinensis* with showy, double pink flowers. When its flowers opened for the first time, perhaps in Hawaii in about 1950, its obscure breeder must have known his plant would soon be in millions of gardens. My guess is he was a modest man, so he named it after his wife: 'Mrs George Davis'. I began chopping down 'Mrs George Davis'. Puss sent me an imploring look. He used this tree to climb up and sun himself on the roof. He began scrambling up what was left of the trunk. Three years later, by then about twenty years old, Puss disappeared. We called out and probed the dark with electric torches. But the Sun King had gone. The flowers of the red frangipani, when it flowered, were a scentless white.

Gail and I ordered a ping-pong table. On fine weekends I played ping-pong on the stone terrace with our next-door neighbour, Steven Jeffery (who had made the New Year's Eve prophecy). His *forte* was to serve with his back to the table. I laughed and could not get the ball back. When he sent me an unplayable shot, he announced it was a 'TS Eliot' or 'This is a Wordsworth'.

Gail was three months pregnant when we went to India. I was delivering a paper about Australian poetry at an academic conference in New Delhi, and Gail was leading a student tour afterwards. On the morning of our flight Gail emptied out her university office – she was giving up teaching Indian studies and about to start a law course. We arrived at Sydney airport twenty minutes before departure and the airline staff checked us through, laughing incredulously. I had never been out of Australia and was forty-two.

As we drove from the airport into New Delhi by bus, I was excited by the fragrant smell of wood fires. An old woman was trudging beside the highway, bent, insect-like beneath a huge load of sticks. She was a small black silhouette against a primrose yellow dusk.

Gail and I were staying in staff accommodation at the University of Delhi. We had an upstairs room with a squat toilet and our own rooftop where we sat in the late afternoon and watched monkeys playing in a stand of silk floss trees at the edge of a lawn.

We called on a friend of hers, the owner of an iron foundry, Chiku – his nickname from the small sweet fruit – and sat in his small office in Connaught Circle and drank small glasses of chai sweetened with condensed milk, a stream of visitors calling in to see Gail, back from Australia for the first time in four years. After dinner one night at Chiku's joint family house, Chiku's chauffeur drove us back in his Ambassador car (the Indian version of a 1950s Morris Oxford saloon) to our university guest house. When we had been let off, the car would not start. The grey-haired chowkidar (nightwatchman) who sat outside all night on the veranda stirred himself. He and I pushed the back bumper while the chauffeur ran alongside with the driver's door open, also pushing, and jumping in when the car started with a puff of blue smoke.

As we travelled through India I learned to drink only from freshly opened bottles or boiled tea, and eat only freshly cooked food. I went looking for puppets for the children. (Sally was looking after them for the five weeks we were away.) I bought Amar Chitra Katha comic books retelling Indian epics and myths at every train station where we stopped. We drank chai out of small earthenware cups which we smashed on the railway platform – that was the local custom – before rejoining the train.

On a bus trip to the thirteenth century redbrick ruins of a Buddhist university at Nalanda we drove across desiccated plains past derelict trucks that had tipped over – our bus driver speaking angrily with peasants who had laid a tree trunk across the road.

On a bus trip to a Madhubani village of lady painters, we were already on our way when we made contact by short wave radio with the government guest house where we were to stay. They had been out of contact for days. There was no booking, the caretaker claimed. We arrived late at night. He gave us a large room with three beds for fifteen Australian students. Most of us slept on the floor. A small boy was perched on a black water buffalo which was cropping the grass when I woke up next morning and looked through a window. There was a bustle as the caretaker organised half a dozen young cooks and served a frugal breakfast. As our bus drove away, he stood on the veranda, bald headed in his long white shirt and dhoti, bowing and waving goodbye, flanked by his retinue of young cooks.

Our bus driver had to stop several times in a flat landscape amidst a jumble of unsignposted, dirt roads and ask directions for our village of lady painters. Eventually, the son of the senior lady painter hailed our bus and led us through clustered houses with thatched roofs and mud walls painted white, and across shiny yellow mud floors, like polished cement. Naming the upper caste women artists, he unrolled his stock of paintings – brightly coloured traditional subjects, populated by small flowers, birds and fish. He unrolled paintings by Harijan women, in duller, raw-earth colours and at lower prices. One of these – 'It is tantric' – had grinning heads branching from a tree trunk. Gail and I bought it and would have liked to pay more.

One night our tour group was waiting for a train. Hundreds of people were milling around. The train was darkened when it arrived, and the windows were shuttered – to reduce the risk of attack by dacoits, we were told. A sudden blackout plunged the station in darkness. A universal cry went up. Our tour organiser agreed to fly us to Calcutta.

In our tour's first week some younger women were in tears, overwhelmed by swarms of beggars, street children selling small items, red splashes of betel nut juice on the cream walls of corridors, peacocks strutting on roofs, whole families riding one pushbike with a child in a basket perched on the handlebars, young men on their way to work urinating against walls, horses with garlands of marigolds pulling carts, and lepers demanding money and flaunting their ruined limbs as we entered a ruined temple complex.

When Gail began at New Delhi's Jawaharlal Nehru University in the early 1970s, with no Hindi, she was the only foreign student. She went on to study there for more than four years and made life-long friends. I would have lasted no more than a week.

Several months after India, Gail was heavily pregnant and we were with the three children, driving down the Pacific Highway. Gail had sold her Mini Moke and I had sold 'Bulk' and we had just one vehicle, a new pale blue Ford Econovan with the initials LLW on the numberplate. A friend suggested we call it 'Leslie Walford' after the fashionable interior decorator. Lucy was eight years old and brooding on one of 'Leslie Walford's' two back benches. She said to Gail, 'When that baby's born, IT's not going to last long. I'm making sure it's just Baby Bones.'

Nicholas was a planned child. When contractions began I drove with Gail to the hospital and stayed. I had brought a transistor radio, and the obstetrician joked it was the first time he had delivered a baby while listening to the 7 o'clock news. It was the first time I had witnessed a birth.

Diana and Iris were now living in an apartment next to the Chatswood shopping centre. Sometimes they came to eat with us. About every three weeks Gail and I, with the three children, went to the Chatswood flat and ate one of my mother's bland evening meals. I was relieved she had no loss of short-term memory as she talked without stopping about recent TV programs. Her vehemence was depressing. I was the 'intellectual son' she had to convince and convert. For her that was a special relationship, not the tranquil companionship she shared with my sister. My mother was afraid of Diana's common sense. Diana could silence her with a look.

They had reluctantly accepted Gail. When we took Nicholas as a baby to their apartment, my mother said how surprising it was to have four grandchildren. Eva, she said, would have been jealous. (Despite having married young and having four children, my mother's deceased sister Eva had no grandchildren. As a child, Eva had danced naked with the postman's children around the hose at Eidsvold.)

My mother may have been having small strokes. She occupied herself with sewing, and Diana noticed she was stitching in the wrong places. One day she had a massive stroke and lost the power of speech. I wondered whether she recognised me when I held her hand in hospital. I was writing children's stories and began reading these to her. She seemed to respond by gripping my hand.

She did not speak again and was taken to a hospice. I do not know if my mother, who was so quiet with strangers, could hear a demented old woman in the next bed, shouting and calling out all day. If she did, it must have been a torment – listening to these endless rages. My mother may have been put next to this woman because she appeared insensible and in any case could not complain. I continued reading her children's stories, talking about what I was doing, sometimes coming with the older children and holding her hand. But her grip was weakening and her eyes did not seem to register anything.

For some months I drove with my sister to the hospice. One afternoon we were standing by my mother's bed and Diana asked,

'Do you notice anything different?' I was puzzled by my sister's question. 'All the tubes have been removed.'

My mother was still breathing. She looked strangely free. Diana had told the hospice to take her off life support. I was silently grateful I had not been consulted. Iris died that night and we visited her next morning in the mortuary. Diana placed a kiss on her forehead and said, 'Goodbye Mother'. I stood by and said nothing. We walked out.

Diana, my children, Gail, a few family members, and Robert Gray came to the crematorium chapel. I was the only person who spoke: about her childhood, her father's death, the difficult years that followed, how she would have liked to be a singer, and her coming to live in Sydney. I sensed that my sister hated every minute of the eulogy as she sat in the small funeral chapel. Her grief was real.

Even when my mother died my impatience about her 'silly ideas', the trivial frictions of family life, were still too raw for me to feel grief. I did not understand how much she was still Bella's victim.

At about the start of the Great Depression Bella conceived the hare-brained scheme of moving to Sydney to be close to Billy, her eldest surviving son, who was single. Now more than sixty years old, she insisted on the move, and Iris had to come with her. Bella uprooted my mother from family and friends and the familiarity of Melbourne. Bella herself was leaving two of her children behind, her youngest son Tom, recently married, and Eva who had children. I find this incomprehensible, particularly abandoning her grandchildren.

Perhaps Bella saw Billy's absence in Sydney as a personal rejection. Rejection by a male is unsettling for women such as Bella. Whatever happened, Bella discarded rationality in pursuit of her son.

Not long after the two women settled in Sydney, and perhaps before, Billy got a girlfriend whom he later married. 'Eileen threw herself at Billy', my mother told me, still upset about it more than twenty years later: 'Billy had only just started seeing Eileen … and after work he used to find her sitting in his car!'

The move to Sydney was a fiasco. Bella and my mother could not compete with Eileen Mumford. Neither Bella nor Iris, as far as I can ascertain, ever formed an intimate friendship in Sydney (apart from Iris marrying Leo). For more than forty years Sydney was an alien city for my mother, and the last sentence of Bella's 'Recollections', written several years after their move is: 'And now I am alone'.

Tony Rainer (Billy's son) told me, 'My father had to come to Sydney if he was ever going to find a wife. None of his girlfriends were good enough for Bella. And my mother wasn't either. Photographs show the hostility. This only changed when Bella found out the Mumfords owned country stores.'

The spell between mother and son was broken for me when Iris told me she had spoken to the mother of the girl next door, and I was to stop playing with her. The girl and I did not speak again. Our friendship had been innocent. We continued living in adjoining houses, and for years neither of us acknowledged the other when we passed in the street.

I never forgave my mother for this exercise of maternal power. She may have told herself she was doing the right thing. She did not want to share her ten-year-old son with a ten-year-old girl.

Diana had no formal legal training, but was working in the Probate Office and prepared all our mother's probate documents. Iris owned a house in Glebe – the house Adrian Heber was going to burn down when he was at a party there – and I purchased Diana's half share. A couple of years later I was having difficulty making payments under the mortgage I took out over the house. I sold it at auction for less than the value Diana and I had assumed when I bought her share. She insisted on refunding what she claimed was my overpayment.

Since our father's death Diana had invested her spare cash in rental properties, several over a decade and a half, and was able to pay for these out of a modest income. She and Iris lived economically – without large expenses such as a car.

Diana had unpredictable expenses on her rental properties and began selling them off and investing in the stock market. She was a joiner – she joined the Australian Shareholders' Association, and although her purchases were limited, subscribed to Choice, a consumers' association, as an act of good citizenship. She had almost no vanity and would not have described it in this way. But she had a forceful personality. About five years after our mother's death, at a time when she was having dinner at the Lindfield house on a weekly basis, Diana and Gail had a falling out. Diana stopped visiting Lindfield and I began meeting with her for lunch in the city two or three times a month.

By that time Gail and I had a second child, something we had always wanted, but felt we could not afford. There was a chain of lucky events, and Harold was literally 'a child of tax reform'.

I became a tax lawyer by accident. I had seen tax as dry and technical. When tax law was offered for the first time to undergraduates in the early 1960s, I dismissed it as having nothing to do with me. My spotty law degree – once a source of perverse pride – was a problem now I was a legal academic. So I took on a 'hard' specialisation: tax.

I was surprised. New cases and new legislation were continuously replacing old law. Tax law was proliferating into specialisations. There was a battle of wits between revenue authorities and taxpayers. The 'progressive income tax' was good at redistributing to the less well off, but high rates were killing off initiative. There were trade-offs between simplicity, efficiency and fairness. Tax was an exhilarating morality play. It was technical, but not dry.

I wrote an article, 'The Income Tax Judgments of Sir Garfield Barwick: A Study in the Failure of the New Legalism'. I had met Barwick once at a student dinner, and had thought him a decent and courteous man. But his income tax judgments as chief justice of the High Court broke with existing precedents. Barwick was a judicial activist pretending to be a literalist. I did a mathematical analysis of his income tax judgments, adopting a methodology from the social sciences. I used income tax judgments of fellow High Court judges as the control group to show Barwick's extreme pro-taxpayer bias.

His casuistry had stripped any practical effect from section 260, the general anti-avoidance provision. With high marginal personal tax rates, this caused an explosion of tax avoidance. Driving to the university, I noticed an expensive car with the numberplate 'TAX 260', and another with the numberplate 'TAX 000'. It was the beginning of personalised numberplates. I saw a young man in a suit waving to a young blonde woman driving past in a navy blue late model Mercedes. Her numberplate was LXIX. It took a couple of minutes before I realised: LXIX was soixante-neuf.

Barwick was a judicial conjuror. Although intellectually thin, he stated a proposition: tax legislation should be precisely worded, otherwise no tax was payable. The *Stanford Encyclopedia of Philosophy* suggests: 'Propositions, we shall say, are the sharable objects of the attitudes and the primary bearers of truth and falsity'.

Barwick's proposition was a bearer of falsity, but in this way he had a permanent influence on how tax legislation was drafted in Australia. The immediate response to his corrosive logic was convoluted legislation plugging obvious gaps. I argued this would have been unnecessary if his court had not neutralised the general anti-avoidance provision. His 'new legalism' was a pragmatic failure as well as bad jurisprudence.

This appeared so when my article was published in 1983. But there was a longer-term effect. Over the next twenty years Australia developed a unique style of tax legislation: detailed rules that needed intensive bureaucratic input and consultation with tax professionals outside government. By the year 2000 about 300 bureaucrats were involved in tax reform. Australia finished up with some of the world's most sophisticated tax legislation. Initial compliance costs were high, but much of it worked well after the settling-in period. Barwick was the catalyst.

When the Hawke Labor government was elected in 1983, Australia got an inspirational Treasurer: Paul Keating. Following on from a Tax Summit, a cascade of tax legislation – capital gains tax, fringe benefits tax and many other measures new to Australia – was about to descend on the accounting firms; they had to educate staff and clients.

I knew Allen Robinson, national head of tax of one of the large international accounting firms, and in late 1985 he telephoned: Did I want to become his national technical tax director? I said no – I was happy with academic life. I telephoned Gail. She told me I was mad – I could take leave from the university. I called

Allen back. Early in 1986 I started with his firm. Gail and I could now afford to have Harry.

I prepared courses for the firm's staff on new tax legislation, gave client presentations and wrote client brochures. One of my press releases, which suggested a capital gains tax provision had an anomalous effect, became front page news in the financial press and the legislation was amended. I was given a bonus.

I was walking past a government publications shop and bought a copy of the recent Research and Development Tax Concession legislation. I gave a press interview suggesting it could be abused, and was telephoned by a government official. We were commissioned to review the concession and I wrote a seventy-page report. My suggested amendments were legislated. I became a member of the government committee set up to oversee the concession and was now an R&D tax expert, writing submissions for industry associations and reports for clients.

In 1987 I was at a course given by two American partners of the firm where I worked. I asked one of them what he did during the day. He said he sat in the firm's national office in Washington and charged his time answering phone queries about tax from the firm's offices around the US. Ten years went by and then I assumed a similar role in another firm.

The editor of *Australian Business*, Trevor Sykes, a legendary journalist who wrote the 'Pierpont' column about shady entrepreneurs, took me to an Indian lunch. I began writing a weekly tax column for his magazine. I was chastened when my first column appeared. My article had to fit on a page and was about 200 words too long. I was used to book reviews of no fixed length. The sub-editor simply excised three paragraphs near the end, and my last paragraph now made no sense.

In 1985 Australia had a National Tax Summit and was lucky to have a young Federal Treasurer, Paul Keating – a connoisseur of antique French clocks, Mahler symphonies and Italian suits – who enthusiastically drove the program of radical tax reforms that came out of the Summit. He was hoping to take over from Hawke as Prime Minister. The main threat to Paul Keating's moving into the Lodge (the prime minister's Canberra residence) was a charismatic Leader of the Opposition, John Hewson, a Ferrari-driving former professor of economics.

I wrote articles for the 1988 and 1989 Christmas issues of *Australian Business*, composed mainly of limericks, in which Paul Keating had a dream. In the Christmas 1989 article I imagined Keating had a dream about a second Tax Summit. Here is an extract:

The Second Tax Summit – Paul Keating's Annual Dream

… The Treasurer found himself addressing a second Tax Summit in the Irish town of Limerick, on the banks of the River Shannon. … [T]he Italian suited Treasurer told the delegates, '… some of my cabinet colleagues are straying from the true religion of the level playing field. They want tax concessions. Well, here we are right next to Shannon Airport, deep in tax concession land. Ladies and gentlemen, I have brought you here so that you can see with your own eyes a countryside that is devastated by tax concessions.

'Just to bring home to you the horrible economic distortions that I've witnessed on my fact-finding mission through this depressed country I've composed a limerick.

In my clapped-out Mercedes Benz
I've been touring the bogs and fens,
But Irish whisky

LEEWARD

In excess is risky.
They don't air-freshen the Mens.

John Elliott [recently retired CEO of Fosters Brewing and former President of the Liberal Party] suggested they adjourn for a snort or two of Fosters in a nearby hostelry. 'That'll be entertainment taxed at only 39 per cent too,' he added with a chuckle. As they did this, Dr Hewson, [the leader of the Federal Opposition] much to the dismay of his retired president, did not order the Australian drop, but a glass of Armagnac. The bar tender, an avuncular fellow, filled the opposition leader's glass and recited:

'*God bless you, ex-Professor Hewson,*
It's easy to see you're new son.
We don't drink shandies
And fancy French brandies.
It's clear you don't know the right brew son.'

The bar spontaneously broke into a chorus:

'*He'll need to get a new Ph. D.*
There's a lot of value-adding in a spree,
With numerous stops
At hops and barley shops
To pick up our depressed economee.'

The last line, particularly the second last word, caused our Prime Minister [Bob Hawke] to drop a blow-wave dryer he was holding in one hand and a pint-glass of lemon squash he was holding in the other [he was temporarily a teetotaller]. Tightening his lips, he scowled:

Gail

*'While I'm PM that word
Is a sound that must never be heard.
You say you're recessed,
And I'm quite impressed,
But that other word's quite absurd.'*

As the drinkers cowered, ashamed of what they had sung, all the doors of the pub were flung open and forty men in dark suits armed with flick knives and stilettos burst into the room, accompanied by press photographers. 'It's a Tax Office raid!' some of the leaders of business said, ducking for cover behind the bar.

'My parents didn't call me Trevor Percy Winston Boucher [the Commissioner of Taxation] for nothing,' the leader of the dark suited brigade announced. 'Stand up like a man and pay your tax!

*Just because you're at the top
Won't cause my auditors to stop.
Corporate squeals and screams
Excite my audit teams
To bring their axes out and chop.'*

'Really, this is all very uncivilised,' Barry Jones [author, Labor parliamentarian and Quiz King] announced. 'You're all frightened because his name means butcher in French.

*'You all should learn to say
'Bon jour, Monsieur Boo-shay.
Here's my last écu,
It's all I can do.'*
And maybe he'd go away.'

As the leaders of business slowly emerged from under chairs and tables, peering at their French phrase-books, Paul Keating struck up a conversation with John Hewson. 'You know John, your name lacks electoral appeal. It's too hard finding rhymes for it. Now my own name is perfect. I could go on endlessly:

'My name is P. J. Keating,
I'll give you a terrible beating.
The Lodge is mine,
It's where I'll dine,
So shut up and stop your bleating.

'Now your own name, John, doesn't have that Damascus steel edge to it. But perhaps if you change from Hewson to Hewsome, you could do more with it.'

John Hewson emptied his Armagnac as he listened to the Treasurer's aspersions and visibly stiffened. Then he said:

'No way that I'll name-change to Hewsome,
I'd win some, but maybe I'd lose some.
I'd consider John Porsche,
And Ferrari of courshe,
But Hewsome's a name that is gruesome.'

༺༻

I stayed eighteen months with the accounting firm that recruited me in 1986. I was approaching fifty and needed a clear pathway to partnership. A friend, Gordon Cooper, helped me negotiate with another firm's tax leader, Robert Oser, and I stayed there for twenty years, becoming a partner despite my age. Through a merger this firm later became the world's largest international accounting firm.

Australian Business stopped weekly publication in 1991 and Paul Kelly, the editor of the *Australian*, asked me to write a weekly tax column. I continued writing these articles for almost a decade, and the firm was paid at normal journalistic rates. My standard fall-back when I could not find a weekly topic was to write a piece recommending a Goods and Services Tax (another name for a value-added tax, where tax is payable to each transaction in the supply chain).

I have never been a political party member, but in late 1990 the Federal Opposition Leader John Hewson invited me to be his capital gains tax expert in the lead-up to the 1993 election. I wrote the chapter (about two pages) on capital gains tax in Hewson's *Fightback!*, his 650-page election manifesto released in November 1991.

The centrepiece of *Fightback!* was a 15 per cent GST. It was at first enthusiastically received. The Labor Prime Minister Bob Hawke seemed unable to counter Hewson. Then Keating replaced Hawke and relentlessly attacked Hewson and *Fightback!*

In March 1993 on the Saturday night of the election, we were ready to print thousands of copies of a hefty GST publication I had written for clients. I was in my office listening to a radio, and at 8.45 pm I decided we should all go home. It was one of the biggest disappointments of my life. My limerick in which Keating told Hewson 'I'll give you a terrible beating' had come true.

Some blamed John Hewson. There was a famous incident (now on YouTube) when he gave a complicated answer about GST on birthday cakes. He confused himself by referring to birthday candles. Only a handful of sales tax experts could have dealt with the obscure issue of the tax on birthday candles before and after a 15 per cent GST. More importantly, *birthday cakes are sold without candles!*

When Keating became prime minister and moved to the Lodge he set up what were known as the Keating awards for mature artists. He had been shocked to discover his son's piano teacher, the pianist Geoffrey Tozer, earned less than a third of what his eighteen-year-old secretary earned. Surprisingly, Donald Horne, who had been Chair of the Australia Council, attacked the Keating awards in the *Sydney Morning Herald* as elitist. I published an article in the *Herald* replying to Horne and supporting Keating.

Keating's commitment to artists has been unusual, if not unique, among Australian politicians. Accomplished mid-career artists are generally poorly rewarded and earn much less than the academics who study their work and publish articles about them, yet they may create work enjoyed by future generations long after their death. It is a classic example of market failure.

In 1994 Peter Coleman, editor of *Quadrant* magazine, commissioned me to write a poem for Barry Humphries's sixtieth birthday. At the birthday party I read twenty-eight lines about his stage characters, every line of the poem rhyming with the syllable 'ate', the easiest rhyme in the English language. Barry kissed me lightly on the cheek and John Howard, then an Opposition backbencher, struck up a conversation – we had not spoken since university debating days – with the words 'We have to get a GST.'

I doubt whether my many press articles over the years arguing for a GST were influential. They were just part of the groundswell resulting from New Zealand's successful GST introduced by a Labour government in 1986. But in July 1994 I published in the *Australian* a duplicitous article attacking the GST, which I suspect did change the nature of the debate.

My intention was to enlist the support of churches and welfare groups for a GST, or at least make them uncomfortable about their hypocrisy in having opposed it, when Hewson lost 'the unloseable election'. My article suggested failure to enact a GST would cause funding for social welfare programs to run out and we would get a social welfare system with many gaps, such as the US had: one of the few large, developed economies without a value-added tax such as the GST. My recantation had to seem genuine. I wrote in my last two paragraphs:

> *Fightback!* was a package of great sincerity and a GST would have provided a number of benefits ... But it would have created an awesome tax raising mechanism, which interest groups in our federal system of government would have exploited to create spending programs.
>
> Business groups may need to consider their long-term commitment to indirect tax reform, and social welfare groups may regret having opposed Dr Hewson.

Not long after my duplicitous article appeared, social welfare groups indicated they were prepared to reconsider a GST. This attitudinal change, in particular, was necessary to persuade the Australian Democrats, who allowed the GST through the Senate several years later when it was introduced by John Howard.

More than 140 countries have a VAT, but no country imposes a VAT on financial services generally. A VAT or GST on financial services has been as elusive as the proof of Fermat's Last Theorem (until it was solved in 1994 after three centuries).

The fact that there is no GST or VAT on many financial services is economically distorting. There was an attempt to remedy this, when the Australian Government proposed introducing a

GST. Technical experts in financial institutions looked at a complex algorithm considered by the Canadian government. This produced a plausible number but did not reflect the actual value added. Eventually they found a true workable basis for taxing general financial services. An approximation of the actual value added by the financial institution could be taxed by using standardised values which are reset annually – a 'pure intermediation margin' for loans, and standardised cost plus profit margin for the other fifty varieties of financial services.

To prove these radical concepts could be turned into legislative words which would apply in the real world, I was asked to prepare draft legislation. There was no Australian GST legislation at the time, so I drafted my thirty-odd pages of legislation as though it was part of New Zealand's *Goods and Services Tax Act*.

None of us could imagine how to tax life assurance. I spoke to a senior actuary I knew – a delightful, thoughtful older man. I explained our methodology and he laughed. The value added by life assurance companies was a simple line in their annual accounts. Taxing life assurance was an extra three-quarters of a page.

When all of this was presented to the Federal Treasurer Peter Costello, the risks and complexity were seen as too great – a decision I think was correct. I may have the last copy of this draft legislation – the VAT aficionado's equivalent of a solution for Fermat's Last Theorem.

In about 1998 Sandra Peacock invited me to join the Consolidation Focus Group, a panel she headed of tax practitioners and government officials who were scoping out the rules for taxing consolidated groups of companies. At that time each company in a related group – there might be hundreds of them – had to calculate its tax and file separately. The proposed regime would allow a group of related companies to file a single tax return, eliminate double tax and prevent company groups co-ordinating their affairs to avoid tax.

I had been involved in the various waves of tax reform since 1986. I was still involved with the GST, but I realised I would soon find it very boring. It was relatively straightforward.

The consolidation regime would be a much bigger challenge. It would be radical and complicated, and almost every difficult tax issue would pass through the gateway of consolidation for our corporate clients. I had not yet become a Washington office–style technical partner at a desk answering interesting questions, but the consolidation regime would allow me to do this.

The main architects of this regime were two middle-level officials: Bill Stock, who had a scholarly manner and was responsible for the asset-based model; and Irene Sim, vivacious and blunt, with a trace of Singapore or Hong Kong in her accent, who was responsible for the rules under which losses of a joining member could be used by the group.

Bill welcomed new ideas. When he disagreed he would crane his neck and smile and start his response with 'Au contraire...' At early meetings of the Focus Group we were all excited. If the model could be made to work, Australia would get a world first – based partly on US rules, but more radical. Ken Spence was one of the private sector representatives who took a leading role in suggesting features of the new legislation. I suggested the rule for the joining time of new members, a rule to cover unrealised losses on joining and what became known as 'tax sharing agreements'. Some of us were also engaged on the government side. I reported on the complex rules that were devised to allow a joining member's losses to transfer to the group.

In 2004 the International Fiscal Association held a meeting in Vienna. There was a session on the taxation of consolidated groups. Ken Spence represented Australia and his paper described our regime, which was far in advance of anything elsewhere in the world. My daughter Lucy was in Vienna and I took her to the IFA's ball at the end of the conference. Ken took a photograph of Lucy and me – Lucy was in a ball gown and I was wearing a tuxedo.

I co-authored a taxation law text with Cynthia Coleman, who taught tax law at Sydney University. Gail and I knew Cynthia and her husband Richard from morning coffees at the Bar Roma. Our first edition was published in 1990 and we wrote four subsequent editions of a 1200-page book. We did not review each other's chapters. I was hypersensitive about errors, after making a bad error in a client brochure in 1986. Perhaps because of this hypersensitivity, over a decade I found only one error in our book – an incomplete sentence, where I may have fallen asleep.

One of the mirages of tax policy is that there is a simple and clear way of identifying taxable income. Boffins within Treasury began work on a Tax Value Method to replace the old common law rules for distinguishing income and capital. I was at first a supporter – I hoped it would bring tax into closer alignment with accounting principles.

Many of us became sceptical as draft legislation appeared. Eventually I was commissioned by the Board of Tax to report on TVM. I presented my fifty-six-page report to a meeting, including the Secretary of Treasury and Commissioner of Taxation. I explained that in its own complicated way TVM was able to duplicate existing income tax rules with remarkable ingenuity. Mixing up the French rococo painter with the jewellery maker Fabergé – but no-one seemed to notice my mistake – I said TVM was 'like a Fragonard toy from Imperial Russia'.

But how it applied was unclear without a detailed explanation from an expert. TVM was a black box. Its seventy-nine pages of 'core rules' compared unfavourably with seventeen pages of core rules in existing legislation, and TVM used many invented concepts and distinctions. It was more complex than what it replaced. By 2002, after almost twenty years of continual legislative change, when the Federal Government decided not to proceed with TVM, the public enthusiasm for tax reform was waning.

My friend Gordon Cooper had helped my move to the large accounting firm where I became a partner. Gordon also nominated me for membership of a discussion group of tax specialist lawyers and accountants. I was a member for twenty years. We met for dinner once a month and discussed a member's paper. Although we were from competing firms, information was freely shared. There was a friendliness within this fraternity that did not exist among poets after the early 1970s.

Gordon also arranged for me to become a member of the Research Committee of the Australian Tax Research Foundation. At that time Sir Harry Gibbs, the retired High Court Chief Justice, was the chairman. Some years later I joined the main board and eventually became chairman myself.

Professor Ross Parsons was a member of the Research Committee. He had initiated the first university tax law course I had scorned thirty years before. Ross lived on the North Shore so I began driving him home.

Ross's roneoed income tax course notes were greatly prized by his students and eventually in 1985 he was talked into publishing these as a 1000 page text: *Income Taxation in Australia*. Ross hated the banal cover which his publisher chose: a photograph of a varnished box for lodging income tax returns inscribed 'Deputy Commissioner of Taxation' in gold letters. Ross's book is still quoted by the courts.

I attended Ross's farewell lecture given to a large audience of legal luminaries. I had been expecting Ross would elucidate some profound issues in his usual way. Instead his lecture became a recital of the brilliant students he had learned from over the previous thirty years, referring to them by name. He was not their teacher, they had had taught him. All of these former students were sitting in the audience. I think they were as surprised as I was – it was typical of Ross's modesty.

In 1993 I published a *Collected Poems*. Ross and I were again driving north after a meeting. We had never talked about poetry. He mentioned he had bought my book. 'I was really surprised', he said. 'I don't read a lot of poetry. It was like reading a novel.'

Along with no-fault divorce, one of the great legacies of the Whitlam Government was its 25 per cent reduction of tariffs in its 1973 Budget. I was in Melbourne when the Centre for Independent Studies held a memorial function for Bert Kelly 'the modest member' of parliament who had written a newspaper column over many years advocating free trade and tariff reductions. One of the speakers was Gough Whitlam.

Afterwards a group of us gathered at a nearby Melbourne restaurant. I could not stay, nor could Gough. We both had to catch a plane. He pressed me to drive out to the airport in his Commonwealth car. As we settled ourselves in the back seat I congratulated him on his speech – how outstanding it was. 'Very po-etical', he said in his deep tones, mocking himself and glancing at me wryly. We talked about the legal profession when he had been younger and his father, the Solicitor-General.

Gail

Les Murray and I had been drifting apart over the 1970s. In 1980 he loaned me a copy of his verse novel *The Boys Who Stole the Funeral*. I did not know how to respond. There were some remarkable poems. But it strained credibility that two city youths would choose to take the corpse of a simple old countryman back to the bush for burial. (I don't think it occurred to either of us that the smell would have made their journey unbearable.)

I did not contact Les for a few days. I was slowly reading the book. He turned up at my house while I was at work. He had an emotional conversation with Gail and took the book back. Our friendship was unable to recover from that moment. (I have said the book was 'loaned'. Until then he gave me a copy of his books when they were published.)

Les decided to make the break between us permanent in a spectacular fashion after *Nero's Poems* was published in 1981. He wrote a long and hostile review in the *Catholic Weekly*. This newspaper was distributed in Catholic churches and was not noted for its interest in literature. I concluded Les had written his critique and then been desperate to get it published – anywhere.

I was embarrassed. I lived four doors down from a Catholic church. Most of my neighbours were Catholic and literate: an English teacher across the road, a large family next to them and the Curtin family next to me. I was also astonished. As editor of *Poetry Australia* Les had published a large batch of these poems – they had taken up almost half an issue.

His close friend Bob Ellis was associated with a periodical, *The Review*. We were chatting and he told me they were publishing a 'big Christian article' by Les. I asked whether he would like to publish my poem about Nero murdering his mother directly under Les's article. I would also choose the most pejorative quotes from Les's review in the *Catholic Weekly* for them to reprint with my poem. Bob loved mischief and immediately agreed. Les's article appeared a few days later under the heading 'Les Murray's journey into the great southern soul' with a poem of Les's, and my poem about Nero murdering his mother directly underneath.

The Review published the following comment above the Nero poem:

> This is one of the more controversial extracts from Geoffrey Lehmann's latest volume *Nero's Poems*. Though many critics liked it, his friend Les Murray said of it: 'It consistently reads as the grubby moral fantasies of a fourteen-year-old trying to shock himself … It is impossible to believe any such thing (as matricide) of Geoffrey Lehmann's little suburban Nero … It is really a teenager burning off some old resentments, not a prince watching the cremation of a mighty parent he has killed. Even the most pedestrian Robert Graves got further into Roman and human darkness than this.'

Some of the more trivial poems may have merited Les's comments, but the long matricidal 'Mother' was the wrong target, and why I chose it to be juxtaposed in *The Review* with Les's article. Les was deeply offended by 'Mother'. He had lost his own mother at age ten and had never experienced the distancing between mother and son that happens to many young men. The last three lines of my poem were partly autobiographical when I had Nero say:

> I don't forget the debt,
> but Nero leaves you drowning, mother,
> not your boy.

Les could not imagine someone not wanting to be his mother's boy.

I was upset by my split with Les. I had always believed we would be life-long friends. But I have not wanted to resume the friendship. Nor, I assume, would he. We stay in touch in a strange way. Piers Laverty, a potter and tree surgeon, is fifteen years younger than us and has become perhaps Les's closest and most loyal friend. For some years Piers and I have had dinner together once every week or fortnight. Les and I continue our friendship by proxy.

In 1979 John Tranter published *The New Australian Poetry* with a cover stating it was 'The work of twenty-four poets from Australian poetry's most exciting decade'. Les Murray and I were already well represented in recent Australian poetry anthologies. I did not mind being left out of Tranter's anthology. However, Tranter had nothing from Geoff Page, Alan Gould, Kevin Hart, Robert Gray, Rhyll McMaster or Jamie Grant, and there was no general anthology representing their work. *The Younger Australian Poets*, which Robert Gray and I edited and which was published in 1983, was intended to correct this. We also included some poets from Tranter's anthology, including Tranter himself.

One interesting aspect of Tranter's anthology was that only two out of his twenty-four poets were women. Earlier 'traditional' anthologies of Australian poetry had a higher proportion of women, but 'Australian poetry's most exciting decade' was a male decade. The anthology Gray and I edited had six women out of twenty-nine poets. We were only slightly less sexist.

In 1991 Gray and I published our second anthology: *Australian Poetry in the Twentieth Century*. As with our previous book, Bob had located a willing publisher and was again the main driving force. He now had an international reputation as one of Australia's major poets. I was surprised (but pleased) he wished to involve me.

Bob may have had an altruistic motive for bringing me in as his co-editor. After my marriage break-up I had become disenchanted with the literary world. He would ask what poems I was writing and made a point of introducing me to younger poets. One of these was Jamie Grant, who stayed at the Lindfield house for several weeks when he moved to Sydney, and later worked with Bob in a bookshop.

Perhaps because Grant is an acerbic critic, his outstanding body of work has been scandalously neglected. Many of his poems use complicated verse forms. His 'Altercation by Owl-Light', about rescuing an owl from a swimming pool, employs the extraordinary verse form of Dylan Thomas's 'Over Sir John's hill'. 'DFC', another exceptional poem, is about Jamie's father landing his flying boat in the dark in a crater lake during World War II.

My interest in poetry revived in the early 2000s. Two things may have helped. My column on tax had become a chore: each week I had to identify a topic and manufacture outrage or enthusiasm. The *Australian* decided to stop my column.

In 2002, following an annual prostate specific antigen (PSA) test, I was diagnosed with prostate cancer and had a radical prostatectomy. Shortly after the operation I wrote 'Self Portrait at 62' recording my 'altered body map'. I had begun writing poetry again, longer poems made up of small snippets, influenced by Wallace Stevens's 'Thirteen Ways of Looking at a Blackbird'. Unlike Stevens's poems, these were autobiographical – mosaic poems about myself, my children and grandchildren.

The experience of cancer was slightly unreal – I had difficulty taking it seriously – as though I was a spectator.

Gail

In July 2008 I retired from my job as tax counsel with the large accounting firm where I had worked since 1988. Bob Gray and I began work on our third poetry anthology. A couple of years later it acquired the title *Australian Poetry Since 1788*. We agreed our roles would be reversed. I would find new material and Bob would be the critic. We would re-use much of our 1991 anthology where Bob had been the main editor.

Australian poetry had changed since our 1991 anthology and we had changed. Perhaps to correct my conservative bias – I am a more conservative poet than Bob – I was keen to explore types of poetry we had not considered for our 1991 anthology. Reflecting a generational change among writers, our anthology has a preponderance of women among poets born after the mid-1950s.

Bob and I met one or two days a week for a couple of years. Our first draft of about 1600 pages had to be cut back. We had a rule that we were collecting poems, not representing poets. The naive poet 'Bellerive' was a beneficiary of this. Bellerive has been regarded as an oddity and does not appear in any other 'serious' anthology of Australian poetry. A committee of poetry experts would have considered themselves daring to include even two or three Bellerive poems in a collection as long as ours. Because I liked them, I initially chose fifteen Bellerive poems. I expected Bob to be apoplectic (in his own quiet way). Much to my surprise, he was not, and we agreed on fourteen.

Including poets such as Bellerive and the Dadaist Jas H Duke meant we had to leave out poets with more established reputations. One of these was Kenneth Mackenzie. I vetoed Mackenzie for the 1991 anthology, although Bob had been an admirer. This time I wrote a long biography of Mackenzie and selected half a dozen of his poems. A few months later, during one of our periodic culls, Bob said one day, 'I think Mackenzie has to go, the way he stands'.

The voice in Mackenzie's poems was grey and poetically conventional. Bellerive's voice was economical and uniquely strange, full of the life around him. Comparing the two voices, we had to choose Bellerive, who had little education and manned his own variety goods stand at Melbourne's Victoria Markets for many years.

One of the pleasures of preparing the anthology came towards the end, when I met with Barry Humphries in his Sydney apartment to discuss our selection of his poems. I wanted to delete a verse from some *vers d'occasion* which referred to the launching of an art exhibition. We sat across a low table, each with a copy of his *Neglected Poems*. Barry was happy with my suggested changes, and wanted several further small changes in other poems. We recorded these in our copies of *Neglected Poems*, then had afternoon tea and talked about the divorces of some mutual friends.

By the time the anthology went to press, it had shrunk to 1086 pages (still twice as long as any previous Australian poetry anthology). Nonetheless, we have been criticised for our 'omissions'. Some uncritically 'representative' Australian anthologies create the impression that Australian poetry is a provincial backwater. Our anthology was cited as one of *The Economist*'s books of 2011.

⁂

I have no wish to live in the suburb where I grew up. But I have a recurring dream about ruined houses. I am walking through derelict rooms with collapsed ceilings, bits of plaster scattered on the floor, and torn drapes hanging across windows filmed with dust. Even when there is no resemblance, I sense these places are the McMahons Point houses. In other dreams they have been restored and I am living in 'Fifty-three', with its grand staircase and doors with yellow cut-glass handles, the house where we never lived.

The painter Peter Kingston is a long-term McMahons Point

resident. I have known Peter's partner Jan Corke for almost fifty years. She sometimes reminds me of a blue velvet jacket I bought not long after I married Gail. Jan liked my jacket. Gail did not. Jan's and my generation of the early 1960s was strangely unpolitical. Vietnam and feminism were yet to happen. Women wore floral dresses and young men acquired a taste for corduroy, which continued with me into the 1980s when I bought my blue velvet coat.

I wrote a poem for Jan which she seems to like:

Men always send roses
To girls with long noses.
To have freckles on one's back
Takes quite a knack.

Gail came of age as the 1960s were ending, taking part in anti-apartheid and anti-Vietnam War demonstrations (but having no sympathy, she tells me, for those who shouted 'Victory for the NLF' – the Viet Cong). As a Queensland University student, she was a member of a feminist collective and wrote for the early feminist newspaper *Mejane*.

Then in 1972, after backpacking by herself on $3 a day around Indonesia and Malaysia, wearing hotpants, she won a scholarship to Jawaharlal Nehru University in New Delhi. Although she was the only non-Indian student on the campus, JNU was international in a way that Queensland University was not. Top American academics visited. Gail met Margaret Mead and Gloria Steinem at JNU during her four-and-a-half years in India. Indians were interested in ideas in a way Australians were not.

In the late 1970s, she was a tutor at the University of New South Wales and completing her PhD. Her mother also died at this time. And one night we met at a party.

She was serious where I was flippant, ordered where I was haphazard. As part of getting to know her, I read her thesis about women and the early twentieth century nationalist movement in India. Its language reflects the academic discourse of the 1970s, a style I was not sympathetic to. But I was attracted to the toughness and objectivity of her argument and an image at its centre.

The female nationalists marched with the men in public protests. Because they were women they gave credibility and respectability to the marches. The men needed them. But the women marched together in a group as though they were still in purdah. They were not treated as equals. Nor did they share in the fruits of political recognition when it came.

When Gail moved into the Lindfield house she brought with her a large library of books about sociology and Indian political history, as well as novels and poetry. I had a bohemian arrangement of bricks and boards along the hallway. Gail ordered in Scandinavian bookshelves, which I secured with an electric drill to the walls of a room we set aside for a library.

Apart from the new bathroom, the house had an air of decrepitude. I had a cedar dining table bought from the Salvation Army, but only an odd assortment of broken-down chairs to set around it. Gail's bentwood chairs from her grandmother Pearson's breakfast room became our dining room chairs. Gail resolved to replace the old and shabby blinds and cheap cotton Japanese rugs I had thrown down on top of June Read's red carpets, which were now threadbare.

Only one of my ancestors had been to a university. All four of her grandparents had a tertiary education. Both grandfathers had headed the Presbyterian Church in Queensland as Moderators General at different times.

The Pearson grandparents' house – a Queenslander on poles

– on a hill in the Brisbane suburb of Greenslopes, was full of nooks not dusted for years, coats hanging on a hook behind a door, books piled on a floor. Its three hallways, five bedrooms, and numerous rooms and verandas housed four children, a billiard table and an old pedal organ on a single level. The children (Gail's father and his three sisters) played tennis on the tennis court. Under the house, their father had a collection of tools and blacksmithing equipment for shoeing the two or three horses that grazed on his hillside.

Breakfast was in the breakfast room. Midday and evening meals were in the dining room at a table always covered with white damask. Despite its many rooms the Greenslopes house had only one bathroom and a spare toilet under the house for emergencies. Six people in the house meant a strict schedule and time limits for morning showers.

The Pearsons came from the New England plateau, where they had lived for generations, slowly accumulating assets and education. (They were unaware they had seven convicts among their ancestors.) This orderly transmission of discipline and assets from generation to generation was foreign to me, with my motley family history.

Gail's maternal grandparents, the Ramsays, were Scottish and equally disciplined. Her grandmother, Joanne Ramsay, was a Scottish Master of Arts, edited the Presbyterian *Outlook*, and wore stylish clothes. She had 'presence'. Unlike Grandmother Pearson who had an aloof, speculative mind, Mrs Ramsay was always ordering the children about, and blew bubbles in the bath when Gail and her sisters bathed there.

Ken, Gail's father, was a young doctor in his mid-twenties when he married Rowena Ramsay, a special needs teacher, who taught the blind, or deaf and dumb children. The young couple moved to Maryborough for a hospital job. Ken was soon asked to join a Maryborough medical practice and bought a house in John Street, a Queenslander, that had two sets of steps descending at the front in a half 'V'. Ken and Rowena soon had five children.

They played in a long paddock of a backyard with banana palms and four varieties of mango trees. The girls became friendly with Jack Blight's girls, who lived over the back fence. (Jack's garden had a red flowering *Eucalyptus ficifolia* which he told me about on his visits to Sydney.) Gail liked riding Sheba, a good-natured grey, and swam twice a day – before and after school – in the town swimming pool, riding there by bicycle.

The children were sent off to Sunday school, but Ken and Rowena became infrequent church attenders. On Sunday afternoons the parents and friends played tennis and their children looked on. At the end of the day the children were allowed onto the court. This seemed like 'an Edwardian summer that would never end', and Gail imagined the parents would still be there when she grew up and moved away.

She got on well with other girls at Maryborough Girls' High School, but felt she was 'different'. With her accent she was asked if she was English or 'from Victoria'. Boarding at Somerville House in Brisbane in her last two school years, she formed her first deep friendships: Judith Wright's daughter Meredith McKinney (Meredith later did the Penguin translation of Sei Shonagon's *Pillow Book*); Judith McKay (later a curator, and author of books, including a monograph on the sculptor Daphne Mayo, who travelled with Lloyd Rees to Italy and later broke off their engagement); and Rosemary Moon and Yvonne Grant, who later moved to Sydney.

Rowena contracted the autoimmune disease myasthenia gravis. Gail was back in Australia and teaching at the University of New South Wales when Rowena had an unexpected crisis. She

Gail

was alone and had died by the time Ken came home from work. Within days of her death he abandoned the practice. The family house, then the farm were sold and he became head of emergency at a city hospital. The ordered world of Gail's childhood fell apart, as though it had never existed.

In photographs of our wedding at the registry office, we look as though we are in our late twenties: Gail in her red and yellow sari and I in a light-coloured suit with a red tie, both of us cheerful and hopeful, with Paul Delprat and Gail's sister Deborah as witnesses.

After Nicholas was born, Gail began a law course. She is now a law professor and author of *Financial Services Law and Compliance*, published by Cambridge University Press, and co-author of two texts on consumer law. If she had not taken her decade-long detour through Indian history, we would not have met when we did. I regret not knowing Rowena. In her photographs she has a look of vulnerable innocence.

Gail's sisters live in Queensland and each week she has long telephone conversations with them. She travels more than I do — she is president of the International Consumer Law Association — and every couple of years returns to India. She likes the music I like — Lutheran church music of the late seventeenth and early eighteenth century and Morton Feldman's 1979 string quartet — but does not share my taste for Conlon Nancarrow's frenetic player piano pieces or for Zappa.

We often read the same books. After a few weeks, a book that is on the floor by one side of the bed changes sides. At night I am usually the last to fall asleep. I take what she is reading, remove her glasses and she briefly stirs as I switch off her bed lamp.

In a recent dream I am sitting in a cafeteria, hundreds of us at small tables, and Gail is finding her way among the tables, looking around. I stand up and wave. The dream re-enacts the many times we arrange to meet at public functions. There is a press of people, we see each other and our faces light up. This has been happening now for thirty-seven years.

BROTHER AND SISTER

In my twenties and sitting in a crowded train, late one afternoon coming home after work, I sneezed. My sister, sitting several rows ahead, recognised my sneeze and turned around. We greeted each other, and later walked home together to the Gordon house.

Diana used to tell me, 'I'm the practical one'. This was not a boast. Sometimes there may have been an edge of desperation to the statement. She would have preferred to be a person like her mother, who did not have to make the hard decisions.

Steven Pinker explained in his 2005 debate with Elizabeth Spelke:

> In the condition called congenital adrenal hyperplasia, girls in utero are subjected to an increased dose of androgens, which is neutralized postnatally. But when they grow up they have male-typical toy preferences – trucks and guns – compared to other girls, male-typical play patterns, more competitiveness, less cooperativeness, and male-typical occupational preferences.

As a child my sister did not display male toy preferences. My father took many photographs of her at her solitary girlish tea parties, sitting at the cream-coloured child's table he made for her, on small cream-coloured chairs which he painted with Minnie Mouse figures. But Pinker's description of the increased dose of androgens reminds me of my sister when we were children: her aggression and competitiveness.

I was aware of her growth spurt when she was ten and grew like Alice in Wonderland and towered over her classmates. Without any understanding of her condition – I was told nothing – in my child's mind she was somehow not a girl.

After her adrenal glands were removed, she had to take artificial cortisone for the rest of her life. She stopped growing and had a longer than normal trunk and slightly short legs. She looked like a normal woman, although stocky. But my childish image of her as not wholly a woman persisted – it was not something I could erase. Diana and I saw each other once at a bistro. I was meeting friends for lunch. I must have shrunk away from her. She said, 'You're avoiding me'. I denied this. But what she said was true.

I inherited only one of the genes, of which she had two. I came within the spectrum of normality. She did not. A more masculine brother may have been able to cajole the woman in her and make her feel protected. My attitude was reprehensible. But it was imprinted in childhood and reciprocated. For my sister, I was not wholly a man. Diana and my mother tried to get me to wear a back brace when I was a teenager – some strips of leather with metal buckles. They were worried by my tendency to stoop.

Diana was attracted to manly men, and I think may have fallen in love a few times – at a distance – but it was not something she discussed. She was thirty-two when our father died. She had lost the only man in her life and dedicated herself to caring for our mother. If I had been a brother who made her feel protected, she would have appreciated this. But nothing would have changed. For the fifteen years that they lived together until Iris's death, she was the man of the house.

Brother and sister

After the split with Gail, she rarely saw the children. I took them once or twice to meet her in Hyde Park. The older children tried phoning her, but she could not sustain a conversation for very long. The androgens *in utero* may have left her lacking the skills to entertain younger people, remembering birthdays and taking them on jaunts. Perhaps she did not want to. I belonged to the childhood when she was a normal little girl and her body had not been tampered with. She wanted to see me and not my children.

I continued seeing her once a week, sometimes once a fortnight, for lunch in the city. I let Diana choose the venues for our lunches. They were take-away food shops where we could also sit, and served food that did not make her sick. Diana suffered from food allergies and sudden illnesses, perhaps from the cortisone. She tried Chinese herbal medicines. At one point she was on two diets at once. I said, 'Diana this is ridiculous. Your two diets may be cancelling each other out.'

It is hard to remember what we talked about during our many lunches over more than fifteen years. I do remember telling her about searching for a commercial-grade orange juicer, with a revolving stainless steel basket. I tracked one down at a restaurant supplies shop. I was now making orange juice at home instead of buying it on my way to work. It would pay for itself in a year. Diana said, 'I hope you are drinking the pulp'.

I heard from her about visits to relatives in Melbourne. She liked reminiscing about her girlfriends from typing school, her first boss when she was a young secretary, and the older female probate solicitor she worked for in a large firm and remembered fondly. She talked about the Probate Office and her current boss, the Prothonotary. He was a contemporary of mine. I imagined her role with him was like that of an older sister.

My tennis partner David McGovern introduced himself to Diana when he was appearing in court. One day she gave David a favourable spot in the list. There must have been a good reason. Diana did not play favourites.

After Iris died, Diana took up ballroom dancing again and made new friends of her own age. (Several of these new friends sent notes when she died, saying how much they had valued her.) Diana told me how she and one of her dancing friends, Heather, sometimes stepped out onto the dance floor together. I kept Heather's name and called my sister 'Wendy' in a *Spring Forest* poem 'Poverty Bush', which ends in this way:

> When sixty-year-old men ran short
> ... Heather was the first to revolt.
> She walked across the floor to Wendy
> without self-consciousness,
> and watching the movements of the males
> guided her among the couples.
> Some girls won't get up without a man,
> so they sit not budging all night.
> But most enjoy dancing with their sex
> when gents are scarce –
> both step forward, no one steps back.

Diana gave a copy of the poem to Heather, who sent a letter of appreciation.

In about 2000 Diana had a heavy cold. By then she had retired from her Supreme Court job. She was still sleeping in the smaller bedroom of the Chatswood apartment where she and Iris had lived. Iris's clothes were undisturbed in the larger bedroom, more than a decade after her death. If I had been the manly brother Diana craved, I would have insisted on a clean-up.

I had not heard from her for a couple of days and phoned her apartment on a Saturday morning. It was too early for her to have gone out. I was annoyed she did not answer. I thought she was being recalcitrant, but decided to investigate.

I drove with my son Nicholas to Chatswood. I had a key to Diana's apartment, and after knocking, we went inside. She was on the floor of the smaller bedroom, unconscious, face down and breathing heavily. Nick phoned emergency. Within five minutes, medics were knocking on the door, ready with a stretcher to carry her down the stairs. I quickly told them her medical history and asked what hospital they were taking her to. A minute later Nick and I were standing alone together in the apartment.

Diana was in a coma for several days in a public hospital where a sympathetic young endocrinologist was looking after her. We talked about her life and I had the feeling he was almost fond of this plain, deeply sleeping older woman. With his help she slowly came out of the coma on about the fourth day. She continued her recovery in a nursing home, and as she became stronger over the next month, reproached me: 'You should have let me die'.

Her next seven years were her happiest. She sold her Chatswood apartment, got rid of all her surplus objects, keeping only what she truly valued, and moved across the road from her apartment to a Uniting Church retirement unit eight stories up. She became perhaps the youngest resident in this multi-storey retirement village. She had finally escaped from her childhood.

Less isolated, she was now was part of a loose community, whose illnesses, deaths and peculiarities she reported to me. They were acquaintances and did not become friends, but life was going on around her. She enjoyed a new freedom. She had never liked cooking and now dined several nights a week at the Chatswood Returned Soldiers Club, which was a ten minute walk away. Her new small unit had a view over an oval and trees – better than her previous apartment's bleak north-facing view of Chatswood's high-rise buildings and shops. I called in on her there, sometimes with children. But she did not resume visits to the Lindfield house.

She used to come in by train to our lunches, which started again in the city. She had never driven a car – to her mind an extravagance. I told her about changes to the Lindfield house. The tennis court had been restored as a lawn tennis court. We had built a swimming pool tiled with half-price blue mosaic tiles. We talked about the things we had always talked about.

Then at one of our lunches – it may have been about nine months after Diana's hospitalisation – I blundered. We were happily discussing her complete recovery from the illness, and I used the term 'diabetic coma'. She reacted fiercely. She was not diabetic and it was not a diabetic coma. I apologised. She phoned later to say that she did not want to see me again. She was saying goodbye. She said she was still fond of me as a brother. It was just that she could not bear to be with me. I protested, saying it was ridiculous for us not to be seeing each other because of my misuse of a term.

Her coma was caused by a lack of cortisone – she may have vomited or forgotten to take her normal dose. Instead of referring to it as just a 'coma', I had pretentiously referred to it as a 'diabetic coma'. I telephoned her several times, asking her to resume our lunches. Eventually she weakened and our lunches began again.

We often talked about the stock market. Diana had a stockbroker called Diane. I called Diane one day when the market was particularly low, introduced myself as Diana's brother and ordered as many stocks as I could afford. Over the next few years Diana warned me against holding certain stocks. She was more knowledgeable, had a much larger shareholding, and bought and sold more often. She kept detailed records, meticulously written up in different coloured manilla files in longhand – not shorthand (which she and Iris sometimes used for reminders, and which Diana had once tried to teach me when I was a teenager).

Diana's literary tastes were unlike our mother's. She remembered fondly the books she read at school, and liked some non-fiction books that caught her attention – the bizarre Gospel of Thomas was one of them. She was interested in the origins of Christianity, while having no clear belief. She also liked books about early Sydney. There was a conversation we did not have. I was unaware that congenital adrenal hyperplasia can be classical or non-classical. The more common, non-classical, form is not manifested at birth, and may be what Diana had. The gene for it is carried by about one in twenty Ashkenazi Jews – something she may have been interested to know.

After her death I found the Reverend Gordon Moyes's short memoir *When Box Hill Was a Village*. I was about to throw this out when I noticed an author's inscription which began 'Dear Diana…' After I read his well-written and moving memoir I felt guilty about my snobbish attitudes. I had underestimated her and him, and have kept the book.

Diana talked about dying. She was emphatic her body was not to be medically examined – there was to be no autopsy and no funeral. She told me she had made a new will. In this I was no longer the sole beneficiary, and the estate was to be divided equally between my five children with a sixth share going to me. I asked why I was still a beneficiary. Her solicitor suggested this, she said – life is uncertain.

We discussed how the estate would be administered. If the shares were distributed in specie to the children, there would only be tax if they sold the shares. In this way there would be an incentive for them to keep the shares and not spend their inheritance.

Diana had laser surgery on her eye in a private hospital and was staying overnight for observation. I visited her in the late afternoon. The ward was overcrowded and she was in a bed tucked into a corner where she could not reach her emergency button. I told the staff my sister had a condition where she could suddenly become ill. She was in danger without access to the emergency button. They had been negligent. We eventually fixed the problem but I was happy to get her out of there next day and drive her home.

I had been planning an overseas trip for May 2007 and had arranged for leave from the accounting firm. Nicholas was graduating from Vassar College in the US. Afterwards he and I would briefly visit several cities. Then I would fly to Tokyo and stay with my son John and meet his fiancée Manami. The three of us – Manami, John and I – were to go on a short tour of the main island and the inland sea.

Diana seemed in good health and her eyesight was restored. I told her about my trip, she had my mobile phone details, and I flew out of Australia.

Nicholas's open-air graduation ceremony was as long as an Orthodox wedding – at its culminating moment students threw hundreds of mortar boards in the air. In Philadelphia we walked along Chestnut Street, where Wallace Stevens once distributed twelve cinnamon buns at a meeting to settle a legal dispute. I did not suggest to Nick we go looking for Lahrs, which still exists and where Stevens bought the buns.

We drove out of Philadelphia to call on a friend of mine, George Reitnour, an American lawyer and poet. That evening George organised a small poetry reading near his home. One of the poems I read was my 'Thirteen Ways of Looking at Twelve Cinnamon Buns'. That night, I saw fireflies for the first time.

We were in Washington when my mobile phone rang. Diana told me she was going into hospital. She would not tell me why. She named the hospital – it was the public hospital where she had been in a coma. I said I would come straight back to Australia. She said not to break my trip. Her stay in hospital was nothing to worry about, she said, and hung up.

Next day I telephoned her in her hospital ward. She would not pick up the phone. I phoned the hospital and asked why she was there. A young male nurse told me he was not authorised to say, and added, 'Your sister is not very well'. I repeated these phone calls every day for ten days – in the US and in Japan. Diana would not pick up the phone and I was told she was not very well. I telephoned Gail. Gail was unable to find out what was wrong. Because of her difficulties with Diana, she was worried a hospital visit would be unwelcome.

On the morning that I got back to Australia, I drove to the hospital. I could not understand why Diana was refusing to pick up her bedside phone. I was concerned she might refuse to see me. As I stepped into her room, her face lit up. I was the first visitor since her admission. She had told no-one else she was there. She had late-stage ovarian cancer. The doctors were recommending a 'debulking' operation to give her a couple of extra months. She had refused.

I began visiting twice a day. I suggested if the doctors recommended debulking, perhaps she should give herself the extra time. I did not expect her to agree with me. She was the 'practical one', her logic was more rigorous than mine and I knew she would not want a lingering death. After a day or so, to my surprise, she changed her mind and decided to have the operation.

She told me she wanted to revoke some pecuniary legacies to charities in her will. She had expected to live longer, when there would be more cash to pay them. The children's need was greater: particularly Julia, she pointed out, who was a widow. She only wished she had died, and not Julia's partner Quinton. She asked me to telephone her solicitors, as she was not strong enough to phone them.

I wanted to be sure she was serious about the codicil to her will and waited for a day. She repeated her request at each visit;

it was a subject she kept returning to, and I telephoned her solicitors.

Gail began coming with me, and they spoke cordially together. My daughter Julia flew up from Melbourne and brought Ada, three years old, to meet Diana. This may have been the happiest moment of Diana's final week, as a proudly smiling grand-aunt.

She asked me to check the terms of her will. There was a copy in her retirement unit. I also noticed on her desk several 'living wills', signed every nine months or so – printed forms, each stating she was not to be kept on life support.

At every visit, twice every day, she asked about her codicil. When could she sign it? I told her the solicitors had agreed to see her – they needed a couple of days – they had to take bedside instructions, prepare the codicil and arrange for her signature. Diana became more insistent and agitated. The time for her operation was approaching – it was in two days' time – and could I do something about the codicil?

I had some sheets of thick grey-blue legal paper left over from my legal practice thirty years earlier. That night after work and my visit to her, I decided to prepare the codicil myself. Time was running out.

Diana knew my tennis partner from her Probate Court days. He now had the illustrious initials 'SC', or Senior Counsel, after his name and I phoned him. He and his wife, Roz, a non-practising solicitor, agreed to be witnesses. We came to the hospital early next morning with the codicil revoking the gifts to the charities. I went in to see Diana and told her what I had done, and that David and Roz McGovern were waiting in the corridor. I said, 'David will read the codicil to you'.

Diana said, 'No. You read it to me first.' I read her the codicil. She nodded. She was happy with it. I left the room. After David and Roz read out the codicil again and witnessed her signature, I joined them by Diana's bed. She was smiling – with the same smile she had had when Ada visited.

At six the next morning I was phoned by the hospital. It was the day fixed for the debulking. Diana's condition had suddenly worsened. I drove to the hospital with Gail. Diana was in intensive care. I went in alone. Diana was surrounded by six or seven medical staff. She muttered something. I asked the nurse, 'What did Diana say?' 'She said, "I want to be killed".' I said, 'Diana, I'll do the right thing by you'. I doubt whether she heard me and it was a feeble thing to say, but all I could think of.

I was told we could be together in a room nearby. There would be just the two of us. I left and a few minutes later was ushered into a small room where my sister was lying propped on a bed, minus all the tubes, already unconscious. I sat with her for a few minutes. She was breathing heavily and then stopped. I saw her eyes roll upwards.

When Diana died, Leo died again. She was her father's child. I was an odd mixture of the two, the practical Lehmanns and improvident Rainers. The pennies Leo collected from the workmen on the *Liberty* for twenty-eight years became real estate, and passed through her and me to my children and grandchildren.

There was no autopsy. Diana had been insistent about no funeral. The female funeral director told me the date and time when her body would be taken to the crematorium early one morning.

Our parents both had funerals and the crematorium had disposed of their ashes. Diana had given me no verbal instruction about her ashes. When they were delivered in a grey plastic container I decided to scatter them at the head of Lavender Bay from the wharf where our father's boat set out and returned daily for almost thirty years. Only family members would be there.

Julia came from Melbourne, John from Tokyo, Nick from Boston and Harry from Canberra. Lucy, who was living in Sydney, was there too. Gail had been with one of her sisters in Brisbane, and was the last to arrive on the winter afternoon. While I was waiting, I walked around the foreshore park and found small Peter Kingston sculptures of Australian comic strip characters of the 1940s: Felix the Cat, Ginger Meggs and my namesake, Boofhead.

The plastic container was tightly sealed. I had a chisel – an old chisel of my father's with a black-painted wooden handle. Turquoise water was bobbing and slopping against the piles of the wharf. Crouching close to the water's surface, I prised the lid open and tipped the container on its side. The ashes kept pouring out. The grains glittered in the sunlit water, rusty shawls revolving and spreading like the great red-brown fans of coral we saw as children on our Queensland holiday.

Lucy said 'Good-bye Diana' – an echo of Diana's words when Iris died – as the last grains trickled out.

CURRARONG

In his biography *John Curtin's War*, John Edwards explains that the Argentine Government's default on payments to British lenders in 1890 threatened the British banking system. This caused a sharp drop in lending to Australia, which triggered a crash in Australian land prices, the collapse of many Australian banks and a fall in output in the 1890s 'deeper and longer … than the Great Depression forty years later'.

Curtin, who became the Australian Labor Prime Minister in 1941, was infected with a deep suspicion of capitalism by his experience of these events when he was growing up. A similar antipathy was inspired in Ben Chifley, Curtin's successor. Chifley (disastrously) introduced legislation to nationalise the banks.

These events, originating in Argentina, also led to the early deaths of both my grandfathers. Johann went to New Guinea and died because his order book was empty, and William Rainer's medical career would have been less tortuous if he had not lost his money. The after-shocks continued in their children's lives, and perhaps my own early mistakes.

Cavafy's poem 'Ithaca' speaks about Ithaca, the end of the voyage, being a poor place when Odysseus gets there. But Ithaca hasn't cheated you, Cavafy says, because it was the 'splendid journey' that mattered, the excitement of dropping anchor in unknown harbours and escaping from man-eating giants; and the ebony, amber and perfumes picked up at Phoenician trading stations.

Cavafy is a romantic pretending to be a cynic. His poem is an evasion. Ithaca is not a poor place. The past is not more glamorous than the present. Most of us get to Ithaca in middle age and live the remainder of our lives there, often the most productive part. If we are lucky, we find partners and have children and grandchildren. It is where most of us find happiness (often unexpected) and do well the things we were learning about on the way. Dramatic events still happen in Ithaca, but they are spaced further apart.

It is quotidian and difficult to write about. William Yeats had reached his Ithaca when wrote 'A Prayer for my Daughter'. In his poem he hoped his daughter would be 'granted beauty, and yet not/ Beauty to make a stranger's eye distraught', so she would not 'Consider beauty a sufficient end' or 'Lose natural kindness'.

He finds 'An intellectual hatred is the worst/ So let her think opinions are accursed.' He prays for custom and ceremony in her future house: 'How but in custom and in ceremony/ Are innocence and beauty born?'

The most rotund and optimistic statement of happiness in later life might be Wallace Stevens's 'Credences of Summer'. He tell us 'The rock ... is the truth', it is not a 'hermit's truth', it is 'visible' and 'audible,/ The brilliant mercy of a sure repose...' We should enjoy the physical world. But its beauty is beyond our control:

> The personae of summer play the characters
> Of an inhuman author, who meditates
> With the gold bugs, in blue meadows, late at night.

Ithaca is not tragic or comic. Shakespeare had reached his Ithaca when he wrote *The Tempest*. His Miranda says:

> How beauteous mankind is! O brave new world,
> That has such people in't!

Shakespeare says through Caliban:

> Be not afeard; the isle is full of noises,
> Sounds and sweet airs, that give delight and hurt not.

Ithaca is full of surprises. The second law of thermodynamics says systems irreversibly trend towards entropy. Astronomers observe a universe speeding up as it is flying apart into heat death. But there is something odd here. We cannot imagine a beginning to time, and if there is no beginning, entropy would have happened already.

The physicist Freeman Dyson is reassured by gravity. Our solar system was once a mass of stellar gas and became an ordered system, and eventually produced intelligent beings. Dyson points out in *A Many-Colored Glass* (at age seventy-six): 'What we see in the real universe is the opposite of a heat death. We see the universe growing more ordered and more lively as it grows older.'

The psychologist Steven Pinker's *The Better Angels of our Nature* shows, through historical and statistical evidence, how human violence has declined over time, century by century. The glamour of the past is an illusion. The past is something we are escaping from.

Roger Penrose in *Fashion, Faith and Fantasy in the New Physics of the Universe* sees entropy as an end that becomes a new beginning and a new Big Bang. He calls this Conformal Cyclic Cosmology and jokes it is Conformal Crazy Cosmology.

He suggests the mysterious magnetic fields in great voids are the ghosts of galaxies that were there in a previous universe.

'People' – beings like us – inhabit these cyclic universes. Intelligent life needs cooperative minds. 'We' – but not the personal pronoun I – have been here before and shall be here again.

As well as thinking intellectual hatreds are the worst, in Ithaca we love the scientific method, numbers and history. They help us understand a little of the universal complexity, but we know there are things we cannot know. Our happiness is illogical. We do not know where it comes from.

One of the most sublimely happy pieces of music in the classical repertoire is Gertrude Stein's and Virgil Thomson's opera *Four Saints in Three Acts*, which Christopher Carroll has described as having 'mesmeric, nonsense language' and 'simple, repetitive, diatonic music'. I got to know it when I was young because it was loved by Richard Meale, a composer, most of whose music sounds unhappy.

Some critics regard this opera as ridiculous words sung to cheerfully vapid tinklings. They seem not to have understood what the younger gay composer and older lesbian poet were about. Thomson said he and Stein 'got along like a couple of Harvard boys'.

There are not three acts, but four; and there are not four saints, but about twenty of these holy men and women with names like Saint Settlement, Saint Plan and Saint Martyr as well as more familiar saints, such as Saint Teresa. Except there is Saint Teresa I and Saint Teresa II, so she can sing duets with herself.

This opera is full of numbers that are sung out, but do not add up. Contradictory stage directions are sung:

CHORUS I
Saint Teresa seated and not surrounded. There are a great many places and persons near together. Saint Teresa not seated.

The libretto is replete with illogical wordplay. I am sure there is logic in this illogic. After an hour and a bit the opera ends as triumphantly and abruptly as it began:

COMPÈRE: Saint Ignatius and left and right laterally be lined.

ALL: All Saints.

COMPÈRE: To Saints.

ALL: Four Saints.

COMPÈRE: And Saints.

ALL: Five Saints.

COMPÈRE: To Saints.

COMPÈRE: Last Act.

ALL: Which is a fact.

Happiness is a fact, and there is no logic to it, except that when self-replicating beings are given the evolutionary advantage of consciousness, they will not want to survive unless they are happy.

The opera's premiere was in Wallace Stevens's home town Hartford, in 1934. The sets were made of shimmering Saran wrap and the cast were all black. Stevens, a difficult modern poet who did not like difficult modern music, was in the audience and found it 'most agreeable musically'. But he wrote to a friend, that there were 'numerous asses of the first water in the audience … people who walked around with cigarette holders a foot long, and so on'.

⁂

Currarong, an old fishing village south of Sydney, is at the heart of my Ithaca. In 1990 Gail and I were staying with Ian and Marilyn Fincham at their beach house in Currarong. We had just finished dinner and at 9 pm there was a knock on the door. Doreen, an estate agent who lived across the road, was standing there in a white nightdress. 'There's a house up the road on the beach front', she told us. 'It's just come on the market.'

We walked up and stood on the road, looking at the house. Before anyone could say anything, I said, 'I'll buy it'. I turned to Ian with embarrassment and said, 'Ian, only if you don't want it'.

The house is on a sand dune and we grow sand-loving Australian plants that do not grow at Lindfield: flannel flowers, and red and yellow kangaroo paws. Currarong is at the end of a long road through uninhabited bush, a naval firing range on one side, and on the other side, beyond some trees and scrub, a long surf beach going for miles, deserted for most of the year.

'Currarong' in the local Aboriginal language is 'place of many winds'. The beach is different every day. Stinging blue bottles sometimes wash up in hundreds. For a week the beach might stink with mounds of kelp. The water is grey one day, and sparkling green-and-blue next morning. Once every few years tens of thousands of dead mutton birds litter miles of beach.

Currarong

Deborah Hope and John Edwards have a house in the next street. Gail and Deborah often go for long walks along the beach and John and I play golf nearby at Callala Bay. Late in the afternoon there are no other players on the course as we finish our game, watched only by kangaroos.

One afternoon Gail was swimming and a dolphin surfaced and startled her, it was so close. She quickly left the water and believes the dolphin was warning her about sharks nearby.

Sea eagles hunt over a wide area and we hear two or three of them calling to each other at dusk, as they fly home. At night we sit on the brick patio gazing out at the garden lit up by lights from the house. We cannot see the ocean, only hear its roaring, when the wind is high, beyond a windbreak of low eucalypts and banksias on the sand dune. Other nights there is a rhythmic murmur of small waves breaking on the beach. When it is free of clouds, the night sky has a hard clarity and brilliance.

The water comes right up to the foot of the dune at high tide. Sometimes after an evening meal on the patio we walk down onto the beach. From our front gate it's a hundred paces along a sandy path through low trees and scrub. Standing on the water's edge we watch the lights of a tanker move almost imperceptibly on the horizon.